THE AMERICAN NEGRO
HIS HISTORY AND LITERATURE

RACE ADJUSTMENT

*

THE

EVERLASTING STAIN

Kelly Miller

ARNO PRESS and THE NEW YORK TIMES

NEW YORK 1968

General Editor
WILLIAM LOREN KATZ

KELLY MILLER WAS A BRILLIANT AND VERSATILE polemicist of the Negro people, and very few important issues affecting their welfare escaped his perceptive comment. His method was that of reason, which he seemed to embrace as the solvent of all problems—so much so that he was once characterized as a "belated rationalist of the 18th Century." The two volumes of essays here reproduced are illustrative of the content and style of his writings during the first decade of this century and during the period following World War I.

The earlier volume reflects Miller's very active role in the storm of controversy around the accommodating policy and program of Booker T. Washington, whom he supported during the 1890's and early 1900's. His polemic in defense of "Washington's Policy," directed mainly at Monroe Trotter, militant Negro leader of Boston, is one of Miller's most celebrated essays. Also notable in this volume is the author's comparative assessment of Frederick Douglass and Booker Washington, in "Radicals and

Conservatives," probably the most trenchant appraisal of these "two superlative colored men" to be found in the literature.

Racist theories and their proponents were among the prime targets of Miller's sharp pen, a fact also evident from the essays in *Race Adjustment*. Especially notable in this regard are his "open letters" to Thomas Dixon, Jr. ("As to the Leopard's Spots") and to John Temple Graves ("An Appeal to Reason on the Race Question").

The Everlasting Stain deals with a wide range of issues confronting the Negro in the aftermath of World War I, many of them still current; and it also reflects the growing catholicity of Miller's interests. Several of the essays relate to problems of education, including school segregation in the North and Federal responsibility for Negro education. There are treatises on lynching ("The Sport of the Ghouls") and radicalism among Negroes. Included also are an "Open Letter to President Wilson" and commentaries on Abraham Lincoln, Lloyd George, Tagore and others. The canvas, world-wide in scope, is much broader than that of the earlier volume.

Miller was a prolific writer, most of whose essays appeared initially in newspapers and journals. The collections which make up these two volumes and two others—*Out of the House of Bondage* (1912) and *Appeal to Conscience* (1916)—are but part of his vast output.

Kelly Miller (1863–1939) was born in Winnsborough, South Carolina, just a few months after the Emancipation Proclamation became effective in that State. He attended Howard University, working to pay the cost of his studies, and completed the preparatory course in Greek, Latin and Mathematics in 1882, and the baccalaureate program in 1886. He studied mathematics under a private tutor during the following year, and at Johns Hopkins University during 1887–1889.

In 1890, after teaching a few months in the public schools of Washington, D.C., Miller accepted the professorship of mathematics at Howard University; and the development of his career and of that institution were very closely entwined for several decades thereafter. At various times he served as professor of mathematics and sociology, dean of the College of Liberal Arts (1907–1919), professor and head of the department of sociology, dean of the Junior College, and Dean Emeritus, from which post he retired in 1934. It was from the congenial intellectual base provided by Howard University that Kelly Miller launched his spirited verbal thrusts into the controversies surrounding the Negro.

Doxey A. Wilkerson
ASSOCIATE PROFESSOR OF EDUCATION
YESHIVA UNIVERSITY

RACE ADJUSTMENT

ESSAYS ON THE
NEGRO IN AMERICA

BY

KELLY MILLER

NEW YORK AND WASHINGTON

THE NEALE PUBLISHING COMPANY

1908

TO

AN AWAKENING RACE

*Struggling Upward from Darkness Through
Twilight
into the Fuller Day*

PREFACE

Several of the essays here listed have previously appeared as magazine articles, or in separate pamphlet form. The reader must not expect to find a consecutive logical treatise, nor a settled solution of the race problem. The author will be satisfied if these papers serve the less ambitious purpose of flashing gleams or even glints of light upon a dark and indefinite background.

The reader will notice the recurrence of phrases and sentences in several of the chapters. The aim has been to preserve as far as practicable the integrity of the several essays originally prepared for widely different occasions, at the risk of occasional overlapping.

KELLY MILLER,
Howard University,
Washington, D. C.

KEY-WORD

"*We continually oscillate between an inclination to complain without sufficient cause and to be too easily satisfied. We have an extreme susceptibility of mind, an inordinate craving, an ambition in our thoughts, our desires, and in the movements of our imagination; yet when we come to practical life, when trouble, when sacrifices, when efforts are required for the attainment of our object, we sink into lassitude and inactivity. Let us not be invaded by either of these vices. Let us estimate fairly what our abilities, our knowledge, our power enable us to do lawfully, and let us aim at nothing that we cannot lawfully, justly and prudently—with a proper respect for the principles upon which our social system, our civilization, is based—attain.*"   —GUIZOT.

CONTENTS

RACE ADJUSTMENT

RADICALS AND CONSERVATIVES

WHEN a distinguished Russian was informed that some American Negroes are radical and some conservative, he could not restrain his laughter. The idea of conservative Negroes was more than the Cossack's risibilities could endure. "What on earth," he exclaimed with astonishment, "have they to conserve?"

According to a strict use of terms, a "conservative" is one who is satisfied with existing conditions and advocates their continuance; while a "radical" clamors for amelioration of conditions through change. No thoughtful Negro is satisfied with the present status of his race, whether viewed in its political, its civil or general aspect. He labors under an unfriendly public opinion, one which is being rapidly crystallized into a rigid caste system and enacted into unrighteous law. How can he be expected to contemplate such oppressive conditions with satisfaction and composure? Circumstances render it imperative that his attitude should be dissentient rather than conformatory. Every consideration of enlightened self-respect impels him to unremitting protest, albeit the manner of protestation may be mild or pronounced, according to the dictates of prudence. Radical and conservative Negroes agree as to the end in view, but differ as to the

most effective means of attaining it. The difference
is not essentially one of principle or purpose, but
point of view. All anti-slavery advocates desired
the downfall of the iniquitous institution, but some
were more violent than others in the expression of
this desire. Disagreement as to method led to personal estrangement, impugnment of motive, and unseemly factional wrangle. And so, colored men who
are alike zealous for the betterment of their race,
lose half their strength in internal strife, because of
variant methods of attack upon the citadel of prejudice. Mr. Booker T. Washington is, or has been,
the storm-center about which the controversy rages,
and contending forces have aligned themselves in
hostile array as to the wisdom or folly of the doctrine of which he is the chief exponent. The unseemly " Boston Riot," in which he was threatened
with bodily violence, served to accentuate the antagonism and to deepen the line of cleavage.

Several years ago a number of New England colored men, " exotics," as some would say, of the New
England colleges, having grown restive under what
they deemed the damaging doctrine of the famous
Tuskegeean, founded the *Boston Guardian* as a
journal of protest. These men declared that the
teachings of Mr. Washington were destructive of
the guaranteed rights and privileges of the Negro
race, especially in the Northern States, and pledged
themselves to spare no effort to combat his political
and social heresies.

Mr. William Monroe Trotter, a Harvard graduate, who is said to have maintained a higher scholastic average than any other colored student of that
famous institution, was head and front of the new
movement. As promoter of the " Boston Riot " he
was convicted and sentenced to the common jail.

His incarceration but served to intensify his animosity.

Mr. Trotter is well suited to play the rôle of a martyr. He delights in a reputation for vicarious heroics. Being possessed of considerable independent means, he willingly makes sacrifices for the cause, and is as uncompromising as William Lloyd Garrison. Mr. Trotter, however, lacks the moral sanity and poise of the great emancipator. With him agitation is not so much the outgrowth of an intellectual or moral comprehension of right and reprehension of wrong, as it is a temperamental necessity. Endowed with a narrow, intolerant intensity of spirit, he pursues his ends with a Jesuitical justification of untoward means. Without clear concrete objective, such as the anti-slavery promoters had in view, he strikes wildly at whatever or whoever he imagines obscures the rights of the Negro race. He has the traditional irreverence of the reformer, an irreverence which delights to shatter popular idols. President Eliot of Harvard University, Theodore Roosevelt, and Booker T. Washington are shining marks for his blunt and bitter denunciation. He sets himself up as the moral monitor of the Negro race. This Negro Puritan is of spotless and austere personal character, and yet he does not scruple to use the weapons of unrighteousness to promote his cherished hopes. He is equally indifferent to the allurements of culture and the blandishments of business; he has sacrificed a business career which was opening up with large prospects, in order to fight the Washington heresy. A Harvard graduate, with a class-standing that puts him easily in touch with the intellectual élite of his alma mater, he has thrown away all the restraints of culture, spurned the allurements of refined association, and conducts

The Guardian with as little regard to literary form and style as if he were a back-woodsman.

By his blunt, persistent assault on Booker T. Washington he has focalized the more radical elements of the Negro race, and has made himself the most forceful personality that the Negroes in the free States have produced in a generation. He is irreconciled to his great foe. This intrepid editor saw clearly that the so-called radical Negroes were wholly wanting in organization and leadership. He chafed under the chide of having no concrete achievement or commanding personality as basis and background of his propaganda. His enemies sought to silence the loudsome pretensions of those of radical persuasion by the cry that they had founded no institutions and projected no practical projects. That the same might have been said of Garrison and Phillips was regarded as a barren rejoinder. It is difficult to found an effective organization on a protest. There is little constructive possibility in negation. Through the influence of *The Guardian*, Mr. Trotter has held together and inspirited the opposition to Mr. Washington. His every utterance leads to the Cato-like refrain: " Booker Washington must be destroyed." Conscious of his own lack of attractive personality and felicity of utterance requisite to ostensible popular leadership, Trotter began to cast about for a man of showy faculties who could stand before the people as leader of his cause. He wove a subtle net about W. E. B. DuBois, the brilliant writer and scholar, and gradually weaned him from his erstwhile friendship for Mr. Washington, so as to exploit his prominence and splendid powers in behalf of the hostile forces.

The author of the " Souls of Black Folk " is also a Harvard man, and possesses extraordinary scientific and literary talent. Few men now writing the English language can equal him in linguistic felicity. He is a man of remarkable amplitude and contrariety of qualities, an exact interrogator and a lucid expositor of social reality, but withal a dreamer with a fantasy of mind that verges on " the fine frenzy."

Dr. DuBois began his career, not as an agitator, nor as a carping critic of another's achievements, but as a painstaking investigator and a writer of remarkable lucidity and keenness. The men who are now extolling him as the peerless leader of the radicals were a few years ago denouncing him bitterly for his restrained and reasoned conclusions. It is almost impossible to conceive how the author of " The Philadelphia Negro " could have penned the " Second Niagara Movement Manifesto," without mental and moral metamorphosis. When DuBois essays the rôle of the agitator, and attempts to focus the varied energies of his mind upon a concrete social emergency, it is apt to result, as did his " Atlanta Tragedy," in an extravaganza of feeling and a fiasco of thought. His mind being cast in a weird and fantastic mold, his place is the cloister of the reflective scholar. He lives behind the veil; and whenever he emerges to mingle with the grosser affairs of life we may expect to hear, ever and anon, that sad and bitter wail. Dr. DuBois is passionately devoted to the welfare of his race, but he is allowing himself to be exploited in a function for which he is by nature unfit. His highest service will consist in interpreting to the white people the needs and feeling of his race in terms of exact knowledge and nice language, rather than as an agitator or promoter of concrete achievement. Trotter is the real guiding power of the " Niagara Movement," for he, almost by his single hand, created the growth that made it possible. Although we may hear the voice of Jacob, we feel the hand of Esau. DuBois ostensibly manages the new movement, but when he dares to deviate from the inflexible intentions of Trotter, there will be war within, and victory will rest with the intrepid editor.

We need not feel surprised, therefore, that such picturesque points as Niagara Falls and Harper's Ferry figured in the " Niagara Movement," under the guiding mind of DuBois. They were planned by a poetic mind. It is a poet's attempt to dramatize the ills of a race with picturesque stage setting and spectacular scenic effect.

At the call of DuBois a number of men met at Niagara Falls, in August, 1905, and launched the " Niagara Movement " amid the torrential downpour of the mighty waters. In this gathering were some of the ablest and most earnest men of the Negro race. The call appealed mainly to those of vehement temperament, every one of whom was an avowed opponent of Booker T. Washington. An address was issued to the country setting forth in manly, pointed terms the rights of the colored race. The platform of the movement contained nothing new, and its dynamic was derived from dissent. It was merely a protest against American color discrimination, based upon Mr. Washington's alleged acquiescence. Many of the subscribers to the new movement had not, up to that time, been known for their activity in behalf of the race, and espoused the cause as " a cult " with all the wonted zeal and intolerance of new converts.

The second manifesto of this body, issued from Harper's Ferry, the scene of John Brown's martyrdom, is scarcely distinguishable from a wild and frantic shriek. The lachrymal wail befits the child, which has " no language but a cry." Verbal vehemence void of practical power to enforce demands in an ineffectual missive to be hurled against the stronghold of prejudice

Another meeting has been called at Oberlin, Ohio, because of its stirring anti-slavery suggestiveness. We may expect a future session at Appomattox, so prone is the poetic temperament to avail itself of episodal and dramatic situations.

When the " Niagara Movement " grows out of the declamatory stage and becomes tempered by dealing with the actualities of the situation it will find its place among the many agencies working together for the general cause.

The radical and conservative tendencies of the Negro race cannot be better described than by comparing, or rather contrasting, the two superlative colored men in whom we find their highest embodiment—Frederick Douglass and Booker Washington, who were both picked out and exploited by white men as the mouthpiece and intermediaries of the black race. The two men are in part products of their times, but are also natural antipodes. Douglass lived in the day of moral giants; Washington lives in the era of merchant princes. The contemporaries of Douglass emphasized the rights of man; those of Washington, his productive capacity. The age of Douglass acknowledged the sanction of the Golden Rule; that of Washington worships the Rule of *Gold*. The equality of men was constantly dinned into Douglass's ears; Washington hears nothing but the inferiority of the Negro and the dominance of the Saxon. Douglass could hardly receive a hearing today; Washington would have been hooted off the stage a generation ago. Thus all truly useful men must be, in a measure, time-servers; for unless they serve their time, they can scarcely serve at all.   But great as was the diversity of formative influences that shaped these two great lives, there is no less opposability in their innate bias of character. Douglass was like a lion, bold and fearless; Washington is lamblike, meek and submissive.   Douglass escaped from personal bondage, which his soul abhorred; but for Lincoln's proclamation, Washington would probably have arisen to esteem and favor in the eyes of his master as a good and faithful servant. Douglass insisted upon rights; Washington insists upon duty. Douglass held up to public scorn the sins of the white man; Washington portrays the faults of his own race.   Douglass spoke what he thought the world should hear; Washington speaks only what he feels it is disposed to listen to.   Douglass's conduct was actuated by principle; Washington's by prudence.   Douglass had no limited, copyrighted programme for his race, but appealed to the Decalogue, the Golden Rule, the Declaration of Independence, the Constitution of the United States; Washington, holding these great principles in the shadowy background, presents a practical expedient applicable to present needs. Douglass was a moralist, insisting upon the application of righteousness to public affairs; Washington is a practical opportunist, accepting the best terms which he thinks it possible to secure.

Booker T. Washington came upon the public stage at the time when the policies which Douglass embodied had seemed to fail.   Reconstruction measures had proved abortive; Negro politicians, like Othello, had lost their occupation, and had sought asylum in the Government departments at Washington; the erstwhile advocates of the Negro's cause had grown indifferent or apologetic, and the plain

intent of the Constitution had been overborne in the
South with the connivance of the North. The idea
of lifting the Negro to the plane of equality with
the white race, once so fondly cherished, found few
remaining advocates. Mr. Washington sized up the
situation with the certainty and celerity of a genius.
He based his policy upon the ruins of the policy that
had been exploited. He avoided controverted issues,
and moved, not along the line of least resistance, but
of no resistance at all. He founded his creed upon
construction rather than upon criticism. He urged
his race to do the things possible rather than whine
and pine over things prohibited. According to his
philosophy, it is better to build even upon the shifting sands of expediency than not to build at all
simply because you cannot secure a granite foundation. He thus hoped to utilize for the betterment
of the Negro whatever residue of good feeling there
might be in the white race. Tuskegee Institute,
which is in itself a marvelous achievement, is only
the pulpit from which Mr. Washington proclaims
his doctrine. Industrial education has become so
intricately interwoven into his policy that his critics
are forced into the ridiculous attitude of opposing a
form of training essential to the welfare of any
people. For reasons of policy, Mr. Washington has
been provokingly silent as to the claim of higher
education, although his personal actions proclaim
loudly enough the belief that is in his heart. The
subject of industrial and higher education is merely
one of ratio and proportion, and not one of fundamental controversy.

Mr. Washington's bitterest opponents cannot gain-
say his sincerity or doubt that the welfare of his
race is the chief burden of his soul. He follows the
leading of his own light. Few men of this genera-

tion have shown such signal devotion, self-abnega-
tion and strenuous endeavor for an altruistic cause.

One of the chief complaints against the Tuskegeean is lack of definite statement upon questions of
vital concern. Mr. Washington is a diplomat, and
a great one. He sinks into sphinxlike silence when
the demands of the situation seem to require emphatic
utterance. His carefully studied deliverances upon
disputed issues often possess the equivocalness of a
Delphic oracle. While he does not openly avow, yet
he would not disclaim, in distinct terms, a single plank
in the platform of Douglass. The white race saddles
its own notions and feelings upon him, and yet he
opens not his mouth. His sagacious silence and
shrewdly measured assertions must be taken, if not
with the traditional grain of salt, at least with a
goodly lump of diplomatic allowance. We do not
usually associate deep moral conviction with the
guileful arts of diplomacy, but we must remember
that the delicate rôle of race statesmanship cannot
be played without rare caution and tactful prudence.

Mr. Washington's popularity and prominence depend largely upon the fact that his putative policy
is acceptable to the Southern whites, because he allows them to believe that he accepts their estimate
of the Negro's inferior place in the social scheme.
He is quiescent, if not acquiescent, as to the white
man's superior claims. He shuts his eyes to many
of the wrongs and outrages heaped upon the Negro
race. He never runs against the Southerner's traditional prejudices, and even when he protests against
his practices the protestation is so palliatory that,
like a good conscience, it is void of offence. Equality
between the races, whether social, political, or civil, is
an unsavory term to the white man's palate, and,
therefore, Mr. Washington obliterates it from his

vocabulary. The higher education of the Negro is in general disfavor, so Mr. Washington gives the approval of his silence to the charge that such pure and devoted philanthropists as President Ware of Atlanta, Patton of Howard, Tupper of Shaw, and Cravath of Fisk, who did more than all others to quicken and inspire the Negro race, have lived, loved, labored, and died in vain. Nor is Washington objectionable to the white man by reason of his self-assertive personality. He is an exact modern counterpart of Chaucer's knight: " Curteys he was, lowly, and servysable." Even when he violates the sacred code of the whites by dining with the President or mingling on easy terms with ultra-fashionable circles, they lash themselves into momentary fury, but straightway proceed to laud and glorify his policy. The North applauds and sustains his propagandism because he strives to be at peace with all men. He appeals to the amity and not the enmity of both races. We are in the midst of an era of good feeling, and must have peace at any price. It is interesting to witness how many of the erstwhile loud-voiced advocates of the Negro's rights have seized upon Mr. Washington's pacific policy as a graceful recession from the former position. The whites have set up Booker Washington as in a former day they set up Frederick Douglass, as the divinely appointed and anointed leader of his race, and regard as sacrilege all criticism and even candid discussion on the part of those whom he has been sent to guide. They demand for him an exemption which they have never accorded their own leaders, from George Washington to Theodore Roosevelt. Nothing could be further from Mr. Washington's thoughts than the assumption of divine commission which the whites seek to impose upon him. He makes no claim to have re-

ceived a revelation, either from burning bush or
mountain top. He is a simple, sincere, unsophisticated colaborer with his brethren; a single, though
signal, agency for the betterment of his race.

Mr. Washington did not start out as a leader of
his people's own choosing; he did not command an
enthusiastic and spontaneous following. He lacks
that magnetic personality that would cause men to
love him and women to adore him. His method is
rather that of a missionary seeking the material and
moral betterment of an unfortunate people, than of
a spontaneous leader voicing their highest self-ex-
pression. He is deficient in the fearlessness, the self-
assertion, the aggressive and heroic spirit necessary
to quicken and inspire. Such a leader must not hold
up for painful contemplation or emphasize to the
outside world the repugnant, grotesque and ludicrous
faults and foibles of his own people, but he must constantly direct their attention to higher and better
ideals. His dominant note must be pitched in the
major key. He must not be of the earth earthy,
with range of vision limited to the ugliness of untoward conditions, but must have the power of
idealization and spiritual vista. Exaggerated self-
importance is deemed an individual fault, but a racial
virtue. It has been the chief incentive of every race
or nation that has ever gained prominence in the
world's affairs. The triumphant, God-sent leader of
any people must be the exponent and expounder of
their highest aspirations and feelings, and must
evoke their manhood and self-esteem, yea, even their
vanity and pride.

Mr. Washington's following was at first very
largely prudential and constrained; it lacked spon-
taneousness and joyance. He was not hailed with
glad acclaim as the deliverer of his people. He

brought good gifts rather than glad tidings. Many
believed in him for his work's sake; some acquiesced
rather than antagonize one who had gained so
large a measure of public confidence; others were
willing to co-operate in the accomplishment of good
deeds, though they inwardly detested his doctrine;
while those of political instinct sought his favor as
a pass-key to prestige and place. Few thoughtful
colored men espoused what passed as Mr. Washington's " policy " without apology or reserve. Many
of the more dispassionate and thoughtful are disposed to yield to his primacy because he has such a
hold on the sentiment and imagination of the white
race that, if for any reason the spell should be broken,
no other colored man could ever hope for like consideration and esteem.

Mr. Washington's critics assert that his leadership
has been barren of good results to the Negro race,
unmindful of the magnitude of the contract he has
promised the American people that he would solve
the race problem. Under his regnancy it is claimed
that the last vestige of political power has been swept
away. Civil privileges have been restricted, educational opportunities, in some States at least, have
been curtailed; the industrial situation, the keystone
of his policy, has become more ominous and uncertain, while the feeling between the races is constantly
growing more acute and threatening. In answer to
this it is averred that no human power could stay
the wave of race hatred now sweeping over the country, but that the Tuskegeean's pacific policy will
serve to relieve the severity of the blow. All of the
leaders before him essayed the task in vain, and gave
up in despair.

The majority of thoughtful men range between
these wide-apart views, appreciating the good and

the limitations of both. They believe in neither surrender nor revolution, and that both forces have
their place and function in the solution of the race
problem. They are joint factors of a common
product, whose relative strength and importance may
increase or diminish with the shifting exigencies of
conditions. While it would be unseemly for those
who breathe the free air of New England to remain
silent concerning the heavy burden borne by their
brethren in the South, yet we must not forget that
Frederick Douglass himself could not to-day build up
an institution in Alabama, nor do the imperative constructive work in that section. The progress of all
peoples is marked by alternations of combat and contention on the one hand, and compromise and
concession on the other, and progress is the result
of the play and counterplay of these forces. Colored
men should have a larger tolerance for the widest
latitude of opinion and method. Too frequently
what passes as " an irrepressible conflict " is merely
difference in point of view.

The Negro's lot would be sad indeed if, under al-
lurement of material advantage and temporary easement, he should sink into pliant yieldance to
unrighteous oppression; but it would be sadder still
if intemperate insistence should engender ill will and
strife, when the race is not yet ready to be "battered
with the shocks of doom." The words of Guizot
never found a more pertinent application than to the
present circumstances and situation of the Negro
race:

We continually oscillate between an inclination to complain
without sufficient cause and to be too easily satisfied. We have
extreme susceptibility of mind, an inordinate craving, an ambition in our thoughts, in our desires, and in the movements of
our imagination; yet when we come to practical life, when

trouble, when sacrifices, when efforts are required for the attainment of our object, we sink into lassitude and inactivity. Let us not, however, suffer ourselves to be invaded by either of these vices. Let us estimate fairly what our abilities, our knowledge, our power enable us to do lawfully, and let us aim at nothing that we cannot lawfully, justly and prudently—with a proper respect for the great principles upon which our social system, our civilization, is based—attain.

Mr. Booker T. Washington's later career is exemplifying more and more the philosophy of this sentiment.

Under the spur of adverse criticism and the growing sense of responsibility which his expanding opportunities impose, Mr. Washington has become so enlarged that his leadership is universally conceded, and well-nigh universally accepted. Few men have shown such power of enlargement. Even those who continue to challenge his primacy confess that they are opposing the Washington of long ago rather than the Washington of to-day. He rises triumphantly on stepping-stones of his dead self to higher things. He began his career with a narrow educational bias and a one-sided championship of industrial training, as offset to the claims of literary culture which had hitherto absorbed the substance of Northern philanthropy. But he has grown so far in grasp and in breadth of view that he advocates all modes of education in their proper place and proportion. He at first deprecated the Negro's active participation in politics, but with broadening vision and increasing courage he now serves as consulting statesman touching all political interests of the race.

Washington's equability of temper is most remarkable. He receives a bequest of a million dollars, dines with the President, listens to the adulation of half the world or the bitter abuse of those whom he strives to serve, with the same modest and unruffled demeanor. His sanity and poise are unsurpassed. In a toast at a banquet given in honor of Mr. Washington in the city of Washington, the present writer proclaimed his conditional leadership, which the Negro race is now accepting with lessening reserve:

"We have as our guest to-night one who has come up from slavery, up from the coal caverns of West Virginia, struggling up against narrow theories, lack of early education and bias of environment, tactfully expanding the prudential restraints of a delicate and critical situation, rising upon successive stepping-stones of past achievements and past mistakes, but ever planting his feet upon higher and higher ground. Sir, you enjoy a degree of concrete achievement and personal distinction excelled by few men now living on this planet. You are not only the foremost man of the Negro race, but one of the foremost men of all the world. We did not give you that 'glad eminence' and we cannot take it away, but we would utilize and appropriate it to the good of the race. You have the attention of the white world; you hold the pass-key to the heart of the great white race. Your commanding position, your personal prestige, and the magic influence of your illustrious name entail upon you the responsibility to become the leader of the people, to stand as daysman between us and the great white God, and lay a propitiating hand upon us both. Some have criticised in the past, and reserve the right to do so in the future. A noble soul is big enough to invite candid criticism, and eschew sycophantic adulation.

"Sir, if you will stand upon the granite pedestal of truth and righteousness, and pursue policies that are commensurate with the entire circle of our needs, and which are broad-based upon the people's will,

and advocate the fullest opportunity of Negro youth
to expand and exploit their faculties, if you will
stand as the fearless champion of the Negro's political rights before the law and behind the law, then a
united race will rise up and join in gladsome chorus:

> " ' Only thou our leader be,
> And we still will follow thee.' "

AS TO THE LEOPARD'S SPOTS

An Open Letter to Thomas Dixon, Jr.

As to the Leopard's Spots—" I regard it as the ablest, soundest, and most important document that has appeared on this subject in many years.

"Geo. W. Cable."

September, 1905.

Mr. Thomas Dixon, Jr.

Dear Sir: I am writing you this letter to express the attitude and feeling of ten million of your fellow-citizens toward the evil propagandism of race animosity to which you have lent your great literary powers. Through the widespread influence of your writings you have become the chief priest of those who worship at the shrine of race hatred and wrath. This one spirit runs through all your books and published utterances, like the recurrent theme of an opera. As the general trend of your doctrine is clearly epitomized and put forth in your contribution to the *Saturday Evening Post* of August 19, I beg to consider chiefly the issues therein raised. You are a white man born in the midst of the Civil War; I am a Negro born during the same stirring epoch. You were born with a silver spoon in your mouth; I was born with an iron hoe in my hand. Your race has afflicted accumulated injury and wrong upon mine; mine has borne yours only service and good will. You express

28

your views with the most scathing frankness; I am sure you will welcome an equally candid expression from me.

Permit me to acknowledge the personal consideration which you have shown me. You will doubtless recall that when I addressed the Congregational ministers of New York City, a year or more ago, you asked permission to be present and listened attentively to what I had to say, although, as might have been expected, you beat a precipitous retreat when luncheon was announced. In your article in the *Post* you make several references to me and to other colored men with entire personal courtesy. So far as I know you have never varied from this rule in your personal dealings with members of my race. You are merciless, however, in excoriating the race as a whole, thus keenly wounding the sensibilities of every individual of that blood. I assure you that this courtesy of personal treatment will be reciprocated in this letter, however sharply I may be compelled to take issue with the views you set forth and to deplore your attitude. I shall endeavor to indulge in no bitter word against your race or against the South, whose exponent and special pleader you assume to be.

I fear that you have mistaken personal manners, the inevitable varnish of any gentleman of your antecedents and rearing, for friendship to a race which you hold in despite. You tell us that you are kind and considerate to your personal servants. It is somewhat strange that you should deem such assurance necessary, any more than it is necessary for you to assure us that you are kind to your horse or your dog and fond of them. But when you write yourself down as " one of their best friends," you need not be surprised if we retort the refrain of the ritual, " From all such proffers of friendship, good Lord deliver us." An astronomer once tried to convince a layman, unlearned in astronomical lore, that the North Star was bigger than the moon. The unsophisticated reply was, " It might be so, but it has a mighty poor way of showing it." The reconciliation of your apparently violent attitude with your profession of friendship is, I confess, too subtle a process for the African intellect.

I beg to call your attention to a fault of temper which may be unconscious on your part. The traditional method of your class in dealing with adverse opinion was " a word and a blow "; with you it is a word and an epithet. Your opponents in the field of opinion are set down as " pot-house politicians," " the ostrich man," " the pooh-pooh man," and " the benevolent old maid." Of course, Theodore Roosevelt, Andrew Carnegie, J. L. M. Curry, Lyman Abbott, Chancellor Hill, John D. Rockefeller and E. Gardner Murphy would fall under the one or the other of your sonorous designations. Your choicest assortment of epithets, I presume, is reserved for Robert C. Ogden and the General Education Board, whom you seem to regard with especial repugnance. For these, doubtless, you intended such appellatives as " weak-minded optimists " and " female men." The most illustrious names in America, living and dead, would fall under the ban of your opprobrium. According to your standard, the only Americans who could be accounted safe, sane and judicious on the race issue would be the author of " The Leopard's Spots," Senator Tillman, and Governor Vardaman.

Your fundamental thesis is that " no amount of education of any kind, industrious, classical or religious, can make a Negro a white man or bridge the chasm of the centuries which separates him from

the white man in the evolution of human history."
This doctrine is as old as human oppression. Calhoun made it the arch-stone in the defense of Negro
slavery—and lost.

This is but a recrudescence of the doctrine which
was exploited and exploded during the anti-slavery
struggle. Do you recall the school of pro-slavery
scientists who demonstrated beyond doubt that the
Negro's skull was too thick to comprehend the
substance of Aryan knowledge? Have you not
read in the now discredited scientific books of
that period with what triumphant acclaim it was
shown that the shape and size of the Negro's skull,
facial angle, and cephalic configuration rendered
him forever impervious to the white man's civilization? But all enlightened minds are now as ashamed
of that doctrine as they are of the one-time dogma
that the Negro had no soul. We become aware of
mind through its manifestations. Within forty years
of only partial opportunity, while playing, as it
were, in the back yard of civilization, the American
Negro has cut down his illiteracy by over fifty per
cent.; has produced a professional class, some fifty
thousand strong, including ministers, teachers, doctors, editors, authors, architects, engineers, and is
found in all higher lines of listed pursuits in which
white men are engaged; some three thousand Negroes
have taken collegiate degrees, over three hundred
being from the best institutions in the North and
West established for the most favored white youth;
there is scarcely a first-class institution in America,
excepting some three or four in the South, that is
without colored students, who pursue their studies
generally with success, and sometimes with distinction; Negro inventors have taken out four hundred
patents as a contribution to the mechanical genius of

America; there are scores of Negroes who, for conceded ability and achievements, take respectable rank in the company of distinguished Americans.

It devolves upon you, Mr. Dixon, to point out some standard, either of intelligence, character, or conduct, to which the Negro cannot conform. Will you please tell a waiting world just what is the psychological difference between the races? No reputable authority, either of the old or of the new school of psychology, has yet pointed out any sharp psychic discriminant. There is not a single intellectual, moral, or spiritual excellence attained by the white race to which the Negro does not yield an appreciative response. If you could show that the Negro is incapable of mastering the intricacies of Aryan speech; that he could not comprehend the intellectual basis of European culture, or apply the apparatus of practical knowledge; that he could not be made amenable to the white man's ethical code or appreciate his spiritual motive—then your case would be proved. But in default of such demonstration we must relegate your eloquent pronouncement to the realm of generalization and prophecy, an easy and agreeable exercise of the mind in which the romancer is ever prone to indulge.

The inherent, essential and unchangeable inferiority of the Negro to the white man lies at the basis of your social philosophy. You disdain to examine the validity of your fondly cherished hope. You follow closely in the wake of Tom Watson, in the June number of his homonymous magazine. You both hurl your thesis of innate racial inferiority at the head of Booker T. Washington. You use the same illustrations, the same arguments, and you set them forth in the same order of recital, and for the most part in identical language. This seems to be an instance of great minds, or at least of minds of the same grade, running in the same channel.

These are your words: " What contribution to human progress have the millions of Africans, who inhabit this planet, made during the past four thousand years? Absolutely nothing." These are the words of Thomas Watson spoken some two months previous: " What does civilization owe to the Negro race? Nothing! Nothing!! Nothing!!!" You answer the query with the most emphatic negative noun and the strongest qualifying adjective in the language. Mr. Watson, of a more ecstatic temperament, replies with the same noun and six exclamation points. One rarely meets, outside of yellow journalism, with such lavishness of language wasted upon a hoary dogma. A discredited doctrine that has been bandied about the world from the time of Canaan to Calhoun, is revamped and set forth with as much ardor and fervency of feeling as if revealed for the first time and proclaimed for the enlightenment of a waiting world. But neither boastful asseveration on your part nor indignant denial on mine will affect the facts of the case. That Negroes in the average are not equal in developed capacity to the white race, is a proposition which it would be as simple to affirm as it is silly to deny. The Negro represents a belated race which has not yet taken a commanding part in the progressive movement of the world. In the great cosmic scheme of things, some races reach the lime-light of civilization ahead of others. But that temporary forwardness does not argue inherent superiority is as evident as any fact of history. An unfriendly environment may hinder and impede the one, while fortunate circumstances may quicken and spur the other. Relative superiority is only a transient phase of human development. You tell us that " The Jew had achieved a civilization—had his poets, prophets, priests and kings, when our Germanic ancestors were still in the woods cracking cocoanuts and hickory nuts with the monkeys." Fancy some learned Jew at that day citing your query about the contribution of the Germanic races to the culture of the human spirit, during the thousands of years of their existence! Does the progress of history not prove that races may lie dormant and fallow for ages and then break suddenly into prestige and power? Fifty years ago you doubtless would have ranked Japan among the benighted nations and hurled at their heathen heads some derogatory query as to their contribution to civilization. But since the happenings at Mukden and Port Arthur and Portsmouth, I suppose that you are ready to change your mind on the subject. Or maybe, since the Jap has proved himself a " first-class fighting man," able to cope on equal terms with the best breeds of Europe, you will claim him as belonging to the white race, notwithstanding his pig eye and yellow pigment.

In the course of history the ascendency of the various races and nations of men is subject to strange variability. The Egyptian, the Jew, the Indian, the Greek, the Roman, the Arab, has each had his turn at domination. When the earlier nations were in their zenith of art and thought and song, Franks and Britons and Germans were roaming through dense forests, groveling in subterranean caves, practicing barbarous rites, and chanting horrid incantations to graven gods. In the proud days of Aristotle the ancestors of Newton and Shakespeare and Bacon could not count beyond the ten fingers. As compared with the developed civilization of the period, they were a backward race, though, as subsequent development has shown, by no means an inferior one.

There were hasty philosophers in that day who branded these people with the everlasting stamp of inferiority. The brand of philosophy portrayed in " The Leopard's Spots " and in *Tom Watson's Magazine* has flourished in all ages of the world.

The individuals of a backward race are not, as such, necessarily inferior to those of a more advanced people. The vast majority of any race is composed of ordinary and inferior folk. To use President Roosevelt's expression, they cannot pull their own weight. It is only the few choice individuals, reinforced by a high standard of social efficiency, that are capable of adding to the civilization of the world.

There is no hard and fast line dividing the two races on the scale of capacity. There is the widest possible range of variation within the limits of each. A philosopher and a fool may not only be members of the same race but of the same family. No scheme of classification is possible which will include all white men and shut out all Negroes. According to any test of excellence that your and Mr. Watson's ingenuity can devise, some Negroes will be superior to most white men; no stretch of ingenuity or strain of conscience has yet devised a plan of franchise which includes all of the members of one race and excludes all those of the other.

Learned opinion on the other side ought, at least, to weigh as much against your thesis as your own fulminations count in favor of it. You surely have high respect for the authority of Thomas Jefferson. In a letter to Benjamin Banneker, the Negro astronomer, the author of the great Declaration wrote: " Nobody wishes more than I do to see such proofs as you exhibit that Nature has given to our black brethren talents equal to those of the other colors of men, and that the apparent want of them is owing merely to the degraded condition of their existence, both in Africa and America."

Mr. William Mathews, a noted author, writing some time ago in the *North American Review*, asserts: "We affirm that the inferiority of the Negro has never been proven, nor is there any good ground to suppose that he is forever to maintain his relative position, or that he is inferior to the white man in any other sense than some white races are inferior to each other."

Prof. N. F. Shaler, a native of the South, and Professor in Harvard University, writes in the *Arena*: "There are hundreds and thousands of black men who in capacity are to be ranked with the superior persons of the dominant race, and it is hard to say that in any evident feature of mind they characteristically differ from their white fellow-citizens."

Benjamin Kidd, in his work on Social Evolution, declares that the Negro child shows no inferiority, and that the deficiency which he seems to manifest in after life is due to his dwarfing and benumbing environment. Prof. John Spencer Bassett, of Trinity College, North Carolina, has had the courage to state the belief that the Negro would gain equality some day. He also tells us that Dr. Booker Washington, whom Mr. Watson takes so sharply to task for hinting that the Negro may be superior to some white men, is the greatest man, with a single exception, that the South has produced in a hundred years. This is indeed a suggestion of Negro superiority with a vengeance. In the judgment of this distinguished Southerner, one Negro, at least, is superior to millions of his white fellow-citizens, including the editor of *Tom Watson's Magazine* and the author of "The Leopard's Spots."

"But," rejoins the objector, "if the Negro possesses this inherent capacity, why has he not given the world the benefit of it during the course of history?" Capacity is potential rather than a dynamic mode of energy. Whatever native capacity the mind may possess, it must be stimulated and reinforced by social accomplishment before it can show great achievement. In arithmetic a number has an inherent and local value, the latter being by far the more powerful function in numerical calculation. The individual may count for much, but the social efficiency counts for most. It is absolutely impossible for a Francis Bacon to thrive among the Bushmen, or a Herbert Spencer among the Hottentots. The great names of the world always arise among the people who, for the time being, are in the forefront of the world's movements. We do not expect names of the first degree of lustre to arise among suppressed and submerged classes.

In confirmation of this view let us turn for a moment to the pages of history. Mr. Lecky tells us in his "History of European Morals":

"I regard it as one of the anomalies of history that within the narrow limits and scanty population of the Greek states should have arisen men who in almost every conceivable form of genius, in philosophy, in ethics, in dramatic and lyric poetry, in written and spoken eloquence, in statesmanship, in sculpture, in painting, and probably also in music, should have attained almost or altogether the highest limits of human perfection."

Mr. Galton in his "Hereditary Genius" tells us: "We have no men to put beside Socrates and Phidias. The millions of Europe breeding as they have done for the subsequent two thousand years have never produced their equals. It follows from all this that

the average ability of the Athenian race is, on the
lowest estimate, very nearly two grades higher than
our own; that is, about as much as our race is above
that of the African Negro."   And yet this intellectual race, this race of Phidias and Homer, of
Plato and Socrates, has continued for two thousand
years in a state of complete intellectual stagnation.
When they lost their political nationality and became
submerged beneath the heavy weight of oppression,
to use the language of Macaulay, " their people have
degenerated into timid slaves and their language into
a barbarous jargon."   Can there be any stronger
proof of the fact that great achievements depend
upon environment and social stimulus rather than
innate capacity?

Where now is the boasted glory of Egypt and
Babylon, of Nineveh and Tyre? Expeditions from
distant continents are sent to unearth the achievements of renowned ancestors beneath the very feet
of their degenerate descendants, as a mute reminder
to the world of the transiency of human greatness.

The Jews seem to form an exception to this rule,
but the exception is seeming rather than real. While
they have lost their political integrity, they have preserved their spiritual nationality. The race of
Moses and Paul and Jesus still produces great names,
though not of the same grade of glory as their prototypes of old.

Our own country has not escaped the odium of
intellectual inferiority. The generation has scarcely
passed away in whose ears used to ring the standing
sneer, " Who reads an American book? " It was in
the day of Thomas Jefferson that a learned European
declared: "America has not produced one good poet,
one able mathematician, one man of genius in a single
art or science." In response to this charge Jefferson

enters an eloquent special plea. He says: "When we shall have existed as a people as long as the Greeks did before they produced a Homer, the Romans, a Virgil, the French, a Racine, the English, a Shakespeare and Milton, should this reproach be still true, we will inquire from what unfriendly cause it has proceeded." How analogous to this is the reproach which you and Mr. Watson, treading the track of Thomas Nelson Page, and those of his school of thought, now hurl against the Negro race? The response of Jefferson defending the American colonies from the reproach of innate inferiority will apply with augmented emphasis to ward off similar charges against the despised and rejected Negro. A learned authority tells us: "Hardly two centuries have passed since Russia was covered with a horde of barbarians among whom it would have been as difficult to find any example of intellectual cultivation and refinement as at this day to find the same phenomenon at Timbuctoo or among the Negroes of Georgia or Alabama." It is well for the good fame of the Russian people that *Tom Watson's Magazine* did not exist in those days.

According to a study of the distribution of ability in the United States, a study made by Hon. Henry Cabot Lodge, the little State of Massachusetts has produced more men of distinction and achievement than all the South combined. "In architecture, agriculture, manufacture, finance, legislation, sculpture, religion, organization, painting, music, literature, science, the wedding of the fine arts of religion," the South is relatively backward as compared with other sections of the country. But this lack of comparative achievement is not due at all to innate inferiority of Southern white men to their brethren in higher latitudes. Mr. Thomas Nelson Page, in his famous book on the Old South, accepts this derogatory fact and explains its cause with much ingenuity. The white people of the South claim, or rather boast of, a race prepotency and inheritance as great as that of any breed of men in the world. But they clearly fail to show like attainment.

It would evidently be unfair to conclude that the white race in Georgia is inherently inferior to the people of New England because it has failed to produce names of like renown. The difference in wealth, culture and bracing tone of environments are quite sufficient to account for the difference in results. I think that you and Mr. Watson will be generous enough to concede to the Negro the benefit of the same argument which the defenders of the South resort to in justification of its own relative backwardness. The Negro has never, during the whole course of history, been surrounded by those influences which tend to strengthen and develop the mind. To expect the Negroes of Georgia to produce a great general like Napoleon when they are not even allowed to carry arms, or to deride them for not producing scholars like those of the Renaissance when a few years ago they were forbidden the use of letters, verges closely upon the outer rim of absurdity. Do you look for great Negro statesmen in States where black men are not allowed to vote? Mr. Watson can tell something about the difficulty of being a statesman in Georgia, against the protest of the ruling political ring. He tried it. Above all, for Southern white men to berate the Negro for failing to gain the highest rounds of distinction reaches the climax of cruel inconsistency. One is reminded of the barbarous Teutons in " Titus Andronicus," who, after cutting out the tongue and hacking off the hands of the lovely Lavinia, ghoulishly chided her for not calling for sweet water with which to wash her delicate hands.

Here is another specimen of the grade of reasoning to which the readers of *Tom Watson's Magazine* are treated:

"Let me repeat to you, Doctor, the unvarnished truth, for it may do you good. The advance made by your race in America is the reflection of the white man's civilization. Just that and nothing more. The Negro lives in the light of the white man's civilization and reflects a part of that light."

Here again we come across the threadbare argument of the advocates of suppression and subordination of the Negro. The aptitude of any people for progress is tested by the readiness with which they absorb and assimilate the environment of which they form a part. I wonder if Mr. Watson would contend that the red Indian shows capacity for civilization because he neither borrows nor imitates. Civilization is not a spontaneous generation with any race or nation known to history, but the torch is handed down from race to race and from age to age, and gains in brilliancy as it goes. The progress made by the Negro has been natural and inevitable. Does Mr. Watson expect the American Negro to invent an alphabet before he learns to read? The Negro has advanced in exactly the same fashion that the white race has advanced, by taking advantage of all that has gone before. Other men have labored and we have entered into their labors. The Japanese did not invent the battleship, modern artillery, or the modern manual of arms, but they use them pretty effectively. The young race, like the individual, must first appropriate and apply what has already gone before. The white man has no exclusive proprietorship of civilization. White man's civilization is as much a misnomer as the white man's multiplication table. It is the equal inheritance of any one who can appropriate and apply it. This is the only practicable test of a people's capacity. I have no doubt that Mr. Watson would say that the million white people of Georgia are a very capable folk. And yet how many of them have added anything to the processes of civilization? They have simply entered into, and carried on the processes already established. When Mr. Watson concedes the Negro's ability to do this much he negatives the whole argument of inferiority.

You and Mr. Watson, by common, unaccountable parallelism, make the same quotation from Buckle's "History of Civilization," and in some mysterious manner endeavor to turn his words to the detriment of the Negro:

> The discoveries of great men never leave us; they are immortal, they contain those eternal truths which survive the shock of empires, outlive the struggle of rival creeds and witness the decay of successive religions. The discoveries of genius alone remain; it is to them we owe all that we now have; they are for all ages and all times; never young and never old, they bear the seeds of their own life, they flow on in perennial, undying stream; they are essentially cumulative, and giving birth to additions which they subsequently receive, they thus influence the most distant posterity, and after lapse of centuries produce more effect than they were able to do even at the moment of their promulgation.

Genius has no age, no country, no race; it belongs to mankind—who cares whether Sir Isaac Newton or Watts or Fulton was red, or white, or brown? Shakespeare means no more to you than he does to me, except in so far as you may have greater capacity of appreciation and enjoyment. Bacon and Darwin appeal to the world. Do you think that when the candle of genius has been lighted by fire from above it can be hid under a bushel of racial exclusiveness? Nay; rather, it is set on a candle-stick and gives light unto all who grope in darkness. The Negro enters into the inheritance of all the ages on equal terms with the rest, and who can say that he will not contribute his quota of genius to enrich the blood of the world?

The line of argument of every writer who undertakes to belittle the Negro is a well-beaten path. Liberia and Hayti are bound to come in for their share of ridicule and contemptuous handling. Mr. Watson calls these experiments freshly to mind, " lest we forget, lest we forget." We are told all about the incapacity of the black race for self-government, the relapse into barbarism, and much more, all of which we have heard before; and yet when we take all the circumstances into account, Hayti presents to the world one of the most remarkable achievements in the annals of human history. The panegyric of Wendell Phillips on Toussaint L'Ouverture is more than an outburst of rhetorical fancy; it is a just measure of his achievements in terms of his humble environment and the limited instrumentalities at his command. Where else in the course of history has a slave, with the aid of slaves, expelled a powerfully intrenched master-class and set up a government patterned after civilized models, which without external assistance or reinforcement from a parent civilization has endured for a hundred years in face of a frowning world? When we consider the difficulties that confront a weak government, without military or naval means to cope with its more powerful rivals, and where commercial adventurers are ever and anon stirring up internal strife, thus provoking the intervention of stronger governments, the marvel is that the republic of Hayti still endures, the only self-governing State of the Antilles. To expect as effective and proficient government to prevail in Hayti as at Washington would be expecting more of the black men in Hayti than we find in the white men of South America. And yet, I suspect that the million of Negroes in Hayti are as well governed as the corresponding number of blacks in Georgia, where, only yesterday, eight men were taken from the custody of the law and lynched without judge or jury. It is often charged that these people have not maintained the pace set by the old master-class, that the plantations are in ruins and that the whole island wears the aspect of dilapidation. Wherever a lower people overrun the civilization of a higher there is an inevitable lapse toward the level of the lower. When barbarians and semi-civilized hordes of northern Europe overran the southern peninsulas the civilization of the world was wrapped in a thousand years of darkness. Relapse inevitably precedes the rebound. Is there anything in the history of Hayti contrary to the law of human development?

You ask: " Can you change the color of the Negro's skin, the kink of his hair, the bulge of his lip, or the beat of his heart with a spelling-book or a machine? " This rhetorical outburst does great credit to your literary skill, and is calculated to delight the simple; but analysis fails to reveal in it any pregnant meaning. Since civilization is not an attribute of the color of skin, or curl of hair, or curve of lip, there is no necessity for changing such physical peculiarities, and if there were, the spelling-book and the machine would be very unlikely instruments for its accomplishment. But why, may I ask, would you desire to change the Negro's heart-throb, which already beats at a normal human pace? You need not be so frantic about the superiority of your race. Whatever superiority it may possess, inherent or acquired, will take care of itself without such rabid support. Has it ever occurred to you that the people of New England blood, who have done and are doing most to make the white race great and glorious in this land, are the most reticent about extravagant claims to everlasting superiority? You protest too much. Your loud pretensions, backed up by such exclamatory outburst of passion, make upon the reflecting mind the impression that you entertain a sneaking suspicion of their validity.

Your position as to the work and worth of Booker T. Washington is pitiably anomalous. You recite the story of his upward struggle with uncontrolled admiration: "The story of this little ragged, barefooted pickaninny, who lifted his eyes from a cabin in the hills of Virginia, saw a vision and followed it, until at last he presides over the richest and most powerful institution in the South, and sits down with crowned heads and presidents, has no parallel even in the ' Tales of the Arabian Nights.' " You say that this story appeals to the universal heart of humanity. And yet in a recent letter to the *Columbia State*, you say you regard it as an unspeakable outrage that Mr. Robert C. Ogden should walk arm in arm with this wonderful man who "appeals to the heart of universal humanity," and introduce him to the lady clerks in a dry goods store. Your passionate devotion to a narrow dogma has seriously impaired your sense of humor. The subject of your next great novel has been announced as " The Fall of Tuskegee." In one breath you commend the work of this great institution, while in another you condemn it because it does not fit into your preconceived scheme in the solution of the race problem. The Tuskegee ideal—" to make Negroes producers, lovers of labor, independent, honest, and good "—is one which you say that only a fool or a knave can find fault with, because, in your own words, " it rests squarely upon the eternal verities." Over against this you add with all the condemnatory emphasis of italics and exclamation point: " Tuskegee is not a servant training-school!" And further: " Mr. Washington is not training Negroes to take their places in the industries of the South in which white men direct and control them. He is not training students to be servants and come at the beck and call of any man. He is training them to be masters of men, to be independent, to own and operate their own industries, plant their own fields, buy and sell their own goods." All of which you condemn by imperative inference ten times stronger than your faint and forced verbal approval. It is a heedless man who wilfully flaunts his little philosophy in face of the " eternal verities." When the wise man finds that his prejudices are running against fixed principles in God's cosmic plan he speedily readjusts them in harmony therewith. Has it never occurred to you to re-examine the foundation of the faith, as well as the feeling that is in you, since you admit that it runs afoul of the " eternal verities "?

Mr. Washington's motto, in his own words, is that " The Negro has been worked; but now he must learn to work." The man who works for himself is of more service to any community than the man whose labor is exploited by others. You bring forward the traditional bias of the slave regime to modern conditions, viz., that the Negro did not exist in his own right and for his own sake, but for the benefit of the white man. This principle is as false in nature as it is in morals. The naturalists tell us that throughout all the range of animal creation there is found no creature which exists for the sake of any other, but each is striving after its own best welfare. Do you fear that the Negro's welfare is incompatible with that of the white man? I commend to you a careful perusal of the words of Mr. E. Gardner Murphy, who, like yourself, is a devoted Southerner, and is equally zealous to promote the highest interest of that section: "Have prosperity, peace, and happiness ever been successfully or permanently based upon indolence, inefficiency, and hopelessness? Since time began, has any human thing that God has made taken damage to itself or brought damage to the world through knowledge, truth, hope, and honest toil?" Read these words of your fellow Southerner, Mr. Dixon, and meditate upon them; they will do you good as the truth doeth the upright in heart.

You quote me as being in favor of the amalgamation of the races. A more careful reading of the article referred to would have convinced you that I was arguing against amalgamation as a probable solution of the race problem. I merely stated the intellectual conviction that two races cannot live indefinitely side by side, under the same general regime, without ultimately fusing. This was merely the expression of a belief, and not the utterance of a preference nor the formulation of a policy. I know of no colored man who advocates amalgamation as a feasible policy of solution. You are mistaken. The Negro does not "hope and dream of amalgamation." This would be self-stultification with a vengeance. If such a policy were allowed to dominate the imagination of the colored race its women would give themselves over to the unrestrained passion of white

men, in quest of tawny offspring, which would give
rise to a state of indescribable moral debauchery.
At the same time, you would hardly expect the
Negro, in derogation of his common human qualities,
to proclaim that he is so diverse from God's other
human creatures as to make the blending of the races
contrary to the law of nature. The Negro refuses
to become excited or share in your frenzy on this
subject. The amalgamation of the races is an ultimate possibility, though not an immediate probability. But what have you and I to do with ultimate
questions, anyway? Our concern is with duty, not
destiny. There are statisticians who can tell you,
to the tick of the clock, when the last ton of coal
in the bowels of the earth will be consumed; but you
will not lower the temperature of your sitting-room
one degree next winter in view of that ultimate contingency. The exhaustion of solar heat is within the
purview of astronomical calculation, and yet we eat
and drink and make merry in supreme indifference
to that far-off calamitous event. Do you not suppose that the future generations will have wisdom
adequate to the problems of their day? We certainly have no surplus wisdom to advance them.
Sufficient unto the day is the ignorance thereof.
Your frantic dread of amalgamation reminds me of
those religionists who would frighten a heedless world
into the belief that the end is at hand. It is conceivable that you voluntarily unfrocked yourself as
a priest of God, where your function was to save the
individual soul from punishment in the next world, in
order that you might the more effectively warn your
race to flee from amalgamation as from the wrath
to come.

But do you know, Mr. Dixon, that you are probably the foremost promoter of amalgamation be-

tween the two oceans? Wherever you narrow the scope of the Negro by preaching the doctrine of hate you drive thousands of persons of lighter hue over to the white race, carrying more or less Negro blood in their train. The blending of the races is less likely to take place if the self-respect and manly opportunity of the Negro are respected and encouraged than if he is to be forever crushed beneath the level of his faculties for dread of the fancied result. Hundreds of the composite progeny are daily crossing the color line and carrying as much of the despised blood as an albicant skin can conceal without betrayal. I believe that it was Congressman Tillman, brother of the more famous Senator of that name, who stated on the floor of the Constitutional Convention of South Carolina that he knew of four hundred white families in that State who had a taint of Negro blood in their veins. I personally know, or know of, fifty cases of transition in the city of Washington. It is a momentous thing for one to change one's caste. The man or woman who affects to deny, ignore, or scorn the class with whom he previously associated is usually deemed deficient in the nobler qualities of human nature. It is not conceivable that persons of this class would undergo the self-degradation and humiliation of soul necessary to cross the great " social divide " unless it be to escape for themselves and their descendants an odious and despised status. Your oft expressed and passionately avowed belief that the progressive development of the Negro would hasten amalgamation is not borne out by the facts of observation. The refined and cultivated class among colored people are as much disinclined to such unions as the whites themselves. I am sorry that you saw fit to characterize Frederick Douglass as " a bombastic vituper-

ator." You thereby gave poignant offense to ten
millions of his race who regard him as the best embodiment of their possibilities. Besides, millions of
your race rate him among the foremost and best beloved of Americans. How would you feel if some
one should stigmatize Jefferson Davis or Robert E.
Lee in such language, these beau ideals of your
Southern heart? But I will not undertake to defend Frederick Douglass against your calumniations.
I am frank to confess that I do not feel that he
needs it. The point I have in mind to make about
Mr. Douglass is that he has a hold upon the affection
of his race, not on account of his second marriage,
but in spite of it. He seriously affected his standing
with his people by that marriage.

Degradation would soonest lead to race blending
through illicitness. Had the institution of slavery
existed for another century without fresh African
importation there would scarcely have remained an
unbleached Negro on the continent. The best possible evidence that the development of self-respect
does not lead to amalgamation is furnished by Oberlin College in Ohio and by Berea College in Kentucky. These institutions have had thousands of
students of the two races, male and female, associating on terms of personal equality, mutual respect,
and good will, and yet in all these years not a single
case of miscegenation has resulted. Contrast this
record with the concubinage of the Southern plantation and the illicit relations of the city slum, and
it is easy to see where the chief stress should be
placed by those who so frantically dread race admix-
ture.

It seems to me, Mr. Dixon, that this frantic abhorrence of amalgamation is a little late in its appearance. Whence comes this stream of white blood

which flows, with more or less spissitude, in the veins of some six out of ten million Negroes? It is due to the bleaching breath of Saxon civilization. The Afro-American is hardly a Negro at all, but a new creature. Who brought about this present approachment between the races? Do you not appreciate the inconsistency in the attitude and the action on the part of many of the loud-mouthed advocates of race purity? It is said that old Father Chronos devoured his offspring in order to forestall future complications. But we do not learn that he put a bridle upon his passion as the surest means of security. The most effective service you can render to check the evil of amalgamation is to do missionary work among the males of your own race. This strenuous advocacy of race purity in face of proved proneness for miscegenation affords a striking reminder of the lines of *Hudibras:*

> "The self-same thing they will abhor,
> One way, and long another for."

I beg now to call your attention to one or two statements of fact. You state that " only one-third of the cotton crop is to-day raised by Negro labor." I would like to ask, what is your authority for that statement? According to the twelfth census, the latest available data on the subject, out of a total cotton crop of 9,534,707 bales for 1899, Negro proprietors alone produced 3,707,881 bales, or 39 per cent. of the total crop. There were 746,715 such proprietors, against 1,418,343 Negro agricultural laborers. If we suppose that these hired laborers were as efficient as the more independent tenants, it will be seen that, instead of raising only one-third, the Negro's immediate labor produced practically all of the cotton crop of the South.

Again, you say that " we have spent about $800,-
000,000 on Negro education since the war." This
statement is so very wide of the mark that I was
disposed to regard it as a misprint, if you had not
reinforced it with an application implying a like
amount. In the report of the Bureau of Education
for 1901 the estimated expenditure for Negro education in all the former slave States since the Civil
War is put down at $121,184,568. The amount con-
tributed by Northern philanthropy during that interval is variously estimated from fifty to seventy-
five millions. Your estimate is four times too large.
It would be interesting and informing to the world
if you would reveal the source of your information.
These misstatements of fact are not of so much importance in themselves as that they serve to warn
the reader against the accuracy and value of your
general judgments. It would seem that you derive
your figures of arithmetic from the same source from
which you fashion your figures of speech. You will
not blame the reader for not paying much heed to
your sweeping generalizations when you are at such
little pains as to the accuracy of easily ascertainable
data.

Your proposed solution of the race problem by
colonizing the Negroes in Liberia reaches the climax
of absurdity. It is difficult to see how such a proposition could emanate from a man of your reputation. Did you consult Cram's Atlas about Liberia?
Please do so. You will find that it has an area of
48,000 square miles and a population of 1,500,000,
natives and immigrants. The area and population
are about the same as those of North Carolina, which,
I believe, is your native State. When you tell us
that this restricted area, without commerce, without
manufacture, without any system of organized in-

dustry, can support every Negro in America, in addition to its present population, I beg mildly to suggest that you recall your plan for revision before submitting it to the judgment of a critical world. Your absolute indifference to the facts, and your heedlessness of the circumstances and conditions involved in the scheme of colonization, well befit the absurdity of the general proposition.

The solution of the race problem in America is indeed a grave and serious matter. It is one that calls for statesmanlike breadth of view, philanthropic tolerance of spirit, and exact social knowledge. The whole spirit of your propaganda is to add to its intensity and aggravation. You stir the slumbering fires of race wrath into an uncontrollable flame. I have read somewhere that Max Nordau, on reading "The Leopard's Spots," wrote to you suggesting the awful responsibility you had assumed in stirring up enmity between race and race. Your teachings subvert the foundations of law and established order. You are the high priest of lawlessness, the prophet of anarchy. Rudyard Kipling places this sentiment in the mouth of the wreckless stealer of seals in the Northern Sea: "There's never a law of God nor man runs north of fifty-three." This description exactly fits the brand of literature with which you are flooding the public. You openly urge your fellow-citizens to override all law, human and divine. Are you aware of the force and effect of these words? "Could fatuity reach a sublimer height than the idea that the white man will stand idly by and see the performance? What will he do when put to the test? He will do exactly what his white neighbor in the North does when the Negro threatens his bread— kill him!" These words breathe out hatred and slaughter and suggest the murder of innocent men

whose only crime is quest for the God-given right
to work. You poison the mind and pollute the imagination through the subtle influence of literature.
Are you aware of the force and effect of evil suggestion when the passions of men are in a state of unstable equilibrium? A heterogeneous population,
where the elements are, on any account, easily distinguishable, is an easy prey for the promoter of
wrath. The fuse is already prepared for the spark.
The soul of the mob is stirred by suggestion of
hatred and slaughter, as a famished beast at the
smell of blood. Hatred is the ever-handy dynamic
of the demagogue. The rabble responds much more
readily to an appeal to passion than to reason. To
stir wantonly the fires of race antipathy is as execrable a deed as flaunting a red rag in the face of a
bull at a summer's picnic, or raising a false cry of
"fire" in a crowded house. Human society could
not exist one hour except on the basis of law which
holds the baser passions of men in restraint.

In our complex situation it is only the rigid observance of law reinforced by higher moral restraint
that can keep these passions in bound. You speak
about giving the Negro a "square deal." Even
among gamblers, a "square deal" means to play
according to the rules of the game. The rules which
all civilized States have set for themselves are found
in the Ten Commandments, the Golden Rule, the
Sermon on the Mount, and the organic law of the
land. You acknowledge no such restraints when the
Negro is involved, but waive them all aside with
frenzied defiance. You preside at every crossroad
lynching of a helpless victim; wherever the midnight
murderer rides with rope and torch in quest of the
blood of his black brother, you ride by his side;
wherever the cries of the crucified victim go up to

God from the crackling flame, behold, you are there; when women and children, drunk with ghoulish glee, dance around the funeral pyre and mock the death groans of their fellow-man and fight for ghastly souvenirs, you have your part in the inspiration of it all. When guilefully guided workmen in mine and shop and factory, goaded by a real or imaginary sense of wrong, begin the plunder and pillage of property and murder of rival men, your suggestion is justifier of the dastardly doings. Lawlessness is gnawing at the very vitals of our institutions. It is the supreme duty of every enlightened mind to allay rather than spur on this spirit. You are hastening the time when there is to be a positive and emphatic show of hands—not of white hands against black hands, God forbid! not of Northern hands against Southern hands, heaven forfend! but a determined show of those who believe in law and God and constituted order, against those who would undermine and destroy the organic basis of society, involving all in a common ruin. No wonder Max Nordau exclaimed: "God, man, are you aware of your responsibility!"

But do not think, Mr. Dixon, that when you evoke the evil spirit you can exorcise him at will. The Negro in the end will be the least of his victims. Those who become inoculated with the virus of race hatred are more unfortunate than the victims of it. Voltaire tells us that it is more difficult and more meritorious to wean men of their prejudices than it is to civilize the barbarian. Race hatred is the most malignant poison that can afflict the mind. It freezes up the font of inspiration and chills the higher faculties of the soul. You are a greater enemy to your own race than you are to mine.

Permit me to close this letter with a citation from

Goldsmith's " Elegy on a Mad Dog." Please note the reference is descriptive and prophetic of the fate of the wreakers of wrath and the victims of it.

> " This man and dog at first were friends,
>   But when a pique began,
> The dog to gain some private ends,
>   Went mad and bit the man.

> " Around from all the neighboring streets,
>   The wondering neighbors ran,
> And swore the dog had lost his wits,
>   To bite so good a man.

> " The wound it seemed both sore and sad
>   To every Christian eye,
> And while they swore the dog was mad
>   They swore the man would die.

> " But soon a wonder came to light,
>   That show'd the rogues they lied,
> The man recovered of the bite;
>   The dog it was that died."

I have written you thus fully in order that you may clearly understand how the case lies in the Negro's mind. If any show of feeling or bitterness of spirit crops out in my treatment of the subject, or between the lines, my letter is, at least, wholly without vindictive intent; but is the inevitable outcome of dealing with issues that verge upon the deepest human passion.

AN APPEAL TO REASON ON THE RACE PROBLEM

AN OPEN LETTER TO JOHN TEMPLE GRAVES

SUGGESTED BY THE ATLANTA RIOT

OCTOBER, 1906.

Mr. John Temple Graves,
    Atlanta, Georgia.

My Dear Sir: The world has read with horror of
the Atlanta massacre and of the part you played
during that awful hour. The outbreak is but the
fruits of the seeds of race wrath which you and
others have been assiduously sowing. They who sow
the wind may expect to reap the whirlwind.

Your open appeal to the passion of the American
people while this riot was yet at its height was
fraught with evil suggestiveness. That half the people of Atlanta were not slain is due to the fact that
other counsel than yours prevailed. The rabble is ever
actuated by sinister influence. It obeys the acquiescent nod of secret understanding. There is a wire-
less communication between the baser elements of
society and the cunning instigator who provokes
them to wrath. Shakespeare with inimitable faith-
fulness has described the inner workings of this subtle and guilty control whereby the obsequious is
prone to take the humor of the mighty for a warrant
" to break within the bloody house of life " on the
winking of authority.

After a wide scanning of the American press,
yours is the only voice which I have heard, South
or North, white or black, still breathing out hatred

57

and slaughter amidst this awful carnival of blood. You alone occupy that " bad eminence." You broke the unanimity of appeal to reason when wild passion had reached its whitest heat.

Your attitude contrasted with that of the foremost member of the afflicted race measures the whole diameter of difference between cruelty and mercy. While Negroes, innocent of any crime, were suffering torture which would cause even the bruised worm to turn, Booker T. Washington, with Christ-like forgiveness of spirit, counseled his people to resist not evil.

The natural impulse of one belonging to the victim race is to indulge in indignant and bitter words. It is almost impossible to repress this natural ebullition of feeling. When human nature is so flagrantly outraged the very stones would cry out if men should hold their peace. It requires the highest self-repression and poise of spirit to refrain from verbal vehemence. But the voice of wisdom counsels only such expression as will tend to relieve rather than to intensify the strain of a critical situation.

I wish to utilize this gruesome occasion to discuss in an epistolary form some of the issues growing out of race relations in this country. I shall strive to be entirely courteous and considerate, and yet I shall abate no whit the fullest candor and plainness of statement demanded of one who speaks for the best interest of his people. Even an ambassador in bonds should speak with becoming boldness. There is a lamentable lack of expression which is at once candid and considerate, as respects the attitude of one race toward the other. We are prone to indulge in either wild, ungoverned onslaught, or diplomatic dissimilation and prudential concealment of real opinion and feeling. Honesty of utterance is usually accompanied with such ruthless and brutal frankness on the one hand, and resentful defiance on the other, as to render rational discussion impossible; while considerate temperament is too often given to indulgence in such fulsome flattery or unmanly yieldance as to make wholesome discussion unprofitable. Several years ago I sat on the platform of a meeting in Atlanta composed of about equal numbers of the two races. If I mistake not, you were present on that occasion. Local representatives on both sides of the race line vied with each other in vowing racial affection and ties of endearment. Words could go no further in expressing friendly relationship. But as I sat there, I divined, as I thought, a hidden spirit not revealed in the spoken words, which seemed to me to be simply verbal civilities and diplomatic platitudes. When the meeting adjourned each went to his own company with no surer knowledge of the real feeling or purpose of the other than when it convened.

Mr. Thomas Nelson Page has suggested in his recent book that the time has come for the best representatives of both races to meet together in conference on matters vitally concerning the common weal. It is needless to say that the value of such conference will depend upon the candor and frankness of spirit on both sides. The strained relation between the races calls for the temper and spirit of a statesmanship which discards wild hysterics and the heated passion of the moment, and sanely safeguards the interests of all the people. We are confronted with a problem whose factors are as intricate and whose outcome is as far-reaching as any that has ever taxed human wisdom for solution.

I am addressing this letter to you not merely because of the leading part which you played in the recent eruption, but also because you stand for a policy and a propaganda whose fatuity it fully reveals. It is a dangerous thing to arouse the evil spirit. It will turn again and rend you. The recent Atlanta outbreak fully illustrates the folly of appealing to the baser passion, especially in a particolored community.

Have you stopped to consider the cause and outcome of Atlanta's shame? The State of Georgia had been lashed into fury for more than a year of bitter race discussion. The atmosphere was ominous and tense. The fuse was ready for the spark. There were assaults or rumors of assaults by black or blackened fiends, upon white women, in and around Atlanta. These were eagerly seized upon and exaggerated by an inflammatory press. They became the alarum and rallying cry about which the pent-up wrath of race found vent. Red journalism ran rife. The terrorized imaginations saw a fiend incarnate in every darksome face. One paper, a little redder than the rest, boldly offered a reward for a lynching bee in the capital of the Empire State of the South. The flaring headlines fanned the fire into a furious flame. The evil passion of a people always finds lodgment in the breasts of its basest members. The half-grown, half-drunk, half-savage descendants of Oglethorpe's colonists can no longer contain themselves. Like the Indian on the war-path, they must have a savage yell. "Kill the Negro brutes!" is the tocsin. They kill and beat and bruise Negroes on sight. The air is filled with ghoulish yells, mingled with the shrieks and groans of the mangled and dying. Although the hollow cry of virtue is ever on the lip, the mob has no more conception of righteousness than a bloodhound set upon a scent cares about the guilt or innocence of his quarry.

The aroused appetite for blood must be satiated.
The police sprinkle the mob with the water hose;
but they laugh at this complaisant impotency and
joke with the mayor over the awful deeds of death,
and cry out louder for blood. The Negroes are in
seclusion; the liquor dens are closed; red headlines
are suppressed in the local press. The fury of the
mob ceases when it has nothing further to feed on.
Twenty innocent Negroes are dead. The guilty escape amid the slaughter of the innocent. Not a
single criminal has been touched. No evil propensity
has been eradicated. As the spasm of delirium re-
laxes the city's name stands tarnished before the
world. The sin of it, the shame of it will abide for
many a day. The Negroes emerge bleeding and torn;
the whites are dumbfounded at the evil possibilities
of their baser class. The race problem still remains
unsolved and the remedy for evil unsuggested. No
knot is untied in the tangled web. Such is the fatuity of your doctrine that the Negro must be controlled through the terror of the senses.

Atlanta may be regarded as the Athens of the
South. It abounds in schools and colleges for both
races. Here is the home of many of the most illustrious names in the South. Here lived the late Henry
W. Grady, the oracle of the New South. Joel Chandler Harris and Clark Howell wield a journalistic
and literary influence second to none of that section.
Among the Negroes Atlanta is noted for its increasing class of cultivated and refined people. Bowen,
DuBois, and Crogman are men of light and leading,
whose influence and power for good have gone out
to all the land; and yet deliberate appeal to race passion may involve this community, with so many influences of refinement and restraint, in riot and ruin
in a single night.

While the Atlanta riot still raged, a hurricane was blowing up from the tropics which destroyed hundreds of lives and millions of property in several Southern cities. But there was no blood-guiltiness. These cities will bury their dead and rebuild their waste places and pursue their path of peace and progress, forgetful and unregretful of this disastrous touch of nature. But the stain of Atlanta will abide. Immigration and capital will shun a mob-ruled city as they would a place infected with pestilence and death. The evil passion of man is more to be dreaded than the terror of earthquake or storm.

You represent the ultra type of opinion and feeling which find lodgment in the breast of the lower order of your own race. You would shut the Negro out from competition on the narrow and intolerant theory that there may not be enough " for you and us." Fearful that the tree of civilization is not big enough to bear fruit for all, you would deny the black man the God-given right to stretch forth his hand and partake of its fullness.

You are a disciple of Senator Tillman, who is the guide, philosopher, and friend of those who worship at the shrine of racial narrowness and hate.

Mr. William Garrott Brown, a scion of the traditional South, tells us in his most interesting book on " The Lower South in American History " that " the triumph of the Tillmanites in South Carolina worked a change in the internal policies of that State deeper than the change in 1776 and 1860." When we study the deep significance of the Tillman movement, we find that these words convey only the sober truth. The Tillman influence is by no means limited to his own State, but is equally potent in all parts of the South. The more cautious and considerate leaders have followed in his wake, while they have not cared openly to acknowledge his regency. Rough, ready, quick-witted, of blunt and bitter speech, unschooled, unrestrained by traditional amenities, Benjamin R. Tillman has become the embodiment and expounder of the rule of the nether whites. In this scheme of government the Negro has no part or parcel, except to be ruled with a rod of iron. The old aristocratic class is accorded only such influence as it may gain by seeming to conform to the spirit of those whom it formerly regarded with scorn. The traditional society of the South was based upon belief in the Negro's complaisant subordination. The Tillman regime is based upon the fear that, after all, the Negro might not be inferior. He is deprived of his rights lest he develop suspected power. Tillman openly proclaims that he intends to keep the serpent frozen. The Devils also believe and tremble. The shifting of the seat of power from the upper to the lower stratum marks indeed a momentous transformation. The Senate seats once held by Calhoun and Jefferson Davis, and later by Hampton and Lamar, are now occupied by Tillman and Williams.

Up to the time of Tillman's advent opposition to the aristocratic regime took the form of combining the cause of the poorer whites with that of the Negroes in bonds of political union. By this means, Mahone won in Virginia, Pritchard and Butler in North Carolina, while Cobb and Watson led their following to glorious and, as they claimed, fraudulent defeat in Alabama and Georgia. Tillman was the first to pitch the poor whites against the Negro in fierce and bitter array. He understood the dynamic power of hatred. He won, and put an end to the aristocratic dynasty in the South. No longer does any faction form political alliance with the Negro. Wade Hampton threw out the olive branch, which was rejected. Now all factions vie with each other in denunciation of this race. Even the lily whites, a new variety of political exotics, which, like their botanical prototype, neither toil nor spin, but array themselves in the victory and spoils of office, have caught the contagion.

A *novus homo*, a Pharaoh, who knows not Joseph the black, is now on the throne. The novice statesmen who are now so frantic about white supremacy are experiencing the first delirium of power. Under the old regime they were rigorously excluded from political authority. They never owned a slave nor anything else. But now the old line aristocrats habituated to governmental control must obey the behests of their new and numerous allies. They are forced to sacrifice both their statesmanlike breadth of view and traditional chivalric spirit.

Mr. E. Gardner Murphy asks with affirmative, though solicitous, intimation: "Is the organization of Democracy in the South never to include the Negro? Is he never to be a factor in the government and heir to a free and generous life?" Senator Tillman answers with a bitter and defiant negative. He declares with vehement asseveration that the black man will ever be excluded from a participating part in the government under which he lives. Race outbreaks in the South are but the outgrowth of this feeling on the part of the half-enlightened whites, but recently conscious of their political power, against the black man, whom they regard as a natural rival and whom they hold in bitter despite. Rumors of assaults but furnish occasions and excuse for the exercise of this pent-up feeling. They are no more the real cause than the gust of wind which topples the mighty oak after the ax-man has plied his last stroke is the dynamic cause of its downfall.

The volcanic eruption breaks through at the point where the mountain crust is thinnest.

A different excuse was found at Wilmington, N. C., where the race passion reached an atrocious climax a few years ago.

But there are two voices in the South to-day. While one preaches hatred and strife, another proclaims justice and humanity. The late Chancellor Hill, Bishop Galloway, Professor John Spencer Bassett, Joel Chandler Harris, and William H. Fleming, and a host of others represent the erstwhile silent South, which has remained tongue-tied under the threat of political and social calamity. When the advocates of a more humane and tolerant doctrine first began to make themselves heard they were regarded as incendiaries, simpletons, or harmless enthusiasts. George W. Cable was banished, Louis H. Blair ignored, J. L. M. Curry was listened to with courtesy, and Dr. Atticus G. Haygood was made a bishop.

But of late this voice has become "something louder than before" and can no longer be ignored as an important, if not a controlling factor in the Southern situation. The fundamental question to-day is which of these voices shall prevail—the voice of Tillman, which you loudly re-echo, or the voice of his vanished adversary, whose dying whisper was, "God bless all the people, white and black." The one breathing out hatred and slaughter, the other proclaiming peace and good will to all the people.

These two principles were exemplified in the Atlanta riot. It was the voice of cunning appealing to baser passion that provoked that shameful outbreak; but it was the firm, stern voice of higher quality and tone that restored peace and quiet. We are told that there was no member of the aristocratic class in that miserable rabble; neither was there any member of the baser element in that deliberate and determined body, composed of the best representatives of both races, which brought order out of chaos. If there is any indication that Providence, in this instance, has overruled the wrath of man for good, it is to be found in the working understanding reached by these two races on the common platform of mutual welfare. For they must live and work and thrive and suffer together for all time, with which you and I are concerned, despite your eloquent and fiery demand for racial separation.

In your address before the University of Chicago, several years ago, you not only justified, but extolled, the lynching of human beings. The punishment of Negroes for crimes committed against white persons furnishes the acutest phase of the race problem to-day. Lynching is apt to follow any serious offense against the person of a male member of the ruling race, and is sure to be inflicted where the complainant is of the other sex. The charge of rape is but one of the excuses for which the Negro suffers swift and summary vengeance. There is a growing understanding that the Negro must be lynched for offenses of certain nature and degree which is hedged about with as much nicety and exactness as the extinct *code duello.*

I am interrupted in the writing of this letter to read on a single page of my daily paper accounts of four lynchings in different parts of the country. In only one instance is assault on woman alleged; and even in this case, there was no judicial determination of guilt. These are fair samples of the nature of the charges upon which Judge Lynch passes sentence upon the black culprit without trial.

"Rape means rope," says the sententious Sam

Jones, and the moral sense of mankind approves the verdict. The only point of contention is whether this rope should be set apart by judicial sanction or extemporized by the bloodthirsty mob to appease ignoble race hatred.

There seems to be a deliberate propaganda on the part of those who appeal to the nether portion of the white South to place the colored race in evil repute in order to justify iniquitous practices. To make a race odious in the eyes of the world is ample excuse for all forms of outrages and cruel treatment. Such is the sinister homage that cunning pays to conscience. It always seizes upon the most sacred instincts and passionate ideals as its palliating cloak. Russia would make believe that the Jews offer up Christian babes in their horrid sacrificial rites to justify the butchery of a meek and lowly race. The lamb below the wolf is always charged with muddying the stream above him. Even among white men in the South the dead man is usually the guilty man. This propaganda has skillfully and willfully exaggerated assaults by colored men so as to give the black race an evil reputation. When all the facts in the case are calmly and carefully considered, due weight being given to all the contributing influences, it will be found that such offenses by Negroes are not greatly out of proportion to like offenses among white men. A careful student of current happenings informs me that he clipped from the newspapers fifteen cases of assaults by white men in one day in a single city. Where the Negro is involved it is the widespread circulation that inflames the popular mind.

Assault by a Negro, actual or alleged, is displayed by the press in the boldest headlines, whereas like offenses by white men are compressed within a half inch space, as part of the ordinary happenings of the day. Whenever a Negro is accused of this crime the Associated Press sends the announcement all over the land. The morning papers proclaim it in bold headlines, only to be outdone by their more reckless evening contemporaries. The weekly journals rehash the same with gruesome particularities, until the whole nation becomes inflamed against the race on account of the dastardly deed of a single wretch.

The Negroes of Atlanta, some forty thousand in number, who had hitherto sustained a good reputation for decency and order, were held up to the abhorrence of the whole civilized world by reason of two or three suspected criminals of their blood. This is as flagrantly unjust to the Negro as it would be to base the reputation of the population of London upon the deeds of Jack the Ripper, or the good name of Englishmen upon the disclosures of William T. Stead. If cases of lightning stroke were proclaimed with such horrifying publicity as heinous crimes committed by Negroes, we should all live in momentary dread of the terror of the sky.

Your chief complaint is not due so much to the heinousness of the assault itself as to the fact that the perpetrators belong to one race and the victims to another. The abhorrence of the deed is intensified by the color and degree of the evil-doer. Shakespeare has painted Caliban and Miranda, the one hideous and depraved, the other fair and pure as the rose of the morning, to illustrate how difference in degree and rank of the offender and the victim adds grievousness to the foulest offense. A nameless assassin, sprung from the scum of the earth and nurtured in a murderous cult, extending his cowardly hand in simulated greetings, struck down William McKinley, the most amiable and beloved of our rulers. This wretch in human form, whose unpronounceable name shall be anathema for evermore, aimed this deadly blow at the idol of the American people, and rolled a heavy stone on the nation's heart. Was ever deed more dastardly or better calculated to excite summary vengeance? This was all but the universal impulse. And yet the anxious solicitude of our dying chieftain was that no harm should come to his assailant not sanctioned by due process of law. Summary vengeance wreaked upon the vilest miscreant answers no worthy end. It neither wipes out the crime committed, nor prevents its repetition. A bitter and bloody experience shows too plainly that vindictive vengeance acts as a suggestive rather than a deterrent to the evilly disposed.

The prevalence of lynching in the South causes a double reaction of feeling. In the first place it causes the whites to hate the Negro, as it is a part of human nature to hate those whom we have injured. In the second place it causes the Negro to hate the whites. It is universally conceded that lynching has no deterrent effect upon the class of crimes alleged to excite its vengeance. On the contrary, it probably has the opposite effect. The criminals and outlaws of the Negro race, who care nothing for life or death, may be thus hardened into resolves of revenge, and lie waiting to strike the hated race where the blow will be most keenly felt.

You ask the Northern press to join in the work of blackening the name of the race by giving two paragraphs to every alleged assault and but scant notice to lynching. You would make it appear that "Negro," "rape" and "lynch" are connotative terms. But you seem to forget, or purposely ignore, the fact that the direst vengeance is often inflicted for other than rapeful assault. In Statesboro, a remote village of your own State, two colored men, intent on robbery, murdered a whole family and set fire to the dwelling to hide their awful deed. The accused were apprehended and sentenced to death within two months after the horrible performance. Race passion ran high. Threats and rumors of lynching flew thick and fast. The bloodthirsty mob vowed summary vengeance. The Governor dispatched State troops to quell the turbulent spirit and vindicate the majesty of the law. But the mob had scented blood and was not to be foiled of its prey by an empty show of force. It snatched the prisoner from the hands of the law, mocked the trial judge, ignored the sheriff, and overpowered the militia, which, like tin soldiers, yielded without inflicting or receiving a wound. Cries of crucifixion filled the air. The sovereign State of Georgia lies prostrate under the feet of the maddened mob, infuriated at the aroused instinct for blood. The culprits are dragged tremblingly through the streets, their bodies saturated with oil, and chained to a decaying tree trunk. The inflammable fagots are piled high, the torch is applied while men, women, and children dance with ghoulish glee at the death groans issuing from the flames. In another instance a woman was burned alive on a gruesome funeral pyre. Such fiendish procedure outrages human nature and hurts the heart of the world. All of this you would palliate and excuse and ask the Northern press to pass over with a scant and hasty paragraph.

I am disposed to hope that you will not be indifferent to the wrongs and injustice inflicted upon a helpless, and, on the whole, rightly inclined people.

The woes and miseries of the Negro race are made to culminate upon the subject of crime and its summary punishment. The black man's political rights, civil privileges, educational opportunities, and the advantage of sympathetic and helpful contact with the white race will be conditioned upon the evil reputation foisted upon him by mob violence, inflicted on account of alleged execrable crimes. No people will tolerate a race of potential rapists in their midst. If this lecherous brand can be fixed upon the Negro's forehead it will be more loathsome than the murderous mark of Cain. The race would be shunned as a colony of moral lepers. No individual of this blood, however upright his personal life, could escape the taint of racial reputation.

This propaganda of evil has so far succeeded as to cool the ardor of those who are disposed to defend the Negro's cause. There is scarcely a single voice in all this land that dares, with undisguised boldness, to defend the rights of human nature for fear of the reproach of encouraging an unworthy people. There has been a sharp change in public sentiment during the last quarter century, which marks the period during which the Negro's alleged evil propensities have been proclaimed to the world with shrewd and unholy design. In 1881 Dr. Atticus G. Haygood, a courtly, pious son of Georgia, wrote a book and styled it "Our Brother in Black." Twenty years later we were startled at the title, "The Negro a Beast." These contrasted titles fairly gauge the drift of sentiment during that interval. So powerful for evil has been the attempt to convince the world that the black man is imbued with a low and evil nature, so despiteful has become the estimate in which the Negro is held, that at the slightest charge against him, the cry, "Lynch the Negro!" leaps spontaneously from the lips of the gathering multitude in the streets of our most populous and peaceful cities. We are so accustomed to the startling headlines in the daily press, "Negro Lynched" or "Negro Burned at the Stake," that the whole American people would become one national nervous wreck were it not that frequently repeated shocks of the same nature render the system insensible to further impressions. There is danger that the national feeling will become numb and the national conscience sear. Clippings from the columns of any leading daily on this subject for the past three months would be sufficient to form a mammoth Sunday edition, with a blood-red supplement of atrocious horrors. The intelligent Negro bears heavily the brunt of this load. The sins of his race, actual and alleged, weigh heavily upon him. Almost every reflecting Negro of my acquaintance is growing prematurely gray.

The Negro complains because of the insistent statement that lynching is resorted to only as punishment for rape, when the plain facts of record show that not more than one case in four can plead the allegement of rape in extenuation. The causes run the whole gamut of offenses, from the most serious crimes to the most trifling misdemeanors. Indeed, lynching is coming to be looked upon as the proper mode of punishment for any offense which the Negro commits against a white person; and yet every time a Negro is lynched or burned at the stake the race is held up to the world as responsible for the execrable crimes.

Mr. George P. Upton, associate editor of the *Chicago Tribune*, has kept records of lynchings in the United States, in itemized form, since 1885. The accuracy of his figures has never been questioned. The following facts are taken from an article contributed by him to the *Independent*, September 29, 1904:

" Between 1885 and 1904 there were 2875 lynchings in the United States. Of these, 2499 were
attributed to the South, 302 to the West, 63 to the
Pacific Slope, and 11 to the East. The alleged causes
were as follows:

For alleged and attempted criminal assault............	564
For complicity and for the double charge of assault and murder	138
For murder	1277
For theft, burglary and robbery......................	326
For arson	106
For race prejudice....................................	94
For unknown reason...................................	134
For simple assault....................................	18
For insulting whites..................................	18
For making threats...................................	16

The remaining cases were inflicted for such offenses as " slander, miscegenation, informing, drunk-
enness, fraud, voodooism, violation of contract, re-
sisting arrest, elopement, train-wrecking, poisoning
stock, refusing to give evidence, political animosity,
disobedience of quarantine regulations, passing
counterfeit money, introducing smallpox, concealing
criminals, cutting levees, kidnapping, gambling riots,
testifying against whites, seduction, incest, and forcing a child to steal." The causes include well-nigh
every offense in the catalogue of human transgression.

In view of these undisputed facts, can you, with
clear conscience, continue to mislead the world into
the belief that the Negro is lynched only for " the
usual crime "? If words are used in their usual sense,
the " usual crime " for which Negroes are lynched
would be other than assault on women.

Again, the Negro suffers injustice in that the mild-
est protest against such red-handed procedure is con-

strued as sympathy for criminals and condonation of crime of the most abominable nature. The Negro race is the gainer by every miscreant that meets his merited doom at the end of a rope. Nor is it particularly concerned as to the manner of his death, nor "the deep damnation of his taking off." If swift, summary vengeance followed as personal punishment for personal transgression, no Negro, as such, would open his lips, albeit he might plead for law and order on the broad basis of humanity. But the vengeance of the mob is not confined to the guilty, if indeed it is aimed at him. Its leading purpose, as you advise, is to strike terror in the whole Negro population. To this end there is little pains to identify the victim or to establish his guilt. The innocent and the guilty are alike objects of its vengeance. Governor Candler of Georgia stated in a public utterance some years ago: "I can say of a verity that I have, within the last month, saved the lives of half a dozen innocent Negroes, who were pursued by the mob, and brought them to trial in a court of law in which they were acquitted." The mob has neither the temper nor the disposition carefully to determine the guilt of the accused. We must not place too much reliance upon the alleged identification of the culprit by the delirious victim, nor upon alleged confession of guilt wrung from the accused by indescribable torture. Although the newspapers glibly tell us of the confession, the courts have never yet been able to determine the identity of the confessor. In many cases it is known that innocent men have suffered death and torture at the hands of the mob. Of the two thousand Negro victims of violence, who can tell how many guiltless souls have been hurled into eternity with the protestation of innocence on their lips? But the innocent equally with the guilty serve to impair the Negro's good name. Several years ago the whole Italian nation was aroused at the lynching of a dozen of its subjects in Louisiana. It was not because of sympathy for or regret at the loss of a few worthless individuals, but because such high-handed procedure served to insult, humiliate, and degrade the entire race and nation to which the unfortunate victims belonged. It is for such reasons that the Negro pleads for the supremacy of law, and not because he has any sympathy for a crime that always excites the wildest passions of human nature.

It is not denied that depraved and vicious Negroes, as of other races, do at times commit these heinous crimes; but it cannot be said that sexual infirmity is an especial failing of the colored race. It is well known that rapeful assault has always been, and is still, a more or less common practice among all races and peoples. Students of the Bible know full well that this practice was not unknown among the Hebrews. Jupiter, father of gods and men, who embodied the vices as well as the virtues of the Greek race, to his numerous epithets might properly have had added the cognomen " ravisher of women." The practice is quite common among all European races to-day. England and Wales, in 1887, furnished 878 prisoners convicted on this charge. From 1871 to 1880 there were in the same country 758 persons convicted for assaults upon girls under thirteen years of age. The eleventh census returns 814 white prisoners in the United States convicted on the charge of rape. And yet to listen to your scathing denunciations of the black man one would be led to believe that a crime as old as human frailty was invented by the American Negro as a new mode of human atrocity.

We must not overlook the fact that where a col-

ored man and white woman are concerned, rape has
a larger definition than is set down in the dictionaries.   Relations are often punished under this head
which, if sustained among members of the same race,
would receive a less abominable, though perhaps an
equally unhallowed name.

There are certain delicate phases of question whose
discussion the seriousness of the situation alone justifies.   The womanhood of the Negro race has been
the immemorial victim of the white man's lascivious-
ness and lust.   The black woman has yielded to
higher authority and superior guile.   A lower will
is overborne by a higher as easily as a weaker by a
stronger physical force.   While breathing out
slaughter against the Negro man, does the white
lord and master ever stop to reflect upon the un-
numbered assaults which he for centuries has made
upon black and bleached womanhood?   The Negro
domestic who must fight daily to preserve her integrity from the subtle guile or forceful compulsion of
her white employer, and who yields only when her
strength of body or will is not sufficient to hold out
longer, is a victim who commands the deepest sympathy.   While the white man is beholding the mote in
his black brother's eye, he should not fail to consider the beam within his own.   This point cannot
be better enforced than by the lines of the poet
Burns:

> "You see your state wi' theirs compared,
>   And shudder at the niffer;
>   But cast a moment's fair regard,
>   What makes the mighty differ:
>   Discount what scant occasion gave,
>   That purity ye pride in,
>   And (what's oft mair than a' the lave),
>   Your better art o' hidin'."

In the refutation of the charge brought against

him the Negro is entitled to every argument that can be brought forward in his behalf.

1. In Africa, the fatherland, or rather the motherland, of this race, rape is almost unknown, and when it does occur, is visited with the severest punishment.

2. We have heard nothing of this abnormal tendency during the days of slavery. When the care and safety of white women of the South were entrusted to the keeping of slaves they returned inviolate all that had been entrusted to them.

3. Some are so careless with facts and reason as to attribute this alleged tendency to the last two amendments of the Federal Constitution. They seem to forget that during the days of reconstruction, when these amendments were in force, such charges were never preferred. It cannot be then, as you affirm, due to the outgrowth of the spirit of equality on the part of the Negro.

4. Of the hundreds of lady missionaries from the North who have and do still entrust their safety to the colored race, not a single case of violation, up to this last day of Christian grace, has been reported to their friends in the North.

5. In South America and the West Indian archipelago, where the Negroes live in largest numbers, " rape and rope " has never become a subject for popular agitation.

What evil spirit then has come upon the present day Afro-American that a people who, from the days of Homer until this generation, have borne the epithet of "blameless Ethiopians," should now be accused as the scourge of mankind? Why has this demoniacal possession held itself in restraint until now, and why does it not manifest itself in peoples of like blood in different parts of the globe?

The self-respecting Negro is upbraided because he

does not exercise a restraining influence over the vicious and criminal members of his own race. As a matter of fact, he has little or no contact with or control over them. He is sought to be made his brother's keeper with no coercive or corrective influence over his brother's conduct. Responsibility implies authority. The Negro is rigorously excluded from governmental power and divested of every semblance of official prerogative. The depraved and criminal Negroes, as of other races, do not go to school, they belong to no church or fraternal order, they are no more influenced by moral agencies than if they were located on another continent. All attempts to interfere on the part of his self-respecting brother would lead to the ancient response, "Who made thee a prince and a judge over us?" Those who occupy places of governmental authority and power are responsible to the world for the punishment of the guilty and protection of the innocent. Moral suasion has little or no influence with hardened criminals—they are answerable to the law alone. The white race, clothed with full authority and power, is confessedly unable to restrain its own vicious classes. It is an extravagant compliment to the Negro to expect him to do by moral suasion alone that which the white man cannot accomplish with moral suasion backed by public power.

The stockades and chain-gangs maintained by the State of Georgia are training schools of crime. Those who enter must leave all hope behind. They are hardened into hatred of society. Have you ever stopped to think that the State may be responsible for the criminal class which you so loudly reprobate?

The Negroes are charged with shielding criminals of their own race. In so far as this charge may have the semblance of truth, it is due to the fact that the black culprit, guilty or innocent, is likely to meet with mob violence, and to assist in the apprehension of the accused is equivalent to joining in a man-hunt for blood. Whenever a Negro is pursued by a posse, charged with a serious offense against a white person, the newspaper headlines usually foreshadow his doom with unerring accuracy: " Will be lynched if caught." The conscientious citizen of the North a generation ago refused to aid the man-hunter in quest of runaways from a cruel bondage, although he was clothed with full authority by an iniquitous law. Every good citizen will uphold and defend the authority and dignity of the law, but he will not aid the mob in quest of vengeance upon a man of unproved guilt. You did not restrain that Atlanta mob of murderers, and yet you censured the Negroes of that city for not suppressing a few suspected criminals, whom even the microscopic eye of the law could not detect. The Negro feels that he cannot expect justice from Southern courts where white and black are involved. In his mind accusation is equivalent to condemnation. For this suspicion the jury rather than the judge is responsible. The very spirit in which, he feels, the law is administered makes it difficult for the colored citizen to exercise cheerful co-operation and acquiescence.

I think I ought to say that after diligent inquiry from colored men in all parts of the South, I am advised that Southern courts are usually fair and often generous to the Negro in cases which do not involve race feeling, but where this issue arises the outcome, in the Negro's mind, is a foregone conclusion. Herein lies the greatest condemnation of existing rule. It fails to make the humble citizen feel safe and secure under the protecting ægis of the law.

In the British Indies, where there is a race situation more complicated than in America, we are told that the behavior toward the whites is exemplary, and the type of crimes so bitterly deplored in this country is unknown. This desirable state of things is due, in my judgment, to the fact that the British Government administers justice with absolute equality as between man and man, without regard to race. Where the Negro sees the white man made amenable to the requirements of the law he is apt to regard it with reverence and respect. On the contrary, in the South a white man is rarely punished for offense against his black brother. Of the thousands of cases of murder of blacks by whites since emancipation there has been scarcely a legal execution, and comparatively few prison sentences. The offender usually escapes with the stereotyped verdict, " Justifiable homicide," or at best with a nominal fine. If the relations were reversed, whatever the provocative circumstances, the Negro would almost certainly be sentenced to death or to life imprisonment, if indeed the mob allowed the case to reach a judicial hearing. To say that these flagrant discrepancies have not their influence upon the black man's attitude toward the law, would be to deny that he is controlled by ordinary human motives. The best example that the South can set for the Negro would be punishment of white men for their crimes according to the requirement of the law. Mean white men will continue to mistreat Negroes just so long as they can do so with impunity by hiding themselves behind the cloak of racial arrogance. Mobs will continue to wreak their wrath on Negro culprits, innocent or guilty, until they are deterred by effective bayonets and bullets at the hands of a firm and unrelenting law. When the Negro sees that the white man can override the law with impunity it begets in him the spirit of desperation, vindictiveness and reprisal. This is the elemental law of human passion. It is firmly lodged in the breast of the ignorant and untutored. The intelligent Negro will be restrained by reason and prudence, but the depraved and the base will follow his wild, untutored human impulse. Good policy requires the placing of the stress of emphasis upon the white offender as upon the black wrongdoer. Judgment in this instance should begin at the house of God. The Negro will follow the pace set by the white man. Reverence and respect for law and order on his part will beget like sentiment in his black brother. Equality before the law is the South's only salvation.

The Negro is by no means the only sufferer from these outrageous practices—the white people are also victims of their own wrath. According to the law of retribution, the perpetrators of wrong must suffer equally with the victims of it. The spirit of violence and lawlessness permeates the atmosphere and is breathed in every breath of air. It has been claimed that the Spanish incurred their blood-thirsty disposition by their fierce struggle in subduing the Moors. The acquired disposition passed into heredity and became a permanent trait of the race.

Is the white South not in danger of such a fate? Some time ago Rev. Sam Jones, with a self-gratulatory spirit, claimed that not one Southerner in ten had ever participated in a lynching. Supposing that these figures approximate the truth. It will be seen that more persons have been engaged in lynching Negroes than there were soldiers in the Confederate army. Every such person has blood on his conscience which cannot be washed away by high-sounding declamation about Anglo-Saxon supremacy.

" Nor florid prose, honeyed lies of rhyme
    Can blazon evil deeds or consecrate a crime."

The evil has reached such alarming proportions as
to become of national importance. While lynching
is confined mainly to the South, it is not wholly so.
Negroes have been lynched in Ohio, Indiana, Illinois,
Colorado, and even in bleeding Kansas, the State of
brave old John Brown, whose soul must for once have
halted in its onward march at such dreadful news.
The " ape and tiger " slumber all too lightly beneath
the thin veil of civilization, whose chief concern is to
keep them subdued under the beneficent sway of reason and law. If they are allowed to break forth and
rave at will in the State of Georgia, will not this savage triumph embolden like spirit throughout the land?
Does not the unrestrained fury of a wild animal that
escapes from a menagerie encourage his encaged fellows to break forth, too, and vent their pent-up rage?
There is no contagion so swift and sure of diffusion
as the baser passion of man. The nation puts forth
a strenuous endeavor to stamp out cholera or yellow
fever, however remote the plague spot where it first
breaks forth. The baleful effect of the burning and
lynching of human beings cannot be limited to any
locality, State or section, but is as widespread as the
nation whose dormant evil passion it tends to encourage, and whose good name it serves to tarnish. The
question is truly a national one, and as such should
appeal to every man, woman and child who loves his
country, and is pledged to uphold its good name and
high ideals.

The infectious germ has inoculated almost every
State in the Union. The list for States and Terri-
tories, from 1885 to 1904, is as follows:

Mississippi	298	Indiana	38
Texas	272	Kansas	38
		California	33
Louisiana	261	Nebraska	33
Georgia	253	Michigan	6
		North Dakota	5
Alabama	232	Nevada	5
Arkansas	207	Minnesota	4
		Wisconsin	4
Tennessee	191	Wyoming	33
Kentucky	148	Colorado	31
		Montana	29
Florida	128	Idaho	21
South Carolina	100	Illinois	19
		Washington	16
Virginia	84	Ohio	13
Missouri	79	Iowa	12
		South Dakota	11
North Carolina	58	Oregon	10
Indian Territory	54	Alaska	4
		Maine	3
West Virginia	43	Pennsylvania	3
Oklahoma	38	New York	2
		New Jersey	1
Maryland	20	Connecticut	1
Arizona	18	Delaware	1
		Massachusetts	0
New Mexico	15	New Hampshire	0
		Vermont	0
		Rhode Island	0
		Utah	0
Total for South	2,499		
		Total for North	376
Total for Nation			2,875

You proclaim the doctrine of State sovereignty
and reprobate federal interference. But every man
lynched or burned in the South furnishes the nation
an invitation to step in and vindicate the national
honor.

What a blot upon our civilization these figures disclose to the foreigner who may still be skeptical as to
the boasts of our free institutions! What will Russia and Turkey and Cuba say? How long will Theodore Roosevelt, bent on setting the world to rights,
keep his hands off?

A large majority of these victims are of the colored race, but a goodly proportion of them are white men. The evil practice cannot be limited to any race or section. A distinguished citizen of Georgia, during the heated anti-slavery discussion, boasted that he would yet call the roll of his slaves under the shadow of Bunker Hill Monument. His boasted prediction would doubtless have been fulfilled had not the institution of slavery been destroyed altogether. Unless the American people stamp out lynching its baleful influence will become as widespread as the national domain. Either the law must destroy lynching or lynching will destroy the law, involving the whole nation in anarchy and red ruin.

You appeal to the North to help separate the races. In this you are speaking in an unknown tongue. The absurdity of the suggestion places it beyond the sphere of practical discussion. I may agree with you that if the Negroes were removed from the South, whether sent to Africa or to some hotter place, there would be no Negro problem left, as such; but I am by no means certain that an equally serious human problem would not spring up in its place. If you should advocate transporting ten million Negroes to the moon your language would be equally intelligible. Even if the races were separated by interstellar space, such separation would last only until some enterprising white man contrived some means of communication. Three hundred years ago the races were absolutely separated. The Negro basked in the sunshine of savage bliss, and was happy, but the white man sought him amid his " sunny clime and palmy wine " and dragged him to the western world. Since then he has become an inseparable part of the two continents, and of the adjacent archipelagos. There are more Negroes in the western world than members of any other race. He is rooted and grounded in the soil; he is here to stay; he is in the South to stay; we need a brand of statesmanship which will adjust itself to this great determining fact.

I beg to suggest that in dealing with the Southern situation you look upon the task as a race problem, rather than as a human problem. The human aspect is ignored and the racial feature over emphasized. We have before us a dual problem of the perfectibility of the people, and of racial peace and harmony.

The South is freighted with an awful load of ignorance and poverty, and resultant degradation. Much of this attaches to the white race, but more to the Negro. There are no nostrums or miracles that will roll away this reproach. It requires the united effort of all the nation to enlighten, upbuild and adjust these neglected people. A wise and far-seeing statesmanship would not seek to isolate and perpetuate these incapacities in one race, but would banish them entirely. Unless ignorance and poverty are destroyed, they will rise up ever and anon to perplex and to trouble. Ignorance and vice are not racial attributes; knowledge and virtue are not racial endowments: they are the outcome of condition. Crime has no color; the criminal no race; he is the common enemy of society. He should be isolated and dealt with according to the desert of his evil deed. It is folly to punish a race for the wrong doings of an individual. The enlightened elements of both races should make common cause with knowledge against ignorance, with virtue against vice, and with law against the lawless.

I must not close this letter without expressing the firm conviction that Negroes of light and leading have grave and serious responsibility. Their race is the victim in every conflict. While they cannot re-

strain the hardened criminal without governmental
authority, yet they are in duty bound to put forth
strenuous efforts to reach and to influence for good
the weak, helpless and neglected elements of their own
race, and to keep them from falling into evil ways.
There is a subtle sympathy of race which renders
individuals more easily amenable to the moral control
of those of their own blood. The Negro school
teacher and minister of the gospel stand in the high
place of moral authority. They should utilize all the
power which they are permitted to wield, and by example, precept and persuasion sustain their weaker
brethren in all right directions. They must bridge
over the widening chasm between the educated and
the more unfortunate by a practical sympathy and
a more vital and brotherly touch. In this great work
of human development we ask and should receive the
hearty good will and co-operation of all those who
believe in the perfectibility of man. The Negro is
impressionable and responsive to kind treatment. If
given the necessary encouragement he will become
a safe, conservative factor, and not the economic or
moral menace which you so vociferously proclaim him
to be. It will not be necessary to ruthlessly override
all human and divine order at the behest of the narrow racial arrogance. All far-seeing and conservative Americans believe that in the final outcome peace
and good will, friendship and amity will prevail, and
that " Ephraim shall not envy Judah, and Judah
shall not vex Ephraim."

Mr. Harry Stillman Edwards, your distinguished
fellow Georgian, in a recent article contributed to the
Century Magazine, expresses the hopeful belief that
the two races can live together in righteous peace.
These are his words: " Neither can settle the questions involved in their lives, but both may, and despite

political riders, I believe both will.   I must either believe this or prepare my descendants for anarchy."

Compared with your doctrine of dread and terror,
subversive of established order and public peace, few
patriotic Americans will fail to feel that Mr. Edwards has chosen the better part.

THE NEGRO'S PART IN THE NEGRO PROBLEM

THE presence of the African element in the United States gives rise to a tripartite problem. The white man of the North, the white man of the South, and the Negro are the parties in interest. The only possible satisfactory solution of this problem must depend upon the united wisdom and conciliatory spirit of this triple alliance, and must be just and honorable to all.

For more than a generation the North alone has directed and controlled our national policies, against the incessant antagonism of the South. This antagonism has been most sharply accentuated over measures intended to promote the black man's welfare. Northern philanthropy and statesmanship have persisted in busying themselves with this problem, despite the resentful hue and cry against meddlesome interference. On the other hand, the South has regarded the Negro question very much as a distinguished politician once characterized the tariff—as a local issue. It has stubbornly and sullenly insisted that it alone possessed the requisite knowledge and experience to deal with its own problems, without the gratuitous assistance of outside busybodies. Nevertheless, the South has not yet put forth any positive, progressive measure toward this end, but has pursued an unbroken policy of negation, protest, and retrogression.

The oft-repeated asseveration of the Southern white man that he understands the Negro better than his Northern brother is not borne out by experience, nor

does it manifest itself in enlightened action. As Mr.
Carl Schurz has so forcibly pointed out, every essential prediction which the South has based upon its
assumed superior wisdom has proved to be erroneous
in the light of subsequent development. It declared
that the black man would die out under freedom; but
the census shows that the four million slaves of 1860
has given rise to eight million freemen in 1900. It asserted that the Negro would not work except by
physical compulsion; but the material progress of
that section, based largely upon Negro labor, renders
the assertion beneath refutation. It once affirmed
that the Negro was uneducationable, but the North
showed the absurdity of the statement by educating
him. The reputation of the prophet is discredited
by the too frequent failure of his predictions.

The Southern white man bases his claim to superior
knowledge upon long association and intimacy of
contact. Long habituation with an environment is
rather apt to deaden than sharpen the critical sense.
Near-sightedness, no less than far-sightedness, is a
serious ocular defect. The three treatises on American institutions which are admitted to show the most
insight and critical acumen were written by a Frenchman, an Englishman, and a German, as a result of
their temporary sojourn among us.

The North has shown superior wisdom on every
phase of our national life, and the most enlightened
minds of the South are now openly avowing that the
salvation of that section depends upon the adoption
of the more enlightened Northern spirit and methods.
Northern knowledge has discovered the industrial possibilities of the South and furnished the means and
directive skill for exploiting them, has demonstrated
the folly of suicidal governmental theories once so
fondly cherished by the South, and has led the way

in every feature of intellectual, material, and social
progress. Is it reasonable, then, to suppose that omniscience, so manifestly withheld in every other domain of knowledge, has been vouchsafed to the white
man of the South on the race problem alone?

Hitherto little attention has been given to the
Negro as a factor whose sensibilities should be regarded and whose voice should be heeded upon questions which affect his own destiny. This race has
been looked upon as an inanimate mass to be exploited
and controlled according to the interest or caprice of
the white lord of creation. But the growing self-
knowledge and self-assertion on the part of the
awakening race adds a new element to the problem
that can no longer be ignored. The wise physician,
however great he may deem his diagnostic knowledge
and therapeutic skill, always encourages the cheerful
co-operation of the patient under treatment. Even
though the patient is not supposed to have any wisdom to contribute, he is at least always accorded the
privilege of saying how he feels. The South and the
North, as attendant and consulting physicians, are
now planning a common line of action; but they will
not wisely leave out the intelligent Negro, whose inside view might at least be supposed to assist external
wisdom.

The fact that the colored race has followed the
guidance of the white man of the North has given
rise to deep and bitter complaint. Ever since the
Negro has begun to animadvert upon his own condition, the North and South have seemed to him to be
as wide apart as the poles on questions touching his
welfare. In the momentous conflict of thought and
conscience which preceded the arbitrament of arms,
the North stood for liberty, the South for slavery.
At countless cost of blood and treasure the North

broke his chains, against the equally strenuous endeavor of the South to rivet them more tightly. The North wrote the last three amendments in our Federal Constitution, while the South protested with all the power at its command. Northern statesmanship placed legislation upon the statute-books recognizing the equality of all men before the law, every line of which met with strenuous opposition and obstruction on the part of the South. Northern philanthropists have given their substance and their service for the intellectual and moral betterment of the black man, while the South, for the most part, has looked on with icy indifference, and often with ill-concealed disapproval. At the present day the North is rather disposed to uphold the doctrine of " a government of laws and not of men," while the South insists on dealing with the Negro as a subject-class.

The law of human passion requites friendship with affection. The black man, perhaps, has not been critical of the motive that has actuated this benefaction toward him. The conduct of the North may indeed have been actuated by economic motive and political policy, as well as by an abstract love of the principles involved. But gratitude is oblivious of motive. The Emancipation Proclamation does not fail to evoke the black man's grateful emotions because he is told that it was merely an incident of a larger policy. It is sufficient for him to know that the slave has been transformed into a freeman, the chattel into a citizen, and that the North has been the chief instrument in effecting this marvelous transformation. It should not occasion surprise or resentment that the black man has given his allegiance to the policies of the North rather than the South, especially when we remember that the African is very largely a creature of affection and is controlled mainly by emotion.

When the Negro aligns himself, on public questions,
with the people of the North, he is accused of spiteful antagonism to his white neighbors. But he is
merely following the impulse that ordinarily governs
human motive. He has put human rights before
economic interest, and righteous public policy before
the blandishments of personal kindliness and individual favor.

It must be conceded, on the other hand, that the
Southern white man frequently displays commendable
personal good-will toward individual Negroes who
come within the circle of his acquaintance or control.
In general, there is the widest margin between his
avowed public policy and his personal demeanor. No
reputable Southerner is half as bad as Senator Tillman talks. The South seizes upon every act of prejudice or proscription practised against the Negro in
the North, and holds it up as proof positive of the
insincerity of its righteous pretensions. The *tu
quoque* argument is never resorted to except in palli-
ation of conduct that is intrinsically indefensible.
The universality of an act does not improve its moral
quality.

Surprise has often been expressed that the Negro
does not move in mass from the South, against whose
public policy he so bitterly complains, to those sections where political and civil conditions are more
liberal and generous. The Negro has an attachment
for locality that almost amounts to instinct. He is
not of a nomadic nature, and lacks the restlessness
and daring spirit of the pioneer. The climatic conditions of the North are not congenial to his tropical
nature, and the strenuous social and economic regime
does not accord with his industrial experience and
aptitude. Six millions of white people from the
South, with their wonted industrial habits and eco-

nomic notions, would find themselves as much disqualified for Northern competition as their less favored brother in black. The Negro also confronts industrial intolerance in the North which shuts him out from the higher forms of endeavor.

Between the relative advantages and discouragements of each section he stands curiously bewildered. The bulk of the race is destined to remain where it was most thickly planted by the institution of slavery. Notwithstanding a continuous stream of immigration toward the North and West for the past forty years, the mass centre of Negro population is moving steadily toward the Gulf of Mexico. The Negro and the Southern white man must live together, in intimate neighborhood, for all time which we are able to foresee. It is essential to the welfare of both that their relations should be characterized by amity and goodwill. But the Negro ought not to be expected to accept with satisfaction any condition that is not honorable and just, and that does not accord with the spirit and genius of American institutions.

The part which the Negro has played in American history has contributed in no small degree to the welfare of the nation. The African was brought to this country for the purpose of performing manual and menial labor. There was no more thought of incorporating him in the body-politic than of thus ennobling the lower animals. His function was intended to be as purely mechanical as that of the ox which pulls the plough. For more than two hundred years he performed this manual mission. He cleared the forests, and planted the fields, and made the wilderness to blossom as the rose. The whole economic and social fabric of the South was built upon his muscular energy under the guidance of the white man's intelligence. Through the discipline of slavery he gained the English language, the Christian religion, a notion of political and civil institutions, and settled industrial habits and methods. His grasp upon these principles is still imperfect and uncertain, and needs to be confirmed and strengthened by the discipline of knowledge and freedom. The institution of slavery exploited the physical capacities of the Negro for the aggrandizement of the white race. Whatever incidental benefit may have accrued to the slave cannot be ascribed to the moral credit of that regime which possessed not the slightest semblance of altruistic intent.

The Negro was transformed from a chattel into a citizen, as it were, in a moment, in the twinkling of an eye. He was thrust into the body-politic with such suddenness and shock as if shot from the cannon's mouth. At the time of reconstruction the race was solidly illiterate, excited with the first excesses of freedom, and without the least experience in governmental affairs. And so the Negro became the natural and inevitable prey of the self-seeker and the adventurer. Grossness and grotesqueness are the inevitable outcome of good-natured ignorance under the control of calculating villainy. The negro merely played the part of bouffe politics. The native Southerner and the carpetbag adventurer vied with each other for public plunder and spoil. It cannot be shown, however, that the Negro ever supported any measure against human liberty or in conflict with the Federal Constitution. The reconstruction constitutions display a higher degree of patriotism and public righteousness than the fraudulently conceived, though cunningly contrived, instruments which have succeeded them.

As an industrial worker the Negro is docile and productive. He does not join in the ranks of the

restless and discontented. He is loyal to the institutions of the country, and strives to become as good
an American as his fellow-citizens will permit him
to be.

The criminal propensity of the Negro is the charge
that is being most widely exploited in current discussion. By fragments of fact and jugglery of argument he is made to appear a beast in human form
whose vicious tendency constitutes a new social
plague. The Negro is held in moral disesteem because
he is being searched and sifted mercilessly for ugly
and uninviting information. All his faults are being
conned and set down by rote. If as diligent search
were made for unseemly and forbidden data concerning any other class, the disclosure might be equally
darksome and damaging. A mental and moral mor-
bidity is acquired by dwelling upon the pathological
side of society. If we listen to the pessimistic wail
of the social purist we would be convinced that the
human race is doomed to speedy destruction through
innumerable physical and social sins. Intemperance,
sexual impurity, and civic corruption are sure to effect our national destruction. And yet society moves
on, like a mighty river, and, despite polluted streams
that flow into it, purifies itself as it goes. Although
the Negro is hampered by an initial weight of social
and moral degradation, yet his upward struggle from
corruption to purity has been marked and unmistakable. Those who are most prone to indulge in wholesale tirade about his moral turpitude do not seek
knowledge from the more progressive and ambitious
element, but preserve a studious ignorance concerning
their higher aims and nobler modes of life. Generalization based upon the study of the most degraded
part is not fair to the whole. This mode of procedure
would blacken the reputation of any people. We do

not judge a society by the misfortune of its submerged members, but by the ideals toward which it
strives and by the potency and promise which it
displays.

Several years ago a colored man of glib rhetorical
facility wrote a book entitled " The American Negro,"
which received the imprint of a leading publishing
house. The Negro author excoriated his race in the
most merciless manner. He held it up to the scorn
of mankind as a breed of moral vipers. These scathing denunciations were supported by no data and upheld by no verifiable reference, but rested solely upon
the pessimistic utterances of a defamer of his own
race. Indeed, the innuendoes were indignantly denied
by white and black alike, who had opportunity for
knowledge and judgment for generalization. These
statements gained plausibility and credence from the
fact that the author was of the same color as the
class which is reprobated; and the book has been
widely appealed to as a buttress to blacken the moral
reputation of the Negro race and to damn a struggling people to everlasting infamy.

Damaging charges against the Negro's social character are usually based upon the following facts and
assumptions:

1. That the Negro shows an overwhelming criminal
record as compared with the white race.

2. That the percentage of crime has increased under freedom and education.

3. That the Negro of the North shows a much
higher criminal average than his more benighted
brother in the South.

4. That the colored man is especially addicted to
crime of an execrable and nameless character.*

* This subject is discussed in open letter to John Temple
Graves.

According to the census of 1890, the Negro constituted only 12 per cent. of the population of the United States and contributed 30 per cent. of the criminals. In Mississippi there were 1,425 colored and 219 white prisoners out of each million of the respective races; while in Massachusetts the numbers were 6,864 colored and 2,262 whites. Such are the facts which, uninterpreted, can be quoted in support of any damaging doctrine that might be advanced. No person of knowledge and candor will deny that the Negro in the South is more readily apprehended and convicted on any charge than the white offender. The Negro constitutes the lower stratum of society, where the bulk of actionable crime is committed the world over. Social degradation is the great contributing factor to his high criminal record. If the lower element of the white race should be segregated and brought under the microscope of sociological investigation, the proscribed class would doubtless reveal like criminal weakness. The foreign element of our population shows a higher criminal average than the native whites, as they occupy a decidedly lower social status.

While the Negro's criminal record exceeds that of the white, it does not appear that his presence in any community increases its criminal quality. In 1890 the Western division of States had 1,300 prisoners out of every million inhabitants; the North Atlantic States, 833.1, and the South Atlantic States, with their heavy Negro element, had only 831.7; Mississippi had 1,177, against 5,227 for Massachusetts. If the Negroes of the South were replaced by a white population there is no statistical indication that the moral character of that section would be improved by the interchange. There is nowhere any traceable casual connection between crime and race, the relation being between crime and condition. It should not occasion surprise that the free Negro shows a higher criminal record than did his slave progenitor. Under the surveillance of slavery there was little opportunity to commit crime, and punishment for offences was personally inflicted by the master without any public record. Slavery suppressed wrongdoing, but did not implant the corrective principle, so that when the physical restraint was removed there was no moral restraint to take its place. The increase in the criminal rate for the United States from 1880 to 1890 was 12.49 per cent. The parallel growth of education and crime is a noticeable phenomenon of the American people as a whole, and cannot be justly urged to the discredit of the Negro alone.

But, says the objector, in the North, where legal processes are acknowledged to be fair, and where the Negro has the fullest educational opportunity, he shows a criminal rate three to four times as great as his ignorant and oppressed brother in the South. And the conclusion is hastily reached that education makes the Negro a criminal. Referring to the above-cited statistics, it will be seen that while the Negro in Massachusetts seems to be five times as criminal as the Negro in Mississippi, it appears at the same time that the white man in Massachusetts is ten times as criminal as the white man in Mississippi. Shall we discount the superior education of the white man in the Bay State because he seems to be only one-tenth as saintly as his less enlightened white brother on the banks of the Mississippi? Or shall we foster the bliss of ignorance only when it is found under a black skin? Ordinarily one would explain the high criminal rate of the Northern States on the ground of congested population and more stringent enforcement of law; but logical processes seem to be of no avail against sweeping assertions to the detriment of the discredited Negro.

It is a common saying that the colored race has made greater progress since emancipation than any other people known to the history in a like space of time. In order to measure this progress, we need a knowledge of the starting-point as well as a fixed standard of calculation. We may say that the Negro began at the zero point, with nothing to his credit but the crude physical discipline of slavery. His progress should be measured in terms of his humble beginning and of the crude instruments with which he has had to work out his own salvation. He cannot be expected as yet to have reached the fulness of the stature of the Anglo-Saxon, who enjoys the advantage of centuries of inheritance and social opportunity.

Moral progress can hardly be gauged in terms of material units. The home lies at the basis of our social morality. The last census shows 60.1 per cent. of the white population of the United States to be single, 36.4 per cent. married, 3.0 per cent. widowed, 0.2 per cent. divorced, and 0.3 per cent. of unknown conjugal status. Among the Negroes 63.5 per cent. are single, 32.4 per cent. married, 3.5 per cent. widowed, 0.3 per cent. divorced, and 0.3 per cent. unknown. There is no glaring discrepancy between the two races as to the relative number of homes, size of family, or the permanence of domestic ties. In 1890 there were 100 Negro church communicants out of every 279 of the population against 100 out of 304 for the whites. The Negro is largely enrolled in patriotic, benevolent, fraternal, and social organizations, the aim of all of which is towards personal, moral, and social improvement. The facts also disclose that the Negro is engaged in settled and orderly industry to a degree that must be promotive of sobriety and good behavior. In 1890 only 36.4 per cent. of the white population were engaged in gainful occupations against 41.1 per cent. of Negroes who were thus engaged. People who but a brief generation ago were in a state of moral and social confusion and who have since formed definite family relations and enlisted themselves under the banner of the Christian church, and settled in regular industrial habits, might well be regarded as having made marvelous social and moral progress. While there remains much grossness and imperfection, yet no candid observer can fail to note the upward trend towards better and nobler modes of life.

In the domain of education the race has made most notable advancement. The rate of illiteracy has steadily declined, until now it is only 44.6 per cent. of persons over ten years of age. There is a school enrolment of 1,096,734, which indicates the eagerness to throw off the shackles of ignorance. When a people pass from an illiterate to a literate stage life takes on a new incentive and meaning. An impulse is imparted which yields ever-increasing momentum. Its influence can never be lost, but is carried forward to remotest generations. The ability to read and write is the minimum requirement of our economic and social scheme. It is the pass-key to social progress, and unlocks the secret and method of civilization. We should not, however, expect the Negro's imperfect grasp upon the literary symbols of knowledge suddenly to transform and uplift him to the level of Aryan attainment. The first effect of symbolic knowledge is necessarily potential rather than practical. It requires time for the new acquisition to become assimilated and to infiltrate into the life and react upon the conduct. The process of education has just begun to do its beneficial work. The urgent task now is to so strengthen and confirm the principles of knowledge that the Negro shall gain an intelligent conception of the object and aim, not merely of labor, but of life.

It has become the fashion to say that the education of the Negro is a demonstrated failure, and that the effort expended upon his mental development has been in vain. The mode of education undertaken by Northern philanthropy has been the chief object of attack. But those who indulge in wholesale assertions are craftily careful to avoid a bill of particulars. They do not tell us that Howard University or Fisk or Atlanta has been a failure; but their chief reliance is placed upon the frequent repetition of the charge, and their only authority is arrogant assumption of infallibility. When we consider that it was through the inspiration of such institutions that the Negro race received its upward impulse; that they trained, for the most part, the teachers who are conducting the public schools of the South; that their graduates and sometime pupils are scattered throughout the race as centers for good and are doing all within their power to enlighten, guide, and restrain the ignorant masses; that they are almost without exception advocates of peace and good-will between the races, it is difficult to see upon what possible fact or argument the assumption is based.

Let us take as an illustration of this type of education Howard University, situated at the National Capital. This institution, during the thirty-seven years of its history, has expended somewhere between two and three million dollars in plant, equipment, and current cost. As returns on this investment, it has sent into the world 700 physicians, pharmacists, and dentists, 300 lawyers, 200 ministers of the gospel, 400 teachers, 600 persons with general scholastic education, together with thousands of sometime pupils who have enjoyed the partial benefits of its course. These graduates and sometime pupils are found in every State and city where the colored population abounds, and are filling stations of usefulness and influence along all lines of high endeavor. They are preaching, practising, pleading, and teaching, and are guiding, directing, and inspiring the masses to a higher and better life. When the facts are carefully and dispassionately analyzed, it will probably appear that nowhere in the history of human experience has the expenditure of a like sum of money resulted in a higher degree of social good than the fifty millions contributed by Northern philanthropy for the enlightenment of this belated race.

But the colored race has received $100,000,000 from the public school funds of the Southern States, and we are told, with all the assurance of infallibility, that this sum has been misapplied because ignorance has not put on enlightenment, poverty has not given way to competence, and purity has not banished corruption. One hundred million dollars is a princely sum when viewed in the aggregate; but it is only when we remember that this amount has been distributed over a period of thirty-five years, scattered over an area of a million square miles, and applied to a population ranging from five to nine million souls, that we can appreciate its woful inadequacy to the task imposed. It would not average two dollars a year for each Negro child of school age. During 1901 South Carolina expended $726,825 for the education of 183,660 white children, and only $211,288 for that of 287,540 colored children. The educational cost of each white child was $3.95 against $0.74 for the Negro child. If, then, the educational facili-

ties for the white children of the South are wofully
inadequate and inefficient, as they are universally conceded to be, what can be said of those for colored
children? If it requires twenty-five dollars a year in
Massachusetts to educate a white boy who has the
stimulus of civilized inheritance and enlightened environment, how can we expect seventy-five cents to do
the same for a black boy in South Carolina who misses
these incentives? The condemnation of Negro education at this stage of the process is merely a preju-
diced pronouncement of judgment in advance of
adequate trial.

That the Southern whites impose a tax upon themselves to educate the Negroes has been so frequently
and so emphatically asserted that it has almost come
to be an accepted maxim. We are told that the whites
pay ninety-five per cent. of the taxes, and that Negro
education is almost a pure gratuity on their part.
This assumption rests upon a false notion of political
economy. According to the fundamental principles
of that science, labor pays every tax in the world.
And the fact that the laborer may not enjoy the
privilege of handing the tribute to the tax-taker is
no reason why he should be deprived of any public
privilege which his labor makes possible. The distribution of public benefits in proportion to tax-pay-
ing ability is widely at variance with the spirit of
American institutions. The public schools were in-
stituted in order to develop and maintain a higher
and more efficient citizenship. To this end the child-
less millionaire is laid under tribute for the educating
of the children of the prolific pauper. The Negro
may not contribute by direct taxation in proportion
to his scholastic requirements; yet, indirectly, public
burdens bear most heavily upon his shoulders. The
Negro is the laborer of the South and contributes his

full share to the public weal. He has a right to demand of the State the education of his children on equal terms with others, not merely as a civic charity, but as a public right. To limit, curtail, or abridge his educational opportunity would be an arbitrary misuse of power without justification on economic or moral grounds.

Ex-Superintendent Glenn, of Georgia, and Superintendent Shields, of Florida, have shown in their published reports that the colored people in these States, at least, pay the full cost of their own education. It would be easy enough to select a comparatively small number of individuals in New York or Massachusetts who pay the bulk of taxation in those commonwealths; but we never hear that they are being taxed for the less fortunate element of the community. The argument runs counterwise. The owners of wealth are rather regarded as the beneficiaries of the burden which is borne by the laboring classes.

Despite the hard industrial disadvantages under which he has labored, the Negro has made steady advancement in the accumulation of property. There is no reliable information as to the value of his holdings except in two or three States. A knowledge of the aggregate of value of this property, however, is of less importance than of its distribution throughout the whole race. In 1890 there were in the Southern States, including Delaware and the District of Columbia, 231,758 Negroes who owned their farms and homes, only 18,000 of which carried a mortgage incumbrance. Estimating five persons to the farm or household, this would give more than a million persons who lived on their own premises. The last census shows 156,372 Negro owners of farms. There were 746,717 Negro farmers, who, either as owner or tenant, operated farms aggregating 37,000,000 acres of land, and yielding in 1899 a productive value of $250,000,000. The Negro operated 13 per cent. of all the farms in the United States. In the South Atlantic States 29.9 per cent. of the farms were operated by Negro farmers, 27.2 per cent. in the South Central States, and 58.3 per cent. in Mississippi. In the State of Governor Vardaman nearly three-fifths of the farms are directed by black proprietors. These 700,000 farms contain a colored population of about four million Negroes who have gained industrial self-direction. There are more Negro farmers than farm hands. These facts give us some indication of the industrial power of the Negro in the Southern States.

A most significant indication of progress is the emergence of a superior class. The talented tenth constitutes the controlling factor in the life of any people. The institution of slavery made no allowance for superior attainment. Yet all slaves could not be kept on the same low level, but there was marked differentiation as to character, intelligence and ambition. The wider opportunities of freedom brought a sudden awakening of power. Negro youths who were deemed incapable of knowledge now dispute academic honors with the choicest collegians of Harvard and Yale. The Negro aims at the same standard of attainment for which the Aryan strives.

There is a growing disposition to ignore the Negro of superior attainment as an insignificant exception or freak of nature, not to be calculated as a factor in the ordinary equation. The white race is characterized by its best powers and capacities, the Negro by his worst. The Southern white man is construed to mean the traditional gentleman, instinct with dignity, comity, and grace, although we are perfectly aware that numerically he represents only a small percentage of the people whom he typifies. But when

reference is made to the Negro we are prone to think
of a composite savage, and banish from the mind the
superior man who has emerged from this dark and
forbidden background.   And yet it would be easy
enough to isolate hundreds of thousands, if not millions, of Southern whites who, in intelligence, thrift
and general respectability, would not rank above a
corresponding number of Negroes that might be
chosen.

Upon the enlightened Negro has been imposed unusual responsibility and opportunity for service. He
becomes the inevitable leader and exemplar of his
people. They look to him as their guide, philosopher
and friend. Any people derive inspiration most readily from men of their own breed who have risen out
of their own environment. When one colored man is
elevated the whole race feels the uplifting effect of
his promotion. As the individual rises he draws the
whole race up toward his own level. Current philosophy seems to suppose that a lever can be put under
the mass of the race and pry it up from the bottom,
whereas the history of human development shows that
races and nations and peoples are uplifted by the
elevation of their choice individuals who draw them
up toward the top. It is the part of sound statesmanship and wise philanthropy to encourage the better
aspirations of this people. There is nothing to fear
from a people who aspire. It is rather a vegetative
race, without a soul that animates and spirit that
strives, that forms a blight upon civilization.

The ignorant must be enlightened, the vicious must
be restrained, the sick and afflicted must be soothed
and healed, the lethargic must be inspired, and the
hungry soul must be satisfied with spiritual solace.
Under the intolerant social policy of the Anglo-Saxon
these ministrations must be directed by members of

the benefited race. A million Negro children are
taught by Negro teachers. Three million church
communicants are led in paths of truth and righteousness by their own ministers; the sick are attended by
sympathetic physicians; the newspapers, magazines,
and other organs of public opinion by which the people are inspired to high endeavor are conducted by
men of their own blood. The members of this controlling class are scattered throughout the entire
race, as diffusive centers of light; and this little
leaven must ultimately leaven the whole lump. These
leaders should be carefully trained and qualified for
this function, which is second to none in its bearing
upon the general welfare of the American people.

It is charged that the enlightened Negro does not
restrain the evil tendency of the most vicious and degraded of his own race. It must always be remembered that the Negro leader is not entrusted with
governmental function. He exerts only moral authority, and has no way of reaching the hardened
criminal, either in church or school or by personal or
social intercourse; for the criminally disposed of
every race shun ennobling contact, and are amenable
only to the rigid hand of the law. The white man
controls the machinery of government, and should
suppress and restrain the vicious and worthless, not
in a spirit of race vindictiveness, but for the common
good of all. The better class of colored people is being
rapidly recruited. In intelligence, thrift, purity of
life and decorum of manners its upward movement is
marked and unmistakable. In spite of obloquy, denunciation, ridicule, doubt and denial, it is steadily
climbing and lifting as it climbs.

The race question in America is a tough and
tangled one. Its issues are as intricate in their relations and as far-reaching in their consequences as any

problem which has ever pressed upon human wisdom for solution. Despite our pride of theory and cock-sure solutions that are so confidently projected and so vociferously proclaimed, it continues to baffle our wisdom and buffet our hopes. While we may not be able to see the distant scene, we should nevertheless proceed step by step in the direction of duty. Justice, intelligence, thrift and character are virtues of undisputed value, and apply to all men under all conceivable conditions. If the white man, North or South, in dealing with his weaker brother, will apply the principle of justice, and encourage him in the development of intelligence, thrift and character, he may safely free his mind from the dread of destiny which now occasions such anxious solicitude.

SOCIAL EQUALITY

A STRANGER to American institutions would be curiously impressed by the separate and distinct social areas which the two races occupy. Here are two peoples, domiciled in the same territory, vested with equal civil and political rights, speaking the same language, loyal to the same institutions, worshiping God after the same ritual, and linked together in a common destiny; and yet in all purely personal and pleasurable intercourse they are as far apart as if separated by interstellar space. "Social equality" is the shibboleth which divides the races asunder. This slogan, like a savage warwhoop, arouses the deepest venom of race, which slumbers only skin deep beneath a thin veneer of civilization. This expression cannot be defined according to the ordinary import and weight of words. Whoever coined it possessed a genius for summoning the evil spirit. The term has no exact lexical status, but it is surcharged with idiomatic meaning. We can no more determine its potency and power from the component words than we can judge the emblematic significance of "Old Glory" by the fabric and dyestuff that enter into its composition. As the sight of the flag evokes the patriotic zeal of the loyal beholder, or as the soldier makes frantic response to the alarm "to arms," so the tocsin "social equality" arouses the pride of class and wrath of race. "Social" and "equality" are two excellent, elegant words; but "social equality" must not be pronounced in good society, like two harmless chemical elements uniting to make a dangerous compound. This phrase has unbounded potency over the passion of the white man of the South. He religiously obeys its behest, at whatever sacrifice or cost of conscience. He bows down and worships before a verbal idol with fear and trembling, as a heathen before his graven God. The sanction of its decree is more binding than that of legal code, religious creed, or the claims of humanity. Pope has given a poetic setting to the moral conviction of mankind that conscience is the rightful arbiter of conduct:

> "What conscience dictates to be done,
>   Or warns me not to do;
> This teach me more than hell to shun,
>   That more than heaven pursue."

If in this elegant quatrain we substitute " social equality " for conscience, although we mar the meter, we adapt the meaning to the social creed of the South. The interpretation which that section places upon " social equality " constitutes the crux of the race problem, and conditions all modes of rights, privileges and opportunity, whether they be political, civil, educational or industrial. By reason of its exactions the Negro is not desired by the white man to vote for the same candidate, work at the same handicraft, enjoy the same public and civic privileges, to worship at the same shrine, or to be buried in the same graveyard. It is indeed the ruling passion strong in death. Race prejudice which this phrase evokes is not amenable to the formulas of logic; it is impatient of fact, and intolerant of argument and demonstration. It does not reason, it asserts and asseverates. Its traditional method is a word and a blow.

At one time it was the avowed policy of the dominant South to furnish the Negro equal public opportunity with the whites, while insisting on the separation of the races in all purely social features. This was the gospel according to the late Henry W. Grady, who, before his untimely death, bid fair to become not only the mouthpiece but the oracle of the New South. Senator D. M. McEnery, of Louisiana, in a notable speech in the United States Senate several years ago, said: " There never has been any disposition on the part of the people of Louisiana to deprive the Negro of his political and civil rights. There has been and will continue to be determination, fixed and unalterable, to deny him social privilege on equality with the whites, and to prohibit him from aspiring to any equality in social life, which nature forbids." Passing by the gracious proffer to assist nature in carrying out her inexorable decree, this deliverance shows plainly that the social policy of the South is regarded as the primary factor, and political and civil regulations are but corollaries of the leading proposition. In society, as in science, the greater includes the less.

But of late we have heard a new voice from the South. It is louder and less considerate of the claims of humanity than the milder tones of the more dignified and decorous leadership which it seeks to supplant. This is the voice of Tillman and Vardaman and Baringer and Thomas Dixon. These new oracles tell us that the Negro must be denied political, civil, educational, and even industrial opportunity, lest " social equality " should be the consummation of it all. The Ten Commandments, the Golden Rule, the Sermon on the Mount, the Declaration of Independence, the Constitution of the United States, and the genius and tradition of American institutions are held in open defiance by a narrow and provincial spirit.

The ethical and political foundations of social order
are ruthlessly overborne by the fiat of a silly phrase.
The question is of vital concern to every loyal American citizen. For if this spirit is allowed to prevail,
and the Negro is, of set policy, suppressed below the
level of American manhood, in deference to an absurd social theory, then his status will inevitably settle into a servile caste as rigid and inexorable as that
which blights Oriental civilization. The enlightened
patriotism that rose up in righteous wrath against
human slavery cannot view with composure the establishment on American soil of an iniquitous caste which
is even more repugnant to the genius of free institutions. The silent South, the survivors and descendants of the better type of the slave-holding class,
the men and women in whose breasts not even the
blighting influence of slavery could sour the milk of
human kindness, are now held, as in a vise, by this
narrow and intolerant spirit. They have no frantic
dread of the social affiliation of the races. Indeed,
according to their traditional social code, intimate
personal association with the uncouth and unculti-
vated whites is almost as distasteful a contemplation.
And yet the cry of social equality has been so per-
sistently and boisterously dinned in their ears that
an imaginary evil has assumed the semblance of a
real danger. Their voice has been hushed; they have
become tongue-tied, and are as completely divested
of freedom, either of action or utterance, as the
poor Negro who bears the brunt of it all. If liberal-
minded Southern white men, like George W. Cable,
or John Spencer Bassett, or Andrew Sledd, though
still yielding allegiance to the prevailing social
dogma, dare lift their voice, even in faintest whisper,
in protest against the evil perpetrated in its name,
they are forthwith lashed into silence by popular fury

and scorn. Race hatred is the most malignant poison
that can afflict the mind. It chills the higher faculties of the soul. The restiveness of the high-souled
sons of the South under restriction imposed by the
less enlightened of their own race is the only hopeful
rift that we can see in the dark and lowering cloud.

Every system of oppression seeks to justify itself.
The institutions of slavery ransacked science, history,
literature, and religion in quest of fact and argument to uphold the iniquitous system. There is almost an exact parallel between the methods employed
in support of human slavery and those that are now
being resorted to in justification of the decrees of
"social equality."

We are told that the separation of the races is
ordained of God, just as slavery used to be called a
" divine institution." It is strange indeed that those
who breathe out hatred and slaughter against their
fellow-men are ever prone to claim divine prerogative
in carrying out their iniquitous scheme. The alliance
of Providence with the type of men who are now
leading the propaganda of race hatred would reverse
all of our received notions of the divine attributes.

Physical dissimilarity is seized upon as a badge of
distinction, and a hasty judgment easily confuses
the index with the indicated potency. But, as is well
known, difference of race and color has never prevented the closest intimacy of personal association.
The gentleman who drives to the station " cheek by
jowl " with his black coachman, but who becomes
furious on being made joint occupant with a black
seat-fellow in a railway coach, is actuated by an impulse other than purely physical repugnance. If race
friction rested solely upon physical basis we should
expect its rigor to be uniform wherever such distinctions prevail. But, as a matter of fact, we find

that it is subject to the widest latitude of variability, and is almost indefinitely modifiable by circumstances and conditions. It presents little of the fixity and inflexible character of natural law. The Teuton manifests it in a different degree from the Latin races, with whom ethnic peculiarities count for little or nothing against moral and spiritual homogeneity. Rio de Janeiro and Richmond, Virginia, are typical illustrations of the two spirits as respects the *entente* of dissimilar races. Prejudice is more pronounced, or at least assumes a different aspect, in the Southern than in the Northern State, being stimulated by the relative number or erstwhile status of the two elements. It becomes mild or virulent, according to incentive or occasion. In individual instances it almost or wholly disappears, and can be aroused only by playing upon class interests, prejudice, and pride. Grant Allen tells us somewhere that the same Englishman who seems to ignore race differences at home becomes the most intolerant of men when he takes residence in the colonies. If the separation of the races is a decree of Providence working through nature, what need of human help in carrying out that decree? The re-enactment of the laws of the Almighty leads naturally to the suspicion that those who so eagerly proffer this assistance are actuated by a wish rather than a conviction. The Negro is not credited with natural repugnance against associating with white men. The charge that they must be restricted in their eagerness for such association is the highest possible unwitting proof that the aversion between the races cannot be wholly accounted for by natural antipathy. The lion and the lamb do not enjoy a common bed, because such social intimacy is doubtless as distasteful to the lamb as to the lion. Natural antipathy is a reciprocal feeling.

There is little room to doubt that the feeling against the Negro is of the nature of inspirited animosity rather than natural antipathy, and can be accounted for, in large part, by the traditional place which he has occupied in the social scheme. A people who have yet made no considerable contribution to the general culture of the human spirit, and whose traditional relation with European civilization has been of a servile sort, are not deemed eligible to the ennobling circle of Aryan fellowship. The violent severance of servile bonds, and the humiliation of the Southern man's tough Teutonic spirit by outside compulsion, engendered deep and long-abiding animosities.

But the chief cause of race estrangement is of a political nature, if we be allowed to use that term, not merely in the technical sense of statecraft, but as comprehending the calculated policy of the ruling class towards the despised element. The cultivation of class consciousness is one of the most familiar phenomena of history. The line of demarcation is drawn at any easily discernible difference, whether it be geographical, racial, natural, political, religious, or minor distinctions of a physical or psychical nature. History is largely concerned with the conflict of antithetic classes. The struggle between Greek and Barbarian, Jew and Gentile, Christian and Mohammedan, Catholic and Protestant, Norman and Saxon, is but prototype of the conflict which now wages about the color line. Evil disposition combined with shrewdly calculated design can always stir up class friction. Two friendly baseball teams can easily be wrought up to a pitch of murderous fury against each other. The yellow press of this country can, within a few months, involve the United States in war with a nation with whom we are now on the closest terms of international friendship. A heterogeneous population, where the elements are, on any account, easily distinguishable, furnishes an easy prey for the promoter of strife. The fuse is already prepared for the spark. The peace and tranquillity of such a community depend upon the highest enlightenment and moral restraint in the leadership of the separable elements.

That the dominant South is determined to foster artificial barriers between the races is clearly seen in the utterances and action of its leaders. It was Henry W. Grady who laid down the platform: " We believe that there is an instinct, ineradicable and positive, which keeps the races apart. We add in perfect frankness, however, that if the South had any reasonable doubt of its existence it would, by every means in its power, so strengthen the race prejudice that it would do the work and hold the stubbornness and strength of instinct." The more recent leadership of the South, without the clear discernment and conscientious restraint of the brilliant Georgian, has seized upon his suggestion for sinister and selfish ends. They have harped upon the chord of race prejudice as a musician upon his favorite instrument. Seemingly dubious of the sufficiency of natural antipathy, they have sought to give it the requisite strength and stubbornness. The fire of race hatred has been fanned until it has become an uncontrollable flame. Sociologists tell us that the collective soul is less sensitive than the conscience of the individual. It responds to the shibboleths and slogans whose refrain is malice and strife. The soul of the mob is stirred by the suggestion of hatred and slaughter, as a famished beast at the smell of blood. Hatred is a great social dynamic, the ever-handy instrument of the unscrupulous demagogue. The rabble re-

sponds so much more easily to an appeal to passion
than to reason. To wantonly stir up the fires of race
antipathy is as execrable a deed as flaunting a red
rag in the face of a bull at a summer's picnic, or
of raising a false cry of " fire " in a crowded house.
And yet this is just what the politician is doing in
order to carry his crafty ends. He has raised the
cry of " Negro domination " when all the world
knows that the Negro is no more able to dominate
the South than the babies in the cradle. But it serves
its purpose by raising race animosity, which easily
overrides all arguments based on tax, tariff, or the
relative value of silver and gold.

The charge that the educated Negro is in quest
of social affiliation with the whites is absurdly un-
true. His sense of self-respect effectively forbids
forcing himself upon any unwelcome association.
Household intercourse and domestic familiarity are
essentially questions of personal privilege.   The
choice of one's friends and intimate associates is the
most delicate phase of the pursuit of happiness.
Such matters are regulated wholly by personal preference and affinity of taste. The social integrity of
the white race is within its own keeping. The social
citadel is not subject to assault and battery.   The
aphorism of Emerson is as true of races as of individuals: " No man can come near me except through
my own act."

The Negro is building up his own society based
upon character, culture, and the nice amenities of
life, and can find ample social satisfaction within the
limits of his own race. President Eliot, of Harvard
University, has told us in a recent utterance that the
white man of the North is not less averse than his
Southern brother to the social mingling of the races.
The Negro, too, has social sensibilities.   He will

never complain against any white man, North or South, because he is not invited to dine at his table, sit in his pew, or dance with his daughter. But the Negro ought not to be expected to accept that interpretation of " social equality " which would rob him of political and civil rights, as well as of educational and industrial opportunity.

For the Negro supinely to surrender his status of political and civic equality would be as unmanly as a silly insistence upon unwelcome social relations would be unmannerly. The Negro and the white man in this country must live together for all time which we can foresee. They must mingle in business and in public life. All their relations should be characterized by mutual respect, courtesy, and good will. In all purely personal and social matters let each, if he will, go unto his own company.

THE CITY NEGRO

THERE are two distinct branches of the Negro problem, viz., the rustic and the urban. The problem of the country Negro may be deferred, that of his urban brother is immediate and imperative. While the former may be preserved indefinitely, embalmed as it were in a state of nature, the latter demands immediate rescue from destruction.

The influx of rural population into large centers constitutes one of the most serious sociological movements of the last half century. The evils which flow in the train of this movement have been universally noted and commented upon. Such evils fall most heavily upon the poor Negroes, who are allured to the destruction of city life as moths by the glare of the candle. These unfortunate people rush from the country where they have a useful status and function to the city where there is no industrial *raison d'être* for them, and inevitably they sink to the bottom of the social scale, where they form the dregs, the scum, and menace of municipal life. A counterstream of tendency which will return this element to the place where it may become a helpful contributing factor is a sociological desideratum devoutly to be wished.

The urban Negro constitutes a larger per cent. of the race than is generally supposed. It is the prevalent belief that 90 per cent. of this race live in direct contact with the soil. There are nearly eight hundred cities and towns in the South, of more than

2500 inhabitants, containing about one and a quarter million Negroes. In Mississippi, Alabama, Arkansas, North and South Carolina the urban element constitutes from 6 to 12 per cent. of the total Negro population; in Georgia, Virginia, Louisiana, Texas, Florida, and West Virginia, from 16 to 20 per cent.; in Tennessee, Delaware, Maryland, Kentucky, and Missouri, from 27 to 55 per cent. It is quite noticeable that the city element is much larger proportionally in the border States than in the far South. It may occasion some surprise to note that more than half the Negro population of Missouri, two-fifths of that of Maryland, and more than a third of that of Kentucky, are found in the towns and cities. In the North and West the cities contain a still larger proportion of the race. When a Negro leaves the South he almost never proceeds to rural surroundings, but makes a bee-line for the large and attractive centers.

According to the census of 1900 there were seventy-two cities containing over five thousand Negro inhabitants; of these, five contained over 60,000; fifteen, over 20,000; thirty-two, over 10,000. Washington heads the list with 86,000; Baltimore, 79,000; New Orleans, 77,000; Philadelphia, 63,000; New York, 60,000, and Memphis, 49,000. The rate of increase for the city Negro during the last census decade was 30 per cent., against 18 per cent. for the country at large. Charleston, Richmond, and Nashville remained almost stationary, while Memphis, Louisville, and Atlanta made surprising gains. On the whole the Northern cities show the largest percentage of growth. Philadelphia increased by 56 per cent.; New York, 66 per cent., and Chicago, 111 per cent. The Negro element of the Windy City, now numbering 30,000, more than doubled itself in a single decade. Already the alarmist has informed us that the great cities of the North are threatened with a black deluge. At the present rate of growth Philadelphia, New York, and Chicago would each contain three-quarters of a million Negroes by the middle of this century. But, as a matter of fact, it is impossible to predict, except in the vaguest and most general terms, the permanent growth of the Negro element in large cities. This growth depends wholly upon immigration. So far as the facts have been ascertained, it appears that the Negro in the North is not a self-sustaining quantity except through fresh reinforcement from the South. The mobile Negro element shifts from place to place according to temporary attraction. A given city will hold just so many of this class in solution before reaching the point of saturation, resulting in a black precipitation. The Negro element in Washington increased by 56 per cent. between 1880 and 1890, but dropped to 13 per cent. during the last decade; the growth in Nashville dropped from 79 per cent. from '80 to '90, to a paltry 2 per cent. for the subsequent decade. It seems quite evident that such cities as Charleston, Nashville, and Richmond have about touched high-water mark so far as the Negro population is concerned, and even the Capital of the nation does not seem subject to much further expansion in that direction. It is misleading to predict the permanent tendency of the Negro population by its spasmodic movement during a decade of unusual commotion and unrest.

The census defines a city as a place of 8000 or more inhabitants. There were in 1900 forty-one places with over 8000 Negroes, making a total of more than a million black souls. This exceeds the city population of the United States in 1830. A clearer idea of the significance of these numbers can be had by the following comparisons: If all the white residents should withdraw from Washington, Baltimore, New Orleans, Philadelphia, New York, and Memphis, the black residue would form municipalities of the respective sizes of Grand Rapids, Seattle, Wilmington, Del., Des Moines, Evansville, and Portland, Me. The Negro element constitutes the majority of the population in Charleston, Savannah, Montgomery, Jacksonville, Shreveport, Vicksburg, Natchez, Baton Rouge, Athens, Ga., and Winston, N. C.

A noticeable feature of the city Negro is the tendency to segregate into certain sections and localities. This is more strikingly apparent in the North than in the South. Every large city has its white wards and its black wards, which the politician understands as well as the seaman knows the depths and shallows of the sea. In 1890, and the tendency has been accentuated since that time, one ward in Philadelphia contained 9000 Negroes, three wards in Chicago contained 9000, and three wards of New York contained 13,000.

The predominance of the female element is perhaps the most striking phenomenon presented by the urban Negro population. The females are in the vast majority in all of the large cities, except Chicago.

About one-half the colored race in cities are engaged in gainful occupations, but are confined mainly to three or four lines of unskilled or menial pursuits. Colored women are engaged almost as extensively as the men, their sphere of gainful activity being confined chiefly to domestic service and "taking in washing." We have not the prescient power to foresee the time when this condition will be materially different. These people should be made efficient along the lines of work that inevitably devolves upon them.

The number of Negroes following mechanical pursuits is quite considerable in the South, but fades away to the vanishing point as we proceed toward the North. Even in the South, the Negro mechanic is fast giving way to conquering European workmen. If we may read the shadow which coming events cast before them, it seems clear that within half a century Negro workmen along lines of higher mechanical skill will be as rare in Atlanta and Richmond as they are in Boston and Philadelphia.

The Negro has hardly as yet entered upon such pursuits as merchant, dealer, and pedler, which perhaps are the chief business of the city. Indications, however, are not wanting that the future will show greater activity in this direction.

Teachers, preachers, doctors, and lawyers enjoy a larger income than any other class of colored wage-earners. Although they constitute an insignificant fraction of the population, nevertheless, it is a signally potential one. There is almost total absence of the merchant, the manufacturer, and the non-professional man of practical affairs, who constitute the ruling power among the whites. This gives the professional class a unique position and influence in Negro society.

The Negro death rate is unmistakably higher than that of the whites; quite enough so to give rise to most serious and searching inquiry as to causes and remedies. New Orleans, Charleston, Savannah, and Richmond show the highest death rates for both races, which is due, we might infer, to the unsanitary situation of these cities. In such Northern cities as New York, Philadelphia, Chicago, and Boston the Negro death rate is not perceptibly higher than in the large centers of the South. It is known, however, that the colored population of these cities is made up largely of young adults who are not subject to high death rate.

Before we become too much alarmed as to this high mortality for the Negro, let us consider several explanatory factors. It is known that the environment of the city Negro is most miserable. He lives in large numbers in byways and alleys that are not fit for human occupation. In spite of all that can be said of the one-room cabin in the South, it possesses one virtue which the city tenement sadly misses, and that is ample ventilation. There is not a cabin in the State of Virginia that is so unfit for human habitation as are scores of blocks of alley houses in Washington City. Dr. John S. Billings tells us that " . . . if we could separate the vital statistics of the poor and ignorant whites, the tenement-house population of our Northern cities, from those of the mass of the white population, we should undoubtedly find a high rate of mortality in this class." The physical and social environment of the city Negro constitutes one of the causes of his high mortality.

The death rate, on the whole, shows a tendency to decrease. But because of the limited data and the fluctuating conditions, little reliance can be placed upon this indication. It is known that the population of these cities has received an enormous reinforcement of Negro adults whose presence would of course lower the general mortality rate. The excess of the colored death rate over that of the whites is due mainly to the great preponderance of infant mortality.

This is the outcome of carelessness, ignorance, and neglect on the part of Negro mothers. As an indication of what proper sanitary treatment will do to lower the rate of infant mortality, the record of the Board of Children's Guardians of Washington, D. C., may be cited. The infants that come to them are mainly abandoned waifs, and therefore the most unpromising of any possible class of children. These infants are placed in homes and subjected to a sanitary and dietary regime under direction of the board, and the result is that the death rate among them is perhaps not half as great as among the corresponding class of the population at large.

The Negro is especially prone to diseases of a pulmonary character. This conclusion does not admit of the least doubt.

While the general death rate for Negroes is much higher than for the whites, the mortality due to pulmonary affections shows the widest discrepancy. This dread enemy of the human race seizes upon the Negro as its favorite victim. It seems to be as prevalent in the most Southern cities as in higher latitudes. Charleston and Savannah are no better off in this regard than Chicago and Boston. Where is to be found deliverance from the effects of this scourge?

The difference between Negro and white mortality in the country at large is a matter of great pertinence to this inquiry. While this matter has not been studied for the entire country, yet the indication is unmistakable that the country negro is more vigorous and healthy than his city brother.

A careful study of census data gives rise to certain clear conclusions: (1) The Negro death rate is nearly double that of the whites in all of our large cities; (2) this rate is due mainly to excess of infant mortality; (3) consumption and allied pulmonary complaints carry off proportionately about three Negroes to one white person; (4) Negro death rate seems to be slightly decreasing, and (5) the mortality of the city Negro is almost double that of his country brother, which is not much in excess of the rate for the white race in rural districts.

The movement toward the cities should be checked; a higher sense of parental duty should be inculcated; simple sanitary and health instruction should be given to the people, and municipalities should be prevailed upon to maintain better sanitary regulations in the alleys and shade places where the Negroes are forced to live.

" The education of the Negro " has become a cant phrase whose sing-song sound is constantly dinged in our ears. By the frequency of its repetition we are led to believe that it stands for a fixed and definite quantity in the educational equation. The Negro race is ever referred to as a unit, and its circumstances and conditions as requiring a unitary mode of treatment. Our educational philosophers seem to think that the whole race stands in need of a single programme of instruction. They make no allowance for discreet differentiation.

The educational needs and circumstances of the city Negro must be carefully differentiated from those of the rustic masses. The general economic conditions are so different from those of the rural districts and the educational provisions are so glaringly disproportional that we must separate the two in any scheme of profitable discussion. In the cities the funds are quite sufficient to maintain the schools for the average length of term, and to provide the requisite appliances and facilities of instruction. The duplication of schools for the two races works to much less economic disadvantage in the cities, where the numbers of both races are sufficient to supply adequate school constituencies, than in the country, where the population is sparse and far between. The education of the city Negro makes no claim on outside philanthropy. The cities are able to educate their own children and do not stand in need of philanthropic aid. There is no more reason for Baltimore, Richmond, New Orleans, and Atlanta to seek outside aid to educate their children than that they should appeal for like support for their police departments.

The teachers in city schools for colored children are generally of the colored race, Baltimore and Charleston forming notable exceptions. In Charleston all such teachers, and in Baltimore the majority of them, are of the white race. The Negro teachers compare quite favorably with their white co-laborers, and Southern superintendents are not sparing in according them the measure of commendation and encouragement which is their just due.

The status of the city Negro seems to furnish a contradiction of the prevalent belief that education will solve the race problems. Experience seems to show that the problems grow in difficulty as general intelligence increases. This is no discredit to education or a derogation of its function. It simply shows that the case was wrongly diagnosed in the first instance. In the city of Washington, and in a corresponding degree the same may be said of other cities, the educational facilities for colored children are practically as good as any offered the most favored class of children anywhere on the face of the earth. These schools have been crowded for a quarter of a century and have now more than fifteen thousand in attendance, a higher average than prevails in white schools. And yet the race problem at the national Capital is not solved. It is a mild criticism of Negro education to say that it has not had satisfactory reaction upon the mass life of the race.

It is on this account that there has recently sprung up such a widespread movement to modify the plan and policy of Negro education so as to bring it into closer relation with the actual life of the people for whom it is designed. In rural districts the pressing problem is better schools and more of them, but in the cities the question is one of readjustment and wise adaptation.

The perfection of the city schools is of the highest importance to the race at large, for it is in the urban centers that the torch must be lighted and passed on to the remotest rural ramifications.

If our great cities were not constantly supplied with fresh life and vigor from the country they would soon wither up for lack of self-sustaining vitality. The tree is cut from the mountain side and shaped and fashioned into instruments of use and ornamentation, but the supply can be sustained only by fresh growth on the original heath. The city constantly draws in fresh supplies of physical, intellectual, and moral energy only to develop, exploit, and exhaust it. The great drawback to the Negro element is that it is exhausted, without being either developed or utilized.

Mr. George W. Cable in a recent contribution has emphasized the importance of what he calls the " citification " of the Negro. The value of this sagacious suggestion must be accepted with a word of caution. The cities are indeed the centers of light, the storehouses of advantage and opportunity. Without the opportunity of urban contact it is hardly possible for one either to develop or exploit his better faculties. The great men of America were, as a rule, born in the country, but nurtured in the city. With the Negro, however, the situation is not so simple. He shares the disadvantages without the benefits. He

does not enter into the larger opportunities of urban
life. There is a certain advantage of education and
contact, but his culture is apt to assume a pale and
sickly cast for lack of the sunlight of opportunity.
The city Negro grows up in the shade. He is completely overshadowed by his overtowering environment. As one walks along the streets of our great
cities and views the massive buildings and sky-seeking
structures, he finds no status for the Negro above the
cellar floor. There is perhaps no place on earth
where so much culture runs to seed, and so much
intelligence goes to waste, as among the Negro element of our large cities. The younger element of
the race at least is practically as well educated as
the whites. And yet they count for almost nothing
in the higher business and industrial life of the community. It is scarcely necessary to inquire into the
cause of this condition of things or to apportion responsibility. The fact cannot be disputed. So far
only the more fortunate class of city Negroes has
been considered. But there are those who are completely crushed by the weight of superimposed conditions and sink to the bottom of the social scale.
These constitute the slum element, and furnish the
hospital and the jail constituency. Let us, however,
be careful to avoid extremes. Large numbers of city
Negroes are sober, industrious, church-going, law-
abiding citizens. There are also exceptional individuals who are able to breast the blows of hard circumstances and have their merit recognized and rewarded. But the picture in its characteristic features
is not too gloomily drawn. The " citification " of
the country Negro as a means of solving the race
problem should be accepted, if not with the traditional grain of salt, at least with prudent hesitation.

On the other hand, the country Negro has very

little opportunity for getting hold of the machinery
of civilization. The discipline of the plantation system has been destroyed. Every well-ordered plantation was a school in which were taught the crude
elements of civilization. Industry, order, and obedience are the cardinal virtues of the industrial world.
The slave regime was based upon false notions of
political economy and therefore encouraged only the
mechanical or marketable virtues in the slave, and
suppressed all higher outcroppings of intelligence
and personal dignity. A black man was looked upon
as a machine and not as a being in whom the image
of God could be made manifest. And so the school
of slavery appealed merely to the physical side, and
left the higher faculties untouched, or, worse still,
smothered and suppressed. As the whites are withdrawing to the cities the Negroes are gaining in
density in the purely rural sections of the South,
and the opportunities for improvement in manners
and methods of life are meager enough. The public
schools hold for only a few months, and with the
most poorly equipped teachers and facilities. The
knowledge thus gained is mostly of the mechanical
sort and has very little potential value. The number
of Negroes who *can* read and write runs up into the
millions. But the number who *do* read and write and
who use these accomplishments as a means of conducting the ordinary processes of life and of acquiring a larger hold on civilization would probably
not amount to ten per cent. of the number who are
reckoned as literate. We must make an immense distinction between the technical and the practical illiteracy of the Negro race. The country schools in the
South cannot qualify their own teachers. The rural
Negro if left to himself would be in a most pitiable
plight. He needs the sympathy and help of his more

fortunate city brother. As the city has need of the
country for new life and fresh physical, moral stamina, just so the country must draw upon the city for
intelligence, system, and civilized method.

The country Negro, however, has certain advantages; he is on terms of equality with his environment. He is not confronted by suggestions of inequality at every turn. Nature is a mother who is
equally kind and beneficent to all of her children.
An acre of ground will yield as much for the black
as for the white tiller. The markets are color-blind.
No one inquires into the color of the producer of
the best produce in the market except as a matter
of idle curiosity. No labor organization has yet
placed a boycott upon Negro farm labor. The farm
offers for the Negro the only really unhampered
field which is open to him on an unlimited scale. The
city Negro of education and culture, on the contrary,
is forced into menial employment, because higher
forms of occupation are pre-empted by the more
favored class. There are plenty of Negro domestics
who have sufficient educational advantages to conduct
independent undertakings. But they find the avenues so crowded, and the competition so fierce, that
the balance of success is on the side of the white
competitor. The best brain and energy of the Anglo-
Saxon race are engaged in the city industries. There
are a dozen competitors for every dollar in sight.
In the great majority of cases the Negro is handicapped by his color. In those branches of business
involving the social feature, as most branches do, he
is placed at a serious disadvantage. His own race
has not yet been educated up to the necessity of
patronizing him, as a sort of race protective tariff.
The white merchant affords the black customer every
facility for spending a dollar. His courtesy is as

expansive as the Negro's pocketbook. But this courtesy turns into coldness and scorn when the Negro
asks the merchant to give his son or daughter a place
in his store so that he may accumulate business
knowledge and experience. In communities where
the Negro constitutes a half, a third, or a fourth of
the population, and where his educational facilities
are practically as good as those of the whites, we
find that he does not conduct one per cent. of the
business. This accumulated intelligence should seek
an outlet. This can be found in the country. It
requires as great intelligence, thrift, and patience to
make a farm productive as to succeed in a city enterprise.

It is to be feared that the city environment too
often develops in the colored boy or girl a love for
leisure and ease and a positive disinclination for
downright hard work. They prefer to affect the
fine manners and fine attire of the ultra-fashionable
of the white race, and are strenuously opposed to
" hanging up the fiddle and the bow and taking up
the shovel and the hoe." Indeed, this is one of the
dangers of superimposing the superficialities of civilization upon a backward race. It indisposes them
to hard work. The Puritans gained the discipline of
work by trying to persuade the rocky hillsides of
New England to yield up a living. This has become
a fixed trait of character and is handed down by
heredity. It is this predisposition to work which
makes the Yankee so great a force in the world.
The work which devolves upon the city Negro is of
an intermittent character, and lacks the discipline
of steadiness and consecutive endeavor.

RELIGION AS A SOLVENT OF THE RACE PROBLEM

RELIGION may be treated as a sociological phenomenon whose manifestation is as evident and whose effect is as easily measured as any other data with which the student of social subjects has to deal. The influence of the church upon the Negro is just as evident as that of the school. In current discussion of the race problem this potent and pervasive factor is all but wholly ignored. The proclaimed purpose of Christianity is to establish· peace and good will among all the children of men. Before discussing the bearing of Christianity upon the Negro let us see to what extent he is susceptible to its influence.

The Negro as we know him in America is of a deeply religious nature. He is widely noted for his emotional and spiritual susceptibilities. His weird, plaintive, melodious longings are fraught with spiritual substances and meaning, not unlike the lamentations of the Jews in captivity; only the Negro does not yearn for an earthly restoration, but for the Promised Land beyond the skies. These plantation melodies, this blind, half-conscious poetry, breaking through the aperture of sound before the intellect had formulated a definite form of statement, reveal the Negro's passive Christian virtues of meekness, humility, and lowliness of spirit, and express the spiritual strivings of his race.

The conversion of the Negro to the Christian faith is as marvelous, and perhaps as momentous, as any event in the history of the church. There were no

133

religious orders devoted to his evangelization, no
zealous missionary propagandism, no concerted movement on the part of his captors to convert the black
heathen whom the lust for lucre had brought within
their gates. Here and there a kindly mistress or
pious planter might have been moved by pangs of
pity to free the soul of the black bondman from the
shackles of sin, if only the body might remain in
subjection to the galling gyves of an iniquitous system. " Servants, obey your masters," was the only
Scripture text which it was deemed prudent to explain in the depth and plenitude of its meaning.
While sitting in the back pews and upper galleries
the Negro caught the suggestion of the Christian
cult, which was so peculiarly adapted to his ethnic
characteristics that it met with an enthusiastic and
ready response. To a race thus spiritually predisposed, the lines of the hymnist convey a special
meaning:

> " This is the way I long have sought
> And mourned because I found it not."

It is doubtful whether any race, however great its
superiority, can impose its intellectual, æsthetic, or
religious cult upon another, either by persuasion or
force, unless the recipient race is ready to adopt the
suggestion and interpret it in terms of its own ethic
aptitude. Culture is a centrifugal as well as a cen-
tripetal process. The inner spring of motive and action must vibrate in sympathetic resonance with the
waves of influence which proceed from without, before they can be awakened into life and power. Mankind had been observing the phenomenon of falling
apples pattering upon the ground ever since the serpent beguiled the first pair; but it was reserved for

Sir Isaac Newton, whose mind was alert on the suggestive, to utilize this familiar occurrence as a key to unlock the hidden mysteries of the universe. This new cult of grace was seized upon by the Negro with Pentecostal enthusiasm and fervor, because it relieved his overburdened soul and satisfied his longings as nothing else could do.

The evangelization of the transplanted African is the only assured fresh conquest of Christianity in modern times, if, indeed, it is not the only undisputed triumph of this faith outside of the range of the Caucasian. For four centuries a continuous stream of missionary influence has been steadily playing upon the American Indian; and yet, to-day, the red aborigine can scarcely be said to be any nearer evangelization than when Columbus first planted his Catholic cross in the virgin soil of a New World. The rise of the missionary spirit is the most unselfish and creditable movement of modern times; but the conversion of the world to the standard of the Cross is discernible only to the eye of faith, which realizes the substance of things hoped for, the evidence of things not seen. On the other hand, the conversion of the Negro is an established fact. The sanction of his religion is as prevalent and as potent as in the case of his white neighbor from whom it was derived. In the United States the Negro has a higher average of church membership than the whites, and constitutes one-fifth of the numerical strength of all the Protestant denominations. This race has a sufficient grasp upon the spirit, meaning, and method of Christianity to propagate and transmit it, although perhaps not yet able to formulate a theological statement of its doctrine. The highest evidence of ignition is furnished by the fact that the lighted torch has become a new center of diffusion, giving light unto all who come within the range of its radiant influence. Several independent Negro denominations in America are supporting foreign missions in the darker continent of Africa, conducted by their own men and means. Where else has Christianity made such manifestation of its power since the rise of the Protestant sect?

But we are accustomed to the reproach that the Negro's religious profession has little beneficial influence upon his practical life. It is unfortunately true that there is a wide discrepancy between creed and conduct. This discrepancy is, of course, intensified by ignorance and grossness of life. At best, the heavenly treasure is placed in earthen vessels. He is indeed a poor judge of human nature who expects to find, in any people, an exact adjustment between practical conduct and religious standard. When we consider the broad function of the Negro church, and the original grossness and degradation with which it has had to deal, it will be seen that, although religion has not yet done its perfect work, the wholesomeness of its influence has been not only manifest, but marvelous. Imagine the moral status of this people if the religious influence had been withdrawn! Who is he that condemneth? The practical conduct of the white Christian furnishes the roughest approximation to the standards of his faith. The keynote and kelson of Christianity is love for God and man. When the white Christian violates the vital precepts of his faith, in his treatment of the Negro, he furnishes an example and an excuse for his weaker brother to transgress, though it may be in a more flagrant manner.

The most notable feature of Negro church life is its tendency toward ecclesiastical independence. After receiving the original suggestion from the white race, the Negro evinced a decided inclination to worship God under his own vine and fig tree. The Baptist and Methodist denominations, representing the independent spirit, contain 98 per cent. of all colored Protestant communicants. The Presbyterian, Episcopalian, and Congregational churches, which have enjoyed the largest measure of white assistance, contact, and control, have flourished, at the expense of much watering, only as a root out of dry ground. Although these churches appeal generally to the more cultivated classes, yet their numerical feebleness is in no wise offset by any superior vigor of spiritual aggressiveness or force. Even in these denominations there is an ambition, expressed or suppressed, for a larger measure of ecclesiastical self-control. Presbyterian and Congregational missionary societies have spent many millions of dollars among the freedmen of the South, but the result is seen rather in the intellectual and moral uplift than in religious proselytism. The real religious advantage consists largely in reflex influence upon the Methodist and Baptist denominations. These churches have flourished because of their ecclesiastical independence, and not on account of any theological tenets or administrative polity.

It is almost as rare to find a white pastor of a colored congregation as to come across the reverse relationship. We see the same tendency in the Northern States. Wherever two or three dozen colored people are gathered together, there will be found a Negro church, of an independent type, springing up in the midst of them. No people take a greater pride in their churches or give so large a share of their means to support them. The church is not merely a religious institution, but embraces all the complex functions of Negro life. It furnishes the broadest field for the exercise of talent, and is the only sphere in which the Negro has shown initiative and executive ability. Frederick Douglass began his public life as a local preacher in the A. M. E. Church, and if a wider career had not providentially opened up to him he doubtless would have risen to a position of ecclesiastical dignity and power.

In politics, education, and business the white man manages and controls the Negro's interests; it is only in the church that the field is undisputed. Upon the failure of the reconstruction governments the Negro politicians sought careers in the church as the most inviting field for the exploitation of their powers. The Negro preacher is a potential politician, whose natural qualities of organization and leadership being denied scope and exercise in the domain of secular activity, seek them in the religious realm. When the Negro preacher makes occasional excursions into the political field we are apt to condemn his conduct as irrelevant to his calling, but he is merely giving vent to pent-up powers on the slightest show of opportunity or pretext of duty.

The Negro ministry is often upbraided for its delinquencies and shortcomings. But when we consider all of the circumstances of the case, there is no more remarkable body of men in America than these black preachers who guide the people in the ways of truth and righteousness. There is a professional body of men, some twenty-five thousand strong, who, like Melchizedek of old, sprang into existence without announcement or preparation. They show unmistakable ability for leadership and guidance. The priesthood has always been upbraided for its carnal imperfections, notwithstanding the high and sacred character of its function. The Negro ministry does not escape blame and censure; but no one can say that

the moral and spiritual trend of its leading has not
been upward. Under the influence of education and
orderly training this ministry is rapidly attaining to
a higher and higher degree of orderliness and spiritual decorum. There are increasing thousands of Negro churches where no breath of suspicion attaches
to the clerical reputation, and where the services are
conducted with intelligence, simplicity, and in the
beauty of holiness.

The Negro church has stood, and still in large
measure stands, for the home, the school, and the
State. It has been and is the greatest enlightening,
uplifting, purifying, and inspiring influence which
actuates the life of the benighted masses.

It was the consolation of religion that solaced and
sustained the Negro slave under burdens as heavy as
any that the human race has ever been called upon
to bear. It was the manifestation of the religious
spirit that gained for him the confidence and sympathy even of his oppressors, and played no small
part in effecting his emancipation. If the Negro had
remained a heathen, and had adhered to the repugnant religious rites of his ancestors, can any one
believe that the Christian sentiment of this nation
would have exerted itself so strongly in his behalf?
Would a race of heathens have ever been incorporated
into the body politic of this nation?

It is probably true that the educated Negro is not
so deeply interested in religion as were his ignorant
forebears. This is due in large part to the revolt of
culture against the grotesque excesses of ignorance,
partly to the cold, critical, intellectual indifferentism
of the times, and in large measure to the haughty
attitude of the white Christian whose spiritual arrogance causes his black brother to offend. But there
still abides that deep subconscious religious feeling

which a larger enlightenment and the sobering influence of adversity will again waken into life and power.

Stern moral qualities are necessary to save a backward race, in contact with civilization, from physical destruction. Such races usually fade before the breath of civilization, as a flower is withered by the chilling blast of autumn. The Indian is gone, the Australian has followed him, the scattered fragments of the isles of the sea are rapidly passing away. These people have not perished so much by force and violence as through the disintegrating influence inherent in the vices of civilization. The backward races cannot stand the vices of the Aryan; what makes the one drunk, but makes the other bold. Vice is destruction; virtue is preservative. The thief, the robber, the murderer, the drunkard, the adulterer, and, not less, those who indulge in the more refined and recondite modes of sin, are destructive of the stability of social order. The criminal and moral status of the Negro race is threatening its physical continuance. After we have made all possible allowance for historic causes and plead all possible exculpatory excuses, the plain, unpleasant, unvarnished fact remains: The American Negro must conquer his vices or be destroyed by them.

It is true that perhaps ninety-five per cent. of the colored people are orderly and well-behaved; but this is not sufficient, any more than it would be satisfactory for a fruiterer to assure us that ninety-five per cent. of the apples in a barrel are sound. It is also true that the Negro has no monopoly of sin. There is no caste in crime which is a failing of weak human nature; and yet the criminal is a special bane and burden to the people to whom his base blood binds him. One might argue the failure of the sort

of Christianity to which the Negro has been subjected, because it has not banished sin and ushered
in the era of righteousness. This religion has been
in the world for two thousand years, and yet history fails to tell us of a single people from whom
it has removed the earth-stains of wickedness and sin.
In portions of Asia and Africa where this gospel once
held sway the surviving influence is so faint as to be
scarcely perceptible. Parts of Europe after many
centuries of Christian endeavor are sunken in the
depths of vileness and iniquity. Many of the cities
of our own country that are covered with a forest of
church towers are, if we believe reports and rumors
of corruption, as rotten as Nineveh and Tyre. Do
we say in such cases that religion is a failure, and
that the people are incapable of understanding and
applying the principles of Christianity? The Negro
needs, what all mankind needs, a higher, purer, and
more effective application of his professed religion
to the daily affairs of life.

Religion constitutes the only effective sanction the
world has yet devised over the conduct of the ignorant and unawakened masses. No enlightened ruler
of backward races, from Marcus Aurelius to Edward
VII, has ever failed to utilize religious adherence as
an aid to wise and salutary control. This conduct
does not always spring from high spiritual motive,
but is resorted to as a matter of administrative prudence. The sneer of the poet Goethe contains a
valuable half-truth:

"Whoso has art and science found, religion too has he;
Who has nor art nor science found, religion his should be."

The value of knowledge, culture, æsthetic taste, and
social pride as aids to conduct is a matter of casuistic

dispute: but all will agree that where such auxiliaries are wanting the absence can be made good only by the mystic power of faith. The combined experience of mankind shows that it is impossible to bring a backward race under a wholesome, moral order without the quickening power of spiritual motive. Intellectual doctrine and moral maxims are not sufficient. China to-day stands as a living, or rather as a dying, embodiment of what a scheme of morality will do for a race without the mystic religious element. Morality, without religion, especially to an unawakened people, is as impotent and void of effect as a cannon ball without the propulsive power of gunpowder.

A new people stand especially in the need of religious guidance. An old-stablished race, as history has often demonstrated, may exist for ages on the forms of faith after the vital spirit has departed. They are carried forward by the spiritual inertia acquired in a more virile and pious period. The foundation of the Roman greatness was laid in the good old days of stern and robust Roman faith and virtue. The anchor-sheet of our own Republic was forged in the furnace of faith. It is absolutely essential for a people to begin right. The opening words of Genesis form the granite foundation of all true race building—" In the beginning, God."

This brings us to the importance of religious instruction in colored schools, whether under public or private control. For the sake of avoiding argument we may hold in abeyance the larger aspect of this question, and limit our discussion to its application to this unfortunate class. The missionaries who came South directly after the war were not educators in the modern significance of that term, many of them were not even educated; and yet they worked wonders in transforming the life of a new people.

They were filled with the love of God and his dark and benighted creatures, and imparted a measure of their moral and spiritual zeal to the people among whom they came to labor. There was not an unbeliever among them. Suppose they had left their Bibles at home; does any one believe that they could have imparted such a lasting and wholesome impulse? In this instance surely the letter killeth and the spirit maketh alive. You do not arouse the lethargic energies of a people seeking a newness of life by imparting information to the mind or skill to the fingers, but by quickening the spirit. The public schools, with their more competent secular agencies, have supplanted the missionary in the educational world; but, alas! the subtle spirit is wanting. It is one of the greatest misfortunes of the race that this moral and spiritual influence was too early withdrawn.

The home, the church, and the school are the only places where religious instruction can formally be imparted. The average Negro home is no more capable of imparting religious than intellectual knowledge. The Sunday school has the child only one hour a week, whereas the ordinary church service is too stiff and formal to be of much advantage to the average child. Thus it can readily be seen that the great bulk of Negro children are growing up in moral and spiritual illiteracy, without a saving knowledge of the truth.

There does not exist the same ground for controversy over introducing the Bible in Negro schools as in the case of the white race. With the Negro there are practically only two religious denominations, with no great diversity of theological tenets. He has no inherited doctrinal bias. Schismatic differences have not been burned into his soul by the hot iron of per-

secution and martyrdom. The Irishman is a Catholic, the Scotchman a Presbyterian, the Yankee a
Congregationalist for reasons whose roots strike deep
in the soil of conflict and suffering. The Negro has
no serious controversy over Scriptural interpretation.
He is never tried for heresy. He does not wrangle
over questions of the higher criticism. After all
these things does the white Christian seek. The
time-honored dispute as to the proper mode of baptism is about the only Scriptural text that the Negro
approaches with controversial heat. The fundamental agreement among the Negro race as to the
interpretation and value of Bible teaching renders
such instruction comparatively easy of accomplishment.

Again, religion furnishes the only sanction that
can enable the overridden races to contemplate
the trend of modern civilization with composure of
spirit. They form an insignificant part in the world's
rivalry for material and political supremacy. The
exceeding weight of humiliation under which the Negro labors can be relieved only by a firm grasp upon
the spiritual and eternal verities. When a contestant
feels that a prize is beyond his grasp he is apt to console himself by depreciating its value. The humble
slave on bended knee, with marvelous sagacity, gave
utterance to a far-reaching philosophy: " You may
have all the world; give me Jesus." Although this
utterance has been made the butt of much ridicule in
recent years, it may yet prove that the intuition of
the soul is a safer criterion than the deductions of
the intellect. Can the heavily handicapped Negro,
with his present enfeebled energies and hereditary
ineptitude for affairs, compete with the Anglo-Saxon,
the modern war-lord of creation, for the power and
glory of this world? Is he not much more likely to

solve his problems by adhering to high moral and spiritual precepts than by joining the great white throng which bows down and worships before the shrine of " the almighty dollar "?

The historic development of races verifies the truth of Scripture: " Seek ye first the Kingdom of God and His righteousness, and all these things shall be added."

There are more than twenty million persons of African blood in the Western Hemisphere. These people have been brought here and are permitted to remain and to insinuate themselves into the civilization and culture of this continent because of their passing Christian graces of meekness and lowliness.

The presence and promise of the Negro in the Western world is a striking fulfilment of that Scripture saying which is at once a beatitude and a prophecy: " Blessed are the meek for they shall inherit the earth." The Negro is not only preserved by his passive virtues, but he holds them as a lash over the conscience of the Anglo-Saxon, to scourge him to the observance of the requirements of the faith to which he avows allegiance. The history of religion abounds in anomalies. The European derived his creed from Jew, but as soon as the transference was finished the new convert turned in persecution upon the race through which the cult had been transmitted. The American Negro secured his first notion of the Christian religion from the Anglo-Saxon, but now, with acknowledged justice, denounces him bitterly for his failure to keep the precepts of the faith which he transmitted to others.

Moral and spiritual qualities are of the essence of eternal good, and carry their own reward. The Negro holds a warmer place in the sympathies of his fellow-men, because it can be said, " Behold, he prayeth."

And what if men should fail to recognize moral and spiritual excellence? They do not depend upon human recognition for their value. For if God is our Father, it matters little whether Abraham affects ignorance of us or Israel acknowledges us or not.

In estimating the benefits of Christianity to the natives of the Sandwich Islands a pious missionary recounted the inestimable blessing in that it had prepared thousands of the dwindling race for their heavenly home. To the Hawaiian this must be bitter irony. The salvation of the soul is an individual and not a collective phenomenon. It is poor consolation to the Indian race to be assured that an encroaching Christian civilization has merely hastened its departure to the happy hunting-ground in the sky. But the mission of Christianity is to bring about social salvation, as well as the salvation of souls. However the complex problems of race may eventuate, whether the Negro is to be absorbed in the great body of the American people, or to be perpetuated in racial integrity, whether he is to be banished to some distant continent, or perish from the face of the earth, religion is absolutely essential either as a solvent or as a salve.

So far we have dealt with the effect of religion upon the Negro alone, but its effect upon the white race is an equally important factor.

The real question is, What power is there in Christianity to wean men from race prejudice? If we listen to some of the good ministers of the Gospel, who with incredible suddenness turn philosophers and propose off-hand solution for all sociological problems, religion has little or nothing to do with this question.

We are led to believe that the white man is all-wise, all-good, and altogether without sin, while the Negro is passively or actively responsible for all of the evils of the situation; that the white man is bearing his burden with fortitude and grace, while the Negro should be thankful for whatever treatment he receives or escapes.

They tell us that the Negro must be patient, that his hand must be trained to work, that the ballot must be taken from him, that his civil privileges must be limited, that he must be constantly impressed with a sense of inferiority; but few indeed have courage to demand of the white race to apply the simple principles and precepts of the religion of Jesus in dealing with their black brethren of the same household of faith.

Mr. James Bryce, in his notable lecture on the world-wide race problem, asserts that religious sanction is less strong than the bond of blood. This is contradictory to the plain letter and spirit of the Gospel. We have fallen upon such evil days that quotation of Scripture, however direct or unequivocal, is not regarded as serious argument. When Jesus was chided with seeming indifference toward His kindred after the flesh, He responded: " Who is my mother and who are my brothers? For whosoever shall do the will of my Father which is in heaven, the same is my brother and sister and mother."

A strong religious sanction can command amity among diverse races or enmity among kindred ones, and it will be so. The Apostle Paul found the new cult of grace sufficient to solve the ethnological problems of his day. For, through the eye of faith, he could discern neither " Jew nor Greek, Barbarian, Scythian, bond or free, but Christ is all and in all."

The unifying power of religion alone can allay the frictional strife among the sons of men.

Mr. James Bryce, in commenting upon this superior pacifying power of Mohammedanism, says: "Can one of the causes be that Christianity achieves less because it aims at more?" Then in answer to his own question he rejoins: "Christians, of course with many noble exceptions, have failed to rise to the level of the higher teaching, while Moslems have risen to the level of the lower." And yet the teachings of the two religions are identical as respects those who are of the same household of faith. There is the crux of the whole question—Christianity has not solved the race problem because Christians, in adequate numbers, have not risen up to the level of their creed. Emerson tells us that "every Stoic was a Stoic, but in Christendom where is the Christian?"

It is worthy of note that the Catholic states are superior to the Protestant countries in controlling the virulence of race prejudice. Macaulay tells us that it was the policy of this church that caused the disappearance of animosity between Saxon and Norman in England. In Brazil the African element is as large or larger in proportion than it is in the Southern States, and yet race friction is unknown. Recently the United States has driven a Catholic power from the Western Hemisphere in the interest of free institutions; but if the victor shall derive from the vanquished the secret and method by which to subdue race prejudice, so that the race relations shall be as kindly and as congenial in Washington as they are in Havana, he will derive from the vanquished Spaniard as valuable a lesson as he can hope to bestow upon his long suffering victim.

In fostering the spirit and power of initiative, in awakening the dominant forces which conquer and control, the Protestant religion clearly leads the van of progress. It solves all physical and natural problems, but seems to fail to produce a harmonious adjustment among the different breeds of men.

But Christianity has not yet been able to wean the Anglo-Saxon of his race prejudice. With him ethnic ties are cherished more fondly than bond of faith or moral and spiritual kinship. Blood is not only declared to be thicker than water, but its consistency and spissitude surpass the cohesive power of civilization, morality, and religion. With him philanthropic interest and personal repugnance are not incompatible terms. While he professedly loves the soul, he avowedly dislikes the bodies of those whose blood differs from his own. He will build schools and colleges, establish asylums and hospitals, give of his substance and his service to carry the light to the darksome places of the earth, but his tough Teutonic spirit balks at the concrete brotherhood of man.

A learned bishop of the Episcopal Church is reported to have said: "I care not if a Negro be as learned as Socrates or as pious as St. John, yet he could not sit down at my table." Such race intolerance would doubtless be astounding both to Socrates and St. John. Household intimacy and the details of personal intercourse may indeed fall outside the sphere of one's Christian duty; but to hold such things to be of higher sacredness and sanction than one's religious creed merely shows the arrogant spirit which actuates those who worship at the shrine of race idolatry.

It required two revelations to convince the Apostle Peter that what God had cleansed was no longer com-

mon or unclean. Will it require still another to teach
the Teuton so?

We read in Isaiah of the type of soul that characterizes the Kingdom of God, as being without form
or comeliness, and when we shall see him there is no
beauty that we should desire him. We did deem him
stricken, smitten of God and afflicted, and hid, as it
were, our faces from him; and we console ourselves
that this has exclusive reference to the attitude of
the stiff-necked Jew toward the Messianic prophecy.
But does it not equally describe the supercilious attitude of the white Christian to-day toward an humble
black people whom he holds in despite? But if the
Christian religion has not overcome, it has markedly
modified this rancorous spirit.

The great work which Northern philanthropy has
accomplished was inspired mainly by religious motive.
Without the love of God the love for man becomes a
dead formulary. For love of knowledge men will
hazard their lives in quest of some new or unknown
fact or process of knowledge; the soldier, in a burst
of patriotic fervor, gives up his life to his country;
the student of science is carried away with zeal and
enthusiasm for screeching things that fly in the air
or creeping things that crawl on the earth or for
slimy things that swim in the sea. But it is only the
man or woman whose soul is full of the love of God
that devotes his life and powers to the salvation of
the souls and bodies of dying men.

It is in matters of religion that the two races will
find the surest basis of mutual helpfulness and co-
operation. Through contact and assistance from
the white race the Negro will be enabled to maintain
a higher standard of concrete morality, thus insur-
ing more rational modes of worship and orderly
habits of life. On the other hand, the white race will

be a great debtor. Culture and refinement are not essential conditions of spiritual enlightenment, but the inevitable outcome. It does not always appear in a pleasing outward garb. The spiritually minded have usually been despised and rejected of men. The haughty Caucasian can learn from the despised Negro valuable lessons in meekness, humility, and forgiveness of spirit, the brightest stars that shine in the galaxy of the Christian graces. The Negro Christian must purify himself of grossness and carnal corruption, and the white Christian must descend from his pharisaical attitude, whose pious hauteur finds vent in the prayer, "I thank the Lord that I am not as other men," until they, too, shall meet upon a common plane of truth and righteousness and brotherly kindness.

Christianity will solve the race problem if, as we profess to believe, it is destined to gain full sway over the innate wickedness of the human heart. Right and wrong may co-exist for ages, but finally the evil will be swallowed up in good. Universal slavery existed for well-nigh two thousand years after the advent of the Christian dispensation, but in the fullness of time the influence of this religion destroyed the iniquitous system wherever its power prevailed. Christianity is incompatible with caste. Spiritual kinship transcends all personal and social relations.

The solution of the race question depends upon the simple recognition of the Fatherhood of God and the Brotherhood of Man, and the application of the Golden Rule to the affairs of life. Let the Negro lay stress of emphasis upon the Ten Commandments and the white man upon the Golden Rule, and all will be well.

PLEA OF THE OPPRESSED

"Lord, Teach us How to Pray"

O Thou who heard the plaintful plea
Of our forebears on bended knee,
And broke their bonds and set them free,
   To Thee we pray,
   To Thee we pray.

In broken word and wailing tone,
In deep, unutterable groan,
They made their tribulations known;
   Hear us, we pray,
   Hear us, we pray.

In this dark day of sore distress,
In deepest gloom of wilderness,
When threatening ills so hardly press;
   Help us this day,
   Help us this day.

If slighting scorn of race would seek
Its vial of wrath to venge and wreak
Upon this lowly folk and meek,
   Spare us, we pray,
   Spare us, we pray.

They need not fear, our Strength and Stay,
Who keep thy Law, walk in the way,
When all the world might look and say:
   " Behold, they pray!"
   " Behold, they pray!"

But when we stray from Thy command,
And feel Thy sore afflicting hand,
We humbly bow; we understand:
      May we obey,
      May we obey.

If some Thy saving help deny,
With wild, inane, distracted cry,
Like Job's wild wife, would curse and die,
      Forgive, we pray,
      Forgive, we pray.

If time-taught wisdom nostrums find
In cunning hand or knowing mind,
Show the blind leaders of the blind
      'Tis vanity,
      'Tis vanity.

Thy righteous Law is all our trust,
Who builds on else but builds on dust;
The Mighty should, the Lowly must
      Rely alway,
      Rely alway.

Lord, since of stones Thou raiseth seed
As choice as any boasted breed,
Vouchsafe to us the larger meed,
      We humbly pray,
      We humbly pray,
        Amen.

THE LAND OF GOSHEN

THERE is much speculation as to the ultimate destiny of the Negro population in the United States. History furnishes no exact or approximate parallel. When widely dissimilar races are thrown into intimate contact it is inevitable that either extermination, expulsion or separate racial types will be the outcome. So far as the present problem is concerned, extermination and expulsion have few serious advocates, while amalgamation has no courageous ones. The concensus of opinion seems to be that the two races will preserve their separate identity as co-inhabitants of the same territory. The main contention is as to the mode of adjustment, whether it shall be the co-ordination or subordination of the African.

All profitable speculation upon sociological problems must be based upon definitely ascertained social tendencies. It is impossible to forecast coming events unless we stand within the pale of their shadow. The Weather Bureau at Washington, discerning the signs of air and cloud and sky, makes probable predictions of sunshine or storm. Such predictions are not for the purpose of enabling us to affect or modify approaching events, but to put ourselves and our affairs in harmony with them. Sociological events have the inevitableness of natural law, against which speculations and prophecies are as unavailing as against the coming of wind and tide. Prescient wisdom is serviceable only in so far as it enables us to put ourselves in harmony with foreknown conditions. Plans and policies for the solution of the race prob-

lem should be based upon as full a knowledge of the
facts and factors of the situation as it is possible to
gain, and should be in line with the trend of forces
which it is impossible to subvert. Social tendencies,
like natural laws, are not affected by quackery and
patent nostrums. Certain of our sociological statesmen are assuming intimate knowledge of the eternal
decrees, and are graciously volunteering their assistance to Providence. They are telling us, with
the assurance of inspiration, of the destiny which lies
in store for the black man. It is noticeable, however,
that those who affect such familiarity with the plans
and purposes of Providence are not usually men of
deep knowledge or devout spirit. The prophets of
evil seem to derive their inspiration from hate rather
than love. In olden times, when God communicated
with man from burning bush and on mountain top,
He selected men of lowly, loving, loyal souls as the
chosen channel of revelation. To believe that those
who breathe out slaughter and hatred against their
fellow-men are now his chosen mouthpiece is to assume that Providence, in these latter days, has grown
less particular than aforetime in the choice of spokes-
men.

The most gifted of men possess very feeble clair-
voyant power. We do not know the changes that
even a generation may bring forth. To say that the
Negro will never attain to this or that destiny requires
no superior knowledge or foresight except audacity
of spirit and recklessness of utterance. History has
so often changed the "never" of the orator into
accomplished results, that the too-frequent use of
that term is of itself an indication of heedlessness and
incaution. It is safe to follow the lead of Dr. Lyman
Abbott, and limit the duration of the oratorical
"never" to the present generation. When, there-

fore, we say that the Negro will never be expelled or amalgamated or that he will forever maintain his peculiar type of race, the prediction, however emphatically put forth, does not outrun the time which we have the present means of foreseeing. The fortune of the Negro rises and falls in the scale of public regard with the fluctuation of mercury in the bulb of a thermometer, ranging alternately from blood heat to freezing point. In 1860 he would have been considered a rash prophet who should have predicted that within the next fifteen years colored men would constitute a potent factor in State legislatures and in the national Congress. On the other hand, who, in 1875, would have hazarded his prophetic reputation by predicting that during the following quarter of a century the last Negro representative would be driven from places of local and national authority, and that the opening of a new century would find the last two amendments to the Constitution effectually annulled? No more can we predict what change in public feeling and policy the remote or near future may have in store. But of one thing we may rest assured, the coming generations will be better able than we are to cope with their own problems. They will have more light and knowledge, and, let us hope, a larger measure of patience and tolerance. Our little plans of solution that we are putting forth with so much assurance and satisfaction will doubtless afford ample amusement in years to come.

> "We call our fathers fools,
>   So wise we grow;
>   Our wiser sons, no doubt, will
>   Call us so."

The late Professor Freeman, in his "Impressions of the United States," suggests a unique solution of the race problem; viz., let each Irishman kill a Negro and get hanged for it. In this way America would be speedily rid of its race problems, both Ethiopic and Celtic. We read this suggestion and smile, as no doubt the author intended we should. And so we smile at the panaceas and nostrums that are being put forth with so much ardor of feeling. Many such theories might be laughed out of existence if one only possessed the power of comic portrayal. While we muse the fire is burning. But alas, we lack the discernment to read aright the signs of the times.

Physical population contains all the potential elements of society, and the careful student relies upon its movement and expansion as the controlling factor in social evolution. It is for this reason that the Federal census is so eagerly awaited by those who seek careful knowledge upon the race problem in America. There are certain definitely ascertainable tendencies in the Negro population that seem clearly to indicate the immediate, if not the ultimate destiny of that race. Amid all the conflicting and contradictory showings of the several censuses since emancipation, there is one tendency that stands out clear and pronounced; viz., the mass center of the Negro population is moving steadily towards the Gulf of Mexico. Notwithstanding the proffer of more liberal political and civil inducements of the old abolition States of the North and West, the mass movement is in the Southerly direction. The industrial exclusion and social indifference of the old free States are not inviting to the African immigrant, nor is the severe climate congenial to his tropical nature. The Negro population in the higher latitudes is not a self-sustaining quantity. It would languish and gradually disappear unless constantly reinforced by fresh blood from the South. Although there has been a steady

stream of immigration to the North for the past
forty years, yet 92 per cent. of the race are found in
the States which fostered the institution of slavery
at the time of the Civil War.   The thirty-one free
States of the North and West do not contain as
many Negroes as Alabama.   There is no likelihood
that the Negro population will scatter itself equally
throughout the different sections of the country. We
should not be misled by the considerable Northern
movement of the last census decade. This period was
marked by unusual unrest in the South, and many
of the more vigorous or more adventurous Negroes
sought refuge in the cities of the North.   But evidently this tendency is subject to sharp self-limitation.

In the lower tier of the Southern States, comprising
Georgia, Florida, Alabama, Mississippi, Louisiana,
Texas and Arkansas, there has been a steady relative
gain in the Negro population, rising from 39 per
cent. of the entire race in 1850 to 53 per cent. in
1900.   On the other hand, the upper tier, including
Delaware, Maryland, Virginia, West Virginia, North
Carolina, South Carolina, Tennessee, Kentucky and
Missouri, showed a decline from 54 to 37 per cent.
during the same interval.   The census shows an unmistakable movement from the upper South to the
coastal and Gulf States. The Negro constitutes the
majority of the population in South Carolina and
Mississippi, and also in Louisiana, outside of the city
of New Orleans.   The colored race forms the more
numerous element in the group of States comprising
South Carolina, Georgia, Florida, Alabama, Mississippi and Louisiana, a contiguous territory of 290,-
000 square miles.   Within this region the two races
seem to be growing at about the same pace.   During
the last decade the Negro rate of increase exceeded
the white in Florida, Alabama and Mississippi, but

fell below in South Carolina, Georgia and Louisiana.

But the State as the unit of area gives us a very imperfect idea of the relative and general spread and tendency of the Negro element. The movement of this population is controlled almost wholly by economic and social motives, and is very faintly affected by State boundaries or political action. The Negro is segregating in the fertile regions and along the river courses where the race was most thickly planted by the institution of slavery. This shaded area extends from the head of the Chesapeake Bay through eastern Virginia and North Carolina, thence through South Carolina, middle Georgia and Alabama and Mississippi to the Mississippi River. Leading off from the main track, there are darkened strips of various width, along the Atlantic Ocean through eastern Georgia and northern Florida and along the banks of the Chattahoochee, Alabama, Mississippi, Sabine and Brazos rivers leading to the Gulf of Mexico. The South is dotted with white belts as well as with black ones. Western Virginia and North Carolina, the southern and northern extremes of Georgia and Alabama, and the peninsula part of Florida are predominantly white sections. There are scores of counties in which the Negro does not constitute ten per cent. of the population. The Negro element not only does not tend to scatter equally throughout the country at large, but even in the South it is gathering more and more thickly into separate spaces. The black belts and white belts in the South are so interwoven as to frustrate any plan of solution looking to political and territorial solidarity. The measures intended to disfranchise the Negro in eastern Virginia operate against the ignorant whites in the western end of the State. The coming political contest in the South will not be between

whites and blacks, but it will be over the undue power
of a white vote based upon the black majority. The
black counties are the more populous, and therefore
have greater political weight. The few white voters
in such counties are thus enabled to counterbalance
many times their own number in the white districts.
This gives rise to the same dissatisfaction that comes
from the North because the Southerner's vote is
given added weight by reason of the black man whose
representative power he usurps. A closer study of
the black belts reveals the fact that they include the
more fertile portions of the South. The master settled his slaves upon the rich, productive lands, and
banished the poor whites to the thin and barren
regions. These belts are best adapted to the culture
of cotton, tobacco, rice, and sugar cane, the staple
productions in which the South has advantage over
other sections of the country. The Negro, by virtue
of his geographical distribution, holds the key to the
agricultural development of the South.

A clearer idea of the distribution of the Negro
population can be had by taking the county as
the unit of area. The number of counties in which
the Negroes outnumber the whites has risen from 237
in 1860 to 279 in 1900. This would make a section
as large as the North Atlantic division of States.
Within these counties there are, on the average, 130
Negroes to every 100 whites. In 1860 there were 71
counties in which the Negroes were more than twice
as numerous as the whites, which number had swollen
to 108 in 1900. The region of total eclipse shows a
tendency to spread more rapidly than the penumbra
surrounding it. The average ratio of Negroes in
these densely black counties is about three to one.
In some counties there are from ten to fifteen Negroes
to every white person. The future of such counties,

so far as the population is concerned, is too plainly foreshadowed to leave the slightest room for doubt.

There seems to be some concert of action on the part of the afflicted States. The revised constitutions have followed with almost mathematical exactness the relative density of the colored element. The historic order has been Mississippi, South Carolina, Louisiana, North Carolina, Alabama and Virginia. Georgia and Florida have not followed suit, for the simple reason that they do not have to. But political action does not affect the spread of population. The Negro finds the South a congenial habitat. Like flora and fauna, that race variety will ultimately survive in any region that is best adapted to its environment. We can no more stop the momentum of this population than we can stop the oncoming of wind and wave. To the most casual observer it is clearly apparent that the white race cannot compete with the Negro industrially in a hot climate and along the miasmatic lowlands. Where the white man has to work in the burning sun, the cadaverous, emaciated body, drooping spirit and thin, nasal voice bespeak the rapid decline of this breed. On the other hand, the Negro multiplies and makes merry. His body is vigorous and his spirit buoyant. There can be no doubt that in many sections the Negro element is gradually driving out the whites. In the struggle for existence the fittest will survive. Fitness in this case consists in adaptability to climate and industrial environment. In the West Indian archipelago the Negro race has practically expelled the proud Caucasian, not, to be sure, *vi et armis*, but by the much more invincible force of race momentum. This seems to be the inevitable destiny of the black belts in the South. For example, in the State of Georgia the number of counties in which the

Negro population more than doubles the whites was 13 in 1860, 14 in 1870, 18 in 1880, 23 in 1890, and 27 in 1900. In the same interval the counties in which the Negro constitutes the majority had risen from 43 to 67. This does not imply that the white population in the Southern States is not holding its own; but the growth of the two races seems to be toward fixed bounds of habitation.

Numerous causes are coöperating toward this end. The white man avoids open competition with the black workman and will hardly condescend to compete with him on equal terms. Wherever white men and women have to work for their living, they arrogantly avoid those sections where they are placed on a par with Negro competitors, and if indigenous to such localities they often migrate to regions where the black rival is less numerous. For this reason European immigration avoids the black belts as an infected region. The spectacle of black and white artisans working side by side at the same trade, of which we used to hear so much, is rapidly becoming a thing of the past. The line of industrial cleavage is almost as sharp as social separation. The white man does not desire to bring up his family amidst a Negro environment. The lynchings and outrages and the rumors of crime and cruelty have the effect of intimidating the white residents in the midst of black surroundings, who move away as rapidly as they can find it expedient to do so. Only a few Jewish merchants and large planters are left. The large plantations are becoming less and less profitable, and are being broken up and let out to colored tenants, to enable the landlord to move to the city, where he finds more congenial social environment for himself and children.

The rise and development of manufacturing industries in the South also adds emphasis to the same tendency. The poor whites are being drawn off in considerable numbers from the rural districts as operatives and workmen along lines of higher mechanical skill. In the black belts the Negro is protected by the masses around him. One may ride for hours in many portions of the South without meeting a white face. The great influx of Negroes into the large cities comes from regions where the Negro is thinly scattered among the whites, rather than from the regions of greatest density. These factors, operating separately and coöperating conjointly, will perpetuate these black belts of the South. The bulk of the Negroes seems destined to be gathered into these dark and dense areas.

If, therefore, we are accorded so large a measure of prevision, it is the part of wisdom to arrange our plans in harmony with the social movement which we have not the power to subvert. The first essential of a well-ordered society is good government, which affords satisfaction to the people living under it. The Negroes in the South are not satisfied with the present mode of government, not only because it was not formulated in harmony with their sensibilities, but because it lamentably fails to protect life and property. Perhaps there is no other government of European type which so ruthlessly disregards the rights and feelings of the governed since the efface- ment of the Boer republics in South Africa. The first need of the South is a brand of statesmanship with capacity to formulate a scheme of government which will command the hearty good will and cheerful coöperation of all the citizens, and at the same time leave the controlling power in the hands of those best qualified to wield it. This is the desideratum devoutly to be wished. The amiable African can be ruled

much more effectively by the wand of kindness than
by a rod of iron. Strange to say, Southern statesmanship has never seriously tested this policy.
European powers in control of tropical races have
found that reconciliation is essential to effective control. The weaker element must feel that they are a
constituent part of the governmental order and are
responsible for the maintenance, authority and discipline. But Southern statesmanship has been characterized by broken pledges and bad faith and open
avowal to humiliate a third of the population. The
Democratic party claimed to have won the election
in 1876 upon a platform which, in clearly avowed
terms, accepted the amendments to the Constitution
of the United States. But the Democratic States
forthwith proceeded to revise their constitutions with
the undisguised purpose of defeating the plain intendment of these amendments. This on the plea
that if the Negro were eliminated from politics, the
government should be equitable and just, guaran-
teeing to all equality before the law. But as soon as
these plans are adopted the very statesmen who were
most instrumental in bringing them to pass are urging more drastic and dreadful measures. They are
demanding the repeal of the Fourteenth and Fifteenth Amendments, which, by indirect tactics, they
have already annulled. Has the Negro any reason to
feel that the demanded appeal would stop this reactionary movement? There can never be peace and
security and permanent prosperity for whites or
blacks until the South develops a brand of statesmanship that rises above the pitchfork variety.

The next great need of these black belts is moral
and industrial regeneration. This can be effected
only through the quickening touch of education.
Outside help is absolutely necessary. These people

unaided can no more lift themselves from a lower to a higher level than one can sustain the weight of his body by pulling against his own bootstraps. The problem belongs to the nation. Ignorance and degradation are moral blights upon the national life and character. They are wasteful of the national resource. The cotton area is limited, and cotton-stuff will become more and more an important factor in our national, industrial and economic scheme. And yet thousands of acres of these valuable cotton lands are being washed away and wasted annually by ignorant and unskilled tillage. The nation is contemplating the expenditure of millions of dollars to irrigate the arid regions of the West. But would it not be a wiser economic measure to save the cotton area of the South through the enlightenment of the peasant farmers? The educational facilities in the black counties outside of the cities are almost useless. The reactionary current against the education of the Negro in the South is deep and strong. Unless the nation, either through statesmanship or philanthropy, lends a helping hand, these shade places will form a continuing blot upon the national escutcheon. There should be better school facilities and social opportunities, not only as a means of their own betterment, but in order that contentment with the rural environment to which they are well suited may prevent them from flocking into the cities, North and South, thus forming a national municipal menace.

The Negro's industrial opportunities lie in the black belts. He occupies the best cotton, tobacco, rice and sugar lands of the South. The climate shields him from the crushing weight of white competition. Agriculture lies at the base of the life of any undeveloped race. The manufacturing stage is a later development. The exclusion of the Negro

from the factories is perhaps a blessing in disguise.
The agricultural industries of the South are bound
to become of greater and greater national importance
and the Negro is to become a larger and larger industrial factor. The cotton area is limited, but the
demand for cotton stuffs increases not only with the
growth of our own national population, but with the
expansion of our trade in both hemispheres. A
shrewd observer has suggested that the time seems
sure to come when a pound of cotton will be worth a
bushel of wheat. When cotton regains its ancient
place and again becomes king, the Negro will be
the power behind the throne.

It is interesting to notice from the last census the
extent to which Negroes are owning and managing
their own farms. The large estates are being broken
up into small farms and let out to Negro tenants at
a higher rate of annual rental. This is but the first
step toward Negro proprietorship. There is a double
field for philanthropy. First, to furnish school facilities so that the small farmer may become intelligent
and skilled in the conduct of his affairs; and second,
to make it possible for him to buy small tracts of
land. The holders of the old estates do not care to
atomize their plantations, but would gladly dispose
of their entire holdings. There is a vast field for
philanthropy with the additional inducement of five
per cent. Already such attempts have been made.
Some Northern capitalists have undertaken such a
movement in the neighborhood of Tuskegee Institute,
which promises to have far-reaching effect upon the
betterment of black belt conditions. There are also
indications of Negro villages and industrial settle-
ments to afford better social and business opportunities. Colored men of ambition and education will be
glad to seek such communities as a field to exploit

their powers. The secret and method of New England may thus be transplanted in these darksome places by the sons of Ethiopia. Thus those that now grope in darkness may yet receive the light.

Mr. John Temple Graves has, in a recent notable utterance, advocated the separation of the races, and has elaborated his doctrine with great rhetorical pains. But mass movement of the Negro race seems clearly to indicate immediate, if not the ultimate, outcome to be separateness rather than separation.

No one can tell what the ultimate future of the Negro is to be; whether it is to be worked out in this land or on some distant continent. We may, however, be permitted to foretell the logical outcome of forces now at work, without assuming the prophet's prerogative.

SURPLUS NEGRO WOMEN

A NOTABLE article entitled "The Duty of Surplus women," * by Mrs. Charlotte Perkins Gilman, excites a deep and abiding interest. The original and unique suggestion that judicious migration from regions of less to regions of greater masculine density might form a panacea for matrimonial helplessness, will doubtless delight the heart of spinsterdom. The practical wisdom of the suggestion has the sanction of historical precedent and high social prestige. Did not the forlorn maidens of old England brave the dangers of the deep in response to the matrimonial demand of a thriving colony? The thrifty farmer, restive under enforced bachelorhood, eagerly resorted to the market place, and gladly exchanged his precious pounds of tobacco for the priceless boon of a bride.

But Mrs. Gilman's article seems to contemplate only that fraction of the female world implied in the somewhat doleful soliloquy: "Here I am, free, white and twenty-one (or over?) " What of the lot of those surplus women who are not white, and not so very free? Is the ennobling sisterhood of woman to be limited to the color line? The struggle of the colored woman towards purity and refinement involves as deep and as dark a tragedy as any that marks the history of human strivings. If any would gain a true knowledge of the inner soul of black folks, let him contemplate the position of their women, whose pathetic situation must fill the soul with infinite pity.

The enormous preponderance of colored females

* New York Independent, January, 1905.

over males, especially in our large cities, is a persistent and aggravating factor which has almost wholly escaped the attention of our sociological philosophers. The census of 1900 gives 4,447,568 Negro females against 4,393,221 Negro males, leaving an excess of 54,347 of the gentler sex in the United States. This gives a residue of thirteen left-over women to each thousand of the male population. But this is utterly insignificant when compared with the excesses revealed by the statistics of the large cities. The predominance of the female element is perhaps the most striking phenomenon of the urban Negro population.

The subjoined figures will show this excess in fifteen cities of more than 20,000 Negroes.

Excess of Colored Females, 1900

CITY	Females	Males	Excess of females	No. females to each 100 males
Washington..........	48,354	38,348	10,006	126
Baltimore............	44,195	35,063	9,132	126
New Orleans.........	42,585	35,129	7,456	121
Philadelphia.........	33,673	28,940	4,733	116
New York...........	33,534	27,132	6,402	124
Memphis...........	25,359	24,551	808	103
Louisville...........	20,297	18,842	1,455	108
Atlanta..............	20,921	14,806	6,115	143
St. Louis...........	18,020	17,496	524	103
Richmond...........	17,878	14,354	3,524	123
Charleston...........	17,552	13,970	3,582	125
Nashville...........	16,775	13,269	3,506	125
Chicago.............	14,077	16,073	*1,996	88
Savannah............	15,344	12,746	2,598	120
Norfolk..............	10,738	9,492	1,246	113
Total,	379,312	320,221	59,091	118

* Surplus Males.

These cities with an aggregate Negro population
of 699,533 show a female excess of 59,091. Chicago
is the only city where the females are not in the majority, which is doubtless due to the fact that a new
city is always first settled by the men, who pave the
way for a subsequent female influx. If every Negro
male in these cities should be assigned a helpmeet
there would still remain eighteen left-over females for
every one hundred couples. In Atlanta this unfortunate residue reaches the startling proportion of 43
out of a hundred. Washington and Baltimore have
respectively 10,006 and 9,132 hopeless females, for
whom there are neither present nor prospective hus-
bands. No such astounding disproportion prevails
anywhere among the white race. The surplus women
who give Mrs. Gilman such anxious solicitude scarcely
exceed one in a hundred even in such man-forsaken
cities as New York and Boston. If then the evil be
a threatening one among the white race with such an
insignificant surplus, what must be said of its multiplied enormity when we turn to the situation of the
black race, where the excess is more than one-sixth
of the male sex? Preponderance of one sex over the
other forbodes nothing but evil to society. The mal-
adjustment of economic and social conditions upsets
the scale where nature intended a balance. The argument of Mrs. Gilman is as correct as it is courageous.
" Where women preponderate in large numbers," she
says, " there is a proportionate increase in immorality, because women are cheap ; where men preponderate in large numbers there is also immorality because women are dear."

This argument is perfectly general in its scope,
and has special application to the Negro only because
aggravated conditions add a graver emphasis. These
left-over, or to-be-left-over, Negro women, falling as

they do in large part in the lower stratum of society, miss the inhibitive restraint of culture and social pride, and, especially if they be comely of appearance, become the easy prey of the evil designs of both races. The question is a painfully delicate one. It is a disordered nature that delights in stirring up filth for the sake of its stench. The only justification for holding up such a dark and forbidden picture to the gaze of the world is that a clear knowledge of the enormity of the evil may lead to the consideration of constructive measures of relief.

The problem is for the most part an economic one, and the treatment must partake of the nature of the disease. It is easier to account for this unfortunate condition than it is to propose a remedy. Negro women rush to the city in disproportionate numbers, because in the country there is little demand for such services as they can render. They cannot remain at the hard, bone-breaking labor of the farm. The compensation of rural workers is so meagre that the man alone cannot earn a reasonable livelihood for the whole family. The girls, when they are of age and become conscious of their great deprivations, are enticed away by the glare and glitter of city life. They would escape the ills they have by fleeing to those they know not of. The situation is anomalous. The Negro man has no fixed industrial status in the cities. He loiters around the ragged edge of industry, and is confined to the more onerous and less attractive modes of toil. He who gives up the freedom and independence of rural life to drive an ash cart or dig in a city sewer surely is not wise. On the other hand, the Negro woman finds an unlimited field of employment in the domestic and household industries. These surplus women can hardly be expected to migrate back to the country in quest of

marriage.   They have just fled from the material
poverty and social dearth of rural environment, and
it is not likely that they will give up the flesh pots of
the city for the dreary drudgery from which they
have just escaped.

In order to forestall mischievous misinterpretation,
it seems necessary to say that which should need no
saying; namely, that the upward ambition and aspiration of colored women is the most encouraging
indication of Negro life.   The women of any race are
the conservators of its moral stamina, which in turn
lies back of all social progress.   Any one who gains
intimate knowledge of the better side of Negro life
must be deeply impressed with the evident superiority of the progressive colored women over the average
man of like opportunity.   This superiority is manifested not only in cultivation and character, but in
their fearless and aggressive attitude towards race
rights and privileges.   In many instances they are
forced to a life of perpetual spinsterhood because of
a dearth of men of the requisite ambition and progressive spirit.   But we should not allow our appreciation of the advancement of the upper ten to render
us oblivious of the needs and necessities of the lower
ninety.

The great bulk of colored women in our cities,
being shut out from higher avenues of work, must
seek employment in domestic service.   A study of the
occupation of colored women in the city of Washington, where the attainments of the upper ten have
been widely exploited, will throw much light on this
subject.

OCCUPATION OF COLORED FEMALES IN THE DISTRICT
OF COLUMBIA, 1900.

All occupations 23,448
Domestic and personal service.................21,018
Dressmaking and needlework................. 1,617
Professional service 519
All other occupations......................... 294

It is interesting to note that nearly one-half of the
females are engaged in gainful occupations, a circumstance which tells its own story. There are ten
thousand surplus women of color at the National
Capital; this fact, together with the low economic
status of the men, renders it imperative that a large
proportion of the women should enter the great
bread-winning contest. Seven-eighths of them are
engaged in domestic and personal service. The 519
assigned to professional service are mainly engaged
in teaching. These figures show us plainly the field
in which these women must labor for all time that we
have the data to foresee. If we take the country at
large it will be found that the Negro woman is confined almost exclusively to agricultural and domestic
pursuits as means of gaining a livelihood.

COLORED FEMALES EMPLOYED IN THE UNITED
STATES, 1900.

All occupations 1 316,872
Domestic and personal service.............. 681,947
Agriculture 582,001
Professional service 15,601
All other occupations...................... 37,323

Thus it will be seen that for the entire country
domestic service absorbs fifty-two per cent. of this
class of wage earners. In the cities it constitutes
almost the exclusive avenue of remunerative work.
If we take the Negro race as a whole, male and

female, it will be found that out of 3,998,963 engaged in all occupations, 2,143,176 are agricultural workers and 1,324,160 are found in domestic
and personal service; these two fields of effort furnished a livelihood for 86 per cent. of the entire race.
It is a hard, but nevertheless a painful, concrete fact,
that an intolerant spirit effectually shuts out the
Negro from manufacturing industries and from trade
and transportation. The two great industrial problems before the Negro are (1) to gain greater efficiency in the two available lines of industry, and (2)
to press upon the borders of the higher mechanical
and industrial pursuits in quest of larger opportunity.

But when we restrict attention to the status of the
colored women in the large cities we find that they
are shut in to a single line of remunerative activity.
Here is a field of labor which is large, wide open,
and undisputed. There is little danger that the
Negro domestic will be banished from the household
by white competition, unless on the score of superior
efficiency. The ultra-fashionable may indulge in the
fad of English servants, but in the long run the
Negro will be found to return to favor. The colored
woman possesses sacrificial virtues and altruistic devotion in the highest degree. In her ignorant and
degraded condition she was able to take the children
of her refined mistress, and by the wealth of her
natural affection, foster for herself a fondness and an
endearment sometimes beyond that they bore their
own mothers. She still possesses that sacrificial quality which gives her the preference, even though she
falls short in point of competency, in close personal
and subordinate relations. The immediate pressing
problem growing out of the situation is how to make
these women more competent and efficient in this
broad field of labor.

There should be in every city with a large Negro population a school of domestic service whose scheme of training should be of such simple and easy character as to be available to every girl of moderate intelligence and ambition. This would indeed be industrial education that counts. It is preparing laborers for a field that is already white unto harvest. There can be no dispute as to the advantage and even the necessity of such training. There is no adequate agency at present devoted to this task. Hampton and Tuskegee do not aim to accomplish it any more than do Fisk and Howard. In the very nature of the case the problem is a local one and must be worked out by local agencies. Here is a wide field for practical philanthropy based upon sound economy. A project looking forward to the higher efficiency of domestic service in our large cities must command the good will and hearty co-operation of all elements, white and black, whatever their school of belief or social opinion. There should be more strenuous and vigilant activity to guard these girls against the dangers of sordid city association, and to surround them with wholesome moral and religious environment. There is no problem of our city life to-day that appeals more imperatively to the religious and charitable agencies that are devoted to civic righteousness and social purity. But after all has been said and done the treatment can only be temporary and palliative. Society cannot contemplate with satisfaction the permanence of any considerable body of unmarried women, whose existence is indeed without " excuse or explanation," in either social or divine economy. It is to be hoped that either city conditions will so improve that men will be attracted in sufficient numbers to claim the surplus city spinsters, or that country conditions will

so improve that they will gladly avail themselves of
rural matrimonial opportunities.

The large and remunerative field of domestic service
has not received adequate attention on the part of the
leaders of the colored race. The contemptuous attitude of the more favored of this race towards this
department of labor has had much to do with the low
estimate in which such service and servants are held.
This feeling is but a survival or reaction of the influence of slavery, which taught the Negro to despise
all those with whom work was a necessity. He saw all
dignity and honor and glory attach to those who
neither toiled nor spun. Even to-day it is hard for
the average Negro to have much respect for a white
man who works with his hands, or to think of him as
other than " po' white trash." Slavery inculcated the
drudgery, but not the gospel of work. This servile
estimate of labor is still potent and persistent. That
all labor is honorable is a formal phrase rather than
a serious feeling with the average Southerner, white
or black. The few Negroes whom circumstances
enabled to rise swiftly above the level of menial labor,
not unnaturally, brought forward the traditional attitude of contempt for those left below. Menial
service served and serves as a reminder of the old
relationship of master and slave. A sharp line of
cleavage suddenly developed between the favored few
and the less fortunate many. There was an absence
of that sympathetic relationship and mutuality of
good-will that prevails in a well-established order
where different ranks and social grades are recognized and understood.

Some negroes still hesitate to advocate preparation
for domestic service for fear of being accused of
proposing menial service for the whole race. The
whites who persist in limiting the Negro's function

in society to the servile sphere impel them to this hesitant attitude. But the plain demands of the situation require the application of sanity and common sense. Class differentiation is becoming a recognized phenomenon of Negro development. No one formula of treatment can be applied to these nine million people with such varied aptitudes and opportunities. The mutual dependence of the more fortunate and the less favored—of the upper ten and the lower ninety—is gaining a wide and deeper appreciation. More than half of the Negro women who are forced to earn a living are employed in the domestic industries. The bulk of the following of the great Catholic Church in America falls among those who are engaged in the humbler spheres of service, but many of them are rapidly gaining wealth, and power, and fame. The wise and far-seeing leadership of this great organization discourages estrangement between the high and low, learned and ignorant, rich and poor, who are of the same household of faith. Nor are the humble workmen led to despise their lowly calling, but rather to dignify their office by diligence and fidelity to duty. A more enlightened leadership among the Negroes will assume a similar attitude towards the toiling masses who look for wise guidance and direction. Those who have been benefited must become enlarged so as to appreciate the obligation that opportunity confers; while those who are left in the humbler places must be encouraged to become workmen " that maketh not ashamed."

Advocacy of adequate preparation for immediate and available service on the part of those who can secure no other is in no sense inconsistent with the higher needs and aspirations of the race. Every American boy and girl who is made of the true metal will make for the highest place within the reach of his faculties or the range of his opportunities. President Roosevelt and Booker T. Washington, alike, will endeavor to procure for their children the highest form of service they are capable of performing. The humblest citizen will, and ought, to do the same. What right can be more sacred than the right to better one's condition? The old-fashioned, homely Negro mother who washed and ironed till her fingers bled and burned, in order that her children might improve their status, exhibited a spirit that should elicit the highest admiration. The Negro woman is handicapped by such an unfavorable environment that it seems almost inhuman to make her the butt of witticism and ridicule as is sometimes done, because from the depth of her lowliness she dares aspire to the highest and best things in life. It is a cheap philosophy and a false leadership that would belittle or ridicule the higher aspirations of the least of these. The Negro women of our large cities, especially the surplus fifth, need all the stimulus of high ideals to sustain them under the heavy burdens which unfortunate social conditions compel them to bear.

These surplus women present a pressing social problem which calls for immediate and special treatment. The remedy suggested is not proposed as a solution of the vexed race problem, but merely as the means of simplifying one of its most serious and aggravating factors.

RISE OF THE PROFESSIONAL CLASS

In a homogeneous society where there is no racial cleavage only the select members of the favored class occupy professional stations. In India it is said that the populace is divided horizontally by caste and vertically by religion; but in America the race spirit serves both as a horizontal and vertical separation. The isolation of the Negro in all social and semi-social relations necessitates independent ministrative agencies from the lowest to the highest rungs of the ladder of service. It is for this reason that the colored race demands that its preachers, teachers, physicians and lawyers shall be for the most part men of their own blood and sympathies. Strangely enough this feeling first asserted itself in the church —that organization founded upon the universal fatherhood of God and brotherhood of man. In the estimation of its founder there is neither Jew nor Greek, Barbarian, Scythian, bond or free. According to a strict construction of its requirements there is no difference in kind among those who are spiritually akin. And yet the organic separation of the races first asserted itself in the matter of religion. Whenever the colored adherents became sufficiently large to excite attention they were set apart, either in separate communion or in separate assignment of place in the house of worship. When the Negro worshiper gained conscious self-respect he grew tired of the back pews and upper galleries of the white churches, and sought places of worship more compatible with his sense of freedom and dignity. Hence arose the Negro church and the Negro clergy. This

179

was the first professional class to arise, and still relatively the most numerous. The religious interests of the race are almost wholly in the hands of the colored clergy. Outside of the Catholic Church it is almost as difficult to find a white clergyman over a colored congregation as it is to meet with the reverse phenomenon. The two denominations, Methodists and Baptists, that are wholly under Negro ecclesiastical control, include well-nigh the entire colored race.

The proportional number of church communicants for the colored race exceeds that for the white race. In 1890 the colored race had one communicant to every 2.79 of the Negro population, while the whites had one out of every 3.04.

This vast host of church members is almost wholly under colored ecclesiastical control. There is need for at least 25,000 trained men to administer to the spiritual needs of this multitude. Herein lies one of the most powerful arguments for the higher education of select members of the Negro race. The tendency of the times is to require of candidates for the professions sound academic training as a preparatory basis for their professional equipment. It is idle to say that because the Negro race is ignorant and undeveloped therefore its clergy need not measure up to the average of professional requirements. It surely requires as much discretion, resourcefulness and sense to meet the needs of the lowly as to administer to those who are already exalted. It is true that the Negroes have been gathered in the church in great multitudes under the guidance of men who had little academic equipment for their work; but we know full well that this is but the first step in their spiritual development, and that their future welfare requires not only men of consecration, but men of

definite training for their work. Let us not forget
also that the Negro church has a larger function
than the white church. Therefore, the Negro preacher
must be not only the spiritual leader of his flock,
but also the general guide, philosopher, and friend.

The rise of the colored teacher is due almost wholly
to the outcome of the Civil War. The South soon
hit upon the plan of the scholastic separation of the
races, and assigned colored teachers to colored schools
as the best means of carrying out this policy. Hence
a large professional class was at once injected into
the arena. As the Negro preacher is responsible for
the spiritual life of the race, so the Negro teacher
is charged with its intellectual enlightenment. The
2,000,000 Negro children of school age constitute
the charge committed to the keeping of the 30,000
Negro teachers. There were at the inception a great
many white laborers who generously entered upon
this work, of whom there still remains a goodly sprinkling. But their function was and is mainly to prepare colored men and women for the responsible
tasks. It was inevitable that many of the teachers,
for whom there was such a sudden demand, should
have been illy prepared for the task imposed. It was
and still is in many cases a travesty upon terms to
speak of such work as most of these teachers were
able to do as professional service. We find here as
strong an argument for the secondary and higher
education of the Negro as was furnished by ecclesiastical necessities. The duty imposed upon Negro
teachers is as onerous and requires as high a degree
of knowledge and professional equipment as that
imposed upon any other class engaged in educational
work. The special needs of their constituency call
for a higher rather than a lower order of training,
preparation and fitness.

The colored doctor and lawyer have only recently entered the field in anything like sufficient numbers to attract attention. The same spirit that demanded the Negro preacher has also operated in favor of the Negro doctor. The relation between patient and physician is close and confidential. The social barrier between the races often operates against the acceptability of a physician of the opposite race. The success of the colored physician has often been little less than marvelous.

The colored lawyer has not been so fortunate as his medical confreres. The relation between client and attorney is not necessarily close and personal, but partakes of a business nature. The client's interest is also dependent upon the court and jury, with whom the white attorney is generally supposed to have greater weight and influence. For such reasons the Negro lawyer has not made the headway that has been accomplished in the other professions.

It must be said for the professions of law and medicine that the applicants are subjected to a uniform test, and therefore colored and white candidates are on the same footing. Colored practitioners, therefore, must have a fair degree of preliminary training and professional preparation.

Macon B. Allen was the first colored attorney regularly admitted to practice in the United States. He was admitted in Maine in 1844. It is claimed by some that the husband of Phyllis Wheatley was a lawyer. Robert Morris was admitted to the Boston bar in 1850, on motion of Charles Sumner, where he practiced with splendid success until his death, in 1882. Prof. John M. Langston was admitted to the Ohio bar in 1854. James Durham was born a slave in Philadelphia in 1762. His master was a surgeon. He purchased his freedom and became one of the most noted physicians in New Orleans. His practice is said to have been worth $3,000 a year. The following account attests the success of a black physician:

" Dr. David Ruggles, poor, blind, and an invalid, founded a well-known water-cure establishment in the town where I write (Northampton, Mass.), erected expensive buildings, won fashionable distinction as a most skilful and successful practitioner, secured the warm regard and esteem of this community, and left a name established in the hearts of many who feel that they owe their life to his skill and careful practice."

Dr. John V. Degrass was admitted in due form as a member of the Massachusetts Medical Society in 1854.

The above are only samples of negroes in the learned professions before the Civil War. Of course, there was a large number of ministers and teachers. Out of such meager beginnings has grown the great number of professional colored men and women of to-day.

The colored preachers are quite as numerous in proportion to the population as the white, and in some cases more so. In West Virginia there are 425 whites and 802 blacks to each minister of the respective races. One might expect a preponderance of colored ministers for two reasons: (1) There is a larger relative church membership; and (2) the colored population has not more than half the density of that of the white in the area under consideration. In the State of Missouri, for example, 735 colored preachers cover the same territory as 3,439 white ministers; and while each of the former has on an average 375 persons to the parish to the latter's 735, yet his geographical area is five times as extensive. If we turn to the States where the Negroes predominate we may expect to find a reversal of conditions. In Mississippi and South Carolina the colored parish is smaller in area but more populous than that of the whites. The clerical demand of the Negro population is fully supplied in a numerical sense, albeit there is much need for a higher standard of professional equipment for its most arduous and delicate duties.

In no case has the colored race as many teachers in proportion to the population as the white. In some cases, like South Carolina and Alabama, the disproportion is glaring, the number of persons to each teacher being 217 to 775 in the former, and 262 to 718 in the latter, in favor of the more fortunate race. It must be said, however, that the number of persons to each teacher does not necessarily represent the actual distribution of work between the races; for it is known that in every Southern State there are white teachers working among colored people. These are mainly in private and philanthropic schools, however, and do not materially affect the general equation, or rather the inequality, of educational conditions. If we take geographical conditions into account, and the fact that the two sets of teachers operate over the same area, it will be seen that the disparity is greatly enhanced. Taking all in all, it appears that the Negro teaching force is in no sense adequate to the task imposed upon it.

The colored lawyers and doctors form so small a proportion of the general population as scarcely to merit mention as a professional class. In Texas there is one Negro doctor in 9,000 and one Negro lawyer in 40,000 of the population, while in South Carolina there are 22,000 and 29,000 Negroes to a colored practitioner in the respective professions. In

Alabama there is one black doctor to look over 24,000 patients, and each colored lawyer has 52,000 clients. The work in these professions is conducted mainly by the whites, although the twelfth census will undoubtedly show a large increase in the colored practitioners. Where numbers are small, proportions are sensitive. The number of persons to each practitioner will be materially reduced. The argument which we sometimes hear that Negroes are leaving the farm and shop to rush into the learned professions is not borne out by the collected facts in the case. In Alabama, for instance, only one Negro in 50,000 has entered upon the practice of law and one in 25,000 upon the profession of medicine. While it is true that there is no large demand for colored men in these professional pursuits, especially outside of the large centers, nevertheless the steady progress of the people in property, intelligence, and diversified material and commercial interests calls for a conservative increase in the number of professional colored men both in medicine and in law.

It cannot be claimed that the colored race has developed superlative names in the several professions. There are not a few ministers of piety and eloquence. The teacher in the public service must maintain the average proficiency of the system to the satisfaction of the white superintendents. The Negro lawyers are in open competition with their white colaborers, and must render satisfactory service, else they would have no clients. Colored physicians generally have a good record for professional skill and integrity. There is no movement affecting the lot and life of the colored race so suggestive of its educational needs as the relative size of the professional class.

EMINENT NEGROES

THE individual is the proof of the race, the first unfoldment of its potency and promise. The glory of any people is perpetuated and carried forward by the illustrious names which spring from among them. As we contemplate the great nations and peoples, whether of the ancient or of the modern world, their commanding characters rise up before us, typifying their contribution to the general welfare of the human race. On the contrary, no people can hope to gain esteem and favor which fails to produce distinguished individuals illustrative and exemplary of its possibilities.

For four centuries the African race has been brought in contact with the European in all parts of the globe. This contact has not been of an ennobling character, but of the servile sort, affording little opportunity for the development of those qualities which the favored races hold in esteem. And yet there have arisen from this dark and forbidding background not a few striking individual emanations. This race, through a strain of its blood, has given to Russia her national poet and to France her most distinguished romancer. Toussaint L'Ouverture, the Negro patriot, is the most commanding historical figure of the entire West Indian Archipelago. In South America persons of Negro blood have gained the highest political and civil renown.

The Anglo-Saxon deals with backward peoples on

a different basis from the Latin races. While he has a keener sense of justice and is imbued with a spirit of philanthropic kindness, yet he builds up a barrier between himself and them which it is almost impossible to overcome. To him personal solicitude and good will and racial intolerance are not incompatible qualities. On the other hand, the Latin races, while possessing a much lower order of general efficiency, accept on equal terms all who conform to the prevailing standards. Under the Latin dispensation color offers not the slightest bar to the individual who exhibits high qualities of mind or soul. We need not be surprised, therefore, to find that the colored men who have reached the highest degree of fame should have sprung from the Latin civilization. The persons of African blood who are most nearly comparable with names of the first order of renown among Europeans are Toussaint L'Ouverture, of Haiti; Alexander Pushkin, of Russia; Alexander Dumas, of France. In France, Italy or Spain color is only a curious incident. The Afro-American, therefore, belongs in a category by himself. His circumstances and conditions are so different from those of his European brother that although of the same color they are not of the same class.

Several lists of distinguished colored men have been prepared, the most important of which, perhaps, was published by Abbé Grégoire, and was prepared to answer the argument of Thomas Jefferson and others, who undertook to prove the Negro's intellectual inferiority. This work contains accounts of Negroes in all countries who have reached eminence and distinction in all lines of endeavor. An account of the part played by colored men in the Revolutionary War contains the deeds and achievements of noted Negroes. Rev. William J. Simmons brings the former work nearer to date and includes many colored men now living. A list of distinguished colored women has also been compiled.

Numerous magazine articles have appeared on this subject from time to time. The two which are perhaps of the greatest importance, and which include the substance of the rest, appeared in the *International Quarterly Review* and in the *North American Review*.

An interesting syllabus has recently been prepared by Mr. A. O. Stafford on " Negro Ideals," which gives a good outline of the efforts of the Negro toward better things.

It is with some hesitancy that a few names of the more distinguished Afro-Americans are here presented. In such a restricted list it is inevitable that many should be omitted who are equally worthy as some who are mentioned. The names here presented have not been selected because of general distinction, but rather for technical, artistic, and intellectual achievements in the scholastic sense.

Only those have been included of whose achievements the world takes account. There is no name in the list which may not be found in Appleton's Cyclopedia of American Biography. Nothing is great or small except by comparison. The names here presented are at least respectable when measured by European standards. It is true that no one of them reaches the first, or even the second degree of luster in the galaxy of the world's greatness. The competing number has been so insignificant and the social atmosphere has been so repressive to their budding aspirations that it would be little short of a miracle of genius if any member of this race had reached the highest degree of glory. It is true that if not one of these had ever been born the bulk and quantity of science, literature, and art would not be appreciably affected.

While these contributors must be measured in terms of European standards in order that there may be a sane and rational basis of comparison, yet there is another measure which takes account of the struggles and strivings out of which they grew. In the light of European comparison it appears that they represent more than the marvelous vision of a one-eyed man among the blind, but rather the surprising visual power of a one-eyed man among two-eyed men. The significance of these superior manifestations, however, must not be measured solely by their intrinsic value. They serve both as an argument and an inspiration. They show the American people that the Negro, at his best, is imbued with their own ideas and strives after their highest ideals. To the Negro they serve as models of excellence to stimulate and encourage his hesitant and disheartened aspirations.

One will be struck by the versatility and range of names in the list. They cover well-nigh every field of human excellence. It will be noticed that the imitative and esthetic arts predominate over the more solid and severe intellectual acquisitions. Is this not the repetition of the history of culture? The poet and the artist precede the scientist and the engineer. This meager fruitage does not furnish cause for self-complacent glorification on the part of the Negro, but is only an index of the promise of the tree of which they are the initial bearings. With its extended range and scope, the rising generation can look upon them in the light of promise rather than fulfilment.

"That which they have done but earnest of the things that we shall do."

Phyllis Wheatley was born in Africa and was brought to America in 1761. She was bought from the slave market by John Wheatley, of Boston, and soon developed remarkable acquisitive faculties. In sixteen months from her arrival she could read English fluently. She soon learned to write, and also studied Latin. She visited England in 1774 and was cordially received. After returning to Boston she corresponded with Countess Huntington, the Earl of Dartmouth, Rev. George Whitefield, and others, and wrote many poems to her friends. She addressed some lines to General George Washington, which were afterwards published in the *Pennsylvania Magazine* for April, 1776. General Washington wrote a courteous response and invited her to visit the Revolutionary headquarters, which she did, and was received with marked attention by Washington and his officers. Her principle publications are " An Elegiac Poem on the Death of George Whitefield "; " Poems on Various Subjects, Religious and Moral," published in London in 1773, and republished as " The Negro Equalled by Few Europeans," two volumes, Philadelphia, 1801. The letters of Phyllis Wheatley were printed in Boston in 1864, collected from the proceedings of the Massachusetts Historical Society.

Benjamin Banneker was born November 9, 1731, near Ellicotts Mill, Md. Both his father and grandfather were native Africans. He attended a private school which admitted several colored children along with the whites. Although his early educational facilities were scanty, young Banneker soon gained a local reputation as a miracle of wisdom. In 1770 he constructed a clock to strike the hours, the first to be made in America. This he did with crude tools and a watch for his model, as he had never seen a clock. Through the kindness of Mr. Ellicott, who was a gentleman of cultivation and taste, he gained access to his valuable collection of books, and was thus inducted into the study of astronomy. In this study he gained great proficiency, and constructed an almanac adapted to the local requirements of Pennsylvania, Virginia and Maryland. This was the first almanac constructed in America, and was published by Goddard & Angell, Baltimore. Banneker's Almanac was published annually from 1792 to 1806, the year of his death. It contained the motions of the sun and moon; the motions, places, and aspects of the planets; the rising and setting of the sun, and the rising, setting, southing, place, and age of moon, etc., and is said to have been the main dependence of the farmers in the region covered. He lived mainly from the royalties received from this publication. Banneker sent a copy of this almanac to Thomas Jefferson, which elicited a flattering acknowledgment on the part of the philosopher and statesman. Banneker assisted the commissioners in laying out the lines of the District of Columbia. A life of Banneker was published by Hon. J. H. B. Latrobe, Baltimore, 1845, and another by J. S. Norris, 1854. That Thomas Jefferson believed in the intellectual capacity of the Negro and appreciated the force of the argument that the treatment of this race found justification in its assumed low state of mental possibility is revealed by his letter to Benjamin Banneker, the black astronomer:

Sir:
   I thank you sincerely for your letter of the 19th instant and for the almanac it contained. Nobody wishes more than I do to see such proofs as you exhibit that nature has given to our black brethren talents equal to those of the other colors of men, and that the appearance of a want of them is owing

merely to the degraded condition of their existence, both in
Africa and America. I can add with truth that nobody wishes
more ardently to see a good system commenced for raising
the condition both of their body and mind to what it ought to
be as fast as the imbecility of their present existence and other
circumstances which cannot be neglected will admit. I have
taken the liberty of sending your almanac to M. de Condorcet,
secretary of the Academy of Sciences at Paris and member of
the Philanthropic Society, because I considered it as a document to which your color had a right for their justification
against the doubts which have been entertained of them.
        I am, with great esteem, sir,
            Your most obedient humble servant,
                                        THOMAS JEFFERSON.
MR. BENJAMIN BANNEKER,
    Near Ellicotts Lower Mills, Baltimore County.

Lemuel Haynes was born in Hartford, Conn., July
18, 1753. His father was an African, his mother a
white woman. He received his honorary degree of
A. M. from Middlebury College in 1804. After com-
pleting a theological course he preached at various
places and settled in West Rutland, Vt., in 1788,
where he remained for thirty years and became one
of the most popular preachers in the State. He was
characterized by a subtle intellect, keen wit, and
eager thirst for knowledge. His noted sermons from
Genesis 3 and 4 were published and passed through
nine or ten editions. His controversy with Hosea
Ballou became of worldwide interest. The life of
Lemuel Haynes was written by James E. Cooley, New
York, 1848.

Ira Aldridge was born at Belair, Md., about 1810.
There is some dispute as to the exact composition of
his blood; some claim that he was of pure African
descent, while others contend that he was of mixed
extraction. He was early brought in contact with
Mr. Kean, the great tragedian, and in 1826 accompanied him to Europe. Mr. Kean encouraged his

dramatic aspiration, and on one occasion, at least, permitted him to appear as Othello, while he himself took the part of Iago. As an interpreter of Shakespeare he was very generally regarded as one of the best and most faithful. He appeared at Covent Garden as Othello in 1833, and in Surrey Theater in 1848. On the Continent he ranked as one of the greatest tragedians of his time. Honors were showered upon him wherever he appeared. He was presented by the King of Prussia with the first-class medal of arts and sciences, accompanied by an autograph letter from the Emperor of Austria; the Grand Cross of Leopold; a similar decoration from the Emperor of Russia, and a magnificent Maltese cross, with the medal of merit, from the city of Berne. Similar honors were conferred by other crowned heads of Europe. He was made a member of the Prussian Academy of Arts and Sciences and holder of the large gold medal; member of the Imperial and Arch Ducal Institution of Our Lady of the Manger in Austria; of the Russian Hof-Versamlung of Riga; honorary member of the Imperial Academy of Arts and Sciences in St. Petersburg, and many others. Aldridge appeared with flattering success in Amsterdam, Brussels, Berlin, Breslau, Vienna, Pesth, The Hague, Dantzic, Konigsberg, Dresden, Berne, Frankfort-on-the-Main, Cracow, Gotha, and numerous other cities in the leading parts of the standard plays of the times. He was an associate of the most prominent men of Paris, among whom was Alexander Dumas. When these two met they always kissed each other, and Dumas always greeted Aldridge with the words " *mon confrere.*" Aldridge died at Lodz, in Poland, in 1867.

Col. George W. Williams was born in Pennsylvania in 1849. He was educated in public and private

schools and completed his theological training at
West Newton Theological Seminary. His "History
of the Negro Race in America" is the sole existing
authority on the subject of which it treats, and
forms, without doubt, as valuable a literary monument as any yet left by a colored man.

Paul Laurence Dunbar died while a young man,
being under thirty years of age. He made an impression on American literature that can never be
effaced. He published "Oaks and Ivy," "Majors
and Minors," "Lyrics of Lowly Life," and "Lyrics
of the Hearthstone," together with half a dozen
volumes of fiction and short stories. Several of his
works have been reprinted in England. Speaking of
his early poems, William Dean Howells says: "Some
of these (poems in literary English) I thought very
good. What I mean is, several people might have
written them, but I do not know any one else at
present who could quite have written his dialect
pieces. There are divinations and reports of what
passes in the hearts and minds of a lowly people whose
poetry had hitherto been inarticulately expressed,
but now finds, for the first time in our tongue, literary interpretation of a very artistic completeness."

Henry O. Tanner, son of Bishop B. T. Tanner, of
the African Methodist Church, was born in Pittsburg, Pa., in 1859. His early educational opportunities were good, having studied at the Pennsylvania Academy of Fine Arts, and subsequently at
Paris. His pictures have been hung on the line in
many a salon exhibition, and now the government of
France has crowned the long list of medals and prizes
which Mr. Tanner has received by buying one of his
most important works, "The Raising of Lazarus,"
for the Luxembourg Gallery. The picture has already
been hung in the Luxembourg Gallery, and in the

course of time will naturally be transferred to the Louvre. Other notable pictures by the same artist are "Nicodemus," owned by the Academy of Fine Arts, Philadelphia; "The Annunciation," which now hangs in the Memorial Hall, Philadelphia; "The Betrayal," in the Carnegie Gallery, at Pittsburg.

Dr. Daniel H. Williams, of Chicago, is widely known throughout the medical profession. He has performed several noted operations that taxed the skill of surgical science. In 1897 Dr. Williams performed an operation on account of a stab wound of the heart and pericardium, a report of which published in the *Medical Record*, March 27, 1897, attracted the attention of the entire medical and surgical fraternity, and was reprinted in the medical journals of nearly every country and language. It has also been referred to in most recent works on surgery, especially in "International Text Book on Surgery" and Da Costa's "Modern Surgery."

An article on "Ovarian Cysts in Colored Women," by Dr. Williams, published in the *Philadelphia Medical Journal*, December 29, 1900, had for its purpose the refutation of the idea that had been almost universal among surgeons, that colored women did not have ovarian tumors. The record of the cases collected by Dr. Williams furnishes sufficient data to sustain his contention. It is also shown in this article that the same may be said of fibrous tumors. This article has been considered of such value to the profession that it has been copied extensively in medical literature, and notably in some of the best German and French medical journals.

Dr. Williams has performed various important operations that have been published in medical journals and widely commented upon in the medical world.

He was surgeon-in-chief of the Freedmen's Hospital at Washington, D. C., from 1893 to 1897.

Charles W. Chestnut was born in Cleveland, Ohio. By his own effort he rose to the rank of court stenographer. Mr. Chestnut has written several works of fiction which, according to competent critics, place him among the foremost story-tellers of the time. " The Wife of My Youth," " The House Behind the Cedars," and " The Marrow of Tradition " are published by Houghton, Mifflin & Co., Boston, Mass.

Prof. W. S. Scarborough was born in Georgia in 1852, was graduated from Oberlin College in 1875, and is President of Wilberforce University. He is a member of the American Philological Society and of the Modern Language Association. He has published " First Lessons in Greek " (New York, 1881), and the " Theory and Functions of the Thematic Vowel in the Greek Verb."

Prof. W. E. B. DuBois was born in Massachusetts about forty years ago. He was graduated from Fisk University and subsequently from Harvard, after which he studied two years in Germany and earned his Ph.D. degree from Harvard. He has been a teacher in Wilberforce University, associate in sociology at the University of Pennsylvania, and professor of history and political economy at Atlanta University. His chief works are " The Suppression of the African Slave Trade," published in the Harvard Historical Series; " The Philadelphia Negro," published under the auspices of the University of Pennsylvania; " The Souls of Black Folks "; and numerous special studies and investigations that have appeared in the proceedings of the Atlanta conferences and the bulletins of the Bureau of Labor, as well as sundry magazine articles. Mr. DuBois has done more to give scientific accuracy and method to the study of the race question than any other American who has essayed to deal with it.

It is generally believed that while the Negro possesses the imitative he lacks the initiative faculty; that while he can acquire what has already been accumulated, he cannot inquire into the unrevealed mystery of things. As an illustration of how easy it is for the achievements of the Negro to escape his fellow co-laborers, the following incident may be regarded as typical. The Patent Office sent out circulars inquiring as to the number and extent of colored patentees. One of the leading patent attorneys responded that he had never heard of the Negro inventing anything except lies; yet the Patent Office record reveals 250 colored patentees and more than 400 patents. Many of these show the highest ingenuity and are widely used in the mechanical arts.

Granville T. Woods was born in Ohio, and is fifty years old. He has more than twenty patents to his credit. Mr. Woods is the inventor of the electric telephone transmitter, which he assigned to the American Bell Telephone Company for a valuable consideration. The transmitter is used in connection with all the Bell telephones.

Elijah T. McCoy, of Detroit, Mich., has taken out thirty patents, mainly devoted to the improvement of lubricating devices for stationary and locomotive machinery. His inventions are in general use on locomotive engines of leading railways in the Northwest, on the Lake steamers, and on railways in Canada.

There are numerous colored people who have achieved distinction in fields calling for practical energy, moral courage, sound intelligence, and intellectual resource. Mr. Frederick Douglass and Prof. Booker T. Washington are, in general average of distinction, the most renowned of their race, although

their fields of exertion are not mainly intellectual, in
the academic sense of the term—and yet Mr. Douglass was one of the most eminent American orators,
and his autobiography forms an integral part of the
literature of the anti-slavery struggle; and Mr.
Washington's " Up from Slavery " is one of the most
popular books printed in the first year of the twen-
tieth century.   As Mr. Douglass's life is woven in
the warp and woof of the great epoch ending in the
Civil War, so Mr. Washington's life and work have
become a vital part of current educational literature,
and his place in the history of education is assured.

WHAT WALT WHITMAN MEANS TO THE NEGRO

WALT WHITMAN is the poet of humanity. He sings the song universal for all who suffer, love, and hope. No class or clique or clan can lay claim to him and say, " He is mine." To his " feast of reason and flow of soul " he invites all mankind.

"Of every hue and caste am I, of every rank and religion."

The processes of nature are uniform in their operations and apply with equal favor to all classes and conditions of men. The rain falls, the grass grows and the sun shines kindly alike for all who place themselves in harmonious relations to their beneficent design. And so comes Walt Whitman, adorning himself to bestow himself upon whoever will accept him, scattering his good will freely over all.

As we ascend higher and higher in the scale of moral and spiritual excellence, the ephemeral distinctions among men, based for the most part upon arrogance and pride, grow fainter and fainter, and finally vanish away. The great moral and spiritual teachings of mankind have always reprobated the spirit of caste. Buddha teaches: " There is no caste in blood, which runneth of one hue; nor caste in tears, which trickle salt withal."

It was revealed to the Apostle Peter in a vision that he should not call any man common or unclean. St. Paul, viewing mankind from his spiritual altitude, saw " neither Greek nor Jew, Barbarian nor Scythian, bond nor free." It is but natural to expect exalted sentiments from Walt Whitman, for he, too, dwells upon " the radiant summit." From this lofty elevation he looks with equal eye on all below. He announces himself " meeter of savages and gentlemen on equal terms." True, it does not require the gift of inspiration to establish the identity of all men when reduced to their lowest terms. Even so unspiritually minded a poet as Shakespeare recognizes the sameness of the fool and the philosopher in their final physical analysis. But Whitman's conception of equality is all-comprehensive in its scope; it is not limited to the lower plane of animal existence, but extends to the higher region of spiritual kinship. Specifying the circumstances of his spiritual illumination with the definiteness of a Methodist convert, he tells us:

"Swiftly arose and spread around me the peace and knowledge that pass all the argument of the earth,
And I know that the hand of God is the promise of my own,
And I know that the spirit of God is the brother of my own,
And that all the men ever born are also my brothers, and the women my sisters and lovers,
And that a kelson of the creation is love."

His cosmic breadth of view is no shallow sentimentality or vain intellectual pretense, but is based upon the unifying power of the love of God.

Let no favored fraction of the human family fancy that they find in him their pet poet or special pleader. He himself rebukes such unwarranted presumption:

"No friend of mine takes his ease in my chair;
I have no chair, no church, no philosophy."

There is no variety of the human race that cannot find in him that which is adapted to its peculiar needs.

Compelled by circumstances to view all objects under a racial angle of vision, the Negro, not unnaturally, seeks in Whitman some peculiar significance and specialty of meaning. The automorphic tendency is so strongly rooted in human nature that a people are apt to form their ideals in their own image and stamp upon them the impress of their own physical and social peculiarities. This circumstance renders any type unsuited to artistic or literary uses among a people of different " clime, color and degree." " Shakespeare," says a learned critic, " ought not to have made Othello black, for the hero of a tragedy ought to be white." But Walt Whitman tells us that in his literary treatment he does not " separate the learn'd from the unlearn'd, the Northerner from the Southerner, the white from the black."

As the Negro is portrayed in modern literature, he usually plays a servile, contemptible or ridiculous rôle. He is sometimes used to point a moral, but seldom to adorn a tale. We find the Negro appearing in several forms of literature.

1. In the unadorned, didactic discussions of the race problem which have filled our newspapers, magazines, and book-stalls, both in anti-slavery times and since the war. Such works are mainly preceptive in their aim, and, strictly speaking, cannot be called literature at all.

2. In the dialect story he is portrayed as being ignorant, superstitious, degraded and clownish, cutting jim-crow capers and apish antics for the amusement and delight of white lookers-on. By a strange literary inconsistency, however, he is made to express the wisest philosophy in the crudest forms of speech. If there be any virtue, or if there be any praise, ascribed to him, it is of the unaspiring, sycophant, servile sort, leaving the world to believe of the race

that " their morals, like their pleasures, are but
low."

3. In anti-slavery poetry the Negro is pictured in
his pitiable helplessness, and is sometimes endowed
with manly qualities and courage, to serve as a more
effective object-lesson of the wrongs and cruelties of
slavery.   Whittier, Lowell, and Longfellow tuned
their lyres to human liberty and did noble service for
freedom by means of their songs.   But on close scrutiny we find that for the most part these have the
patronizing or apologetic tone.   They are not intended to please, but to teach.   They do not appeal
to the taste, but to the moral judgment.   The ser-
monic purpose is apparent in every line.   This class
of poetry reaches the high-tide mark in the kindly
conceived lines of the poet Cowper, who, with conscious satisfaction of feeling, pays the Negro the
negative compliment of not being outside of the pale
of humanity:

> " Fleecy locks and black complexion
> Cannot forfeit nature's claim."

It is no depreciation of the kindly intent and useful purpose of this class of poetry to say that it is
" sicklied o'er with the pale cast of thought."   Contrasted with it, how refreshing are the lines of Whitman:

> "You whoever you are!
> You daughter or son of England!
> You of the mighty Slavic tribes and empires! you Russ in
>   Russia!
> You dim-descended, black, divine-soul'd African, large, fine-
>   headed, nobly-form'd, superbly destin'd, on equal terms
>   with me!"

4. In recent years it has been quite customary to
discuss the race question through the agency of the

novel. Authors of no less distinction than Grant Allen, W. D. Howells, and Paul Bourget have handled the subject in this fashion. The Negro is made the tragic representative of his own fate. These stories usually breathe the spirit of despair and death. They hold up no model, no ideal, no ambition, no aspiration for the youth of this race.

The growth and expansion of modern literature is co-extensive with the rise and development of African slavery. This literature is tinged throughout with the contemptuous disdain for the Negro which he is made to feel in all the walks and relations of life. In it he finds himself set forth in every phase of ridicule, and derided in every mood and tense of contempt. It appears in our text books, in works of travel, in history, fiction, poetry, and art.

The same spirit does not obtain in the Oriental and classical literatures. These never refer to the Negro except in terms of endearment and respect. The gods of Homer are not too fastidious to spend a holiday season of social intercourse and festive enjoyment among the blameless Ethiopians.

It is true that many of the choicest works of the human mind have been produced during this modern period. This literature possesses all of the qualities which Macaulay ascribes to the works of Athenian genius. It is " wealth in poverty, liberty in bondage, health in sickness, society in solitude." " It consoles sorrow and assuages pain and brings gladness to eyes which fall with wakefulness and tears." But for the Negro to derive therefrom such wholesome, beneficial effects, he must be " self-balanc'd for contingencies," so as to steel his feelings against rebuff, insult, and ridicule. He must exercise the selective instinct, which " from poisonous herbs extracts the healing dew."

The poet Virgil paints a pathetic picture. After the wandering Æneas had suffered many vicissitudes by land and sea, he came at length to Tyre, the land of the ill-fated Dido; and while waiting in the sacred grove an audience with her Sidonian majesty, he feasted his mind on the works of art which embellished the temple of Juno. But when he saw, represented in art, the woes and miseries of his race; when he saw the Trojan forces fleeing before the Greeks, and beheld the body of the god-like Hector dragged around the walls of Troy, and saw the aged Priam extending his feeble hands in helpless pity, his heart failed him and his eyes melted with tears. Out of this pathetic fullness of soul he exclaimed to his faithful companion in woe: "O Achates, what spot is there, what region is there, throughout the whole earth, which is not full of our misfortunes?"

Like father Æneas, the Negro sees that his woes and misfortunes are universal, confronting him everywhere—in art and literature, in statue and on canvas, in bust and picture, in verse and fiction, in song and story. But in the literary realm of Whitman all are welcome; none are denied, shunned, avoided, ridiculed, or made to feel ashamed. Indeed, Whitman's whole theory is a protest against such exclusion. He has in his inimitable way described the degrading effects of European literature upon America. This degradation holds with added force when we apply it to modern literature and the Negro. Whitman says:

No fine romance, no inimitable delineation of character, no grace of delicate illustration, no picture of shore or mountain or sky, no deep thought of the intellect, is so important to a man as his opinion of himself is; everything receives its tinge from that. In the verse of all those undoubtedly great writers —Shakspere just as much as the rest—there is the air which to America is the air of death. The mass of the people, the laborers and all who serve, are slag, refuse. The countenances of kings and great lords are beautiful; the countenances of mechanics ridiculous and deformed. What play of Shakspere as represented in America is not an insult to America, to its marrow and to its bones?

As a matter of course the Negro can get no standing in that school of literature which runs wild over the " neck, hair, and complexion of a particular female."

Walt Whitman's poetic principle does not depend upon superficial distinctions, but upon the eternal verities. He does not believe the " jay is more precious than the lark because his feathers are more beautiful, or the adder better than the eel because his painted skin contents the eye." He is " pleased with the homely woman as well as the handsome." This concession would bankrupt almost any other poet by depriving him of half of his stock in trade. Truly his poems " balance ranks, colors, races, creeds, and sexes." He does not relegate the Negro to the backyard of literature, but lets him in on the ground floor.

But let none imagine that because Whitman includes the weak as well as the mighty, the lowly and humble as well as the high and haughty, the poor as well as the rich, the black as well as the white, that he depreciates culture, refinement, and civilization. Although he widens the scope, he does not lower the tone. True, he is " no dainty *dolce affettuoso*." He hates pruriency, fastidiousness and sham. " He is stuff'd with the stuff that is coarse and stuff'd with the stuff that is fine."

I know that his bold, bald manner of expression sometimes gràtes harshly upon the refined sensibilities of the age. But he speaks with the unblushing frankness of nature. To the pure all things are pure. "Leaves of Grass" must not be judged by isolated lines, but we must consider the general drift of its purpose and meaning. Whitman does not despise the perfumeries, graces, and adornments of life, but he will not be intoxicated by their exhalations. He maintains his soberness and sanity amid these enticing allurements.

> " He says indifferently and alike, How are you, friend? to the
>   President at his levee,
> And he says, Good day, my brother, to Cudge who hoes in
>   the sugar-field,
> And both understand him and know his speech is right."

And yet he urges us to preserve all the solid acquisitions of civilization.

> "Earn for the body and for the mind whatever inheres and
>   goes forward."

> "Produce great persons, the rest follows."

> "Charity and personal force are the only investments worth
>   anything."

All truly great souls spend themselves in selfless service. Whitman would drag none down, but would lift all up. He would ring in for the world " the nobler modes of life, with purer manners, sweeter laws." He would bring mankind everywhere " flush " with himself.

America has broken the shackles which bound four millions of human beings to a degraded life. But the bondage of the body is nothing compared with the slavery of the soul. Whitman sounds the keynote of the higher emancipation. A great poet is necessarily a great prophet. He sees farthest because he has the most faith. The time must come when color will not be interchanged for qualities. When all other considerations will not wait on the query, " Of what complexion is he?"—when men and women

cease to make graven images of their physical idiosyncrasies, and cease to bow down to them and serve
them—then the accidental will yield to the essential,
the temporary and fleeting to those things which
abide.

The providence of God is mysterious and inscru-
table, but His ways are just and righteous altogether. Suffering and sorrow have their place in divine economy. If the woe and affliction through
which this race have passed but lead to the unfoldment of their latent æsthetic and spiritual capabil-
ities, then the glory of tribulation is theirs. But can
it be that they are to be forever the victims of contempt, caricatured in literature, and despised in all
the ennobling relations of life? Can it be for the
purpose of making a race despicable in the eyes of
mankind that this people have endured so much and
suffered so long? Was it for this that their ancestors were ruthlessly snatched from their native land,
where they basked in the sunshine of savage bliss and
were happy? Was it for this that they endured the
hellish horrors of the middle passage; that the ocean
bed was calcimined with the whiteness of human
bones, and ocean currents ran red with human blood?
Was it for this that they groaned for three centuries under the taskmaster's cruel lash? that their
human instincts and upward aspirations were brutal-
ized and crushed? Was it for this that babes were
inhumanly torn from mothers' breasts; that the holy
sentiment of mother-love—that finest, that divinest
feeling which God has embedded in the human bosom
—was stifled and smothered? Was it for this that
our Southland was filled with sable Rachels " weep-
ing for their children and would not be comforted
for they were not "? Was it all for this? In the
name of God I ask, was it for this?

Whitman points to a higher destiny. He looks through the most degraded externals and forecasts the glorious possibilities of this people. He leads the Negro from the slave block and crowns him with everlasting honor and glory.

" A man's body at auction,
   (For before the war I often go to the slave-mart and watch
      the sale),
   I help the auctioneer, the sloven does not half know his
      business.
   Gentlemen, look on this wonder,
   Whatever the bids of the bidders they cannot be high enough
      for it,
   For it the globe lay preparing quintillions of years without
      one animal or plant,
   For it revolving cycles truly and steadily roll'd.
   In this head the all-baffling brain,
   In it and below it the makings of heroes,
   Examine these limbs, red, black, or white, they are cunning
      in tendon and nerve,
   They shall be stript that you may see them.
   Exquisite senses, life-lit eyes, pluck, volition,
   Flakes of breast muscle, pliant backbone and neck, flesh and
      flabby, good-sized arms and legs,
   And wonders within there yet.
   Within there runs blood,
   The same old blood! the same red-running blood!
   There swells and jets a heart, there all passions, desires,
      reachings, aspirations,
   This is not only one man, this the father of those who shall
      be fathers in their turns,
   In him the start of populous states and rich republics,
   Of him countless immortal lives with countless embodiments
      and enjoyments."

No Negro, however humble his present station, can read these lines without feeling his humanity stirring within him, breeding wings wherewith to soar. Whitman has a special meaning to the Negro, not only because of his literary portrayal; he has positive lessons also. He inculcates the lesson of ennobling self-esteem. He teaches the Negro that " there is no sweeter fat than sticks to his own bones." He urges him to accept nothing that " insults his own soul."

"Long enough have you dream'd contemptible dreams,
Now I wash the gum from your eyes."

"Commence to-day to inure yourself to pluck, reality, self-
esteem, definiteness, elevatedness."

Surely he would lead this race " upon a knoll."

He has also taught his fellow-men their duty concerning the Negro. Catching his inspiration from
the hounded slave, he has given the golden rule a
new form of statement which will last as long as
human sympathies endure:

"I do not ask the wounded person how he feels, I myself
become the wounded person."

"Whoever degrades another degrades me."

He will accept nothing that all cannot have a
counterpart of on equal terms with himself. Listen
to his " Thought":

"Of quality—as if it harm'd me giving others the same chances
and rights as myself—as if it were not indispensable to
my own rights that others possess the same."

These are the lessons that Whitman would teach the
world.

But one asks, What did he do practically in his
lifetime for the Negro? Beyond the fact that he
imbibed the anti-slavery sentiment of his environments, and that this sentiment distills throughout
"Leaves of Grass," I do not know. Nor does it matter in the least. Too large for a class, he gave himself to humanity. These are his words:

"I do not give lectures or a little charity,
When I give, I give myself."

"I give nothing as duties, what others give as duties I give
as living impulses."

He knows no race, but scatters his charity alike

over all the families of the earth. He believes in Euclid's axiom that the whole is greater than any of its parts. He does not love a race, he loves mankind.

I am a Christian and believe in the saving merits of Jesus Christ to redeem mankind, and to exalt them that are of low degree. It is nevertheless true that

> "In faith and hope the world will disagree,
> But all mankind's concern is charity."

Whitman has given the largest human expression of this virtue.

On this first meeting of the Walt Whitman Fellowship all men can equally join in celebrating the merits of their great comrade, who, in robust integrity of soul, in intellectual comprehension and power, in catholic range of sympathy, and in spiritual illumination, is to be ranked among the choicest of the sons of men.

FREDERICK DOUGLASS

The highest function of a great name is to serve as an example and as a perpetual source of inspiration to the young who are to come after him. By the subtle law known as " consciousness of kind " a commanding personality incites the sharpest stimulus and exerts the deepest intensity of influence among the group from which he springs. We gather inspiration most readily from those of our class who have been touched with the feeling of our infirmities and have been subject to like conditions as ourselves. Every class, every race, every country, and indeed every well-defined group of social interests has its own glorified names whose fame and following are limited to the prescribed sphere of influence. Indeed, human relations are so diverse and human interests and feelings so antagonistic that the names which command even a fanatical following among one class may be despised and rejected by another. He who serves his exclusive class may be great in the positive degree; the man who serves a whole race or country may be considered great in the comparative degree; but it is only the man who breaks the barrier of class and creed and country and serves the human race that is worthy to be accounted great in the superlative degree. We are so far the creatures of local and institutional environment, and so disposed to borrow our modes of thought and feeling from our social medium, that even an appeal to the universal heart must be adapted to the spirit and genius of the time and people to whom it is first made. Even the Saviour of the world offered the plan of salvation first to the Jews in the traditional guise of the Hebrew cult.

It is essential that any isolated, proscribed class should honor its illustrious names. They serve not only as a measure of their possibilities, but they possess greater inspirational power by virtue of their close sympathetic and kindly touch. Small wonder that such people are wont to glorify their distinguished men out of proportion to their true historical setting on the scale of human greatness.

Frederick Douglass is the one commanding historic character of the colored race in America. He is the model of emulation of those who are struggling up through the trials and difficulties which he himself suffered and subdued. He is illustrative and exemplary of what they might become—the first fruit of promise of a dormant race. To the aspiring colored youth of this land Mr. Douglass is, at once, the inspiration of their hopes and the justification of their claims.

I do not on this occasion intend to dwell upon the well-known facts and circumstances in the life and career of Mr. Douglass, but deem it more profitable to point out some of the lessons to be derived from that life.

In the first place, Mr. Douglass began life at the lowest possible level. It is only when we understand the personal circumstances of his early environment that we can appreciate the pathos and power with which he was wont to insist upon the true measure of the progress of the American Negro, not by the height already attained, but by the depth from which he came. It has been truly said that it required a greater upward move to bring Mr. Douglass to the status in which the ordinary white child is born than is necessary on the part of the latter to reach the presidency of the United States. The early life of this gifted child of nature was spent amid squalor, deprivation and cruel usage. Like Melchizedek of old, it can be said of him that he sprung into existence without father or mother, or beginning of days. His little body was unprotected from the bitter, biting cold, and his vitals griped with the gnawing pangs of hunger. We are told that he vied with the dogs for the crumbs that fell from his master's table. He tasted the sting of a cruel slavery, and drank the cup to its very dregs. And yet he arose from this lowly and degraded estate and gained for himself a place among the illustrious names of his country.

We hear much in this day and time about the relative force of environment and heredity as factors in the formation of character. But, as the career of Mr. Douglass illustrates, there is a subtle power of personality which, though the product of neither, is more potential than both. God has given to each of us an irrepressible inner something, which, for want of better designation, the old philosophy used to call the freedom of the will, which counts for most in the making of manhood.

In the second place, I would call attention to the tremendous significance of a seemingly trifling incident in his life. When he was about thirteen years of age he came into possession of a copy of the "Columbian Orator," abounding in dramatic outbursts and stirring episodes of liberty. It was the ripened fruit of the choicest spirits, upon which the choicest spirits feed. This book fired his whole soul and kindled an unquenchable love for liberty. It is held by some that at the age of puberty the mind is in a state of unstable equilibrium, and, like a pyramid on its apex, may be thrown in any direction by the slightest impression of force. The instantaneity of religious conversions, which the Methodists used to acclaim with such triumphant outbursts of hallelujah, may rest upon some such psychological foundation. When the child nature stands at the parting of the ways, between youth and adolescence, it yields to some quickening touch, as the fuse to the spark, or as the sensitized plate to the impressions of sunlight. There are "psychological moments" when the revealed idea rises sublimely above the revealing agent. According to the theory of harmonies, if two instruments are tuned in resonant accord the vibrations of the one will wake up the slumbering chords of the other. Young Douglass' soul was in sympathetic resonance with the great truth of human brotherhood and equality, and needed only the psychological suggestion which the "Columbian Orator" supplied. In a moment, in the twinkling of an eye, it burned deep into his soul and made an ineffaceable impression upon his consciousness of the gospel of brotherhood and equality of man. It was the same truth which could only be impressed upon the Apostle Peter in the rhapsodies of a heavenly vision. The age of revelation is not past, and will not pass so long as there remains one soul that yearns for spiritual illumination. There comes at times into our lives some sudden echo of the heavenly harmony from the unseen world, and happy is that soul which beats in vibrant harmony with that supernal sound. When the gospel of liberty first dawned upon the adolescent Douglass, as he pursued the pages of the "Columbian Orator," there is no rendition of either the old or the new school of psychology that can analyze the riot of thought and sentiment that swept through his turbulent soul. This was indeed his new birth, his baptism with fire from on high. From that moment he was a possessed man. The love of liberty bound him with its subtle cords and did not release him until the hour of his death on Anacostia's mist-clad height.

Our educational philosophers are ransacking their brains to prescribe wise curricula of study for colored youth. There is not so much need of that which gives information to the mind or cunning to the fingers as that which touches the soul and quickens the spirit. There must be first aroused dormant consciousness of manhood with its inalienable rights, privileges, and dignity. The letter killeth, the spirit maketh alive. The "Columbia Orator" contributed more towards arousing the manhood of Mr. Douglass than all the traditional knowledge of all the schools. Of what avail is the mastery of all branches of technical and refined knowledge unless it touches the hidden springs of manhood? The value of any curriculum of study for a suppressed class that is not pregnant with moral energy, and that does not make insistent and incessant appeal to the half-conscious manhood within is seriously questionable. The revelation to a young man of the dignity, I had almost said the divinity, of his own selfhood is worth more to him in the development of character and power than all the knowledge in all the de luxe volumes in the gilded Carnegie libraries.

In the third place, Negro youth should study Mr. Douglass as a model of manly courage. In order to acquire a clear conception of principles let us discriminate sharply in the use of terms. Courage is that quality which enables one to encounter danger and difficulties with firmness and resolution of spirit. It is the swell of soul which meets outward pressure with inner resistance. Fortitude, on the other hand, is the capacity to endure, the ability to suffer and be strong. It is courage in the passive voice. True courage sets up an ideal and posits a purpose; it calculates the cost and is economic of means, though never faltering in determination to reach that end. Bravery is mere physical daring in the presence of danger, and responds to temporary physical and mental excitation. He who is eager to fight every evil which God allows to exist in society does not display rational courage. Even our Saviour selected the evils against which He waged war. The caged eagle which beats his wings into insensibility against the iron bars of his prison-house is accounted a foolish bird. On the other hand, " the linnet void of noble raze " has gained the everlasting seal of poetic disapproval. It is not genuine courage to go through the world like the knight in the tale with sword in hand and challenge on lips to offer mortal combat to every windmill of opposition.

Mr. Douglass was courageous in the broadest and best significance of the term. He set before him as the goal of his ambition his own personal freedom and that of his race, and he permitted neither principalities nor powers, nor height nor depth, nor things present nor things to come, to swerve him from the pursuit of that purpose.

When we speak of moral courage we indulge in tautology of terms; for all courage is essentially moral. It does not require courage to go with your friends or against your enemies; it is a physical impulse to do so. But true moral courage is shown when we say no to our friends.

Mr. Douglass reached the climax of moral courage when he parted with William Lloyd Garrison, his friend and benefactor, because of honest difference of judgment, and when for the same motive he refused to follow John Brown to the scaffold at Har-

per's Ferry. It required an iron resolution and sublime courage for Douglass to deny the tender, pathetic, paternal appeal of the man who was about to
offer up himself as a sacrifice for an alien race. John
Brown on the scaffold dying for an alien and defenseless race is the most sublime spectacle that this
planet has seen since Christ hung on the cross. That
scaffold shall be more hallowed during the ages to
come than any throne upon which king ever sat. Who
but Douglass would decline a seat on his right
hand?

In the fourth place, Mr. Douglass stands out as
a model of self-respect. Although he was subject to
all of the degradation and humiliation of his race,
yet he preserved the integrity of his own soul. It
is natural for a class that is despised, rejected and
despitefully used to accept the estimate of their
contemners, and to conclude that they are good for
nothing but to be cast out and trodden under foot.
In a civilization whose every feature serves to impress a whole people with a sense of their inferiority,
small wonder if the more timid and resigned spirits
are crushed beneath the cruel weight. It requires
the philosophic calm and poise to stand upright and
unperturbed amid such irrational things.

It is imperative that the youth of the colored race
have impressed upon them the lesson that it is not
the treatment that a man receives that degrades him,
but that which he accepts. It does not degrade the
soul when the body is swallowed up by the earthquake or overwhelmed by the flood. We are not
humiliated by the rebuffs of nature. No more should
we feel humiliated and degraded by violence and
outrage perpetrated by a powerful and arrogant social scheme. As a man thinketh in his heart, so is he.
The inner freedom of soul is not subject to assault

and battery. Mr. Douglass understood this principle well. He was never in truth and indeed a slave; for his soul never accepted the gyves that shackled his body.

It is related that Mr. Douglass was once ordered out of a first-class coach into a " Jim Crow " car by a rude and ill-mannered conductor. His white companion followed him to the proscribed department, and asked him how he felt to be humiliated by such a coarse fellow. Mr. Douglass let himself out to the full length of his robust manhood and replied, " I feel as if I had been kicked by an ass." If one will preserve his inner integrity, the ill-usage and despiteful treatment others may heap upon him can never penetrate to the holy of holies, which remains sacred and inviolable to an external assault.

The fifth lesson which should be emphasized in connection with the life of Mr. Douglass is that he possessed a ruling passion outside the narrow circle of self-interest and personal well being. The love of liberty reigned supreme in his soul. All great natures are characterized by a passionate enthusiasm for some altruistic principle. Its highest manifestation is found in the zeal for the salvation of men on the spiritual side. All great religious teachers belong to this class. Patriots and philanthropists are ardently devoted to the present well-being of man. The poet, the painter, and the sculptor indulge in a fine frenzy over contemplative beauty or its formal expression. The philosopher and the scientist go into ecstasy over the abstract pursuit of truth. Minds of smaller caliber get pure delight from empty pleasure, sportsmanship or the collection of curios and bric-à-brac. Even the average man is at his highest level when his whole soul goes out in love for another. The man who lives without altruistic enthusiasm goes through the world wrapped in a shroud.

There have been few members of the human race that have been characterized by so intense and passionate a love for liberty as Frederick Douglass. His love for liberty was not limited by racial, political or geographical boundaries, but included the whole round world. He believed that liberty, like religion, applied to all men "without one plea." He championed liberty for black men, liberty for white men, liberty for Americans, liberty for Europeans, liberty for Asiatics, liberty for the wise, liberty for the simple; liberty for the weak, liberty for the strong; liberty for men, liberty for women; liberty for all the sons and daughters of men. I do not know whether he permitted his thoughts to wander in planetary space or speculated as to the inhabitability of other worlds than ours; but if he did, I am sure that his great soul took them all in his comprehensive scheme of liberty. In this day and time, when the spirit of commercialism and selfish greed command the best energies of the age, the influence of such a life to those who are downtrodden and overborne is doubly significant. Greed for gain has never righted any wrong in the history of the human race. The love of money is the root, and not the remedy of evil.

In the sixth and last place, I would call attention of the young to the danger of forgetting the work and worth of Frederick Douglass and the ministration of his life. We live in a practical age when the things that are seen overshadow the things that are invisible.

What did Douglass do? asks the crass materialists. He built no institutions and laid no material foundations. True, he left us no showy tabernacles of clay.

He did not aspire to be the master mechanic of the colored race. The greatest things of this world are not made with hands, but reside in truth and right-eousness and love. Douglass was the moral leader and spiritual prophet of his race. Unless all signs of the times are misleading, the time approaches, and is even now at hand, which demands a moral renaissance. Then, O for a Douglass, to arouse the conscience of the white race, to awaken the almost incomprehensible lethargy of his own people, and to call down the righteous wrath of Heaven upon injustice and wrong.

JEFFERSON AND THE NEGRO

THE recurring anniversaries of the birth of
Thomas Jefferson elicit expressions of gratitude and
esteem second only to that for George Washington.
For strength and intensity of discipleship and for
attachment to the tenets that he taught, his name
is honored beyond all names in American politics.
The authorship of the Declaration of Independence
has fixed his fame forever among those who love
liberty and hate oppression. The vital clause in
this world-renowned document transcends the narrow exigencies of the situation with which it spe-
cifically dealt, and makes it the greatest state paper
of all times. The specific charges against the British
monarch are caustic enough, and adroitly drawn,
but they no longer burden our memory nor quicken
our emotion. If we should strike from the document
the appeal to the universal heart touching the inalienable right to liberty and equality of privilege, it
would rarely be disturbed from its resting-place in
the appendix of our school histories. Abraham Lincoln, who, after Jefferson, possessed perhaps the most
illumined understanding of any American statesman,
deemed it the crowning proof of the political genius
of the author of the great Declaration that " in the
concrete pressure of a struggle for national independence, he had the coolness, foresight, and capacity to introduce into a merely revolutionary document an abstract truth applicable to all men and
all times, and so embalm it there that to-day and in

all coming days it shall be a rebuke and a stumbling-block to the harbingers of appearing tyranny and oppression."

It is among the glaring anomalies of our national history that the political party which from the days of Jefferson to the present time has stood for the enslavement and suppression of the Negro race professes the greatest admiration for his teachings and assumes almost the exclusive right to cherish his memory. And yet the welfare of this unfortunate race, not merely its release from physical bondage, but, to use his own felicitous expression, "the emancipation of human nature," was ever a burden upon the heart of this great apostle of liberty. It is doubtful whether among all the tributes of praise and honor which these anniversaries of his birth evoke one word will be said about his devotion to that cause for which he labored as strenuously as for any other. Indeed, the Negro race is the chief beneficiary of his doctrine. The luminary which he lit in the sky of liberty can never be blotted out till all men shall be blessed by its kindly light. Though for a time it may be obscured by the shifting mists of doubt, evasion, and denial, it will endure as long as sun and moon and stars.

It is said that the Northern States, after finding slavery unprofitable in their barren clime and ice-bound latitude, disposed of their slaves at a profit and turned abolitionists for easement of conscience. However this may be, it is well known that economic principles and moral notions are so closely interwoven that it is hard to say where the one begins and the other ends. It is a sad comment upon human nature that no people, as such, have ever cried out against the oppression of the weak so long as it inured to their material profit. "Go sell all thou

hast and give to the poor " is the hardest condition
the Saviour imposed upon His followers. Idolatry
will never be destroyed by the makers of images, nor
the rum traffic by saloon-keepers. There were, indeed, a number of choice spirits like Edward Coles,
of Virginia, a devoted disciple of Jefferson, who had
the courage to make the sacrifice which his conscience
demanded. There were thousands of individuals who
did the same thing; but never enough to make it a
general policy.

Those who make a close study of the economic condition of Virginia during the latter half of the eighteenth century are easily persuaded that the Old Dominion was ready to follow closely upon the heels of
New England in the matter of the emancipation of
the slaves. The agricultural resources of the colony, under a century and a half of reckless tillage,
had been well-nigh exhausted. The old baronial estates were rapidly falling to pieces, and were passing
through the hands of the sheriff. The production of
tobacco by slave labor had ceased to be a bonanza.
Under such conditions it was inevitable that enlightened public sentiment would animadvert to the moral
evil of slavery; the same moral leaven that had leav-
ened the conscience of New England was at work in
Virginia. The Negro element in Virginia has scarcely
more than doubled itself in one hundred years. Unless the estates of Washington and Jefferson were
cared for because of sentimental reasons, they would
now be the homes of the owl and the bat. If it had not
been for the rise of the lower Southern States and
the new valuation put upon slaves by the invention
of the cotton-gin, Virginia would have early arrayed
herself in the column of the anti-slavery States.
But just as New England carried on the slave trade
with Southern neighbors for many years after the

system had ceased to be profitable on her own soil, so Virginia became the slave market for the newer and richer States to the South of her. The close geographical touch and ties of blood kinship strengthened, no doubt, by the rise of a meddlesome spirit in the North, kept Virginia in sympathy with the slave regime. The rise of the anti-slavery spirit, however, was not the sole product of Puritan principles, but had an exact counterpart in the more southern colony. The moral sense of a community does not rest upon geographical latitude, but upon a long chain of cause and consequence, which the careful student can trace as clearly as the causal connection in the more exact domains of knowledge.

Jefferson was of Welch and Scotch extraction, with little of the Anglo-Saxon in his makeup. His passionate devotion to moral principle, which was redeemed from fanaticism only by his robust intellectual sanity, may be considered in part at least as an attribute of blood. As with George Washington, the circumstances of his blood and birth would hardly entitle him to rank with the exclusive aristocratic set. Like Washington also, by force of personal worth and dint of strenuous endeavor, he made his merits known and received the fullest recognition among circles of the highest social consideration; but, unlike Washington, he was never completely assimilated by the upper set among whom he moved. He never forgot the rights and privileges of the under man. It was the ambition of his life to found an aristocracy upon character and culture, instead of lineage and wealth. No one ever gave the aristocratic pretensions of his day such rude shocks as he. It was Jefferson who abolished the law of entail and primogeniture in Virginia, and disestablished the Church of England. He never failed to exert his influence for the curtail-

ment and even for the abolition of slavery. The
aristocrats hated him with bitter and malignant
hatred.

The struggle against the oppression of the mother
country and the wrongs and cruelties of slavery were
in harmony with the impulse of his soul. Perhaps no
man ever lived who has done so much to impress
the minds of the common people, whom others were
disposed to ignore and despise, with a sense of liberty and personal dignity, as the author of the
Declaration of Independence. This he was able to
do without the gift of oratory, without the glamour
of military glory, without the potent spell of religious mystery, but by sheer force of intense conviction and intellectual acumen.

It is generally believed that Jefferson was himself a wealthy slaveholder, who inconsistently enough
gave occasional utterance against the system of
which he was a beneficiary; but that his serious and
sustained endeavor lay wholly in other directions.
As a matter of fact, the question of emancipation
and the subsequent welfare of the Negro race was
one in which he never lost a vital interest. It is
known that this was one of the first questions to
which he gave attention at the beginning of his career, and at the age of eighty-two, just one year
before his death, we find him writing to an Aboli-
tionist: " My own health is very low, not having
been able to leave the house for three months. At
the age of eighty-two, with one foot in the grave,
and the other uplifted to follow it, I do not permit
myself to take part in new enterprises, even for bet-
tering the condition of men, not even the great one
which is the subject of your letter, and which has
been through life one of my greatest anxieties."

In the early part of his public career he proposed

an amendment to the Constitution of Virginia for the emancipation of slaves born after a certain date, and that they should be educated at public expense " in tillage, arts, and sciences, according to their geniuses." His marvelous foresight comprehended the entire scheme of industrial preparation of the Negro, which is nowadays being exploited with as much gusto and freshness of enthusiasm as if it were a new discovery. As a member of the Legislature, in 1778, he brought in a bill forbidding the further importation of slaves in Virginia, which was adopted without opposition.

The last article of the Declaration of Independence as the author drafted it was an indictment against the King for his complicity in the slave trade. This article, which was rejected by his more conservative colleagues, contained the only underscored words in the whole document: " He has waged cruel war against human nature itself, violating its most sacred rights of life and liberty in the persons of distinct peoples, who never offended him; captivating and carrying them into slavery in another hemisphere to incur miserable death in their transportation thither. This piratical warfare, the opprobrium of infidel powers, is the warfare of the Christian King of Great Britain. Determined to keep open market where MEN should be bought and sold, he has prostituted his negative for suppressing every legislative attempt to prohibit or to restrain this execrable commerce."

There is much dispute as to whether the Declaration of Independence was intended to include the Negro race. The language of this clause leaves not the slightest room for doubt of its intendment, at least so far as the author was concerned. He intended nothing short of the " emancipation of human nature."

Speaking of a temporary check placed upon the slave traffic in Virginia, he said: " This will in some measure stop the increase of this great political and moral evil while the minds of our citizens are ripening for the complete emancipation of human nature." As still further proof that Jefferson included the Negro in his universal scheme of liberty and equality, we read from a letter written to Edward Coles in 1820: " I had hoped that the younger generation, receiving their early impressions after the flame of liberty had been kindled in every breast, would have sympathized with oppression wherever found, and proved their love of liberty beyond their own share of it."   And again: " What a stupendous, what an incomprehensible machine is man!   Who can endure toil, famine, stripes, imprisonment, and death itself, in vindication of his own liberty, and the next moment be deaf to all those motives whose power sustained him through his trial, and inflict on his fellow-men a bondage, one hour of which is fraught with more misery than ages of that he arose in rebellion to oppose."

If such unmistakable utterances by the author of the instrument do not make clear its intendment. then all the laws of critical interpretation are of no avail. In a recent political controversy we heard this great document reduced to an airy abstraction .by the leaders of a party that was supposed to espouse its principles.   But the spirit of Jefferson must surely rise up and condemn all those who would deprive any race or class of the blessings which flow from this great Declaration.

Jefferson presented a plan for the government of

the great Northwest Territory, according to which
slavery was to be abolished after the year 1800. This
provision was lost by a bare majority of one. The
author, commenting bitterly upon the miscarriage
of his propaganda of liberty, said: " Thus we see
the fate of millions unborn hanging upon the tongue
of one man, and heaven was silent at that awful moment!" With characteristic sagacity he clearly
foresaw the strategic value of gaining the great
Northwest country to the side of liberty. It was,
indeed, in this region that the issue became most
acute, and the struggle between the two economic
regimes became most intense.

Jefferson adopted two principles that the modern
statesman would do well to heed: (1) That the Constitution should be liberally interpreted where human
rights are involved, and (2) that a just cause, if
persisted in, will prevail in the long run. It is the
policy of this day to make the most lax constitutional interpretation, not in favor of, but against
the rights of man, and there is also danger of forgetting that old homely motto that truth is mighty
and in the end will prevail.

Thomas Jefferson loved humanity and did not
despise it because of the outward semblance that it
wore. On one occasion he had as his guest at Monticello a colored man of education and taste, by name
of Julius Melbourn. There were in the company
at dinner Chief Justice Marshall, Mr. Wirt, Mr.
Samuel Dexter, of Boston, and Dr. Samuel Mitchell,
of New York. On this occasion the race question
was the theme for discussion. About the same arguments as to the Negro's incapacity and the decrees
of Providence which are still resorted to were brought
forward and ably presented. Mr. Jefferson showed
clearly the faith that was in him by declaring that,

"As regards personal rights, it seems to me most palpably absurd that the individual rights of volition and locomotion should depend upon the degree of power possessed by the individual. I should hardly be willing to subscribe to the doctrine that because the Chief Justice has a stronger mind or a more capacious and better-formed brain than I that, therefore, he has the right to make me his slave." Jefferson informed his colored guest that it was his intention to make instruction at the University of Virginia free to all sects and colors. In a letter to Benjamin Banneker, the Negro astronomer, Mr. Jefferson expressed his interest in the moral and intellectual improvement of the colored race, and wished them every opportunity to demonstrate to the world their intellectual and moral worth.

Mr. Jefferson in his notes on Virginia expressed the conviction that there were irreconcilable differences between the races, and that they could not live together on terms of amity. In defining the shortcomings of the Negro, however, he makes full allowance for unfavorable circumstances and lack of opportunity, and hazards his statements with great hesitancy and caution. There is entire absence of that cock-sureness and assumption of omniscience of which we hear so much nowadays. Jefferson's plan for the colonization of the emancipated race was a much more simple, sensible and humane project in his day than at the present time. It should not be without significance, however, that Jefferson, De Tocqueville, and Abraham Lincoln, all three of whom were men of as great a degree of enlightenment as any who have ever discussed American policies, were of the same mind as to the final solution of the race problem.

But how could a man be a slaveholder and at the

same time entertain such doctrines of liberty and equality? This charge has stood for more than a century, not only against the author of the Declaration of Independence, but against all those who participated in the great events leading up to and growing out of the Revolutionary struggle. Jefferson was a man of glaring inconsistencies, even above his fellow. Indeed, every man who thinks great thoughts and does great deeds is apt to encounter the charge of inconsistency. The man of one idea who never puts even that one into execution can easily be consistent, because he has no hosts of conflicting thoughts and deeds among themselves. But the man of thoughts and deeds always repels the charge of inconsistency with the retort, " Do I contradict myself; well, then, I contradict myself; I am large, I contain multitudes." When a great American President wants to place the fiscal scheme of the country on a firm basis he simply does so, and would gladly forget that he at one time advocated free silver. When a great party wants to annex some distant island of the sea, without their let or hindrance, it proceeds to do so, even though it once professed to subscribe to the Declaration of Independence. Jefferson was a man of superlative political genius, and at the same time possessed a high order of talent for well-nigh every other branch of human pursuit. You cannot fetter genius by the delicate cords of consistency. It breaks them violently asunder, and follows the freshly imparted impulse. When President Jefferson saw that the purchase of Louisiana would inure to the lasting good of his country he struck the bargain with the great Napoleon, although it ran counter to all of his political teachings.

No man more keenly appreciated the inconsistency of the American attitude on the question of slavery than did Thomas Jefferson. The above recital shows this most plainly. And yet he retained the slaves which came to him as patrimony. Slavery on the Jefferson estate was of the mild, patriarchal sort, and the owner continued it partly from the force of inertia, and partly as a duty to those thrust upon his charge. To use his own words: " My opinion has ever been that until more can be done for them, we should endeavor with those whom fortune has thrown in our hands, to feed and clothe them well, protect them from ill uses, and require such reasonable labor only as is performed voluntarily by freemen." Mr. Bacon, who was for twenty years the manager at Monticello, has given us a splendid account of the kindly and patriarchal dispensation that prevailed on Mr. Jefferson's estate. When the British soldiers carried off some thirty or forty of his slaves he complained of their unnecessary harshness and severity, but did not forget to add that if they would give the men their freedom it would be right.

We do not hold men responsible for participating in the prevailing customs of their time, although it must ever be a source of regret that the author of the Declaration of Independence did not personally set the example which he never failed to urge upon the conscience of his fellow-men.

THE ARTISTIC GIFTS OF THE NEGRO

WHAT contribution has the Negro race ever made
or ever can make to the general culture of the human
spirit? asks the critic, with a scornful disdain that
allows no answer. Ridicule and contempt have characterized the habitual attitude of the American mind
toward the Negro's higher strivings. The faintest
suggestion as to his higher possibilities is received
either with a sneer or with a smile. The African
was brought to America to be a hewer of wood and
a drawer of water. Requisition was made upon his
physical faculties alone to perform this manual and
menial mission. His function was supposed to be
as purely mechanical as that of the ox which pulls
the plow. No more account was taken of his higher
susceptibilities than of the mental and moral faculties of the lower animals. Indeed, the Negro has
never been regarded in his own right and for his own
sake, but merely as a coefficient which is not detach-
able from the quantity whose value it enhances. The
servant exists for the sake of his master. The black
man's status is fixed and his usefulness is recognized
on the lower level of crude service. His mission is
to administer to the wants of the higher, or as it is
more fitting to say, the haughtier race. " The Negro
is all right in his place " phrases a feeling that is
deep seated and long abiding. This historical bias
of mind is brought forward in current discussion. It
is so natural to base a theory upon a long-established
practice that one no longer wonders at the prevalence
of this belief. The African has sustained servile

relations to the Aryan for so long a time that it is easy, as it is agreeable to the Aryan pride, to conclude that servitude is his ordained place in society. The dogma of Carlyle that " the Negro is useful to God's creation only as a servant " still finds wide acceptance. Much of our current social philosophy on the race problem is but a restatement of the ancient prejudice in terms of modern phraseology. Why awaken the higher faculties of the race when only the lower ones are demanded in our scheme of economy? What boots it to develop higher taste and finer feelings in a people who must of necessity perform the rougher grade of the world's work? Is it not preposterous that black men should ponder over Shakespeare and Dante and black maidens pursue music and painting when th·y might earn a dollar a day at useful, productive toil? Such arguments are as familiar to us as the more orthodox doctrine drawn from the curse of Canaan used to be in days gone by. To an attitude thus predisposed, manifestation of higher qualities on the part of the people held in despite is both unwelcome and embarrassing. The justification of oppression is always based on the absence of higher faculties. Phyllis Wheatley and Frederick Douglass were more persuasive and potential anti-slavery arguments than all the flood of eloquence poured forth in behalf of an oppressed race. There was serious hesitation in admitting that the Negro possessed a soul and was entitled to the rites of baptism, on the ground that it was not right to hold a Christian in slavery. There is a sneaking feeling in the breast of humanity that the ennobling circle of kindly sympathy should include all persons and peoples who display aptitude for the higher intellectual and spiritual cult.

Despite traditional theories and centuries of cruel

usage, there have been more or less continual outcroppings of the Negro's suppressed and stunted
soul. Any striking emanation from this dark and
forbidden background was at one time called a freak
of nature not to be calculated in the ordinary course
of events. But when freaks become too frequent
they can no longer be ignored in any rational scheme
of philosophy.

Music is the easiest outlet of the soul. The pent-
up energy within breaks through the aperture of
sound while the slower and more accurate deliberations of the intellect are yet in process of formulation. Plantation melody, that blind, half-conscious
poetry that rose up from " the low ground of sorrow," was the first expression of the imprisoned soul
of an imprisoned race. It was the smothered voice
of a race crying in the wilderness, " with no language
but a cry." These weird, plaintive, lugubrious longings go straight to the heart without the interven-
tions of cumbersome intellectual machinery. They
came from the unsophisticated soul of an humble and
simple-minded black folk and make the strongest appeal to the universal heart. There can be no stronger
argument of the sameness of human sympathy. " As
in the water face answerest to face, so the heart of
man to man." Negro melody has been called the
only autochthonous music of the American Continent. The inner soul of the red man is not preserved
to us in song. The European brought his folk-
thought and folk-song acquired by his ancestors in
the unremembered ages. It was reserved for the
transplanted African to sing a new song racy of the
soil, which had been baptized with his blood and wa-
tered with his tears. This music is the spontaneous
expression of the race soul under new and depress-
ing environment. It is the folk-genius of the Afri-

can, not indeed on his ancestral heath, but in a new though beloved land. Unlike the captive Jew, who, under like circumstances, hung his harp upon the willow tree and sat down by the rivers of Babylon and wept, the transplanted African made a contribution to the repertoire of song which moistens the eye and melts the heart of the world. These songs are not African, but American. The scene, circumstances and aspirations are not adapted to some distant continent, but to their new environment in a land, not of their sojourn, but of their abiding place. Shall they not immortalize the soil from which they sprung? Robert Burns has gathered the superstitions, the sorrows, the sufferings, the joys, the strivings of the lowly life of Scotland and woven them into soulful song, and has thus rendered old Scotia ever dear to human memory. The tourist makes his eager pilgrimage around the world to view " the banks and braes o' bonnie Doon " where the peasant lass poured out her soul in anguish. What halo of glory hovers over that ghostly route traversed that dreary night by the tippled Tam O'Shanter! The glory of a locality rests as much upon the folk-song or folk-story that grows out of and gathers about it as upon the tradition that this or that great man was born there. If the human heart ever turns with passionate yearning to our own Southland, it will not be so much in quest of the deeds and doings of her renowned warriors and statesmen, as to revel in the songs, the sorrows, the sighings, the soul strivings of her humble black folk and to realize the scenes amid which these pathetic melodies took their rise. Which of their musical achievements would the American people not gladly give in exchange for " Steal Away to Jesus " or " Swing Low, Sweet Chariot "? What song yet ascribed to the glory of " Hail Co-

lumbia!" equals in power of pathetic appeal and
strength of local endearment the yearnful quest of
the slave for his home land, " 'Way Down Upon the
Suwannee River "? The motif of the world renowned
" Dixie," the musical inspiration of the Southern
Confederacy, is based upon the yearning of a slave
removed from his native Sunny South for the land
where he was born. The South is the home of the
Negro, not merely because he has aided in the development of its resources by his strong and brawny
arm, but also because he has hallowed it by the
yearnings of his soul.

There is a dispositon on the part of the more
sensitive members of the colored race to affect to feel
ashamed of these melodies which solaced and sustained their ancestors under burdens as grievous as
any the human race has ever been called upon to
bear. They fear to acknowledge a noble influence
because it proceeded from a lowly place. All great
people glorify their history, and look back upon
their early attainment with spiritualized vision.
What nation is there that cannot find in its earlier
struggles those things which, if interpreted in light
of present conditions, would count for humiliation
and shame? But through the purifying power of
spiritual perspective they are made to reveal a
greater degree of glory. However trying and perplexing experiences may be while we are in the midst
of them, yet a longer range of vision gives us the
assurance that " it will afterwards please us to remember even these things." A race that is ashamed
of itself or of its historic humiliation which has been
overcome makes a pitiable spectacle in the eyes of
the world to which it appeals for sympathy and tolerance. A people who are afraid of their own shadow
must forever abide in the shade. These plantation

melodies represent the Negro's chief contribution to the purifying influences that soften and solace the human spirit. Can the oyster be ashamed of the pearl, or the toad of the jewel in its head? For the Negro to despise his superior natural qualities because they differ from those of another class would be of the same order of folly as if the female sex, in derogation of its natural endowment, should refuse to sing soprano, because the males excel in baritone.

This music is indeed inimitable. Its racial quality is stamped on every note. The writer remembers the anomalous spectacle of a white principal trying to lead his colored pupils in the rendition of jubilee glees. The requisite melodic, pathetic quality of voice is a natural coefficient which is as inalienable as any other physical characteristic. It rings out from the blood. As we listen to its sad, sighing cadence, we naturally expect to look and see, and say, "These are they who have come up through great tribulation." A white man attempting a plantation melody is as much a racial anomaly as a Negro affecting to feel in his soul the significance of that line of a celebrated hymn in which the singer passionately avows that he will never " blush to speak His name."

Immediately after the war troupes of Negro singers invaded the North and sang the songs whose melodic pathos melted the heart like wax. The Fisk Jubilee singers carried the ministration of this music to the remotest ends of the earth; and kings and emperors have wept before these soul-moving wailings. Many a school in the South owes its endowment to this sweet, sad singing. The plantation melodies possess the quality of endurance. It fulfils Keat's definition, " A thing of beauty is a joy forever." Whenever and wherever they are faithfully rendered, the people are moved mightily.

Transition from plantation melody to the standard tunes of Watts and Wesley was as easy as the second step in walking. Indeed, the Negro's gift for psalmody and his wonderful melodic and harmonic endowment is the marvel of the musical world. The wonder is how these people can sing so well without having learned. To listen to a Negro campmeeting in the backwoods of the Carolinas rendering the good old songs of Zion is almost enough to "rob the listening soul of sin."

The rise of rag-time music, which for the past few years has been the rage, marks another stage of Negro music. The potency of its spell has been all-pervasive. Half the world has been humming its tunes. The small boy whistles it on the street; the Italian grinds it from his music box while the urchins gambol on the commons; it jingles in our ears from the slot machine while we wait for the next train or sip a glass of soda; it has captivated the European capitals; the ultra dilettante and his alabaster lady in the gilded palace of wealth glide gracefully over the tufted fabric to the movement of its catchy, snatchy airs. The critics may indeed tell us that music is one thing and rag-time another, but the common people, and the uncommon ones as well, hear it, not only gladly, but rapturously. Rag-time is essentially Negro in motive, meaning, movement, and indeed, in composition. It is neither serious nor soul deep, like its plantation prototype, but is rather the outcome of a silly, flippant, dilettantism of the "new issue." The scene is in the city, not the country. Indeed it might well be called "city airs" in contradistinction from "plantation melodies." While this music portrays faithfully the Negro race in a certain phase of development, and while some of it bites deep into the experiences of human nature, yet it lacks the element of permanence, and seems destined to pass away, like the jingles of the variety stage which tickle the ear only for a season. It is here for the first time that the Negro figures as a composer of music. The words and music of the plantation melodies are attributed to no definite authorship. The "coon songs," a sort of connecting link between the old and the new, were composed mainly by white authors. It is not generally known that such famous songs as "Ben Bolt," "Listen to the Mocking-Bird," and "Rally Round the Flag, Boys" bear the stamp of Negro workmanship, as respects either words or music. But the Negro's chief musical distinction, up to the rise of rag-time, rested upon rendition, rather than upon composition. For the past few years, however, music sheets by Negro authors have been flying from the press as thick as the traditional autumn leaves. There has scarcely been a musical collection, so the critics tell us, during that interval that has not contained songs by Negro authors. Colored troupes in the rôles of Negro authorship or improvisation have crowded the largest theaters in all parts of the land. Several such troupes have undertaken European tours with marked success. There is a group of Negro composers in New York whose works bear the imprint of the best-known publishing houses. Some of them have accumulated fortunes from their composition and performance. Such famous pieces as "All Coons Look Alike to Me," "Under the Bamboo Tree," and "Go 'Way Back and Sit Down," are sung between the oceans and, indeed, around the

world. Gus L. Davis, the most famous Negro composer, died a few years ago. He belonged to the
era of the "story-song" and did not attempt any
piece of purely Negro sentiment. Whenever the
world plays or thrums, or hums, or whistles, or sings
"The Light-House by the Sea," "The Baggage
Coach Ahead," or "The Fatal Wedding," it pays
homage to the musical genius of the Negro race.

The Negro race is indeed a highly musical people.
The love of music crops out everywhere. The back
room of every Negro barbershop is a young conserva-
tory of music. In the ordinary Negro household the
piano is as common a piece of furniture as the rock-
ing-chair or center-table. That rosewood piano in a
log cabin in Alabama, which Dr. Booker T. Washington's burlesque has made famous, is a most convincing, if somewhat grotesque, illustration of the
musical genius of the Negro race. Music satisfies
the Negro's longing as nothing else can do. All human faculties strive to express or utter themselves.
They do not wait upon any fixed scheme or order of
development to satisfy our social philosophy. When
the fires of genius burn in the soul it will not await
the acquiring of a bank account or the building of a
fine mansion before gratifying its cravings. The
famished Elijah, under a juniper tree, was the purveyor of God's message to a wicked king. Socrates
in poverty and rage pointed out to mankind the path
of moral freedom. John the Baptist, clad in leather
girdle, and living on the wild fruits of the fields,
proclaimed the coming of the kingdom of God.
Would it be blasphemy to add, that the Son of Man,
while dwelling in the flesh, had not where to lay His
head? Our modern philosophy would have advised
that these enthusiasts cease their idle ravings, go to
work, earn an honest living, and leave the pursuit of

truth and spiritual purity to those who had acquired a competency. Is it a part of God's economy that the higher susceptibilities of the soul must wait upon the lower faculties of the body? Should Tanner paint no pictures because his race is ignorant and poor? Should a Dunbar cease to woo the Muses till every Negro learns a trade? The Negro in poverty and rags, in ignorance and unspeakable physical wretchedness, uttered forth those melodies which are sure to lift mankind at least a little higher in the scale of spiritual purity.

There are scattered indications that the Negro possesses ambition and capacity for high-grade classical music. The love of music is not only a natural passion, it is becoming a cultivated taste. The choirs of the best colored churches usually render at least one high-grade selection at each service. Blind Tom and Black Patti are at least individual instances of the highest musical susceptibility. There are numerous colored men and women who have completed courses, both instrumental and vocal, in the best American conservatories, and several have pursued their studies under famous European masters. In almost every center where a goodly number of cultivated colored people are to be found, there is a musical organization devoted to the rendition of the standard works of the great composers.

But music is only one of the forms of art in which the Negro has given encouraging manifestations. Frederick Douglass was among the foremost orators of the anti-slavery crusade, the second great oratorical epoch in the annals of American history. Booker T. Washington, according to some, is the most effective living orator that speaks the English tongue. Phyllis Wheatley, the Black Daughter of the Sun; and Dunbar, the peerless poet of lowly life, wooed the Muse of Song, who did not disdain their suit because their skin was dark. Pictures by Tanner adorn the walls of many a gallery in two hemispheres, one of which is on its way to the Louvre. If we might be permitted to cross the ocean and include those whom the Negro race can claim through some strain of their blood, Pushkin stands as the national poet of Russia, and the Dumas as the leading romancers of France. It is noticeable that the names which the Negroes have contributed to the galaxy of the world's greatness are confined almost wholly to the fine arts. Toussaint L'Ouverture stands almost alone among Negroes of whose fame the world takes account, whose renown rests upon solid deeds.

The Negro's order of development follows that of the human race. The imaginative powers are the first to emerge; exact knowledge and its practical application come at a later stage. The first superlative Negro will rise in the domain of the arts. The poet, the artist and the musician come before the engineer and the administrator. The Negro who is to quicken and inspire his race will not be a master mechanic nor yet a man of profound erudition in the domain of exact knowledge, but a man of vision with powers to portray and project. The epic of the Negro race has not yet been written; its aspirations and strivings still await portrayal. Whenever a Dunbar or a Chestnut breaks upon us with surprising imaginative and pictorial power, his race becomes expectant and begins to ask, " Art thou he that should come, or do we look for another? "

Mr. W. D. Howells, writing in the introduction of Mr. Dunbar's first volume of poems, says: " I said that a race which had come to this effect in any member of it, had attained civilization in him, and

I permitted myself the imaginative prophecy that the hostilities and prejudices which had so long constrained his race were destined to vanish in the arts; that these were to be the final proof that God had made of one blood all nations of men. I accepted them as an evidence of the essential unity of the human race."

THE EARLY STRUGGLE FOR EDUCATION

A FULL knowledge of the education of the Negro cannot be had without making some reference to the earlier educational efforts. It is well known that slavery discouraged the dissemination of literary knowledge among persons of African descent, and, in most cases, this discouragement amounted to a positive prohibition. But despite the rigid regulations of the slave regime there were many kind-hearted slaveholders who taught their slaves to read and write. Many others picked up such knowledge in ways which it is mysterious to comprehend. The fact that book information was withheld from the Negro made him all the more anxious to acquire it. Stolen waters are sweet, and the fact that they are forbidden leads those from whom the privilege is withheld to suspect that they possess mysterious efficacy. Such hungering and thirsting after knowledge amid dark and dismal discouragements is surely a compliment to the intellectual taste of the African. The antebellum struggle of the free colored people and the more ambitious slaves to acquire the use of printed characters is almost incomprehensible in view of the liberal educational provisions of these latter days. The experience of Frederick Douglass was not without many parallels and counterparts. In his autobiography he tells us:

The most interesting feature of my stay here (in Baltimore) was my learning to read and write under somewhat marked disadvantages. In obtaining this knowledge I was compelled to resort to indirections by no means congenial to my nature, and which were really humiliating to my sense of candor and uprightness. My mistress, checked in her benevolent designs toward me, not only ceased instructing me herself but set her face as a flint against my learning to read by any means.

She would rush to me with the utmost fury, and snatch the book or paper from my hand with something of the wrath and consternation which a traitor might be supposed to feel on being discovered in a plot by some dangerous spy. The conviction once thoroughly established in her mind that education and slavery were incompatible with each other, I was most narrowly watched in all my movements. If I remained in a separate room from the family for any considerable length of time, I was sure to be suspected of having a book, and was at once called to give an account of myself. Teaching me the alphabet had been the "inch" given; I was now waiting only for the opportunity to take the "ell." Filled with determination to read at any cost, I hit upon many expedients to attain my desired end. The plan which I mainly adopted, and the one which was most successful, was that of using my white playmates, with whom I met in the streets, as teachers. I used to carry almost constantly a copy of Webster's Spelling Book in my pocket, and when sent on errands, or when playtime was allowed me, I would step aside with my young friends and take a lesson in spelling.

Meanwhile I resolved to add to my educational attainments the art of writing. After this manner I began to learn to write. I was much in the shipyard, and observed that the carpenters after hewing and getting ready a piece of timber to use, wrote on the initials of the name of that part of the ship for which it was intended. When, for instance, a piece of timber was ready for the starboard side, it was marked with a capital S; a piece for the larboard side was marked L; larboard aft marked L. A.; starboard aft S. A.; starboard forward S. F. I soon learned these letters, and for what they were placed on the timbers. My work now was to keep fire under the steambox, and to watch the shipyard while the carpenters had gone to dinner. This interval gave me a fine opportunity to copy the letters named. I soon astonished myself with the ease in which I made the letters, and the thought was soon present, if I can make four letters, I can make more. With playmates for my teachers, fences and pavement for my copy-books, and chalk for my pen and ink, I learned to write.

This was the university training of the most illustrious American Negro, which could be duplicated in the experience of thousands of his fellow-slaves who remained "mute and inglorious."

A different and less strenuous phase of early educational opportunities may be found in the experience of another distinguished colored American, the late Prof. John Mercer Langston. Mr. Langston thus recounts the early schooling of his brother:

His father (a Virginia white man), manifesting the deepest interest in him, sought by his own efforts and influence to give him such thorough English education, with general information, and mental and moral improvement, so as to make him a useful man. He (at 7 years) was required to appear for his recitations in his father's special apartments the year around at 5 o'clock in the morning.

A second brother was put through the same regime, and John M., though too young for definite training when his father died, had ample provision made for his education.

These citations represent two phases of Negro education before the Civil War. The one gives a picture of the dauntless, self-impelling determination to gain knowledge at any cost; the other, the kind and genial disposition of a father-master, in spite of the rigorous requirements of the law. These instances may be regarded as typical, and might be multiplied by hundreds and thousands. There were also organized efforts for the education of the colored race. Schools were established for the free colored people within the limits of the slave territory. These were mainly in the large cities. A careful and detailed study of such early educational efforts for the several States and cities affords a rich field for interesting and valuable monographic writing. This chapter attempts little more than to present some of the hindrances, embarrassments, personal and economic sacrifices under which the Negro in the slave territory labored during the dark days of slavery, in order to secure what he considered the talismanic power of knowledge.

In Alabama the law of 1832 provided that " any person or persons that shall attempt to teach any free person of color, or slave, to spell, read, or write, shall upon conviction thereof by indictment, be fined in a sum of not less than $250, nor more than $500."

In 1833 the mayor and aldermen of the city of Mobile were authorized by law to grant licenses to such persons as they might deem suitable to instruct for limited periods the free colored creole children within the city and in the counties of Mobile and Baldwin, who were the descendants of colored creoles residing in said city and counties in April, 1803, provided, that said children first receive permission to be taught from the mayor and aldermen and have their names recorded in a book kept for the purpose. This was done, as set forth in the preamble of the law, because there were many colored creoles there whose ancestors, under the treaty between France and the United States in 1803, had the rights and privileges of citizens of the United States secured to them.

Arkansas seems to have had no law in the statute book prohibiting the teaching of persons of African descent, although the law of 1838 forbade any white person or free Negro from being found in the company of slaves or in any unlawful meeting, under severe penalty for each offense. In 1843 all migrations of free Negroes and mulattoes into the State was forbidden.

There was no law expressly forbidding the instruction of slaves or free colored people in the State of Delaware until 1863, when an enactment against all assemblages for the instruction of colored people, and forbidding all meetings except for religious purposes and for the burial of the dead, was made.

While the free colored people were taxed to a certain extent for school purposes, they could not enjoy the privileges of public instruction thus provided, and were left for many years to rely principally upon individual efforts among themselves and friends for the support of a few occasional schools. In 1840 the Friends formed the African School Association in the city of Wilmington, and by its aid two very good schools, male and female, were established in that place.

In 1828 the State of Florida passed an act to provide for the establishment of common schools, but white children only of a specified age were entitled to school privileges.

In Georgia the following law was enacted in 1829:

If any slave, Negro, or free person of color, or any white person, shall teach any other slave, Negro, or free person of color to read or write, either written or printed characters, the said free person of color or slave shall be punished by fine and whipping, or fine or whipping, at the discretion of the court; and if a white person so offend he, she, or they shall be punished with a fine not exceeding $500 and imprisonment in the common jail, at the discretion of the court.

In 1833 a penalty not exceeding $500 was provided for the employment of any slave or free person of color in setting up type or other labor about a printing-office requiring a knowledge of reading or writing. The code remained in force until swept away by events of the Civil War.

In 1833 the city of Savannah adopted an ordinance that if any person shall teach or cause to be taught any slave or free person of color to read or write within the city, or who shall keep a school for that purpose, he or she shall be fined in a sum not exceeding $100 for each and every such offense; and if the offender be a slave or free person of color, he or she may also be whipped not exceeding thirty-nine lashes.

Notwithstanding this severe enactment, there were, nevertheless, several schools for colored children clandestinely kept in Augusta and Savannah. The poor whites would often teach Negro children clandestinely. If an officer of the law came round the children were hastily dispatched to the fictitious duty of " picking chips." The most noted Negro school was opened in 1818 or 1819 by a colored man from Santo Domingo. Up to 1829 this school was taught openly. The law of that year made concealment and secrecy a necessity.

In Kentucky the school system was established in 1830. In this provision the property of colored people was included in the basis of taxation, but they were excluded from school privileges.

Louisiana, in 1830, provided that whoever should write, publish, or describe anything having a tendency to produce discontent among the free population or insubordination among the slaves, should upon conviction be imprisoned at hard labor for life or suffer death, at the discretion of the court. It was also provided that all persons who should teach or permit or cause to be taught any slave to read or write should be imprisoned not less than one month or more than twelve.

In 1847 a system of public schools was established for the education of white youth, and one mill on the dollar upon the ad valorem amount of the general list of taxable property might be levied for its support. Prior to the Civil War the only schools for colored youth in Louisiana were a few private ones in the city of New Orleans among the creoles.

St. Francis Academy for colored girls was founded

in connection with the Oblate Sisters, in Baltimore, Md., and received the sanction of the Holy See October 2, 1831. There were many colored Catholic refugees who came to Baltimore from Santo Domingo. The colored women who formed the original society which founded the convent and seminary were from Santo Domingo. The Sisters of Providence is the name of a religious society of colored women who renounced the world to consecrate themselves to the Christian education of colored girls. This school is still in successful operation. A colored man by the name of Nelson Wells left by will to trustees $7,000, the income of which was to be applied to the education of free colored children. The Nelson Wells school continued from 1835 to the close of the Civil War.

Dr. Bokkelen, State superintendent of education, recommended in 1864 the establishment of colored schools on the same basis as those of the whites, and states in his recommendation:

I am informed that the amount of school tax paid annually by these [colored] people to educate the white people in the city of Baltimore for many years has been more than $500. The rule of fair play would require that this be refunded unless the State at once provided schools under this title.

By an act of January, 1833, the legislature of Mississippi provided that the meeting of slaves and mulattoes above the number of five at any place or public resort or meeting-house in the night or at any schoolhouse for teaching reading or writing in the day or night was to be considered an unlawful assembly. In 1846 an act was passed establishing a system of public schools from all escheats and all fines, forfeitures, and amercement from licenses to hawkers and all income from school lands. These schools were for the education of white youths.

The legislature of Missouri in 1847 provided that no person should teach any schools for Negroes or mulattoes.

In North Carolina until 1835 public opinion permitted the colored residents to maintain schools for the education of their children. These were taught sometimes by white persons, but frequently by colored teachers. After this period colored children could only be educated by confining their teaching within the circle of their own family or by going out of the limits of their own State, in which event they were prohibited by law from returning home. The public system of North Carolina declared that no descendant of Negro ancestors to the fourth generation, inclusive, should enjoy the benefits thereof.

In 1740, while yet a British colony, South Carolina took the lead in directly legislating against the education of the colored race:

Whereas the having of slaves taught to write, or suffering them to be employed in writing, may be attended with inconvenience, be it enacted, That all and any person or persons whatsoever, who shall hereafter teach or cause any slave or slaves to be taught, or shall use or employ any slave as scribe in any manner of writing whatever, hereafter taught to write, every such person or persons shall for every such offense forfeit the sum of £100 current money.

In 1800 free colored people were included in this provision. In 1834 it was provided:

If any person shall hereafter teach any slave to read or write, or shall aid or assist in teaching any slave to read or write, or cause or procure any slave to be taught to read or write, such person, if a free white person, upon conviction thereof, shall, for each and every offense against this act, be fined not exceeding $100 and (suffer) imprisonment not more than six months; or if a free person of color, shall be whipped not exceeding 50 lashes. . . . And if any free person of color or slave shall keep any school or other place of instruction for teaching any slave or free person of color to read or write, such free person of color shall be liable to the same fine, imprisonment, and corporeal punishment.

And yet there were colored schools in Charleston from 1744 to the close of the Civil War.

In 1838 Tennessee provided a system of public schools for the education of white children between the ages of 6 and 16, but the colored children never enjoyed any of its benefits, although the free colored people contributed their due share to the public fund.

Texas never expressly forbade the instruction of Negroes, although the harsh and severe restrictions placed upon the race made a provision scarcely necessary.

In 1831 the general assembly of Virginia enacted, among others, the following provisions:

That all meetings of free Negroes or mulattoes of any schoolhouse, church, meeting-house, or other place for teaching them reading or writing, either in the day or night, under whatsoever pretext, shall be deemed an unlawful assembly. . . . If any white person or persons assemble with free Negroes or mulattoes at any schoolhouse, church, meeting-house, or other place for the purpose of instructing such free Negroes or mulattoes to read or write, such person or persons shall, on conviction thereof, be fined in a sum not exceeding $50, and, moreover, may be imprisoned, at the discretion of a jury, not exceeding two months.

It is known, however, that schools for the colored children were established and maintained in such cities as Petersburg, Norfolk, and Richmond.

The early educational efforts of the colored people of the District of Columbia have been studied with more fulness than those of any other Southern community. He who presents the movement in Baltimore, Richmond, Louisiana, Charleston, and other Southern centers with as much detail and accuracy will render no inconsiderable service to the history of education.

There does not seem to have been any express law forbidding the education of colored people in the District of Columbia. In 1807 the first schoolhouse for the use of colored pupils was erected by three colored men,—George Bell, Nicholas Franklin, and Moses Liverpool,—not one of whom knew a letter of the alphabet. They had been former slaves in Virginia, and, like others of their condition, had an exalted notion of literary knowledge. A white teacher was secured. From this time to the opening of the new regime, brought on by the Civil War, there was a tolerably adequate number of schools, supported mainly by the colored people themselves, but not without assistance from Northern philanthropy. But that these schools did not always have plain and smooth sailing may be gathered from the fact that in 1835, on account of an alleged indiscreet utterance of a colored resident, colored schools were attacked by a mob, some of them burned, and property destroyed, while the most conspicuous Negro teacher, Mr. John F. Cook, was compelled to flee for his life. This outbreak is known as the " Snow Riot."

Many of the best-known names in the District were both products of and factors in these early schools, the most noted of whom, perhaps, is Mr. John F. Cook, who subsequently became a tax collector of the District of Columbia. For substance, dignity and influence he stands as one of the conspicuous names of the National Capital, regardless of race distinction. His brother, George F. T. Cook, who was both a pupil and a teacher in the antebellum schools, subsequently became superintendent of the colored public schools of Washington and George-town, which position he held for thirty years.

This survey has been limited to the Southern or slave States. In the free States of the North the Negro had a more picturesque and exciting educational experience. The Northern States did not expressly forbid the education of colored persons, but the hostility to such movements is attested by many a local outbreak.

It was amid such dangers and difficulties that the Negro began his educational career. It must not be for a moment supposed, however, that the laws above referred to were rigidly enforced. It is known that pious and generous slaveholders quite generally taught their favorite slaves to read, regardless of the inexorable provisions of law. Quite a goodly number also learned the art of letters somewhat after the furtive method of Frederick Douglass; in the cities, schools for Negroes were conducted in avoidance, connivance, or defiance of ordinances and enactments.

In 1865 there was to be found in every Southern community a goodly sprinkling of colored men and women who had previously learned how to read and write.

The censuses of 1850 and 1860 give the number of free colored people attending school in the several States. These figures, for obvious reasons, represent only a small fraction of the Negroes, free and slave, who were openly or furtively gaining the elements of literary knowledge. The decline in avowed school attendance between 1850 and 1860 is due to the growing intensity of feeling which culminated during that decade.

FREE NEGROES ATTENDING SCHOOL

STATE	1850	1860	STATE	1850	1860
Delaware	187	250	Texas...........	20	11
Maryland	1,616	1,355	Arkansas........	11	5
District of Columbia	467	678	Tennessee	70	92
			Kentucky	288	205
Virginia.........	64	41	Missouri	40	155
North Carolina ..	217	133			
South Carolina ..	80	365	Slave States	4,414	3,661
Georgia.........	1	7	Free States	28,213	22,800
Florida..........	66	9			
Alabama	68	114	Total,	32,627	26,461
Mississippi......		2			
Louisiana	1,219	275			

It will be noticed that most of the enactments against the education of the Negro were made subsequently to 1830. The Nat Turner insurrection and the opening up of the anti-slavery campaign in the North had a decidedly reactionary effect in the slave territory.

A people who have made such sacrifice and run such risks for the sake of knowledge, who of their own scanty means were ever willing to support schools for the education of their children, although their property had been taxed for the support of an educational system from which they were excluded, surely deserve a larger and fuller draught of that knowledge of which the regime of slavery permitted them to gain only a foretaste. The Civil War wiped out all of these restrictions, and at its close the Freedmen's Bureau, religious and benevolent associations, and the reconstructed governments of the former slave States threw wide open the gate of knowledge.

The avidity and zeal with which the erstwhile suppressed population seized upon the new opportunity furnish the most interesting chapter in the history of American education. Educational opportunities were thus thrown open to a people who desired and needed them above all, and who had shown by long and persistent endeavor that they were fully worthy and deserving of them.

A BRIEF FOR THE HIGHER EDUCATION
OF THE NEGRO

RIDICULE and contempt have characterized the habitual attitude of the American mind toward the Negro's higher strivings. The African was brought to this country for the purpose of performing manual and menial labor. His bodily powers alone were required to accomplish this industrial mission. No more account was taken of his higher suscepti-bilities than of the mental and moral faculties of the lower animals. As the late Mr. Price used to say, the white man saw in the Negro's mind only what was apparent in his face, "darkness there, and nothing more." His usefulness in the world is still measured by physical faculties rather than by quali-ties of mind and soul. The merciless proposition of Carlyle, that the Negro is useful to God's creation only as a servant, still finds wide acceptance. It is so natural to base a theory upon a long-established practice that one no longer wonders at the preva-lence of this belief. The Negro has sustained servile relation to the Caucasian for so long a time that it is as easy as it is agreeable to Caucasian pride to conclude that servitude is his ordained place in so-ciety. When it was first proposed to furnish means for the higher development of this race, some, who assumed the wisdom of their day and generation, en-tertained the proposition with a sneer; others, with a smile.

MANIFESTATIONS OF HIGHER QUALITIES

As the higher susceptibilities of the Negro were not wanted, their existence was at one time denied.

The eternal inferiority of the race was assumed as a part of the cosmic order of things. History, literature, science, speculative conjecture, and even Holy Writ were ransacked for evidence and argument to support the ruling dogma. While the slaveholder had proved beyond all possibility of doubt the incapacity of the Negro for knowledge, yet he, prudently enough, passed laws forbidding the attempt. His guilty conscience caused him to make assurance doubly sure by re-enacting the laws of the Almighty.

For three hundred years the Negro by his marvelous assimilative power and by striking individual emanations has been constantly manifesting the higher possibilities of his nature, until now whoever assumes to doubt his susceptibility for better things needs himself to be pitied for his incapacity to grasp the truth. The same Carlyle who regards the Negro as an "amiable blockhead," and amenable only to the white man's "beneficent whip," also declares: "That one man should die ignorant who had capacity for knowledge, this I call a tragedy, were it to happen forty times in a minute." When it is known that the Negro has capacity for knowledge and virtue there can be no further justification for shutting him out from the higher cravings of his nature.

IS THE HIGHER EDUCATION OF THE NEGRO WORTH WHILE AS A PRACTICAL PHILANTHROPY?

The education of the Negro is not of itself a thing apart, but is an integral factor of the general pedagogic equation. Race psychology has not yet been formulated. No reputable authority has pointed out just wherein the two races differ in any evident mental feature. The mind of the Negro is of the same nature as that of the white man and needs the same nurture. The general poverty of the Negro, however, and his inability to formulate and direct his own scheme of culture, render the question not so much one of abstract pedagogics, as of practical philanthropy. The philanthropist is supremely indifferent as to whether an individual, white or black, should study Kant or Quaternious, except in so far as the resulting development reacts beneficially upon the common welfare. Does the higher education of the few capable Negroes possess sufficient advantage to the race at large to justify its continuance by a wise and discriminating philanthropy? The great missionary societies, representing the philanthropic arms of the Congregational, Presbyterian, Methodist and Baptist denominations after forty years of arduous, earnest endeavor and the expenditure of many millions of dollars in this field, answer this question emphatically in the affirmative. An ounce of opinion from such sources should be worth a ton of speculation from those who reach their conclusions by a process of " pure reasoning."

THE FUNCTION OF EDUCATION TO A BACKWARD RACE

The African was snatched from the wilds of savagery and thrust into the midst of a mighty civilization. He thus escaped the gradual progress of evolution. Education must accomplish more for a backward race than for a people who are in the forefront of progress. It must not only lead to the unfoldment of faculties but also equip for a life from which the recipient is separated by many centuries of development. The African chieftain who would make a pilgrimage from the jungle to Boston might accomplish the first part of his journey by the original modes of transportation—in the primitive dugout or on the backs of his slaves; but he would complete it upon the steamship, the railway, the electric car and the automobile. How swift the transformation and yet how suggestive of centuries of toil, struggle and mental endeavor. It required the human race thousands of years to bridge the chasm between savagery and civilization, which must now be crossed by a school curriculum of a few years' duration. In a settled state of society the chief function of education is to enable the individual to live the life already attained by his race, but the educated Negro must be a pioneer, a progressive force in the uplifting of his race, and that, too, notwithstanding the fact that he belongs to a backward breed that has never taken the initiative in the progressive movements of the world.

THE HIGHER TRAINING OF CHOICE YOUTH

The first great need of the Negro is that the choice youth of the race should assimilate the principles of culture and hand them down to the masses below. This is the only gateway through which a new people may enter into modern civilization. Herein lies the history of culture. The select minds of the backward race or nation must receive the new cult and adapt it to the peculiar needs of their own people. Japan looms up as the most progressive of the non-Aryan races. The wonderful progress of these Oriental Yankees is due in a large measure to their wise plan of procedure. They send their picked youth to the great centers of western knowledge; but before this culture is applied to their own needs it must first be sifted through the sieve of their native comprehension. The graduates of the schools and colleges for the Negro races are forming centers of civilizing influence in all parts of the land, and we confidently believe that these grains of leaven will ultimately leaven the whole lump.

SELF-RELIANT MANHOOD

Another great need of the race, which the schools must in a large measure supply, is self-reliant manhood. Slavery made the Negro as dependent upon the intelligence and foresight of his master as a soldier upon the will of his commander. He had no need to take thought as to what he should eat or drink or wherewithal he should be clothed. Knowledge necessarily awakens self-consciousness of power. When a child learns the multiplication table he gets a clear notion of intellectual dignity. Here he gains an acquisition which is his permanent, personal possession, and which can never be taken from him. It does not depend upon external authority; he could reproduce it if all the visible forms of the universe were effaced. It is said that the possession of personal property is the greatest stimulus to self-respect. When one can read his title clear to earthly possessions it awakens a consciousness of the dignity of his own manhood. And so when one has digested and assimilated the principles of knowledge he can file his declaration of intellectual independence. He can adopt the language of Montaigne, " Truth and reason are common to every one, and are no more his who spake them first than his who speaks them after; 'tis no more according to Plato than according to me, since he and I equally see and understand them."

Primary principles have no ethnic quality. We

hear much in this day and time of the white man's civilization. We had just as well speak of the white man's multiplication table. Civilization is the common possession of all who assimilate and apply its principles. England can utilize no secret art or invention that is not equally available to Japan. We reward ingenuity with a patent right for a period of years upon the process that has been invented; but when an idea has been published to the world it is no more the exclusive property of the author than gold, after it has been put in circulation, can be claimed by the miner who first dug it from its hiding-place in the earth. No race or nation can preëmpt civilization any more than it can monopolize the atmosphere which surrounds the earth, or the waters which hold it in their liquid embrace.

I have often noticed a young man accommodate his companion with a light from his cigar. After the spark has once been communicated, the beneficiary stands upon an equal footing with the benefactor. In both cases the fire must be continued by drawing fresh supplies of oxygen from the atmosphere. From whatever source a nation may derive the light of civilization, it must be perpetuated by the exercise of the nation's own faculties. Self-reliant manhood is the ultimate basis of American citizenship.

TRAINING FOR LEADERSHIP

The work of the educated colored man is largely that of leadership. He requires, therefore, all the discipline, judgment and mental equipment that long preparation can afford. The more ignorant and backward the masses the more skilled and sagacious should the leaders be. If a beneficial and kindly contact between the races is denied on the lower plane of flesh and blood, it must be sought in the upper region of mental and moral kinship. Knowledge and virtue know no ethnic exclusiveness. If indeed races are irreconcilable, their best individual exponents are not. All dignified negotiation must be conducted on the high plane of individual equality.

"For east is east, and west is west, and never the twain shall meet,
Till earth and sky stand presently at God's great judgment seat;
But there is neither east nor west, border nor breed nor birth,
When two strong men stand face to face, though they come from the ends of the earth."

Irreconcilables become reconciled only after each has manifested the best possibilities of a common nature. The higher education tends to develop superior individuals who may be expected to exercise controlling influence over the multitude. The individual is the proof, the promise and the salvation of the race. The undeveloped races which, in modern times, have faded before the breath of civilization have probably perished because of their failure to produce commanding leaders to guide them wisely under the stress and strain which an encroaching civilization imposed. A single red Indian with the capacity and spirit of Booker T. Washington might have solved the red man's problems and averted his pending doom.

THE MORAL IMPOTENCY OF ELEMENTARY AND MECHANICAL KNOWLEDGE

Again, the higher education should be encouraged because of the moral impotency of all the modes of education which do not touch and stir the human spirit. It is folly to suppose that the moral nature of the child is improved because it has been taught to read and write and cast up accounts, or to practice a handicraft. Tracing the letters of the alphabet with a pen has no bearing on the Golden Rule. The spelling of words by sounds and syllables does not lead to observance of the Ten Commandments. Drill in the multiplication table does not fascinate the learner with the Sermon on the Mount. Rules in grammar, dates in history, sums in arithmetic, and points in geography do not strengthen the grasp on moral truth. The ability to saw a line or hit a nail aplomb with a hammer does not create a zeal for righteousness and truth. It is only when the pupil comes to feel the vitalizing power of knowledge that it begins to react upon the life and to fructify in character. This is especially true of a backward race whose acquisitive power outruns its apperceptive faculty.

THE SOCIAL SEPARATION OF THE RACES

The Negro has now reached a critical stage in his career. The point of attachment between the races which slavery made possible has been destroyed. The relation is daily becoming less intimate and friendly, and more business-like and formal. It thus becomes all the more imperative that the race should gain for itself the primary principles of knowledge and culture.

The social separation of the races in America renders it imperative that the professional classes among the Negroes should be recruited from their own ranks. Under ordinary circumstances, professional places are filled by the most favored class in the community. In a Latin or Catholic country, where the fiction of " social equality " does not exist, there is felt no necessity for Negro priest, teacher, or physician to administer to his own race. But in America this is conceded to be a social necessity. Such being the case, the Negro leader, to use a familiar term, requires all the professional equipment of his white confrere, and special knowledge of the needs and circumstances of his race in addition. The teacher of the Negro child, the preacher to a Negro congregation, or the physician to Negro patients certainly requires as much professional skill as those who administer to the corresponding needs of the white race. Nor are the requirements of the situation one whit diminished because the bestower is of the same race as the recipient. The Negro has the same professional needs as his white confrere and can be qualified for his function only by courses of training of like extent and thoroughness. By no other means can he be qualified to enlighten the ignorant, restrain the vicious, care for the sick and afflicted; administer solace to weary souls, or plead in litigation the cause of the injured.

THE PROFESSIONAL NEEDS OF THE CITY NEGRO

According to the census of 1900, there were 72 cities in the United States with a population of more than 5,000 persons of color, averaging 15,000 each, and aggregating 1,000,000 in all. The professional needs of this urban population for teachers, preachers, lawyers and physicians call for 5,000 well-equipped men and women, not one of whom would be qualified for his function by the three R's or a handicraft.

THE EFFECT OF HIGHER EDUCATION UPON THE RURAL MASSES

The supreme concern of philanthropy is the welfare of the unawakened rural masses. To this end there is need of a goodly sprinkling of well educated men and women to give wise guidance, direction and control. Let no one deceive himself that the country Negro can be uplifted except through the influence of higher contact. It is impossible to inaugurate and conduct a manual training or industrial school without men of sound academic as well as technical knowledge. The torch which is to lighten the darksome places of the South must be kindled at the centers of light.

THE IMPORTANCE OF CULTIVATED TASTE

Rational enjoyment, through moderation, is perhaps as good a definition as can be given of culture. The reaction of culture on conduct is a well-known principle of practical ethics. The Negro race is characterized by boisterousness of manner and extravagant forms of taste. As if to correct such deficiencies, his higher education, hitherto, has largely been concerned with Greek and Latin literature, the norms of modern culture. It is just here that our educational critics are liable to become excited. The spectacle of a Negro wearing eye-glasses and declaiming in classic phrases about the "lofty walls of Rome," and the "wrath of Achilles" upsets their critical calmness and composure. We have so often listened to the grotesque incongruity of a Greek chorus and a greasy cabin and the relative value of a rosewood piano and a patch of early rose potatoes that if we did not join in the smile in order to encourage the humor, we should do so out of sheer weariness. And yet we cannot escape the conviction that one of the Negro's chief needs is a higher form of intellectual and esthetic taste.

THE RELATIVE CLAIMS OF INDUSTRIAL AND HIGHER EDUCATION

Whenever the higher education of the Negro is broached, industrial training is always suggested as a counter-irritant. Partisans of rival claims align themselves in hostile array and will not so much as respect a flag of truce. These one-eyed enthusiasts lack binocular vision. The futile discussion as to whether industrial or higher education is of greater importance to the Negro is suggestive of a subject of great renown in rural debating societies: which is of greater importance to man, air or water. We had as well attempt to decide whether the base or altitude is the more important element of a triangle. The two forms of training should be considered on the basis of their relative, not rival, claims.

THE HIGHER EDUCATION STIMULATES INDUSTRIAL ACTIVITY

Indeed, one of the strongest claims for the higher education of the Negro is that it will stimulate the dormant industrial activities of the race. The surest way to incite a people to meet the material demands of life is to teach them that life is more than meat. The unimaginative laborer pursues the routine rounds of his task, spurred on only by the immediate necessities of life and the taskmaster's stern command.

To him, it is only time and the hour that run through the whole day. The Negro lacks enlightened imagination. He needs prospect and vista. He does not make provision because he lacks prevision. Under slavery he toiled as the ass, dependent upon the daily allowance from his master's crib. To him the prayer, Give us this day our daily bread, has a material rather than a spiritual meaning. If you would perpetuate the industrial incapacity of the Negro, then confine him to the low grounds of drudgery and toil and prevent him from casting his eyes unto the hills whence come inspiration and promise. The man with the hoe is of all men most miserable unless, forsooth, he has a hope. But if imbued with hope and sustained by an ideal, he can consecrate the hoe as well as any other instrument of service, as a means of fulfilling the promise within him. When a seed is sown in the ground it first sends its roots into the soil before the blades can rise out of it. But is it not actuated by the plant-consciousness to seek the light of heaven? For what is the purpose of sending its roots below, if it be not in order to bear fruit above? The pilgrim fathers in following the inspiration of a lofty ideal developed the resources of a continent. Any people who attempt to reach the sky on a pedestal of bricks and mortar will end in confusion and bewilderment as did the builders of the Tower of Babel on the plains of Shinar in the days of Eld. It requires range of vision to stimulate the industrial activities of the people. The most effective prayer that can be uttered for the Negro is, "Lord, open thou his eyes." He cannot see beyond the momentary gratification of appetite and passion. He does not look before and after. Such stimulating influence can be brought to bear upon the race only through the inspiration of the higher culture.

MEN OF HIGHER TRAINING THE LEADERS OF INDUS-
TRIAL EDUCATION

It requires men of sound knowledge to conceive and execute plans for the industrial education of the masses. The great apostles of industrial education for the Negro have been of academic training, or of its cultural equivalent. The work of Hampton and Tuskegee is carried on by men and women of a high degree of mental cultivation.

DR. BOOKER T. WASHINGTON AN EXAMPLE OF HIGHER
CULTURE

Dr. Booker T. Washington (note the title) is the most influential Negro that the race under freedom has produced. He is the great apostle of industrial training. His great success is but the legitimate outcome of his earnestness and enthusiasm. And yet there is no more striking illustration of the necessity of wise, judicious and cultivated leadership as a means of stimulating the dormant activity of the masses than he who hails from Tuskegee. His success is due wholly to his intellectual and moral faculties. His personal opportunities of association and contact have been equivalent to a liberal education. Several of America's greatest institutions of learning have fittingly recognized his moral and intellectual worth by decorating him with their highest literary honors. Mr. Washington possesses an enlightened mind to discover the needs of the masses, executive tact to put his plans in effective operation, and persuasive ability to convince others as to the expediency of his policies. He possesses no trade or handicraft; if so, he has never let the American people into the secret. Nor can it easily be seen what possible benefit such trade or handicraft would be to him in the work which has fallen to his lot. Tuskegee has been built on intellect and oratory. If Mr. Washington had been born with palsied hands, but endowed with the same intellectual gifts and powers of persuasive speech, Tuskegee would not have suffered one iota by reason of his manual affliction. But, on the other hand, had he come into the world with a sluggish brain and a heavy tongue, whatever cunning and skill his hands might have acquired, he never could have developed the institution which has made him justly famous throughout the civilized world.

THE DEFICIENCY OF THE SLAVE MECHANIC

Slavery taught the Negro to work, but at the same time to despise those who worked. To them all show of respectability was attached to those whom circumstances placed above the necessity of toil. It requires intellectual conception of the object and the end of labor to overcome this mischievous notion. The Negro mechanics produced under the old slave regime are rapidly passing away because they did not possess the power of self-perpetuation. They were not rooted and grounded in rational principles of the mechanical arts. The hand could not transmit its cunning because the mind was not trained. They were given the knack without the knowledge.

MONEY SPENT FOR THE HIGHER EDUCATION OF THE NEGRO NOT WASTED

The charge has recently been made that money spent on the higher education of the Negro has been wasted. Does this charge come from the South?

When we consider that it was through Northern philanthropy that a third of its population received their first impulse toward better things; that these higher institutions prepared the 30,000 Negro teachers whose services are utilized in the public schools; that the men and women who were the beneficiaries of this philanthropy are doing all in their power to control, guide and restrain the South's ignorant and vicious masses, thus lightening the public burden and lifting the general life to a higher level; that these persons are almost without exception earnest advocates of peace, harmony and good-will between the races; to say nothing of the fact that these vast philanthropic contributions have passed through the trade channels of Southern merchants, it would seem that the charge is strangely incompatible with that high-minded disposition and chivalrous spirit which the South is so zealous to maintain. Does this charge come from the North? It might not be impertinent to propound a few propositions for their consideration. Is it possible to specify a like sum of money spent upon any other backward race that has produced greater results than the amount spent upon the Southern Negro? Is it the American Indian, upon whom four centuries of missionary effort has produced no more progress than is made by a painted ship on a painted sea? Is it the Hawaiian, who will soon be civilized off the face of the earth? Is it the Chinese, upon whom the chief effect of Christian philanthropy is to incite them to breathe out slaughter against the stranger within their gates? It is incumbent upon him who claims that this money has been wasted to point out where, in all the range of benevolent activity, the contributions of philanthropy have been more profitably spent.

It is true that forty or fifty millions of dollars

have been thus spent, but when we consider the magnitude of the task to which it was applied, we find that it would not average one dollar a year for each Negro child to be educated. Why should we marvel, then, that the entire mass of ignorance and corruption has not put on enlightenment and purity?

NOT MERE THEORIZERS

We often hear that the advocates of higher education are mere theorists without definite, tangible plans and propositions. There has recently sprung into prominence a class of educational philosophers who deny the value of stored-up knowledge. We are informed that only such information as will be honored at the corner grocery or is convertible on demand into cash equivalent is of practical value, while all else is an educational delusion and a snare. The truth is, that all knowledge which clarifies the vision, refines the feelings, broadens the conception of truth and duty and ennobles the manhood is of the highest and most valuable form of practicability. An institution which sends into the world a physician to heal the sick, a lawyer to plead the cause of the injured, a teacher to enlighten the minds of the ignorant, or a preacher to break the bread of life to hungry souls, is rendering just as practical service to the race as those schools which prepare men to build houses and plant potatoes.

NEED FOR THE NEGRO COLLEGE

It is sometimes claimed that the few capable Negroes can find opportunity for higher training in the institutions of the North. It is by no means certain as to what extent these institutions would admit colored students. The Northern college is not apt to inspire the colored pupil with the enthusiasm and fixed purpose for the work which Providence has assigned him. It is the spirit, not the letter that maketh alive. The white college does not contemplate the special needs of the Negro race. American ideals could not be fostered in the white youth of our land by sending them to Oxford or Berlin for tuition. No more can the Negro gain racial inspiration from Harvard or Yale. And yet they need the benefit of contact and comparison, and the zeal for knowledge and truth which these great institutions impart. The Negro college and the Northern institutions will serve to preserve a balance between undue elation for want of sober comparison, and barren culture, for lack of inspirational contact with the masses.

DOES THE HIGHER EDUCATION LEAD AWAY FROM THE RACE?

It is often charged that the higher education lifts the Negro above the needs of his race. The thousands of graduates of Negro schools and colleges all over the land are a living refutation of this charge. After the mind has been stored with knowledge it is transmitted to the place where the need is greatest and the call is loudest, and transmuted into whatever mode of energy may be necessary to accomplish the imposed task.

The issues involved in the race question are as intricate in their relations and far-reaching in their consequences as any that have ever taxed human wisdom for solution. No one can be too learned or too profound in whose hands are entrusted the temporal and eternal destiny of a human soul. Even if the educated Negro desired to flee from his race, he soon learns by bitter experience that he will be thrown back upon himself by the expulsive power of prejudice. He soon learns that the Newtonian formula has a social application: "The force of attraction varies directly as the mass."

ROOSEVELT AND THE NEGRO

THE late Senator Ingalls, in one of his luminous flashes, defined politics as " the metaphysics of force." This definition fits with philosophic fineness the nature of Theodore Roosevelt, who is its most strenuous exemplar. In effective political dynamics and intensity of accelerative energy, he easily surpasses all the present-day rulers of the earth. He has no reserved physical or psychical potencies. All the energies of his nature are in the active voice and present tense. With him pure reasoning is a burden, and disquisitional niceties a waste of while and a weariness of flesh. His one superlative passion is how to bring things to pass. His mind works with the celerity of feminine intuition. He reaches conclusions and settles issues with a swiftness and self-satisfying certainty that startles the more cautious statesmen who rely upon the slower processes of reason and deliberation. He has diagnosed the case, prescribed the remedy, and cured, or killed, the patient before the ordinary physician has finished feeling the pulse. After the deed is done, he leaves to the college professor or the senile moralist discussion of the moral quality of the method employed. If he has not a Jesuitical disregard of means, he at least considers them as but subsidiary processes, which must not too seriously embarrass the righteous end in view. He is the greatest living preacher of righteousness; but it is always righteousness as it is in Roosevelt. He holds to his conception of public duty with the tenacity of infallible assurance. If others are too stubborn to accept or too dull to appreciate his more enlightened point of view, the worse is the perversity, or the more the pity. He never reaches either intellectual or moral sublimity, but is transcendent only in action. His deeds are never dull. Even in dealing with the commonplaces of life he infuses into them the energizing spirit of his own nature. He dramatizes the Ten Commandments and vitalizes time-worn moral maxims with a spirit and power as if they were fresh pronouncements to arouse the energies of a lethargic world. A man almost or wholly without Anglo-Saxon blood, he is the ideal embodiment of the Anglo-Saxon spirit which glorifies beyond all things else the power of doing things.

> " The Celt is in his heart and hand,
> The Gaul is in his brain and nerve."

He is absolutely self-centered, and believes that he was sent into the world to set things right. The world has accepted him at his own appraisement, as it is prone to do with all ardent natures, especially if they be serious and incessant in the advocacy of their high pretensions. He accomplishes his sovereign purposes while his fellow-citizens stand amazedly at gaze, as an astronomer when a new luminary flashes suddenly upon his vision and pursues its uncomputed orbit across the skies.

HIS EARLY CAREER

He begins his public career by defying James G. Blaine, the magnetic statesman, who, like Agamemnon, was a born king of men. He leads a little hand-

ful of rough and ready dare-devils up a little hill in
a little skirmish, and is covered with the military
glamour and glory of a great hero in a great conflict.   Our party captains, fearing the exorbitancy
of his foreshadowed power, force him into the Vice-
Presidential office as a sure political quietus, but it
proved to be merely an instance of the folly of men
trying to defeat a career marked out by destiny. The
assassin's bullet takes off McKinley, the beloved, and
installs Roosevelt, the strenuous.   His high place but
affords a vantage ground for the exercise of his
strenuousness and power.   By the word of his might,
he commands two powerful nations engaged in Titanic struggle to stay their strife and sue for peace,
and forthwith they obey him.   He commands peace
or war, according to the dictates of his high conception of righteousness.   With one bold Roosevel-
tian stroke he acquires a canal connecting the mighty
waters which had washed separate shores since recorded time, a consummation which American statesmanship had sought for half a century in vain.   He
regulates railroads, throttles trusts, defies labor
cliques, and holds in leash both the millionaire and
the mob.   He makes even the wrath of Tillman to
praise him, and the remainder of his wrath he holds
in contempt.   The universality of his sway was never
more strikingly illustrated than by the grotesque
spectacle of the last session of Congress, where the
spectator might look and see Roosevelt's mighty
hosts advancing against the stronghold of plutocracy, with Tillman leading on!   There is no question of human interest whose magnitude or minuteness
is beyond his strenuous handling.   He gives the
American women salutary advice as to their domestic
function and duty; with an off-hand stroke of the
pen seeks to reform English orthography, which has

been slowly modifying from Chaucer to Mark Twain; sets up as expert detective of nature fakirs; while Americans, of however high reputation and standing, who persist in seeing things under other than his own angle of vision, may regard themselves as lucky indeed if they escape being relegated to his famous "Index Prævaricatorum."

THE WEAK AND HELPLESS

When one considers what manner of man is this whom the strong and mighty hold in awe, the man who gives the word and the nation obeys, he who speaks and it is done, he might feel disposed to ask who is the despised Negro that he should be mindful of him, or that he should bestow upon him one moment of his august consideration and regard! There is little room for the weak and helpless in a strenuous philosophy which glorifies the valiant man. What hope has the feeble and the heavy laden in a dispensation whose gospel relegates the hindermost to the mercy of his satanic captor? Roosevelt has never been the champion of manhood rights. But rather, like Lyman Abbott, he believes in manhood first and rights afterward. He has little of the humanitarian sentimentalism that would stoop to the infirmities of the weak. His motto is " all men up " who can get up and stand up. But if some men allow themselves to be pushed down, the overthrowers rather than the overthrown command his higher respect because they manifest the greater degree of power. Had he been born at an earlier season he doubtless would have opposed the reconstruction scheme as he now opposes independence for the Philippine Islands. His very nature revolts at the idea of clothing weakness with authority.

ROOSEVELT NOT BAPTIZED WITH THE FIRE OF OUR CIVIL WAR

He is the first commanding statesman of his party who was not baptized with the spirit of the Civil War. The political and civil equality of all men was burned into the soul as the outcome of that great struggle. Orthodoxy in this doctrine was at one time the one determinative test of patriotism, the only passport to public favor and power. But now we have a new Pharaoh who knew not Joseph the black. With the new issue have come new issues. Tax and tariff, trade and transportation, plutocracy and trusts, expansion and subjugation, now monopolize public attention. The issues of life to-day are material rather than moral, and are placed on a hard, unsentimental metallic basis. The dollar is the highest common divisor of values, in terms of which we measure all forms of excellence—yea, even human rights. Indeed, whoever is so archaic in this material day as to insist on the political doctrine of a generation ago is apt to be waived aside as a doctrinaire enthusiast, or perhaps as a moral mollycoddle. Roosevelt embodies the new spirit rather than the old, which he espouses with a moral enthusiasm and a preachment of a type of righteousness which well befits the new faith.

ALTERNATION OF GOOD AND ILL WILL

Roosevelt's relations with the Negro have been marked by an almost whimsical alternation of good and bad impressions. At one time he elicits his highest praise, only at the next turn to evoke his bitterest curses. He is a man of instantaneous impulse and promptitude of action, and is unhampered by the tedium of logical coherence or consistency of procedure. He follows the latest impulse. The Negro is by no means the only alternate beneficiary and victim of his impulsive caprice. The Southern whites have also experienced like vicissitudes. No President has been so bitterly abused or so highly extolled by the white South as its half-son who claims a national poise by reason of the balance of his blood. The people who but yesterday were heaping upon him maledictions which exhaust the lexicon of malignity, are now proclaiming him their hearts' idol and chief delight. The praise and blame which he receives at the hands of the white South and the black race are at the same time antithetical and complementary. Like the illumined and bedarkened portions of the moon's surface, the one increases at the expense of the other. In dealing with the delicate questions complicated by race antagonisms he has not as yet found a policy that is satisfying to all—a statesmanlike consummation devoutly to be wished. And so whites and blacks alike have experienced, with fluctuating humor, the variable phases of the amplitude of his impulse.

> " But through the shift of mood and mood
>   Mine ancient humor saves him whole,
> The cynic devil in his blood
>   That makes him mock his hurrying soul."

AS CIVIL SERVICE COMMISSIONER

Theodore Roosevelt entered upon his public ministry as an ardent advocate of administrative purity. He believed in righteous methods applied to public business. It was as Civil Service Commissioner that he first came in practical contact with the race issue. He served as Commissioner under the second administration of Grover Cleveland, who himself was a consistent disciple of administrative reform. It was the boast of many of the supporters of the new administration that they would take the departments at Washington out of mourning by removing all the darksome embellishments in the shape of colored employees. But Grover Cleveland was made of the same sort of stern, dogged integrity as his doughty young Commissioner. Mr. Roosevelt strenuously insisted that all applicants should be treated according to their degree of fitness on the established scale of merit, to the utter disregard of such extraneous issues as race, color or political alignment. It was due in large part to the courageous insistence of this intrepid Republican official under a Democratic administration, backed up by the stubborn honesty of his chief, that black applicants for clerical positions were not blackballed by a party which had posed as their traditional political adversary. It cannot be claimed that Commissioner Roosevelt assumed this attitude out of any special regard for the brother in black, or rather the brother in colors, but to preserve the integrity of his principles. It is a very imperfect philosophy which breaks down at the color line. That scheme of political or moral ethics which awaits answer to the query, "Of what complexion is he?" before applying its beneficence cannot be entertained by a noble nature or a broadly enlightened mind. There is nothing in Roosevelt's strenuous philosophy that would cause him to propound this query or await its answer. If the Negro can drink of the cup of which the white man drinks and be baptized with the baptism with which he is baptized withal, he holds that he should share with him the glory, honor, and power of his kingdom. If his faith in the Negro is small it is only because he has not been impressed with sufficiently numerous examples of strenuosity and success to guarantee it as a race characteristic.

AS ROUGH RIDER

Roosevelt's second point of contact with the Negro race was during the Spanish War. In that famous charge up San Juan Hill—or was it Kettle Hill?— the courage and intrepidity of the Negro troops saved Colonel Roosevelt and his Rough Riders from utter destruction. Had it not been for their courageous intervention he would have been cut off in the flower of his youth, and his dazzling career lost to the American people. Gratitude is not characteristic of a self-centered nature. When one is overburdened with a sense of his ordained primacy, he naturally looks upon lesser men as being put into the world as auxiliaries to his higher mission. While the whole world was extolling the prowess of the Negro soldier, it was reserved for the chief beneficiary of that prowess to sound the sole discordant note. In a notable magazine article, where our present-day warriors are wont to fight their battles with an ingenuity and courage rarely equalled on the tented field, Colonel Roosevelt either discredited their valor or damned them with such faint praise as to dim the luster of their fame. This ungenerous criticism dumbfounded the Negro race. Disparagement of the Negro soldier, as subsequent developments have clearly shown, touches the pride and arouses the resentment of this race as nothing else can do. The Negro's loyalty and patriotism, as exemplified in all the nation's wars, is perhaps the chief tie of endearment that binds him to the heart of the American people. If that tie becomes tenuous his hold upon

the nation's affection would be precarious indeed.
For a time there was no more unpopular man in
America throughout Afro-Americandom. But election time was approaching. Political exigencies
made him the available candidate for the governor-
ship of the Empire State of New York. The chief
factor in this availability was the military glamour
that gathered about him because of San Juan Hill,
where the colored troops fought so nobly. The results at this election depended upon the colored vote,
whose resentment he had aroused. Candidate Roosevelt so mollified and qualified the strictures of Colonel Roosevelt as to take away much of the keenness
of the sting. By the use of such blandishments as
the politician knows well how to apply to salve the
sores of an aggrieved class during the unrest of a
heated campaign, the injury was forgiven, or at
least held in abeyance. Under the rallying cry of
the Grand Old Party the Negro vote came to the
rescue and supported him almost to a man. The
slender margin of his victory showed that his success
was due to that support. Had the Negro persisted
in a spiteful spirit and sought vengeance at the polls
his political career doubtless would have been cut
short and the pent-up energies of his nature must
have sought outlet through a different channel. It
was thus that the Negro saved his political life at the
ballot-box as he had saved his physical life on the
battlefield.

AS GOVERNOR OF NEW YORK

During his brief service as Governor he appointed
one or two colored men to unimportant positions and
entertained a colored artist at the gubernatorial
mansion. He accepted an invitation to deliver the

dedicatory address at the unveiling of the Frederick Douglass monument at Rochester. Perusal of this address enables one to sympathize with an official who feels forced to perform a ceremony in which he has little spirit or zest, in order to accommodate a constituency whom it is desirable to keep in good humor. On the whole his administration as Governor preserved the general attitude of his party toward its black allies without any notable departure either to their benefit or disadvantage.

As candidate for Vice-President and for President he not only secured the black man's loyal support, but commanded his enthusiastic, yea, rapturous applause.

THE APPOINTMENT OF CRUM

Toward the latter part of McKinley's administration there were mutterings of disquiet and unrest among the Afro-American contingent. After the unfortunate outcome of the Lake City horror, it was reported that the President had abandoned the policy of appointing colored men to Federal offices in the South. It was also whispered that he was giving aid and encouragement to the propaganda of the Lily Whites, a breed of political exotics which neither toils nor spins, but delights to array itself in all the spoils and splendor of office. An open revolt was narrowly averted during the campaign of 1900. When Theodore Roosevelt became President the Negro's hopes revived. Here was a man of granitic character whose courageous righteousness on all national questions admitted of no variableness nor shadow of turning. The test was not long in coming, and Roosevelt stood it unfalteringly. Dr. William D. Crum, a most highly capable and respected citizen of Charleston, South Carolina, became his party's choice for collector of that ancient and honorable port. His name was sent to the Senate for confirmation. The whole white South became enraged and lashed itself into fury. Was this a reopening of the issue at Charleston supposed to have been settled at Lake City? Political agitation, especially when tinged with race antagonism, never obeys the formulas of logic. It booted nothing to point out that colored men had held throughout the South the highest Federal places since the days of Grant. It was also shown that both at Savannah and Wilmington, more important ports environing Charleston on the south and on the north, colored men sat at the receipt of customs.

All sorts of direful predictions filled the air. The ear of the nation tingled with the choice of bloodshed, race war, Negro domination, Anglo-Saxon superiority, and like rhetorical fustian which such an occasion is calculated to evoke. But Roosevelt stood by his guns as he always does while the firing continues. The sleepy old city by the sea had not had so much national attention focused upon it since the firing upon Fort Sumter. The Republican leaders became frightened. Some were disposed to balk, others to dodge. It was Roosevelt who applied the whip and inspirited his party to stand by its great traditions. In the midst of this raging controversy he took occasion to announce to the world that he would not shut the door of hope upon any class of American citizens. The principle was established. Crum was confirmed. The door of hope still stands ajar; albeit few there be who enter thereat. The swarthy collector now sits calmly at his window overlooking Fort Sumter, straining his eyes for sight of an occasional ship in quest of unlading or clearance

at his port.   The citizens are again tracing their
favorite phantoms.   The good old city has sunken
into its traditional ways, reveling in the glory of by-
gone days, dreaming of things of yore in the shadow
of Calhoun's Monument, and basking in the soft, sil-
very moonlight over the Battery.   No more heed is
taken of the racial personality of the dignified and
leisurely collector than of the cut of his coat or the
color of his necktie.

THE INDIANOLA POST OFFICE

At Indianola where an irascible community defied
the national authority because of the unfashionable
color of a Federal official, the President upheld the
national dignity and prestige with a firm and un-
flinching hand.

THE BOOKER WASHINGTON DINNER

A simple act of civility on the part of the President toward an eminent colored American called
down upon his head the fires of wrath of his white
brethren in the South.   Dr. Booker T. Washington,
the consulting statesman for the Negro race, was
invited to dinner at the White House.   There is, perhaps, no other person in America of like standing
and relation to public questions who has not received such semi-official courtesy.   But immediately
a mighty storm arose.   Had the President suddenly
turned traitor and flagrantly violated our most
sacred religious or moral code he could not have been
more bitterly or blatantly denounced.   That two
gentlemen of world-wide reputation and of congenial
temperament should occasionally sit together at meat
might naturally be expected anywhere outside of the

Brahmin caste. Mr. Washington is our only domestic ambassador.

He has been picked out and set up as the representative of an overshadowed nation surrounded by an overshadowing one. An ambassador usually has immediate access to the presence of the chief ruler to whom he is accredited without the intermeddling of official understrappers. Nice courtesies and high civilities usually accompany diplomatic procedure. Should the representative from Corea or Hayti or Turkey be invited to dine alone with the President at the White House the act would hardly be construed into one of social intimacy, but it would be regarded merely as a convenient opportunity to consult over some weighty matters of state. Indeed, only a few days after the famous Washington dinner a red Indian chief who had not passed beyond the blanket and feather stage of civilization was received by the President and the incident only excited curious pleasantry. Mr. Washington has mingled in close pleasant personal touch with princes and potentates of the Old World and with merchant princes and money barons of the New. He is entirely familiar with high social favors. The colored race has not the slightest concern with whom Mr. Washington, in his personal capacity, may or may not be invited to dine. A man's dinner list is his private affair. It is the prerogative of every citizen to extend, accept, or decline such invitation, according to the dictates of his own taste and pleasure. But to affirm as a principle that the man who is looked upon as the chiefest among ten millions, in his ambassadorial capacity, is not eligible to the established modes of courtesy, at the high court of the nation, cannot be accepted with satisfaction by any manly man of the blood thus held in despite.

These acts on the part of the President evoked the highest plaudits from the colored race. It was felt that his views were broad, based upon the fundamental principle of our institutions which accord to all classes of citizens the same official consideration and courtesy. Indeed, these laudations became so loud and fulsome that they must have proved embarrassing to one who did not pose as the special champion of an unpopular class.

POLICIES NOT SUSTAINED

But it must be said that these evidences of friendship and good will have not been systematic and sustained, nor followed up to their logical conclusion. Roosevelt never surrenders, but often seems to evacuate his stronghold as soon as he has demonstrated the enemy's inability to capture it. In the final estimate of history, if his reputation falls short of superlative greatness, it will be because he lacks consecutiveness and persistence of purpose and policy. He is not permanently wedded to any one question as the dominant note of his career. He suddenly takes up a measure, settles it and drops it, and goes in quest of issues new. And so in dealing with the Negro. He has established the principle, but has desisted at the point of practical operation. Crum was made collector of Charleston in face of a frowning South, but he makes no more such appointments against local opposition. He closed the post office at Indianola, but it was shortly reopened in substantial harmony with the contentions of its white patrons. He preserved a dignified and becoming silence while the storm of wrath raged over the Booker Washington dinner, but no more do he and the famous Tuskegeean break pleasant bread and shake the friendly glass while conferring over weighty matters of the nether state.

SOUTHERN REFEREES

The tentative policies which President Roosevelt has pursued concerning the political welfare of the race have not been calculated to command their cordial co-operation and cheerful acquiescence. These may be considered under three distinct heads.

1. His scheme of selecting referees with whom to consult on political dealings in the South is something new under the political sun. While he has sought diligently to find men of the highest standing and character to serve in this consultive capacity, yet his selections have usually been of the Democratic persuasion, and sometimes of strong anti-Negro bias. According to the universal method of American politics, the administration is controlled in its local matters by the leaders of the organization of the same party faith. When an administration discards its own party supporters and seeks advice from its political adversaries it may not expect the approval of the regular workers who have borne the brunt and burden of battle. This feeling is by no means confined to the Negro race, but is shared in or perhaps it would be more accurate to say is directed by the white manipulators of the shattered Republican fragments in the South.

BOOKER WASHINGTON AS SPOKESMAN

2. Dr. Booker T. Washington has been chosen as referee at large and as the sole spokesman for the entire Negro race. His selection was not due to his

political activity or experience, for the whole tenor of his teaching has been to persuade his race to place less proportional stress on politics and to concentrate its energies upon things economic and material. But by reason of his general prominence and the world-wide esteem he was put in command of political forces, to the relegation of war-scarred veterans who had borne the heat and burden of the day. Othello naturally objects to his loss of occupation. Most of them have yielded, but only after they learned that the only road to official favor was the straight and narrow path that leads to Tuskegee. No Negro, whether in Vermont or Texas, whatever has been his service to the party, can expect to receive consideration at the hands of the President unless he gets the approval of the great educator. It should, in all fairness, be said that this position was not of Mr. Washington's own seeking. It has on more than one occasion caused him serious embarrassment. It might seem that active participation in politics would impair his usefulness along other lines to which he has devoted the chief energies of his life. It is needless to say, as some are wont to aver, that Mr. Washington's function as adviser to the President does not make him a practical political participant. The procurement of office and the manipulations incident thereto are the chief concern of the typical politician. Mr. Washington was impressed into this service on the demand of the President, which no patriotic citizen feels inclined to refuse. Indeed, there is no prominent Negro who would not have accepted the assignment upon the slightest intimation that he might be the Presidential choice. That Mr. Washington has filled the assignment with an eye single to the best interest of his race is wholly aside from the merits of the question. Mr. Roosevelt would readily assent to the proposition that the political boss is an undesirable person. And yet he has set up Mr. Washington as the boss of ten millions, and commanded the rest to obey him on penalty of political disfavor. He has put at his disposal the means by which all bosses retain their influence—the persuasive power of public patronage. For where the patronage is, there the subserviency of the politician will be also. This policy is not calculated to teach the Negro the needed lesson in self-government and manly political activity.

Should succeeding administrations follow Mr. Roosevelt's example in this regard, the Negro would remain in perpetual thraldom to an intermediary boss set up at the whim or caprice of whoever happens to be President. We cannot hope that every administration will be as fortunate in its selection as Mr. Roosevelt has been. Contemplation of the continuance of such conditions is repugnant to every principle of manly American politics.

FEDERAL OFFICES FOR NORTHERN NEGROES

3. Strangely enough, one of the most significant moves of the President affecting the political life of the Negro has almost or wholly escaped attention. He has shifted the center of gravity from the South to the North. Hitherto the important Federal places accorded the race have gone to persons below the Mason and Dixon line. This recognized the race as a factor in local Republican organizations and gave some prestige at national conventions. It also recognized the potential political rights of the Negro which neither suppression nor temporary nullification can take away. To withhold recognition because suppression has rendered non-effective the exercise

of political power seems to be equivalent to an abandonment of the principles for which the Republican party has stood from the days of Grant until now. The Minister to Hayti, the Register of the Treasury, the Fourth Auditor of the Treasury, the most conspicuous positions given to the race, are filled by Negroes from the North. Such appointments have not been made solely on the basis of the local weight and influence, but as recognition and satisfaction of the claims of the entire race. But one commanding national position is now held by a Southern Negro, and that is the recordership of deeds for the District of Columbia, a purely local office which has widespread fame as being the conceded allotment to the Negro, whether Democrats or Republicans are triumphant. The favorites of political fortune have come from the North and from the South, from the East and from the West, and ensconced themselves in this snug office, while the voteless sons of the District have been ignored. Dame Rumor has it, or had it, that among the first acts of the present administration was the shifting of the colored collector of the port of Wilmington, N. C., to the District of Columbia to relieve embarrassment to the Lily White propaganda, which he at that time is said to have encouraged. Judge Peter C. Pritchard, who was then the administration's intermediary in Southern politics, could write an interesting inside account of this transaction. It would seem from present tendency that there are to be no more new Negro appointees in the South, but merely a continuance in office of those officials against whom local Democratic protest is not too loud and boisterous. It requires little power of prevision to foresee the outcome of this policy. In a few years there will not be a Negro Federal official south of the Mason and Dixon line.

This would prove to be a blow to the race, for which
the appointment of Northern Negroes were but a
poor compensation.   When the Southern Negro has
been eliminated from the political equation with the
connivance and implied sanction of the party of
Grant and Sumner, it will not be long before his
Northern brother will begin to feel its baleful effect.
With a rare political sagacity the Northern Negro
feels that in order to preserve his own liberties he
must insist upon the rights of his brethren in the
South.   Shifting the stress of political emphasis from
the region where the Negro is, to the section where
he is not, is like placing the center of gravity outside
the basis of support.   The result must be unstable
political equilibrium.   But here again the President
is displaying his characteristic disposition which
glorifies the effective component of force, and takes
little heed of power, reserved or suppressed, which
fails of effective expression.   The Negro vote in the
North is a practical present political dynamic.   In
the South it is an inert potentiality, whose unfoldment, like faith, is the substance of things hoped for,
the evidence of things not seen.   The President deals
with the real and the tangible rather than the remote
and the contingent.   While this policy may seem to
answer the immediate demands of political exigencies,
it will prove disastrous to the Negro political outlook and vista.

THE BROWNSVILLE AFFAIR

The chief irritating issue between the President
and the Negro race is the outcome of a most deplorable incident.   The Negro soldier has ever been
an object of detestation to the Southern whites.   The
soldierly spirit is incompatible with the status to

which the black man is assigned in their political and social scheme. Every Southern State has disbanded its colored militia. This feeling was accentuated by the Spanish War, where Negro and Southern white troops were placed on a footing of soldierly equality, and where the black troops gained the higher meed of glory. Occasional friction between local authorities and Negro troops passing through the South to and from the front but added fuel to the flame.

In face of this feeling a Negro battalion was quartered in an obscure town on the remote frontier of Texas. The air about Brownsville became tense with trouble. Citizens goaded soldiers to the point of acute irritation. One dark night some shooting was done in the streets, resulting in the death of a barkeeper and the wounding of an officer of the law. The alarm was sounded that the Negro soldiers had " shot up the town." Race passion was stirred to the utmost. Brownsville would have been drenched in blood had it not been for the firm attitude of the gallant commander of the fort. The local grand jury could not find sufficient regular evidence for indictment of the hated troops quartered among them. Word was flashed to the commander-in-chief at Washington, who forthwith proceeds to deal with the matter out of hand. The army inspector was dispatched to the scene to investigate and report. Unfortunately the inspector was a man of Southern birth and bias. The distress cry of the city through the undercurrent of communication made its subconscious appeal with Masonic secrecy and force. Every thoughtful student knows that where race passion is aroused the judicial temperament takes flight. Suspicion or even suggestion of wrongdoing on the part of the Negro if reiterated with loud outcry and demand for blood is assumed to be confirmation strong as holy writ. Instantaneously every white man aligns himself on the side of his race. Where racial instinct is appealed to the laws of evidence have little weight. "Lynch the brutes!" was on the lips of every citizen, and the execution was stayed only by the too fearful aspect of Uncle Sam's bayonets. In the midst of this inflammable state of things a son of Georgia, as inspector-general, repaired to Brownsville. Instantly he assumed the feeling of the community. The investigator acted the rôle of prosecutor with preconceived conviction of guilt. He accepted the representation of the citizens of Brownsville and propounded a few shrewdly calculated questions to the suspected soldiers, whose answers were designed to confirm their guilt. No opportunity was afforded them to prove their innocence. Assuming the existence of a criminal conspiracy, he demanded of the non-commissioned officers the names of their guilty companions. Compliance with this request would inevitably have been self-incriminatory, convicting the respondent of murder if personally involved, or of guilty knowledge if a non-participant. Following the method of the mob in dealing with a black culprit, he declared them guilty, and graciously offered them the opportunity to confess. Affirming their innocence, they refused to confess; and declaring their ignorance, they declined to inform on their fellows. The inspector hastened to Washington and reported to the President that some fifteen or twenty men out of a total of one hundred and sixty-seven had shot up the town, murdered and maimed its citizens, while the rest had guilty knowledge of the deed, but were disposed to shield their companions in crime. The city of Brownsville had worked out the case with such cir-

cumstantial confirmation of detail as to deceive even
the commanding major, who reluctantly assented to
the findings of the inspector-general. On fuller investigation, however, Colonel Penrose changed this
opinion and now stoutly affirms his belief in the innocence of his men.

When this report was presented to President
Roosevelt he was bound to accept in good faith the
findings of the inspector-general, the regularly authorized agent for such service, and especially so
when concurred in by the chief officers of the command.

A flood of righteous indignation welled up within
him at this outrage upon the national arm. He would
teach the wrongdoers a lesson which would never be
forgotten. The color of the offenders, he stoutly
avers, neither mitigated nor magnified the character
of the offense in his mind. The discipline of the
army must be upheld. It is easy to believe that the
President's conduct at this stage was not based upon
consideration of color. He is himself of a military
mold of mind. In military matters, as elsewhere, he
is a law unto himself and has little reverence for
those above, around, or beneath him. He shatters a
military idol with as little hesitancy as he would
reprimand a common soldier. Did he not criticise
and discredit the sagacity of his own commanding
general with a little round robin? The man who
spoke disparagingly of the troops who saved his life
on the battlefield, who unceremoniously reprimanded
General Miles, the gallant head of the army and
hero of many battles; who imputed cowardice to Ad-
miral Schley, our only naval hero who has triumphed
with modern guns over modern armor, might naturally be supposed to act vigorously in case of reported wrongdoers at Brownsville.

Basing his action on General Garlington's report, the President with ruthless hand, though righteous purpose, ignored all forms and precedents of military, judicial, or executive procedure, and proceeded to mete out drastic punishment. Although there was no pretense at determination of individual guilt, and although not more than ten per cent. of the battalion could possibly have participated in the outrage, the whole number were dismissed without honor, and in the hot indignation of his wrath he imposed upon them serious civil disability by executive fiat. The disqualifying feature of his order was flagrantly *ultra vires* and void by virtue of its own nullity. It was afterwards rescinded, but its original issuance stands as a memorial of the state of mind actuating the President at the time.

This order of the President violates every principle of our jurisprudence. It assumed that the men were guilty and imposed upon them the onus of proving their innocence; it condemned them without even the formality of a trial; it imposed punishment without proof of individual culpableness; by it one hundred and fifty probably innocent men were made to suffer in order that fifteen possibly guilty ones might not escape.

The President must have foreseen or forefelt the tumult which the issuance of this order was calculated to excite, for with prudent political sagacity he held it up till the day after the election, in which the Negro vote might prove a determining factor, and especially in the congressional district where the political fate of his son-in-law was involved. In the meantime he had betaken himself to the high seas, planning to return, it would seem, after the clouds had rolled by.

But instead of rolling by to accommodate the return of the President, the clouds continued to gather in density and ominousness. The whole Negro race was dazed. Theodore Roosevelt had for the second time struck at the Negro soldier, the pride and idol of the race. Protest, indignation, cries of outrage flew thick and fast from the Negro press, pulpit, and platform. The great papers of the country with practical unanimity condemned the order as one of unusual and unnecessary severity. Those versed in constitutional lore declared that the President had set a precedent which might prove dangerous to the principle of American liberty. It was reserved for Senator Tillman to describe the act as executive lynching, a description which characterizes the deed with his wonted picturesque aptness of language. It possesses the essential characteristics of mob vengeance. It inflicts punishment on demand of the rabble rather than by judicial process. It furnishes victims to appease popular vengeance without nice regard to the identity of the perpetrator. The punishment of the possibly innocent effectually destroys the evidence by which the guilty might subsequently be apprehended. The Secretary of War with political forethought sought to have the order suspended until further investigation, but to no avail. What was written was written. " The moving finger writes and having writ Moves on; nor all your piety nor wit Shall lure it back again Nor all your tears blot out a line of it."

From a racial point of view it was doubly unfortunate that the President should have selected the weak and helpless Negro, the increasing object of the nation's contumely and despite, upon whom to make this drastic departure from the usual procedure. The disciplinary value of the example would doubtless have been more effective had he applied it in the first instance to the white troops guilty of the offense charged against the colored troops in Ohio some months previous. Coming, too, as it did, swiftly upon the heels of the Atlanta riot, it added the color of justification to that awful slaughter. Indeed, John Temple Graves, the justifier of this atrocious murder of innocent men, employs the same line of justificatory argument as that used to defend the President's position. But the most unjust and unkindest cut of all occurs when the President, acridly assuming a defensive attitude, holds the race up to the world, by executive decree, as fostering a criminal fellowship.

ANNUAL MESSAGE

In the meantime, the session of Congress was approaching. In his annual message the President undertook to discuss the subject of lynching. In this document he imputed to the colored race a lecherous tendency which is not justified by the infrequent occurrence of clearly proved cases of assault. He placed upon the whole race the responsibility of restraining and controlling the wild passion of the dastardly few. In his eagerness to effect the wished-for consummation he overlooked the absurdity of imposing upon a race studiously deprived of governmental power and authority, without the means of inflicting punishment, the obligation of reaching, correcting, and coercing the criminally disposed. This vicarious burden is imposed upon no other class of citizens. The alleged infirmities of the Negro race are thus set forth and embalmed in an official document and held up to the gaze of all the world. However holy and righteous may have been the President's intentions, this message is calculated to do the

Negro more harm than any other state paper ever issued from the White House. Construed as it was in connection with the Brownsville order and the recent Atlanta barbarities, this message seemed to accentuate the Negro's rapidly culminating ills.

With the opening of Congress the Brownsville order assumed the character of political discussion. It threatened to split in twain the triumphant Republican party. The President's closest personal and political friends felt forced to uphold his contentions, though not without apology. The Southern Democrats, with a single and grotesquely singular exception, reversed the tenor of their teachings and traditions and upheld the President in the unwarranted exercise of executive power. The aroused passion of race has twisted their immemorial political doctrine. Then came Senator Foraker, like a gallant knight of old, and stepped into the arena as the champion of the helpless and overborne. The voice of ten million Americans, unheard and unheeded in the conduct of the nation's affairs, found expression in this eloquent and fearless Ohioan. And yet not so much he proclaimed because the victims were black, but because the method employed was violative of the principles of American jurisprudence and liberty. He assumed neither the innocence nor guilt of the accused, but planted himself firmly on the bed-rock principle of the law, that a full and fair trial should precede conviction and punishment. The country and the Senate sided with Mr. Foraker, although by the nice amenities of legislative verbiage they refrained from wounding the Presidential pride. An inquiry by the Senate was ordered. In the meantime the President had dispatched a law officer to Brownsville in quest of confirmatory evidence. He found what he was sent for.

By a prudential intuition these government agents seem to divine the conclusion of the Presidential mind. His method was of the same *ex parte* character as that of the army inspector, and of course the foregone conclusion was confirmed. The President became incensed at the persistent attitude of the colored race, and in several special messages reiterated his inuendoes with redoubled vim and emphasis. Senator Foraker became the principal object of his wrath. It was rumored that at a social function, where secrecy was imposed upon all present, a personal colloquy between the two was sharp and bitter. All of this served to make Senator Foraker the hero and idol of the Negro heart. Foraker gained what Roosevelt lost. The Ohio Senator is the only commanding statesman of our day who has risked his public career on an issue involving the Negro's cause. Whatever may be the immediate outcome of the issue, he has, and will have, his reward, for no one who devotes his powers to the defense of the helpless will fail to receive the highest meed of praise when the rancor and hate of the conflict have passed away.

FORAKER, THE NEGROES' CHAMPION

Under the guidance of Senator Foraker the Senate inquiry has now proceeded for several months. At the instance of the President several eminent Republican Senators reluctantly consented to reinforce the Democrats in upholding his hand. The accused soldiers have been given a hearing. Their straightforward, manly, unwavering testimony in their own behalf has raised in the public mind a reasonable doubt of their guilt. That one hundred and sixty-seven men, ignorant and unlettered, unskilled in the art of double-tongued dialectics, should unite and persist in one straightforward tale and suffer loss of livelihood and honor without one confessing or informing voice would be the most remarkable psychological phenomenon in the history of criminal procedure.

FAR-SIGHTEDNESS AND MYOPIA

On the other hand the citizens of Brownsville have given the most positive and circumstantial evidence of guilt. These far-sighted witnesses have testified under oath that they saw these men in the act and distinguished their uniform, color, and visage at a distance of a hundred yards on a dark night, when the trained eyesight of army officers could not recognize a brother officer ten feet away. The weight of this testimony is weakened by the prepossessions of the witness as well as by its inherent incredibility. Aroused race passion is as heedless of fact as it is of reason and logic. It blunts the physical as well as the moral sense. For any white citizen of Brownsville to say one word contradictory of the popular prejudice means permanent banishment or sure and sudden death. The wealthiest man of the town was assassinated because he had the temerity to question the accuracy of certain of this testimony. Had these Springfield rifles in the hands of men who have never failed to use them when ordered by their commanders proved less dissuasive from violence, and had half a dozen Negro soldiers been lynched on the broadest street of Brownsville in broad daylight, neither the army inspector, nor the President's law officer, nor the Senate committee could have found a single citizen who was able to see such happenings under the bright sunlight of a Texas sky. These same citizens with far-sighted vision in the gloom of night would have developed suddenly cases of myopia that could not distinguish objects of their own handling in open day.   The rule works both ways.   A witness who will not see that which he does not want to see can easily compound for the failure by seeing things which do not exist in obedience to the demand of prejudice or passion.

The Senate Committee, after prolonged and exhaustive inquiry, brought in a majority report upholding the President's contention as to the guilt of the accused soldiers, with a strong dissentient minority report under the leadership of Senator Foraker.   The majority findings were made possible by the solid vote of the Southern members of the committee, whose attitude, it is not unjust to say, had no relation to the judicial merits of the case under inquiry. The minority party often assumes the privilege of casting their vote so as to produce the greatest political embarrassment to the responsible majority. That the vote of these Southern Senators was prompted by racial and political motives and was wholly void of ethical or judicial weight, is seen from the fact that they voted at one time with Foraker to embarrass the administration and at another time, on the same measure, they voted with the administration to embarrass Foraker.

Before the report of the committee could be presented to the Senate, President Roosevelt, by one of his surprising strategic strokes, proclaimed his " vindication," and proposed, through the unsearchable depth of administrative mercy, that the accused might be restored to the service if they could convince him of their innocence.   These dismissed and dishonored soldiers might be remanded, not for trial, but for reconsideration of sentence, if they could prove their innocence in the estimation of the man who had served as their judge and executioner and had denounced them in the utmost vehemence of language as murderers and criminal conspirators. Senator Foraker aptly characterized this recommendation as " the most remarkable proposition ever submitted to a civilized legislature."

As the matter now stands before the bar of public opinion, this black battalion is at least entitled to a Scotch verdict—" not proven." There is all but a universal concurrence in this verdict except among those whose racial sentiment renders them incapable of considering the case with judicial calmness and poise. But whatever may finally be proved as to the guilt or innocence of some or all of these men, they have not received a " square deal " at the hands of its author, who borrowed the phrase from the gaming table and consecrated it to a higher and worthier ideal.

This affair has shaken the prestige of the President as has no other occurrence in his public career. It gives him no end of keen concern. There is every reason to believe that he could wish the deed undone. He has sought to conciliate the Negro with the blandishment of office, but to no avail. With the double view of disconcerting Foraker and reconciling the colored brother, at the psychological moment, when the Ohio Senator was booked to make a strategic move in the Brownsville affair, announcement was made of the intention to appoint a colored citizen to the leading Federal office in the Senator's own State and home city. But as this move seemed to embarrass the President's own friends, including his son-in-law, as much as it did the offending Senator, it was abandoned. But not to be outdone, on the day of the evening that Senator Foraker was announced to sound the keynote of his position in a speech to his constituents, the Associated Press announced to the country that Ralph W. Tyler, a worthy colored citizen of Ohio, had been appointed Auditor of the Treasury Department at Washington. But this conspicuous appointment had not the slightest effect upon racial sentiment, except to intensify it against the President. A nice young man got a nice fat office without changing the attitude of a single Negro in or out of Ohio. The whole race is wounded and sore. There is no division of sentiment. Never before has there been such unanimity. The balm of office cannot heal it. Even the colored members of the President's official household can only preserve a prudent and salutary silence.

When Senator Foraker found that he was unable to get through Congress a simple measure of justice to the dismissed soldiers against the united opposition of the South and the President's personal supporters in his own party, by a skillful parliamentary move, he had the whole issue deferred until after the pending presidential election. A considerable fraction of the Negro voters in the North and West will undoubtedly desert the Republican party on account of the stubborn attitude of the President. This may result in the defeat of his party and of the policies which bear his personal brand. So great a matter the Brownsville fire kindleth.

THE NEGRO'S JUST GRIEVANCE

There has recently appeared a cartoon by a clever Negro artist representing the " Black Man's Burden." It is in the form of a cross, not a crown of thorns, but a cross of skulls. At the top of the vertical upright is the head of Roosevelt; Hoke

Smith and Tom Watson are arranged underneath; on the left of the crosspiece are Thomas Dixon and John Temple Graves; on the right, Tillman and Vardaman. An athletic Negro with broken body is bowed beneath this awful load. Theodore Roosevelt, America's most passionate civil patriot, whose every impulse beats in sympathetic resonance with the welfare and betterment of the nation, who had stood firmly by the Negro at Charleston and Indianola, and who had proclaimed to the race the gospel of a "square deal" and an open door, is placed as chief among those who breathe out hatred and slaughter against the Negro with every vital breath. It is the law of human passion that friendship which lapses or seems to lapse begets the bitterest hate. The good deeds are forgotten; the hurtful act rankles in the soul. A deliberate and candid judgment would declare this attitude unjust; but it would be equally uncandid to deny that it is real.

President Roosevelt is easily the most popular man in America. The whites who join issue with him on the Brownsville incident regard it as a thing apart. With the Negro it overshadows all else. With a consenting nod he could have been re-elected President almost by acclamation. Not only so, but he is easily the foremost man of all the world to-day. Had the Peace Congress while sitting at The Hague ushered in Tennyson's prophesied "Parliament of man, the Federation of the world," Roosevelt, by unanimous consent of the participating nations, would have been chosen speaker of this world-controlling body. And yet he has so wounded his colored fellow-citizens that to-day they stand apart from this world acclaim. As he treads the dizzy highway of universal fame, he must feel a certain sad, unsatisfied something prompting him to become reconciled to his black brother who may justly have aught against him.

THE EVERLASTING STAIN

THE EVERLASTING STAIN

BY

KELLY MILLER

HOWARD UNIVERSITY, WASHINGTON, D. C.

THE ASSOCIATED PUBLISHERS
WASHINGTON, D. C.

PRINTED IN THE UNITED STATES OF AMERICA

CONTENTS

PREFACE

The essays in this collection center about the issues growing out of the World War and the Negro's relation to them. Several of the titles have appeared in separate pamphlet form and as magazine articles. The reader will note that the articles are presented as of date of writing. There appear some duplications, due to the fact that the productions herein assembled were prepared for various occasions.

KELLY MILLER.

INTRODUCTION

For nearly a generation Kelly Miller has been the Negro's chief intellectual protagonist. Others have formulated programs, peddled nostrums and elaborated panaceas; but he, dealing with the concrete issues, has conducted our defenses. It is true that from the point of view of the theorist he has seemed to shift from position to position—one has not the choice of position in defensive combat. Now upon one frontier, now upon the other as the issues of attack have shifted, he has been found in valiant logical defense. His very virtuosity in this has often been judged a fault: with an ax for every occasion he has at times seemed to be chiefly engaged in sharpening his own wits. But there is more than the edge of practice upon the sharp and readymindedness of this man; there is the edge of science and in his heart there has always been a loyalty of a feudal kind and degree to the interests of his race. Here in this volume are gathered together not merely the sundry whitlings of the fray, but some of the substantial rail-splitting which has cleared obstruction from our racial path and made clearings where there were forests, and roads where there was but jungle growth of misunderstanding and folly. Nor has it been solely a struggle against natural circumstances and natural enemies; in advance of others and with the courage of promptness, Kelly Miller has entered single-handed many an ambush of hostile cunning, intrigue and hate, and has emerged with unscathed sanity and a more or less notorious scalp.

Centered as they have been upon the transitory phases and issues of the race problems, Professor Miller's writings would inevitably pay the usual penalty of the polemic—a lusty youth and an early grave, but for two redeeming traits—style and comprehensiveness. The style of his essays is a conceded and well-known fact. What is not so generally realized this collection should especially make manifest— that is, the historically representative character of his work as year by year it has followed and registered the changing issues of the discussion of race within his generation. They constitute from decade to decade a history of the discussion of the problem. They register first of all the shift from the purely theoretical discussion of the late reconstruction period to the practical scientific analysis and statistical comparison of today. They trace the successive levels of

interest upon which the race problem has rested
from the moralistic and theological to the political, from that to the ethnological, from that
again to the sociological, and then to the educational and economic planes upon which most of
our contemporary discussion rests. One can
nowhere find so complete a history of thought
on the Negro question during the period covered
as that contained in Professor Miller's four
volumes of published essays—*Race Adjustment,* 1908; *Out of the House of Bondage,* 1912;
Appeal to Conscience, 1916, and the present
title, *The Everlasting Stain.* As through a long
line of canal locks, this heavy laden barge of
controversy has passed until now it seems in
the advent of the discussion of race as a world
issue and problem to have reached the sea upon
which it must meet its final buffetings and perhaps its final haven of rest.

Oddly enough the discussion of today finds
itself back to a theoretical phase. When the
moral issues lapsed in the decline of the aboli-
tionist spirit and interest and the idealistic
yielded to the social pragmatism of Booker
Washington—who, by the way, is more aptly interpreted in Professor Miller's short essay than
in the several extant volumes of biography put
together—it seemed that the theoretical aspect
of the problem was permanently obscured.

Throughout this moral and idealistic eclipse, however, Kelly Miller has held up the lamp of reason, and during the ebb of indifference has confidently predicted the return of the moral and theoretical flood-tide of interest and concern. This has now come about, and we find the appeal to reason and the appeal to conscience more possible and more hopeful than perhaps ever before.

One will instinctively ask two questions as the touchstones of such work as is represented in these essays. First, has there been consistency—and then, what is the proposed solution? As to the first there has been polemical versatility of an almost too casuistic sort, but back of it a redeeming moral consistency which has always championed the right and condemned the wrong. There has been, of course, as is proper for an approach essentially intellectualistic, the tendency to see and even to state both sides. The workmanship has therefore been sound. And then as to the solution, there has been a singularly consistent and almost unpopular insistence on the solvent of reason. One might almost regard Kelly Miller as a belated rationalist of the eighteenth century or a Jesuit strayed from the cloisters into the arena, but for his very modern and practical preoccupations. He believes in the essential efficiency of reason and common sense. Surely he can scarcely be said to have had any creed beyond "A man's a man for a' that" or any formula on the race question except two and two are four. And, after all, if there is to be any solution to social problems can we afford to abandon the hope in reason tempered with sanity and common sense, and in a not over-sentimental humanism?

ALLAIN LEROY LOCKE, PH.D.,
Professor of Philosophy, Howard University.

July, 1923.

THE EVERLASTING STAIN

CHAPTER I

THE EVERLASTING STAIN

A dying and desperate political party clutches at the straw of race hatred as its last gasping hope. Bourbon democracy is true to its ruling passion strong in death. The crafty politician psychologized the public, and felt assured that the cry of Negro blood would throw it into a spasm of delirium. The infamy of this taint was deemed to be more detestable than the murderous brand upon the forehead of Cain. It was thought to outweigh in public estimation the entire catalog of intellectual, moral and political virtues. To charge an American with murder would be a mild accusation as compared to this.

The time was set with dramatic cleverness. The iron must be struck while it is hot. There must be no margin of time to refute the charge or to reconcile public sentiment. The cry of "Wolf! Wolf!" on first alarm, stampedes the crowd, even if there be no wolf. But the bun-

1

gling dastard did not know his game. Righteous
strategy triumphed over dastardly cunning.
With amazing celerity of action the charge was
refuted as soon as made. The dastardly deed
redounds to the shame of the doer. Never before, and let us hope, never again, will any political party sink to such a low level of infamy.
"Blessed are ye when men shall revile you, and
say all manner of evil against you falsely."
With righteous indignation against the methods
of the character assassin, the American people
with all but one voice swept Harding into the
White House, assured that his purity of blood
was as unblemished as his spotlessness of character. The country is safe, the Republican
party is victorious, and the honor of the white
race is secure.

But what of the Negro? Is he supposed to be
endowed with ordinary human pride and sensibilities? To him the defense is, if anything,
more insulting than the attack. Why should it
be considered more heinous than any crime to
possess a trace of Negro blood? I doubt
whether any race since human civilization began, has ever been placed under any such ban
of opprobrium. It is the boast of statesmen and
of men of renown that they carry in their veins
a blend of Indian blood. But one drop that
flows from African veins vitiates ten times its

own volume of any other strain. Against this assumption the Negro rebels with all the ardor and indignation of which his nature is capable. Can the Negro be expected to share in the derogation of his own blood? Is his color of his own choosing? He is wholly guiltless of the stain for which he is stigmatized.

Pigmentation affects the color of the body, but not the equality of the soul. Were Dumas, Douglass, and Dunbar accursed of God and unworthy of honor and esteem because of their sable hue? Shall we be expected to give a higher meed of glory to Plato and Shakespeare and Jesus because their skins were white? Perish the thought! Such self-abasement would compromise the Negro's self-respect and hypothecate all hope.

The Ten Commandments assure us that the Father of all races and breeds of man visits the sins of the fathers upon the children unto the third and fourth generation of them that hate, but shows mercy unto thousands of them that love. The Constitution of the United States forbids the attaint of blood, so that the political and legal sins of the fathers may not be visited upon the children. Must the Negro of all men stand doomed to eternal infamy from the foundation of the world unto the end of time?

There can be no satisfactory solution of the

race problem while this notion prevails. In the face of its inexorable exactions, our palliatives and programs are as ineffectual as the application of emollients to the hopeless consumptive. From the inherent sense of self-respect and in vindication of the essential claims of humanity, the Negro must insist that his blood is as good as any which courses through human veins.

CHAPTER II

RADICALISM AND THE NEGRO

Revolution accelerates evolution. Gradual advance is expedited by epochal upheavals. Social progress is wrought through change. Stability begets stagnation. Perfection is an ideal of perpetual approximation. Traditional values must ever and anon be restated in terms of contemporaneous demands.

The world today is in process of radical readjustment. The relationship of the rich and the poor, the laborer and the overlord of labor, the strong and the weak, the white and the non-white races of men, must be adjusted in harmony with the progressive spirit of the times. The germ of the new idealism has inoculated the blood of the world and thrown it into throes of delirium. The social fabric is being battered with the shocks of doom. Riot and revolution are rife. Action and reaction are always equal, but in opposite directions. The whole creation groaneth until now. It is the travail of the new birth.

5

WORLD RESTLESSNESS

The World War has upset everything, and, so far, has settled nothing. The upset world must now be set to rights. Germany has been physically overpowered but not inwardly conquered. Her tough Teutonic spirit has not been broken. She is writhing under the sting of defeat, and planning troubles anew. Russia is in the hands of the riotous "Reds." France is trembling in the balance of insecurity. Italy is dominated by the Socialists. The Laborites in England are waiting the next election for a conceded victory. The fate of the British Empire will soon fall into the hands of a class unaccustomed to exercise power and domination. Neutral states are not immune from internal confusion. The Balkan States are breathing out hatred and slaughter. China and Japan are pitted against each other by connivance of the white man's cunning to divide and control. Ireland is in revolt against the tyranny of Anglo-Saxon dominion. Egypt and India are dreaming of the hour when they shall be able to throw off the yoke of British overlordship. There is no abatement of customary turbulence in the South American Republics. The United States is seething with internal turmoil and confusion. Labor is all but ready to try conclusions with capital. We have seen the Labor unions shake the finger of defiance in the face of the Government, and wrest the demanded concessions. The advice and counsel of the President of the United States have been flouted, and his good offices and kindly suggestions rejected with scorn. The decree of the courts has been regarded as little more than a scrap of paper. Strikes everywhere abound. We have seen race riots raging along Pennsylvania Avenue, the national thoroughfare which runs from the Capitol where the laws are made to the White House where they are supposed to be executed. Surely the times are out of joint.

Surface sores are but the outward manifestations of inner disease. The scourge of war with its grewsome toll of blood and treasure was not the cause but the consequence of world-wide social dissatisfaction and unrest. Indeed the war in all probability relieved the severity of the shock. The upheaval might have come with greater suddenness and virulence had not the war intervened. The violent cough is the outcome of the irritation of the lungs. Sagacious statesmanship, both in Europe and America, clearly foresaw the coming of the evil day. William Jennings Bryan, like blind Cassandra, prophesied its coming, but none would believe him. Theodore Roosevelt was the greatest

American who has lived since Lincoln died. Through clear foresight and courageous conservatism he staid the revolution for half a generation.

WOODROW WILSON AND THE NEGRO

The late Woodrow Wilson believed that he could hold a restless world in poise by the soothing balm of pleasing phraseology. His single-track, double-acting mind moved with equal celerity, sometimes with and sometimes against the onsweeping current which he sought to guide and control. He was no whit abashed at the tangle of moral paradoxes in which he frequently found himself enmeshed. He followed the lead of events only long enough to gauge their tendency and trend in order that he might make himself appear to guide them. He frequently reversed his course, and proceeded to the new goal with utter disregard of logical sequence or ethical consistency. It is utterly impossible to tell whether he underwent a genuine conversion of heart or a prudent shift of mind. The same lack of consecutiveness and consistency appeared in every great issue which he was called upon to handle. Elected the first time upon a platform which condemned renomination, he accepted a second term, and connived at a third with convenient forgetfulness. He forced his party to change its declared attitude on the Panama Canal by threats of calamity which he alone foresaw. Habitually opposed to national female suffrage, after the propaganda had gained significant proportions, as belated entrant, he then outran the other disciples. He kept the nation out of war while the presidential campaign was on, and without additional provocation plunged it into war when the election was over. After Germany had committed every atrocity with which she has subsequently been charged, he issued a proclamation to the American people urging them to refrain from discussing the moral issues involved lest they disturb the serenity and composure of the German mind. At first an ardent advocate of the Washington policy of no entangling foreign alliances, he sat at the head of the Council Table and tied his country to alliances which are unentangleable. The apostle of new freedom for mankind ignored its application to the freedom in America. The high priest of democracy in Germany became the obligated beneficiary of oligarchy in Georgia. He played at peace and war successively with Huerta, Villa and Carranza, and yet our Southern neighbor remained untranquillized and defiant. In one breath he declared that politics should be adjourned during the progress of the war, with another he urged the country to return a Democratic Congress as more easily pliant to his imperious will. As head of the nation he congratulated the Republican Governor of Massachusetts upon his victorious stand for law and order, and as head of the Democratic Party he felicitated the successful Governor of his own State and party, who won the election on the declaration that he would make the nation as wet as water, thus subverting all law and order. The highest world exponent of derived powers, he swiftly overleaped all precedents in the assumption of unauthorized power. Elected President of the United States, he made himself the chief magistrate of mankind. He reversed the world motto; his charity began abroad rather than at home. He believed in democracy for humanity but not for Mississippi. Abraham Lincoln's gospel of freedom was immediate; Woodrow Wilson's was remote. The one believed in the freedom of the Negro; the other in the freedom of nations. President Lincoln wrought for the United States of America, Woodrow Wilson for the United States of the World. The former never uttered one insincere or uncertain word; the utterances of the latter rarely escape the imputation of moral ambiguity. By marvelous assumption of superior insight, he propounded preachments and compounded idealistic theories as infallible solvents of all social ills. He retired into the secrecy of his inner consciousness and evolved his famous Fourteen Points—the new "tetra decalogue," which he was the first to violate and ignore. The advocate of open covenants openly arrived at proceeded to the Peace Conference enshrouded in the sacredness and secrecy of Sinai, and returned with the League of Nations written upon the tablet of his own conception with the finger of finality. Although the newly conceived League of Nations transcends the Constitution and Declaration of Independence, "anathema, maranatha" be upon the head of that impious statesman who would add or subtract one jot or one tittle from the law oracularly vouchsafed by the ordained lawgiver of the world.

President Wilson was indeed the greatest phrase-maker of his age, although each preceding phrase was apt to have its meaning nullified by a quickly succeeding one. "The Nations should be permitted to shed all the blood they please"; "we are too proud to fight"; "there must be peace without victory," have already taken their places in the limbo of innocuous desuetude. Such lofty expressions as "to make the world safe for democracy"; "overridden peoples must have a voice in the governments which they uphold''; ''the only way to stop men from agitation against grievances is to remove the grievances'' still await vindication in light of sanctioned and condoned practices. To the Negro these phrases seemed to possess the sinister suggestion of hollow mockery under the guise of holy democracy. Mr. Wilson would strengthen the chain by ignoring the weakest links. His abstract doctrine broke down at the point of concrete application. The Negro question, the most aggravating moral issue of American life, was avoided or thrust aside as hopelessly impossible. He handled this issue with less positiveness and moral aggression than any president since James Buchanan. Under pressure of political exigency or military exaction he indited several of his customary notes on this question, but their lukewarmness indicated that they might have been written with the left hand as the easiest riddance of a disagreeable issue. On promise of political support, he pledged Bishop Walters the full recognition of the Negro's claims. Shortly after election he sent the name of a Negro as Register of the Treasury. His Southern partisans protested. The nomination was withdrawn. The promise was ignored. It must be said that the President's change of attitude or shift of mind was usually in the di-

rection of progress, aggression and courage; on
the Negro question it was in the direction of timidity, negation, and reaction. President Wilson
appeared to be at once the greatest radical and
the greatest conservator of the age. Under
such leadership the American people—white
and black—had to face the issues which then
confronted the world.

The Old Order and the New

But the struggle grows apace. No man can
move very far forward or backward the hand
of the clock of time. The fullness of the hour
has come; the conflict is irrepressible. A better
dispensation is at hand. Human relations must
be adjusted on the broad basis of righteousness
and brotherhood. Shall the process of adjustment be peaceful or violent? Can the old bottle
hold the new wine? Can the tree of liberty be
saved by pruning away the dead limbs or must
the ax be laid at the root of the tree? The awful
sacrifice of the past six years will have been in
vain unless it results in a securer fabric of social order than the one that has been shaken
down. The new order must be ushered in; the
old order must pass away. The passing régime,
based upon the divine right of kings, the ava-
rice of power and the arrogance of race, dies
hard. The new order must rest upon liberty,

fraternity, equality for all the children of men. Conservatism is the inertia of human nature. An imparted impulse tends to move forever unaccelerated in speed and unmodified in direction. Innovation is universally denounced and condemned. Tradition is the dead hand of human progress.

Despite the terrible ordeal through which the world has just passed, there is a persistent tendency to revert to the previously existing status in government and social polity. The vanquished nations may enter the kingdom of freedom ahead of the victorious allies. Realignment in Germany is moving more rapidly than in England, and with amazing illogicality adheres to the exploded tradition of King and hereditary class. America, with scarcely less blind devotion, bows down to the idols of the past. Standards and methods of a hundred years ago cannot fix the guidance of the people to the end of days. The fathers laid the foundation on the eternal bedrock, but left the structure uncompleted. The war has not yet wrought a radical change in the heart of the nation. The old ideals still seek to perpetuate themselves. The Civil War radically readjusted social opinion and conduct; but the World War so far has brought forth only vacuous phraseology. The old spirit still persists with stubbornness. The nations are vying with each other in selfishness and greed. The world is held in equilibrium by the parallelogram of forces rather than the paragon of principles. The strong exploit the weak; the rich oppress the poor; the white lord it over the black, the yellow and the brown.

The belabored League of Nations, which Mr. Wilson relied upon with amazing optimism to cure all human ills from militarism to the measles, is based upon the dominance of five great powers over a score of weaker ones. England still holds Ireland, Egypt and India in the clutches of her overlordship. The United States has a strangle-hold upon Hayti and San Domingo, Japan insists upon supremacy in the Orient. France demands the spoils of victory. Britannia still rules the waves. Labor is still interpreted in terms of money rather than manhood. The laborer is besought to be satisfied with whatever the generous overlord, who exploits his labor, may graciously dole out to him in the form of wages or under the guise of philanthropy. The Negro is expected to resume his wonted place of inferiority as if he had not felt the moral energy and self-elation of the new awakening. The world has been bathed in blood, but not baptized with the spirit. Religion has functioned, but feebly. The church has looked on with pitiful impotency, while every principle which it professed has been trampled under foot. The voice of conscience has been crying in the wilderness with no language but a cry. No great leader in church or state has yet arisen with moral virility to meet the new demand. Archaic platitudes and worn-out moral maxims will not cope with the new situation. The doles of charity will profit but little. There must be quickened a keener appreciation of the inherency of the manhood of man. All programs of reconstruction not based on this conception are but soothing syrup to relieve the delirium; leaving the internal malady untouched.

BOLSHEVISM

The one distinctive dispensation which has come out of the conflict, decisively different from existing conditions, appears in Russia. The new philosophy proclaims that those who work with the hand shall exercise exclusive right to rule. This is a radical departure from the aristocratic theory wherein those who work with the hand were excluded from participation in government. Bolshevism is the antithesis of autocracy. It is democracy run mad. The pendulum swings with equal ease to either extreme and finally rests at the middle point. The true order of things lies midway between

Russia under Nicholas, the Czar, and Russia under Trotzky and Lenin, the ruthless Radicals. Bolshevism has thrown the world into a spasm of convulsion for fear its example might become contagious and imperil the foundation upon which social order rests. The first effect of release from autocracy is, naturally enough, extreme experiment in democracy. The Russian peasants being crushed for centuries under the iron heel of tyranny, are over-elated with the first taste of self-direction. Liberty is the medium between license and oppression. Moderation is the golden mean between the extremes of indulgence and deprivation. The term Bolshevism, etymologically considered, means the rule of the majority and it is equivalent to democracy in the Russian tongue. Menshevism, the rule of the minority, corresponds to the detested term, oligarchy, in the English speech. The world extols democracy and detests oligarchy; but when these expressions are translated into Russian speech and practice, the feeling is reversed. The rule of the majority in Massachusetts is called democracy; the rule of the majority in Mississippi would be condemned as Bolshevism. We should not allow ourselves to be frightened at a phrase. It is not the word itself that disturbs the world, but rather the abuse in the hands of radical expounders who would push it to the verge of unmitigated madness. We are reminded of the attitude of the European monarchies when the democratic spirit began to exert itself a hundred and a half years ago. Conservative thought and feeling of that day believed that it threatened the stability of social order and was destructive of accumulated values of all generations that had gone before. The old monarchies bound themselves in alliances, holy and unholy, to stamp out the doctrine of democracy which threatened the destruction of the world order. History repeats itself. Order will rise out of chaos.

The denunciation of Bolshevism rests upon the familiar charge that when government is placed in the hands of the peasant class without traditional inhibition and self-restraint, it will inevitably pull down the Temple of Liberty and Justice, involving all in common ruin. This argument is parallel in every particular to the justification for the overthrow of reconstruction governments in the South. The French Revolution passed through the same range of experiences. Majority controlling a complex constituency always entails serious difficulties. Its seeming failure is always greatly exaggerated and ridiculed and condemned in terms of loud denunciation.

MACAULAY ON LIBERTY

Lord Macaulay declares: "The final fruition
and permanent fruits of Liberty are wisdom,
moderation and mercy. Its immediate effects
are often atrocious crimes, conflicting errors,
skepticism on points the most clear, dogmatism
on points the most mysterious. It is just at this
crisis that its enemies love to exhibit it. They
pull down the scaffold from the half-finished
edifice. They point to the flying dust, falling
bricks and comfortless homes, and frightful ir-
regularity of the old appearance and then ask
with scorn where the promised splendor and
comfort are to be found. There is only one cure
for the evils which newly acquired freedom produces. That cure is more *freedom*.

"Many politicians of our time are in the
habit of laying it down as a self-evident proposition that no people ought to be free till they
are fit to use freedom. The maxim is worthy of
the fool in the old story who resolved not to go
into the water till he learned to swim. If men
are to wait for liberty till they become wise
and good in slavery, they may indeed wait forever.

"Ariosto tells a story of a fairy who by some
mysterious law of her nature was condemned to
appear at a certain season in the form of a foul

and poisonous snake. Those who injured her
during the period of her disguise were forever
excluded from participation in the blessing
which she bestowed; but to those who in spite
of her loathsome aspect pitied and protected
her, she afterward revealed herself in the beautiful and celestial form which was natural to
her, accompanied their steps, granted all their
wishes, filled their houses with wealth, made
them happy in love and victorious in war. Such
is the spirit of liberty. At times she takes the
form of an atrocious reptile. She grovels, she
hisses, she stings, but woe to those who in disgust shall venture to crush her! And happy
are those who having dared to receive her in
her degraded and frightful shape, at last shall
be rewarded by her in the time of her beauty
and her glory.''

The world today might well take this lesson
to heart as it applies to the retarded and belated
peoples of all lands struggling to set themselves
free. American institutions have nothing to
fear from this neo-democracy which for the moment is delirious in the first flush of release
from an intolerable tyranny. There is no
ground in America upon which Bolshevism may
grow. Our people are too intelligent and understand too well the beneficence of free institutions. Our danger lies in failure to live up

to the platform of our own principles. The
best way to make vice odious is by making virtue odorous. We will most surely discredit the
vices of Bolshevism by exemplifying the virtues
of Democracy. Our Ship of State, if kept
headed straight to the Haven of Liberty, will
weather every gale.

COMMON CAUSE OF AGGRIEVED GROUPS

The American Negro, representing a suppressed and aggrieved class, cannot be incu-
rious or indifferent to the effort which any
struggling people is making to throw off the
yoke of tyranny and oppression. He has no interest in or sympathy for Bolshevism or any
other radical doctrine excepting so far as it may
seem to suggest relief from existing evils. It
is perfectly natural for any new propaganda
to seek support among the dissatisfied groups
wherever they may be found. The greatest reformer of all time appealed to the restless, the
despised, the rejected and the aggrieved peoples
of his day: "Come unto me all ye that labor
and are heavy laden and I will give you rest."
The French nation during the American Revolution encouraged the colonists to revolt
against the mother country and helped them to
throw off the yoke of oppression. Lafayette
and Washington joined forces because of a

common grievance against England. The descendants of these glorious heroes joined hands with the descendants of their ancient foe, by reason of the common grievance against Germany. The German nation, logically enough, sought to encourage Irish revolt against Great Britain and met with hospitable reception. The hanging of an Irish peer with a silken cord may put an end to the unholy alliance, but not to the deep-seated grievances of the irrepressible Celt. The Germans also sought to foster dissatisfaction among American Negroes because of the alleged grievances against democracy's illogical attitude towards them, but the seed fell on stony ground. President Wilson, supposing that the German people entertained grievances against the Prussian autocracy, advised them to join with him to rid themselves of their tyrannical government, but subsequent events proved that he failed to fathom the Teuton's deep-seated love for overlordship.

There is a widespread belief that the Bolsheviki of Russia are disseminating their doctrine among the American Negroes and are finding converts among them. A new propaganda is always persuasive in its promises to the oppressed to whom it appeals. The Bolsheviki of Russia have made an American Negro a Cabinet officer under the Soviet Government. This

is in striking contrast with our Democratic
Policy, which accords no Negro an office of first-
class importance, although this Government is
supported and upheld by ten million loyal
people of this race. The Socialists and Industrial Workers of the World, it is said, are making overtures to the Negro workingman by holding out more flattering considerations than
those which he received at the hand of organized labor. Any new party is apt to write a better platform than an old one. Political parties
degenerate in moral quality and tone when they
are harnessed with concrete responsibilities.
These appeals will find little lodgment in the
mind of the Negro. His conservative nature
makes him for a long time bear the ills which
he has before flying to those which he knows
not of. There are doubtless a few minds of the
race to whom such doctrine might appeal. This
is not surprising for there are many white
Americans, native and foreign-born, who give
hospitable ear to the new doctrine. In every
race there are to be found men of a certain type
of moral temper and mental oddity who will be
swayed by the wind of any new doctrine; but
the wind of false doctrine will pass away with
its own blowing. There would be no Negro
radicals if the wise policy were pursued by those
who would vindicate the beneficence of Ameri-

can institutions for all the peoples who are true
and loyal to them. If the American people
would only follow the advice of President Wilson, "the only way to stop men from agitation
against grievances is to remove the grievances," there would not be found a single one
of the ten million of this race in the ranks of
restlessness and discontent.

ALIEN PROPAGANDA AMONG NEGROES

It is the policy of cunning to make a doctrine
detestable by casting odium upon its advocates.
It appears that the leaders in this new agitation against existing order are recruited in
large part from the ranks of dissatisfied foreigners who do not understand or appreciate
the beneficence of American institutions. They
fly from the oppression of the old world to the
freedom of the new; but abuse the asylum which
offers them shelter and protection. America
cannot be expected to receive hospitably foreign radicals who would destroy the house that
gives them shelter. Insidious attempt is being
made to align the Negro with the restless and
dissatisfied foreigners, a thing which would at
once deprive him of the tolerance which he has
always received because of his unfaltering patriotism and loyalty, whatever the circumstances of his lot. But it does not require the

persuasion of the Bolsheviki to make the Negro dissatisfied with injustice. He does not need the advice of the Industrial Workers of the World to feel keenly the sting of industrial discrimination. No foreign propaganda is required to cause him to denounce Jim Crow cars. His feelings are not so numb that he must await the urgency of Socialism to make him cry aloud against lynching. Such supposition would prove the Negro is not a normal human being and does not voluntarily feel the sting of cruelty, injustice and wrong which should meet with universal condemnation. It used to be thought that the Negro, if left to himself without outside intermeddlers, would be satisfied with any condition that might be imposed upon him. That day is past. His self-insurgency of spirit rebels. But if external stimulus were necessary to excite a quickened sense of resentment and resistance to the iniquities which he suffers, it need not be looked for in the plausible and specious pleas of the Bolsheviki, Industrial Workers of the World, or the propaganda of native or foreign Socialists. He absorbs it from the new atmosphere which the World War has created. President Wilson became the mouthpiece of the new freedom of humanity. His high declarations quickened the spirit of resentment and resistance of every aggrieved group in the world.

SUPPRESSION OF FREE SPEECH

Attempt is made to throttle the expression of dissatisfaction on the part of the Negro against the wrong and injustice which he suffers. A proposition has been made on the floor of Congress to shut off free speech of the Negroes who would give vent to their just complaints. It must be conceded that in times of war the Government has the right to commandeer the life, property, and the conscience of the people in order to save itself from destruction. Beyond this, universal experience proves that the suppression of complaint against grievances is the very best way to advertise them. During the anti-slavery controversy the South used every endeavor to shut out freedom of speech. The detested agitators were bodily banished. *Uncle Tom's Cabin* and other literature baring the evils of slavery were forbidden circulation; but such prohibition did not prohibit full and free discussion of the merits of that moral issue. William Lloyd Garrison, the chief apostle of freedom, went so far as to denounce the Constitution as being "a covenant with death and an agreement with hell." For such assertion today, he might be given free passage

on the ark of the Soviets or lodged in jail with
Eastman and Debs. But the result of free discussion was to vindicate the integrity of the
Constitution, and to purge it of this alleged evil
alliance. Any attempt to limit free speech on
the part of the Negro, except for the purposes
of war, would merely serve to make martyrs of
those whose voice is suppressed and further
disseminate the doctrine which they declare.
The best way to promote any doctrine is by
persecution and martyrdom.

Kindness and Cruelty

The Negro's soul is prepared soil for the
sowing of good seed which quickly takes root
and springs forth into abundant harvest, but
the seed of destruction and discord finds un-
congenial reception. Denmark Vesey and Nat
Turner had few followers and no successors.
On the other hand, the seed of the Christian religion found Negro nature a congenial soil
where, without cultivation, it has grown into
luxuriant harvest. The Negro masses can
easily be aroused to frenzy by religious or patriotic appeal, but respond very slowly—if at
all—to the appeal of hatred, animosity and revenge. The race is slow to anger and plenteous
in mercy. The Department of Justice would
more effectively perform its function by using

strenuous endeavor to secure justice for the Negro rather than by trying to stop his complaint against injustice.

RADICALS AND CONSERVATIVES

Since time began, mankind has been divided into two groups of temperament—the radical and the conservative. The radical is habitually dissatisfied with the existing order and seeks change through revolution. He would rather prove all things than to hold fast to what is good. The conservative is disposed to be content with things as they are and deprecates effort at reform. Social progress is the resultant of these two conflicting tendencies. In the fundamental sense, there are comparatively few Negro radicals. The Negro nature possesses the conservatism of inertia. Some Negroes are cautious, while others are courageous in the expression of their conservatism. The cautious conservative believes in amelioration through moderate modification, as distinguished from the radical who advocates change for the love of innovation. The Negro who is content with existing conditions is a satisfied simpleton, while the Negro who advocates the destructive radicalism is a distracted idiot. Before the World War, the race leadership was divided into two hostile camps based upon quiescence on the one side and assertion on the other. There never has been a Negro conservative in the sense of satisfaction with existing status, but merely in the sense of prudential silence in the face of wrong. All right-minded Negroes everywhere and at all times must want equal and impartial laws, equally and impartially applied. Any other attitude is simply unthinkable. Every Negro today who is using his brain above the dead level of a livelihood is pronounced in demanding the full measure of manhood rights. He would not be a worthy American if this were not so. Any individual or group of individuals who are willing to accept without protest less than the fullness of the stature of American citizenship is not fit material for the new order of things now about to be ushered in. The leaders of any suppressed people should speak boldly, even though they be ambassadors in bonds. It is not impossible for the Negro to be courageous and sensible at the same time. He must recognize conditions which he may not be able to overcome, but he must not let such conditions cow his spirit or sour his soul.

THE VOICE OF THE NEGRO

The highest function of the higher education of the Negro is not merely to produce a set of

educated automatons who can ply a handicraft
or practice a profession with creditable cleverness, but to develop a class of men who can state
the case and plead the cause of the masses in
terms of persuasive speech and literary power.
Their voice should not be controlled or constrained by any outside coercion. Their attitude must be candid and courageous if they
would fulfill the high function of interpreting
to the world the feelings, hopes and aspirations
of the people who look to them for leadership
and direction. Every institution of learning,
North and South, has produced its quota of
leading Negroes who are now insisting upon the
fulfillment of the Declaration of Independence
and the Constitution of the United States.
This courageous attitude is shown by Trotter
of Harvard; Dubois of Fisk and Harvard; the
Grimkes of Lincoln; Frazier Miller and Murphy of Howard; Johnson and Hershaw of Atlanta; Ferris and Whaley of Yale; Hurst and
Ransom of Wilberforce; Pickens of Talledega
and Yale; Daly of Cornell; Abbott of Hampton;
Brawley of Morehouse; and Barber and Owen
of Virginia-Union. It is no reflection to say
that those Negroes today who take any other
public attitude are operating on a lower level
of moral courage and intellectual understanding, and are moved by motives of thrift or con-

straint of prudence. This spirit is not limited to the educated Negro, but pervades the entire mass of the race—the man between the plow-handles, the mechanic applying his tools, the miner in the bowels of the earth, the waiter standing behind the chair while his white lord and master sits at meat, the barber with his razor, the menial in the humblest service—all feel and are actuated by the same spirit, and are moved by the same impulse. Although they may not be able to give voice to the sentiment which they feel, they quickly respond when it is expressed and interpreted for them. The new Negro has arrived. The war has developed a new spirit. In the time of revolution there is but a tenuous partition between timidity and cowardice. If Booker T. Washington were living today with all the high prestige of his personality, patronage and power, he would not be able to hold the Negro to his avowed doctrine of prudential silence on the issue of manhood rights.

Hopes Aroused by the War

During the war the nations relied upon the forgiving spirit and patriotic emotion of the Negro and that reliance was not in vain. Although he had just cause for deep dissatisfaction, he held his grievances in abeyance, but not in oblivion. He was a good American while the war was on and wishes to be considered as an American now that the war is over. His valor and courage contributed in full measure to the consummation of the struggle. The slogan of democracy was harmonious to his ear. It aroused in him hopes and ambitions that he would enter as a full participant in the fruition of that democracy which he was called upon to sustain and perpetuate. He was given every assurance that the nation would no longer deny him a just share in the new democracy which his courage helped bring to the world. Andrew Jackson advised the Negro troops who won the belated victory behind the fleecy breastworks of New Orleans to return to their masters, and be loyal, obedient servants, but no one now expects the Negro soldiers of the World War to revert with satisfaction to the status they occupied before the war for the emancipation of mankind.

RACIAL EQUALITY

The final outcome of the war must be the fulfillment of the Tennysonian prophecy:

"Where the common sense of most shall hold a fretful world in awe;

And the kindly earth shall slumber lapped in universal law."

Four hundred million members of the white race today are dominating twice their number of the non-white peoples of the world. They are at present superior in the development of concrete and concerted power and lay arrogant claim to superiority as inherent race endowment. By some sort of divine favor it is claimed that they are predestined to rule over their darker brethren for all time to come. The darker and at present the feebler races cannot recognize the justice of this claim, and would seriously question the justice of that providence which ordains one-third of the human race to rule over the other two-thirds to the end of days.

The Negro a Natural Conservative

The conservative elements of the nation— white and black—who would test the values of American institutions must unite in determined effort to withstand reckless revolution which threatens to shake the foundations of existing world order. It will require united effort of all men of sound judgment and conservative temper to uphold and vindicate the integrity of our laws and institutions, purged as they must be of injustice and inequity. The nation looks to the Negro as a great storehouse of conservatism. Before entering upon the war the Government began to count upon its reliable resources. The devotion and loyalty of the Negro were regarded as a certain asset. In the past this has been the loyalty of inertia—the blind altruistic devotion to flag and country. In the future this loyalty will not be less emotional or ardent, but more intelligent and self-enlightened. The Government said to itself that the good-natured and unresentful Negro will quickly forget all of the indignities and outrages heaped upon him and join with his white fellow-citizen in upholding the glory and honor of the flag which he has never failed to magnify and adore. The Negro has been prone to exhibit the spirit of humility and forgiveness— the crowning glory of the Christian graces. He has loved his enemies. He has done good to them that despitefully use him. He has returned love for hate and good deeds for despiteful usage. Booker T. Washington, the personal embodiment of the blamelessness of the Negro, has declared that no white man could be so mean as to make him hate him. However cruelly and unjustly the nation might treat the black man, he has always responded, "Though you slay me, yet will I serve you." But the acerbity, not to say the bitterness, of W. E. B.

DuBois very strongly indicates that this sub-missiveness of spirit is not universal and may not be everlasting.

CIRCUMSTANCES ALTER RACIAL CHARACTER

Although these characteristics have prevailed up to the present time, and are still operative, we cannot rely upon their everlasting continu-ance. Circumstances not only alter cases, but characteristics as well. There is no such thing as unchangeable racial character. The Hebrew race possessed the spiritual genius of the world as long as they were shut in to a peculiar en-vironment which encouraged the development of spiritual talent, but when they became scat-tered abroad among the gentiles they forthwith lost their spiritual ascendancy. There has not arisen a single Jew with transcendent spiritual genius or originality since St. John died. The Greek mind reached the loftiest pinnacle of thought and genius as long as the environment favored the development of this peculiar form of culture, but the lapse of two thousand years does not indicate that this race possesses today the slightest trace of that intellectual subtlety which gave rise to "the glory that was Greece." God has made of one blood and of one mind and of one spirit, all nations to dwell on the face of

the earth, and has set as the bounds of their
habitation no geographical lines or racial limitations, but the natural boundaries of land and
sea which fix the confines of human habitability.
Race and color are physical and geographical
attributes, and do not permanently determine
mind and spirit. All races in the long run will
respond to the same stimulus in the same way.
The Negro is perhaps the most adaptable and
chameleon-like of all the races of man. He
takes on the quality of the environment in
which he is involved. He is a Mohammedan
in Turkey; a Catholic in South America; a
Protestant in the United States; a Frenchman
in France; an Englishman in Jamaica. He
helps Peary find the North Pole and assists
Goethals in digging the Panama Canal. There
is no type of human culture which he does not
readily absorb and assimilate. He has learned
the white man's language, borrowed his religion, and conformed to his political policy in
all the ends of the earth. He reads his literature, and is quickened by his ideals, hopes, and
aspirations. He has also absorbed a goodly
measure of the white man's blood, carrying
with it an asserted quantum of disposition and
spirit.

The Negro cannot, therefore, develop meekness and humility in an environment of resentment and aggression. The white man will not let him do so. Hatred begets hatred, as love begets love. It is an imperfect knowledge of human nature that expects the white man to preserve his attitude of overlordship, revenge and disdain while the Negro, nourished with the same nature, will forever remain passive and forgiving. It is too much to hope that he will forever requite cruelty with kindness and hatred with love and mercy. The nation cannot expect to humiliate the Negro eternally with Jim Crow cars, disfranchisement, segregation, and lynching, and expect him to assign his love and devotion in perpetuity. If the victims of mob violence were equally distributed throughout the nation, there would be standing a blood-stained tree in every county in the United States as a ghastly reminder to the Negro of the crucifixion of his race. Unless this barbarous tendency is checked, lynching will become ingrained in the warp and woof of the national character. Would the nation, then, have the moral right to demand the Negro's love and devotion? The nation must destroy lynching or lynching must destroy the nation. Let us fondly hope that the Negro will be forever true to the nation; but let us fervently pray that the nation will prove itself worthy of his affection.

RACE RIOTS

We have heard of late very much about the so-called race riots in several parts of the country. Although these riots do not indicate an aroused spirit of revenge, they do suggest an awakening purpose of self-defense. But these outbreaks were perpetrated by a small element of lawless whites against the Negroes who merely acted on the defensive. Mr. Dooley has complained that the Negro is "too easily lynched." To paraphrase the famous statement of Frederick Douglass, "The people who are lynched easiest, will be lynched oftenest." But there has not been, and let us hope that never shall be a race riot in the full sense of the term, where all the members of one race will be arrayed in violent hostility against the other. In these recent happenings we have had the conservative masses of both races, white and black, uniting to quell the riot and put down lawlessness. In acting on the principle of self-defense, the Negro has but followed the advice of Abraham Lincoln, who in the Emancipation Proclamation advises the people set free to refrain from all violence except in necessary

self-defense. The moment the Negro goes beyond the limit of self-defense, aggressive violence will mean self-destruction. But there is
no likelihood that the Negro will ever become
the aggressor. He is the victim, not the perpetrator. The wolf always has some sinister
purpose when he accuses the lamb of muddying
the stream above him. It is entirely probable
that all conservative elements of this nation
will be appealed to in the approaching Presidential election to uphold the integrity of the
courts. The finality of the courts lies at the
basis of free institutions. We have already
seen two of the most distinguished Americans
leading campaigns to upset this doctrine. The
Negro complains that he can hardly secure justice at the hands of the courts. The white man
precipitates race riots, the Negro is punished
by the courts. A recent survey has been made
showing how difficult it is for a poor man to
receive justice, but there is a double difficulty
when the applicant is both poor and black.
And yet when this appeal is made, the Negro,
although it places a severe tax on his devotion,
will be found standing shoulder to shoulder
with his conservative white fellow-citizen in
vindicating the majesty of the law and upholding the finality of the judiciary as the last word
in the settlement of human issues.

The Integrity of American Institutions

As outcome of the World War, every nation
except our own will probably have its governmental structure radically modified and readjusted. Our institutions are pedestaled upon
the Declaration of Independence, and though
the winds of revolution may blow, they will
withstand the fury of the storm, because they
are founded upon the eternal Rock of Ages.
No other foundation can be laid than that which
has been laid. We may hope to live up to but
can never transcend the conception therein contained. The spiritual genius of the Hebrew
race gave the world the everlasting, never-
changing religious truth. Through inspiration
of the intellect, the Greeks have given us the
formal laws of thought which never can be
changed. The founders of our government
with no less political genius have formulated
for all time the right law of political procedure.
The Constitution was founded in the midst of
slavery, but the founders had the projected discernment to transcend these regrettable incidents which they knew would pass away with
time. Had their vision been fully caught by the
immediately succeeding generations, the Thirteenth, Fourteenth and Fifteenth Amendments
would have been unnecessary. But when the

first test came to justify their faith and vision, there sprang up a new set of political thinkers with a double portion of the spirit of the old. They completed the purpose of the founders by the necessary addenda to the Charter of Liberty. Abraham Lincoln justified the faith of Thomas Jefferson. The Emancipation Proclamation was the fulfillment of the Declaration of Independence.

NOT TO DESTROY, BUT TO FULFILL

And now in this day of world dissatisfaction and unrest, we need not doubt the validity of the foundation on which we rest. The way has been left open for progressive adjustments to meet the requirements of events. Orderly amendments may be added in harmony with the progressive need of the human race. But unless the new additions are in alignment with the old foundation, the superstructure will topple and fall. The Negro has no hope outside of the Declaration of Independence and its embodiment in the Constitution of the United States. There is no other power under Heaven whereby he might be saved. It is the greatest human instrumentality for the profound development of mankind. The world revolution will but disseminate the blessing of American institutions among the other nations of the earth. This is

the light that lighteth the path of every struggling people of the world. The Negro must
insist, with incessant insistence, upon the exact
fulfillment of the declared purpose of American
institutions. Not only his own self-interest,
but the integrity of their high purpose as well,
demands that he should do this. Let him insist
upon every American right with the "i" dotted
and "t" crossed, but woe be to him who would
lay destructive hand to tear down this Temple
of Freedom. The Negro will be the last of all
to give hospitality to such unholy thought.
When it is considered what American institutions have done, and are calculated to do for
this race, despite the past disappointment and
present hopes deferred, he might well exclaim,
"Though all men should forsake you, yet will
not I." The Negro will seek remedy for his
grievances under the flag, and will uphold the
institutions which it symbolizes and extols.
There is a divine discontent, but there is also
a diabolical spirit of disturbance. The Negro
will not be allured by the arguments of distracted, destructive radicals who, like Job's
wild wife, would curse and die. The reckless
radical is without the restraint of law and reason and is guided only by the license of a disordered imagination. He would strike at the
chastity of women, the integrity of the home,

and the regnancy of law and order, and the beneficence of divine providence, while setting up a materialistic dispensation which begins in appetite and ends in death. The Negro will have none of this, but joins with the courageously conservative forces of this nation, not to destroy the law, but to fulfill.

CHAPTER III

THE NEGRO IN THE NEW WORLD ORDER

The inherent rights of man receive emphasis and new assertion at moments of social stress and strain. When society is in travail, liberty is born. During the long eras of leisure, the spirit of liberty languishes. Existing order is transformed, and all things made new amidst the fire and smoke of revolution. In times of quietude and peace, social evils accumulate and crystallize. The acquisition of wealth and the attainment of culture and refinement constitute the goal of endeavor. Discontent is decried and the soul seeks its ease. The voice of the reformer is denounced as tending to disturb social placidity and repose. The troublesome issues of the rights of man are banished from consciousness. Inequalities arise, aristocratic prerogative is asserted, and divine sanction assumed as the ordained scheme of social adjustment. When reform becomes impossible, revolution becomes imperative. It requires periodic upheavals to startle the soul from its complaisant slumber, discredit the dominance of material aims, frustrate the assumption of arrogance and pride, and vindicate the rights of man as the highest attainable human value.

History abounds in convulsive epochs when the acute evils of society are eradicated. We have but to recall the tremendous outburst of moral energy during the Revolutionary Struggle and the Civil War, to bring to mind the operation of this principle within our own national experience. Each of these great upheavals served to curb the arrogant assumption of irresponsible power, and to give impulse to the doctrine of the inherent claims of man as man. The titanic struggle which has just engulfed the whole world in red ruin of revolution is but another act in the drama of human liberation, and the uplifted curtain shall fall on a world transformed.

REVOLUTIONS NEVER GO BACKWARD

Revolutions never go backward. When a nation puts its hand to the plow of liberty, although it might wistfully reverse its vision, yet the furrow which marks the forward path can never be effaced. Revolutions always lessen the domain of oppression and increase the area of liberty. By the inexorable logic of events, the poor and oppressed receive the chief benefits of these great movements of history. The world convulsions precipitate the showers of liberty whose droppings fall upon the needy and neglected of the children of man. The despised Jew of Europe, the oppressed millions of Asia, the Negro in Africa and America, and the under-man throughout the world will be the beneficiaries of the blessings which flow from the greatest epoch in the history of social evolution.

POWER AND PRINCIPLE

The fundamental issue involved in this struggle is but the consummation of the age-long struggle between power and principle. The Central Powers, under the compulsion of Germany, espoused the ancient dogma of the dominance of power and the divine right of the strong. Through their ruthless acts, which spoke louder than their arrogant words, they defiantly declared that the weak has no rights which the strong is bound to respect. When the Belgian border was crossed, the die was cast. The Allies were forced, willingly or otherwise, to accept the challenge. Right and might once more met in open conflict. There is in the human. heart a deep-seated conviction of the indomitability of right. The universal and spontaneous response to this appeal confirms the same conviction. Power may seem to triumph for a while; might may be enthroned while right is enchained; but final defeat is never accepted until the verdict is reversed, and right is crowned victor. If it appears that God is on the side of the heaviest battalion, a deeper insight and closer scrutiny reveal the fact that ultimately the heaviest battalion gets itself arrayed on the side of right. Power may put on efficiency and seem to work wonders for a while, but conscienceless efficiency is no match for efficiency quickened by conscience. The victorious outcome of this titanic struggle has given to the cause of right a sanction that can never again be shaken. The inviolability of the rights of man has become a sacred principle for all time to come.

THE OVERRULING PURPOSE

Shakespeare was not uttering threadbare theological dogma, when he declared that "there is a divinity which shapes our ends." This belief is in harmony with universal human experience. No statesman or philosopher was able to foresee or guide the trend of events during these five foregone fateful years. The wise statesmen have but followed the flow of events. The foolish tried to stem the tide. Men and nations have been moved, as it were, by an unseen hand, as pawns upon the chessboard of the world. Those who were at first impelled by the traditional motives of greed, ambition, animosity, and revenge, have been led to a broader vision as the involved purpose of the great drama was unfolded. If there have been hesitation, indecision, and revised or substituted statements of the objects and aims of the war, it has been only in proportion as a constantly clarifying vision has been vouchsafed to those who were sincerely seeking after the right way, if haply they might find it. The wrath of man has been made to serve the great consummation, and the remainder of wrath has been held in restraint. The offense must needs come, but woe unto that man or nation by whom t cometh. The Serbian assassin of an Austrian Prince fired the shot that shocked the world. But we have already forgotten the name of the prince and assassin, in the momentous results which transcended the part which these unwitting participants were made to play. The little fire kindleth a great matter, when the fuel has already been accumulated for the flame. This tragedy was but the exciting occasion of a deep-seated cause. The idle gust overtopples the giant oak only when the foundation has already been undermined. The fullness of time had come. The world was ripe for a great moral revolution. The rapid scientific and material advancement had outrun ethical restraint. Culture had supplanted conscience. Deeds had become glorified over ideals; the thing counted for more than the thought. Success meant more than righteousness. The rights of the weak were subordinated to the interests of the strong. Religion had become silent in the face of wrong. The church with pious cant continued to repeat archaic phraseology, while the world plunged headlong into sin.

The Failure of Prophecy

It is a sad commentary on the human understanding that the so-called wise men and seers of the time were proclaiming the era of universal peace and the end of war, at the moment when the world was on the edge of a precipice. Their eyes were holden, so that they could not discern the signs of the times nor see the shadow of coming events. They proceeded in the even tenor of their satisfied way. Moral maxims were mouthed without moral meaning. The church preached a lukewarm gospel and a tepid righteousness that had reconciled itself with arrogance of class and prejudice of race. It attempted the forbidden rôle of trying to serve God and Mammon. The moral deluge engulfed the complaisant world with suddenness and shock as completely as the Mosaic flood startled and overwhelmed the convivial devotees in the days of Noah. The fountain was suddenly swept away by that hand which rules over events and brings to naught the purposes of man. The highest human wisdom has little predictive value. We can with no greater assurance foretell what the next five years will bring forth than, in 1914, we could predict the momentous movements of the intervening quinquennium. Czar and Kaiser, King and Mikado, Sultan and President, were made to play their assigned parts. The Kaiser of the Germans may be considered the Pharaoh of modern times, whose heart had been hardened, in order that the dominance of right over might might be vindicated anew. The voice spoke through the mouthpiece of the Allies to the heart-hardened leader of the hosts of oppression, saying, "Let my people go." The horse and rider have been overthrown in the Red Sea of destruction, as a modern reminder to kings and nations of the fate of those who would stand between the people and liberty which is their due.

A Righteous Cause

It is not necessary to invoke the doctrine of perfection in order to justify the part which the Allies are playing in this great issue. A righteous cause may be better than any man or na-

tion involved in it. An evil propaganda may
be worse than its most wicked advocate. Christianity, in nineteen hundred years, has not yet
produced a single Christian according to the
rigid exactions of the cult. Nor has the kingdom of evil produced a single unmitigated devil.
The modern crusade of liberty is better than
any allied nation which espoused it. The doctrine of oppression is more detestable than its
most wicked adherent. Not one of the allied
nations could pose as model of the virtue which
is espoused, nor yet claim freedom from the evil
practices which were so bitterly denounced in
the adversary. A nation without sin cannot
be found to cast the first stone. In the readjustment of historical wrongs of nation against
nation and race against race, the victorious Allies will be forced by considerations of prudence to choose a comparatively recent date as
point of departure, to save themselves from
serious embarrassment. In order to make ourselves worthy devotees of a righteous cause it
is not necessary that we should be free from
sin, but that we acknowledge our sin, and promise to do so no more. Any nation that enlists
in the crusade of humanity with vainglorious
assumptions of self-righteousness thereby proclaims its own insincerity. They who would
prepare themselves for vicarious and sacrificial

service, must first submit themselves to serious self-searching with deep humiliation and contrition of soul.

Abraham Lincoln was the one commanding moral genius that has arisen in the Western Hemisphere. He followed the leading of the inner light. He heard and heeded the call, and accepted the commission to lead the unrighteous hosts in behalf of righteousness. But he was all the while deeply conscious of our national unworthiness, and accepted the chastening hand of affliction with a groaning of spirit that was too deep for utterance. In an outburst of moral anguish he exclaims: "Yet if God wills that it (the war) continue until all the wealth piled up by the bondsmen's two hundred and fifty years of unrequited toil shall be sunk, and until every drop of blood drawn with the lash shall be paid by another drawn with the sword, as was said three thousand years ago, so still it must be said, 'The judgments of the Lord are true and righteous altogether.' "

The vital difference between the Central Powers and the Allies, all of whom had fallen far short of the standard of national rectitude, consisted in the fact that the Allies stood ready to acknowledge their faults and prayed forgiveness as moral preparation for the great contest. On the other hand, the Ger-

mans valued the discarded methods which the
Allies repudiated. They had the foolish hardi-
hood to justify their misdeeds as a part of their
code of national morality. Great indeed is the
condemnation of that man or nation who breaks
the moral law and justifies its transgression.
A nation cannot wait until it has become perfect before espousing right ideals. But a declaration of high purpose arouses the conscience
and reacts upon the conduct. Nations, like individuals, rise on stepping stones of their dead
selves to higher things. But all moral progress
is estopped when misdeeds are justified. The
American people were not in favor of the emancipation of the slave when they entered upon
the Civil War. England was not committed
to the doctrine of world democracy when she
joined hands with Russia, the most autocratic
state in Europe, to protect a violated treaty.
But just as the battle-cry of freedom soon became the dominant motive in our Civil War, so
the World War had not progressed far before
it became imperative that the allied cause be
impelled by the dynamic power of a moral
watchword. To Woodrow Wilson was vouchsafed the high privilege of uttering this word.
All the nations of the world have been made
nobler and worthier by reason of the righteous
doctrine which they have espoused and ex-

tolled. Never again can the weak peoples of the world be ruthlessly overridden by arrogant power. The United States has assumed the world's spokesmanship for the doctrine of human liberty. Never again can the American Negro be dealt with in ruthless disregard of this declared doctrine without discrediting our righteous advocacy and making our high pretensions of non-effect.

The Power of Right Doctrine

Historic epochs enounce dynamic doctrines surcharged with pent-up revolutionary power. These doctrines epitomize and express the oppressive burden under which the people have been laboring and embody their ideals of relief. The doctrine is more than the deed. The thought precedes the thing. The issues of life flow from the fountain-head of thought and belief. The Christian church, not unwisely, emphasizes the supreme importance of orthodox belief, which serves as the standard by which right conduct is regulated and controlled. If the people's ideals are right, their conduct cannot be wrong. If the people's ideals are wrong, their conduct cannot be right. A pure fountain cannot send forth a corrupt stream. The world is ruled by opinion. Revolutions always emphasize the right opinion concerning human liberty and the equality of man. "Liberty, fraternity, equality"; "all men are created equal"; "no distinction on account of race and color," are maxims which epitomize the outcome of the three great social revolutions of modern times. These maxims have become axioms and are appealed to as self-evident principles in all subsequent social progress. Revolutionary fervor heats the thermometer of public sentiment many degrees beyond its normal registry. Great truths are uttered by the entranced prophets of reform which transcend the calculated and cautious judgment of calm and quiet reflection. Like the enraptured apostle on the Mount, they utter words of marvelous wisdom, though they wist not what they say. The moral watchword of the French Revolution was principally intended for Frenchmen who were oppressed beneath the heavy heel of haughty autocracy. The author of the Declaration of Independence was a slaveholder, and must have penned that immortal document with serious reservation of mind or disquietude of conscience. The abolition of race and color in civil and political procedure marks the most daring concrete application of this abstract philosophy of human rights to which this doctrine has yet been subjected. The world is still amazed at the moral audacity of the great apostles of human liberty who made the despised Negro a citizen and clothed him with political and civil prerogative and power.

The Inherent Truth of Sound Doctrine

The value of doctrine does not depend upon its interpretation by the one who first uttered it, but rather upon the meaning which it suggests and the response which it evokes in the minds of those who receive it. The telling sermon depends upon the meaning which the minister imputes to his text. Shakespeare, who fathomed the depths of human thoughts and feelings, was incapable of profound intellectual or moral convictions. His maxims of wisdom were called forth to meet the requirements of mimic art. We read into his words a profundity of thought and meaning of which the author never dreamed. A word once uttered can never be recalled. He who sends it forth cannot retract or limit its meaning and interpretation to his narrow interest or intention. The early apostles of Christianity were profoundly impressed with the conviction that the gospel dispensation was limited to the Jewish race. It required a divine revelation to convince its chief spokesman of its higher intent and purpose to embrace all mankind. Universal truth enforces universal application, despite the narrow judgment of men who may not be able to see beyond the circle of their own circumstances. The story runs, that a colored citizen of a southern state became sorely perplexed as to a practical definition of the word "democracy," which had recently become current in the discussion of the issues of the day. The dictionaries at his disposal furnished no satisfactory relief from his dilemma, in view of the proscriptive civil and political policy of which he was made to bear the brunt. In the midst of his bewilderment he decided to write to his senator, who is far-famed for his reactionary attitude towards manhood rights of the Negro race. This distinguished senator, not knowing that the request came from a colored constituent, replied: "Democracy means that you are as good as I am." He was thus beguiled into telling the truth, which no subsequent qualification can affect, though he may expostulate until the day of judgment.

WORLD DEMOCRACY

Democracy for the world, and the world for democracy, has become the keyword of the convulsive struggle in which the nations and races of mankind are involved. This instantly appeals to the moral energy of those who labor and are heavy laden in all the ends of the earth. It is needless to speculate as to what reservations of thought or qualifications of judgment lay in the mind of the statesman who first gave utterance to this expression, or to point out inconsistency between word and deed. It is more important to know that those who stand in need of the beneficence of the great truth hear it gladly. All races, colors and creeds have fought under the inspiration of its banner. It has become the battle-cry of those who yearn for freedom, the tidings of great joy for those who sit in the shadow of arrogance and power.

Divine Right

The dominance of power over weakness was the only sanction that primitive man needed for his overlordship among his feebler fellows. As soon as the troublesome qualms of conscience emerged, they were assuaged by assumption of divine right. All of the historical evils of nation against nation, and race against race, and class against class have sought justification on this ground. The overbearing attitude of the Germans toward the other nations of Europe was based primarily upon might backed up by assumed divine sanction. Because this nation had reached certain superior attainments, it asserted the right to impose its imperious will upon others without let or hindrance. The arguments which the German apologists used to justify their conduct towards other European nations are paralleled in every particular by the assertions of the anti-Negro propagandists in the United States, who would hold the Negro in everlasting subordination to the white race. One distinguished German philosopher declared:

"As the German bird, the eagle, hovers high over all the creatures of the earth, so also should the German feel that he is raised high above all other nations who surround him, and whom he sees in the limitless depths beneath him."

Another tells us:

"One single highly cultured German warrior, of those who are, alas! falling in thousands, represents a higher intellectual and moral life-value than hundreds of the raw children of nature whom England and France, Russia and Italy, oppose to them."

With the proper substitution of terms, these citations might be adopted bodily by those American publicists who believe that God has appointed the Negro an inferior place in his all-wise scheme of things. It was but logical that the German nation should raise the race issue in the world conflict. They first appealed to England on the basis of a common Teutonic blood to refrain from entering the conflict in behalf of the inferior Celts and Slavs. The invited participation of the yellow and black races was reprobated as the crowning act of apostasy against the ordained superiority of the white race. It is interesting to note that a certain type of southern opinion which is welded to the divine theory of race relationship agreed with the German point of view, and denounced the enlistment of the black and yellow races to fight against the lordly white race as a crime against humanity.

Deep-Seated Evils

There are certain evils which get themselves so firmly lodged in the human mind that they can be eliminated only by shot and shell. Men at one time sincerely and honestly believed in the right of the strong to own the weak, as master and slave, especially if the strong man were white and the weak one black. This doctrine was shot to death at Appomattox. The last important public utterance of Senator Benjamin R. Tillman, the oracle of a certain school of opinion, was to the effect that he was glad that the Civil War was resolved in favor of the Union, and that the Negro was made free. The mind of the defeated reactionary gives its tardy assent to the righteous judgment enforced by the sword. The German people sincerely believed in the divine right of kings and the German nation. But this doctrine received its death wound at the battle of the Marne. Enlightened German opinion will soon express gratification that the World War was resolved in favor of the Allies, and that the detested doctrine of divine right of kings and nations has been shot out of the minds of men forever. It is the lost cause that never can be revived. The anti-slavery advocates used to declare that whenever a practice became too despicable for human responsibility, it sought vindication under the shelter of divine sanction. It is noticeable that those who assume familiarity with divine intendment, exhibit least of the divine spirit in dealing with their fellowmen. To suppose that there could be any traceable connection between an All-wise and All-good Providence and the workings of the minds of those who have been loudest in denying the inalienable rights of man, on both sides of the Atlantic, would reverse all our received notions of the divine attributes.

The Divine Right of Race

But along with the divine right of kings must go every other semblance of the divine right, including divine right of race. There is no more reason to suppose that God has chosen the white race to exercise lordship over the darker races of men than that He has chosen Germans to lord it over the other European nations. There exists in the minds of many the deep-seated opinion that the white race has some God-ordained mission to which the weaker breeds must bow in humble submission. Rudyard Kipling's *White Man's Burden* is but the modern refrain of the exploded conceit that God has given his chosen race the heathen for their possession to be broken to pieces with a rod of iron. The divine right of kings is a more acceptable doctrine than the divine right of race. It is more consoling to be required to submit to one ruler of divine designation than to be compelled to bow in subjection to a whole race of persons so designated. Most of the unjust and unrighteous discriminatory regulations against the Negro are based upon the assumed or implied superior claim of the white race. Wherever and whenever the white man is accorded a single advantage because he is white and the Negro subjected to a single disadvantage because he is black, it represents a discrimination without any reasonable justification, human or divine. A social fabric built upon this basis rests upon the foundation of sand which will surely be shaken down when the wind and rain of democracy blow and beat upon it; and great will be the fall thereof.

KINSHIP IN INIQUITY

The advocates of race discrimination are spiritual descendants of the defenders of human slavery, who in turn bear close kinship of spirit with the Germans who believe in the divine right of kings. It is a tragedy to see men of genius prostituting their power on the side of human oppression instead of liberty. The most tragic chapter in history is the collapse of the Germans, the most highly favored of nations. They misjudged their mission and misapplied their powers. It will never again be possible for the black man and the yellow man, who fought side by side with the better element of the white race against the outrageous pretensions of the minor and meaner fraction, to believe that color confers any divine favor. By what possible process of logic can it be claimed that one-third of the human race, because it happens to be white, should exercise lordship forever over two-thirds which happens to be colored?

NOBLESSE OBLIGE

Some individuals, some nations and some races have present advantages over other individuals, nations and races. If there is any divine attribute to whose appeal the human conscience responds, it requires that the strong should encourage and strengthen the weak, and not aggrandize their own conceit at the expense of those more helpless and hapless than themselves. Germany might have uplifted the whole human race to a higher level of science and achievement, had she chosen the way of liberty rather than oppression. The strong will fulfill their mission in the world by playing the rôle of the big brother rather than that of the big bully. The divine right of kings, the divine right of race, the divine right of class, the divine right of power must go the way of all wicked and detestable dogmas. The only divine right that will be acceptable to a democratic world is the divine right of each individual to make the most of himself.

RACE PREJUDICE

Human history abounds in deep and bitter political, religious and social animosities. The dawn of history breaks upon a world at war. Society, like nature, has been red in tooth and claw. The ape and tiger have had little time to slumber. But race prejudice, as it is understood in the world today, is the product of comparatively modern times. It has sprung

up during the past four hundred years, since
the Western European has forced himself upon
the weaker breeds of man in all parts of the
world.   Ancient literature contains little or
nothing of this form of race prejudice, under
which eligibility is based upon the flesh and
blood rather than upon mind and spirit.   The
Germanic races are more seriously afflicted with
this idolatry of blood than those of Latin or
Slavonic origin.   The Latin races have had as
wide and varied contact with weaker peoples
as the Teuton or his Anglo-Saxon cousin.   But
the Latin dispensation, despite its manifest imperfections, has never sown the seeds of race
hatred in the portions of the world where its
power held sway.   In South America and in the
West Indian Archipelago where the Latin
blood and authority dominated for centuries,
the people live and move in racial peace and
good will.   But in the Teuton cult, color is more
than creed, race counts for more than religion.
The Negro in France may rise to the level of
his talent or genius in the civil, social or military life, but race intolerance among the Germanic races would restrict his aspiration on the
mere ground of race and color.   A Negro soldier
might rise to superior command in the French
army; but should a Negro possess the military
genius of Alexander, Cæsar and Napoleon com-

bined into one, he could not rise above a designated level in the armies regulated by this restrictive spirit. Some one has written a book entitled *If Christ Came to Congress*, and pointed out the strange contradiction which He would witness among those who profess to follow in His footsteps. But should the Man of Sorrows return to earth under the similitude of a man of color, in many parts of the world, He would be denied communion with the saints in His own church which He died to establish; or at most, restricted to spiritual relationship with those of His own assumed complexion.

An Anomaly

It is one of the curious anomalies of history that in the recent World War the climax of bitterness was reached between German and Anglo-Saxon of kindred blood and spirit. The German nation translates its doctrine of intolerance into logical and unmitigated action. The Anglo-Saxon rose up in his might to defeat the logical conclusion of his own intolerant attitude. His good sense has redeemed his bad logic. The spirit of intolerance based on race and blood has received a shock at the hand of its own adherents from which it can never recover. Italy, Spain, France and Russia and the Balkan States do not show the same aversion of

race as the Teuton and the Saxon. The Saxon
who is but a Teuton of diluted blood is better
than the Teuton. Some Saxons are better than
others. Race aversion whose stubbornness and
strength override considerations of conscience
does not characterize the entire white race, but
only a lesser fraction of that race. Of these the
Germanic element is the dominating force of the
world today. But this tough Teutonic intolerant spirit must yield by attrition with the
milder and more human disposition of the great
majority of the human race whether European,
Asiatic or African. For the first time in the
history of the world, all elements of the European peoples have come into council with representatives of other races and colors to
deliberate upon the fate of the world. This
council will be brought to naught unless it is
based upon the underlying principles of the
brotherhood of man. The Japanese, the foremost section of the Asiatic peoples, are now
speaking with authority for the yellow races.
They have already put the world on warning
that the intolerant spirit of the more arrogant
portion of the white race can never be accepted
as the final basis of peace on earth and good
will among men. Race prejudice is the greatest
evil that afflicts the world today. Animosities
growing out of greed, religious schisms, and

political ambition may be made amenable to reason of force. Those who foster race hatred are defeating the millennium of world civilization, whatever form of value their contributions to human culture may take. What profit is it to gain the whole world at the expense of the soul? German efficiency dwindles in importance when weighed against her accompanying arrogance and intolerance of spirit. Unless the higher soul values shall be universally recognized as transcending the intolerant exactions of flesh and blood, the moral unity of mankind cannot be attained, the devoutly hoped for brotherhood of man is a delusive dream, and Jesus Christ, as Savior of the world, has lived and died in vain.

Moral Consistency

The Allied Nations will be bound in ethical consistency to live up to the doctrines which they espoused to meet the great moral emergency. All permanent progress depends upon the stability of law. The Savior tells us: "Till heaven and earth pass, one jot or one tittle shall in no wise pass from the law, till all be fulfilled." This is characteristic of all universal law, whether spiritual or scientific. It is independent of time and place. This is true of the multiplication table. It cannot be varied or modified to satisfy human arrogance or pride. Great indeed is the condemnation of that one who violates law and justifies the violation. The business man who would misapply the multiplication table in his dealings and justify his conduct, must be placed under drastic penalty, or else our economic fabric would fall. When the German nation would ruthlessly destroy weaker nations for its own aggrandizement and justify the destruction, it was establishing a new code of morality which must not be allowed, lest civilization be imperiled. There cannot be one law for the weak and another for the strong, or one law for black men and another for white men. The ethical principles have no respect for geographical latitudes nor for the conventional pride of men or nations. What is wrong in Germany, is equally wrong in Georgia. Atrocities in Texas and atrocities in Turkey call for like condemnation. The United States, as sponsor for the moral issue upon which the world struggle is waged, will be bound to treat all of its citizens with the equal justice which it is now proclaiming as the saving doctrine for the world. The nation cannot longer permit its own Constitution to be violated with impunity, while insisting that other nations shall observe the letter and spirit of international law. It must practice and inculcate the principles of justice and equality at home, as preparation to serve as moral monitor of mankind.

RECONSTRUCTION OF THOUGHT

The only reconstruction worth while is a reconstruction of thought. Permanent reforms grow out of a change in the attitude of mind. The weaker element is always governed by the attitude of the stronger. Programs proceed from principles. As long as man looked upon woman as a plaything and a toy, she was a nullity in the state. But in proportion as his more enlightened view leads him to regard her as a co-equal in the equation of life, she will be accorded a larger and larger measure of privilege and prerogative. The Negro was at first regarded as representing an inferior order of creation, fit only for drudgery and rough toil. Under the dominance of this idea, he was made a slave. So long as this notion prevailed, he could hope for no other status. But when it began to dawn that he was a man, with all the involved potentialities of manhood, his captors began to become unquiet concerning the inhuman treatment heaped upon him.

The anti-slavery struggle resulted in profoundly changing that attitude of the people toward the Negro race, which finally resulted in emancipation. Chief Justice Taney's name has been damned to everlasting fame by a single sentence that failed to synchronize with the sentiment of the nation at the time it was uttered. The institution of slavery rested upon the foundation of the dogma that the Negro had no rights that a white man was bound to respect. The leaven of the Declaration of Independence and the anti-slavery propagandists had wrought a great change in public sentiment concerning the place and function of the Negro. It was in view of this altered attitude of mind that the Negro was set free and clothed with the prerogative of citizenship. As the American mind began to grow cold and indifferent on this issue, a strong sentiment was arising which demanded the annulment or abolition of the reconstruction amendments to the Federal Constitution. But at this juncture the World War was precipitated, which reëmphasized the doctrine of the rights of man. The gallant part which the Negro played in bringing victory to the side of liberty has also served to liberalize the feelings and sentiment in his behalf. The new reconstruction, therefore, in so far as it may affect the Negro, will grow out of this new attitude of mind. According to the present state of sentiment, the Negro has some rights which the white man is bound to respect, but others which he is privileged to ignore. The moral revolution must create a new heart and renew the right spirit. All the rights of every man must be respected by every other man. It is needless to attempt to formulate in detail the particular forms which this reconstruction will take. If the spirit of democracy prevails, the statutes, articles, and clauses will take care of themselves.

THE AFRICAN COLONIES

The future government of the African colonies will form a chapter in the new reconstruction of the greatest interest and concern to the American Negro. During the past four hundred years the European has been brought into contact with the African. But the one motive has been exploitation of the weak for the aggrandizement of the strong. The poet Pope has embalmed the deep infamy of motive which has dominated the European in his contact with the weaker breeds of men. Lo, the poor Indian, is described as seeking release from it all in his happy hunting grounds beyond the skies,

"Where slaves once more their native land behold
No thieves torment, no Christians thirst for gold."

But a new note has been uttered. The beneficence of democracy is extending even to the

man farthest down. The enlightened statesmen have united in declaring that, hereafter
colonies must be governed in the interest of the
people themselves, and not for the aggrandizement of their exploiters. The haughty Germans, relying on the ancient dogma of divine
right, have ruthlessly ruled the African colonies
with iron efficiency, with sole reference to gain.
It is agreed on all sides that these colonies must
be taken over by the Allies in the interest of
humanity. They are to be governed, as far as
practicable, on the basis of self-determination.
The United States is under heavy moral obligation to the African continent and its people.
Under the spell of the old dogma, America
reached out her long arm across the sea and
captured helpless African victims and subjected them to cruel bondage. The Peace Conference will be confronted with the question of
requiting the historic wrong of one nation
against the other; the American can never
requite the Indian whose land she despoiled and
whose race she extinguished; nor yet the African, whose simple-souled sons and daughters
were snatched from their native land and made
to labor for centuries in unrequited toil. But
the adjustment of grievances of French against
German, and Italian against Austrian, suggests
the deep moral obligation to this helpless and

expatriated people. The United States represents the highest type of democracy among the nations. Democracy will never justify itself as a world influence unless it can be becomingly related to the backward and belated peoples of the world in such a way as will lead to their speedy development and reclamation. Indeed the immediate, persistent problem of civilization is the satisfactory adjustment of the advanced sections of the human race to their less fortunate fellowmen. The infamy which has hitherto characterized this relationship stands in everlasting discredit against the claims of Christianity and civilization. While the Constitution of the United States does not bestow authority of government over subject races and peoples, nevertheless, we have taken over Hawaii, Porto Rico and the Philippines on the ground of national necessity and benevolent assimilation. The United States is under both moral and political obligation to assume responsibility for the future welfare of the African colonies taken from Germany for reasons of humanity. It might be well for the United States to assume complete responsibility over a section of the German colonies as an example to the world of how a backward people can be governed without exploitation, and lifted to higher planes of civilization under the guidance of the democratic spirit. This government would naturally enough utilize the talents and attainments of its Afro-American element to help sympathetically in the government and development of their African kinsmen.

SELF-DETERMINATION

No people, however lowly and backward, can be effectively governed unless an element of self-determination is involved in their government. There are ten million Americans of African descent in the United States. They have naturally a vital interest in the welfare of their motherland. The Afro-American, on the whole, constitutes the most advanced section of the African race to be found anywhere in the world. He is best qualified to utter the voice of two-hundred million black people in the continent of Africa and scattered over the face of the globe.

RACE LEADERSHIP

All true leadership must be autochthonous. It must spring from the midst of those to be led. The real leader must be of the same blood and sympathies and subjected to the same conditions and linked to the same destiny as his followers. No race can speak for another or give utterance to its striving of soul. Before an individual of one class can assume to be spokesman for another, he must forego his former allegiance and naturalize himself in the class for which he aspires to speak. He must leave the one, and cleave to the other. Should a conflict arise between the two, he must eschew the old and espouse the new. Napoleon Bonaparte was by blood an Italian. He became not only the mouthpiece but the oracle of the French people; but he must first become a Frenchman by adoption. The white man is not disposed to become naturalized in the Negro race, nor to forego the privilege and prestige which his class and color confer. The Kaiser is the most detested white man on the face of the earth today. And yet the Anglo-Saxon *amour propre* would revolt against the suggestion of subjecting him to the humiliating conditions which without compunction of conscience it forces upon the Negro.

THE LIMIT OF PHILANTHROPY

In the days of slavery when the black man's tongue was tied, noble champions arose to plead his cause. The voices of Phillips, Garrison and Sumner, ringing with righteous indignation, quickened the conscience of the nation. This race can never repay the debt of gratitude for this vicarious service. But the slave has been made a freeman. His sons and daughters have been taught the art of disquisition and persuasive appeal. The black man must now plead with his own voice and give tongue to his own complaints. The white man can yet do much to champion the cause of the Negro, and to arouse the conscience of his own race against injustice and wrong heaped upon the defenseless head of the weak and helpless people. Altruistic advocacy, however genuine, fails to arouse the desired response in public feeling and judgment. The people who fail to produce their own spokesman can hardly convince the world that they feel a deep-seated sense of injustice and wrong. The man who feels the wound must utter the groan. Although the retained advocate may have a genuine interest in the welfare of his clients, the persuasive power of his plea is weakened by the thought that his own destiny is not involved in the verdict. It was necessary that Moses should be one in flesh and blood and spirit with the oppressed people of Israel, to qualify him to stand before the court of Pharaoh, and plead their cause with plenary power and unimpeachable moral authority.

The Voice of the Negro

The white man, with amazing assumption of wisdom and goodness, has undertaken to set the proper régime for the Negro without consulting his advice or consent. The all-wise physician disdains inquiry of the patient of the nature of his ailment. But experience proves that the civilized man is not enlightened enough to govern the savage; that the saint is not sanctified enough to govern the sinner; the philosopher is not wise enough to govern the fool, without involving the consent and participation of the one to be governed. John Locke was a keen expert in the workings of human understanding, and yet he was unable to draft a satisfactory constitution for the people of South Carolina. It is now conceded that the European, with all of his assumed power, has woefully failed in establishing efficient and satisfactory government of weaker races and peoples. This failure has been in proportion to his neglect to consult the interest and feelings of those to be governed. There can be no good government where the principle of self-government is not involved and invoked.

The Negro represents one-eighth of the population of the globe. The Peace Conference now sitting at Paris has assumed the function of the Parliament of Man. The common sense of most must hold the fretful world in awe. All classes and races with just grievances to be remedied or wrongs to be righted are seeking a hearing before this tribunal of law, justice and peace. The laboring men throughout the world, the Irish, the Jews, dissatisfied elements of every race and class, are demanding a hearing through voices of their own choosing. Shall not the voice of the Negro be heard and heeded, if the world is to establish an enduring peace or equality and righteousness?

THE NEW RECONSTRUCTION

The United States belongs to the victorious nations, and is not subject to technical reconstruction. Our whole fabric, however, economic, political, social and moral, will be transformed by the new democratc spirit. The Negro need not expect to be made the subject of special legislation, but may expect to be included in the program of social justice and human opportunity. Proscriptive and restrictive regulations will be nullified under the mollifying influence of these ideals.

RIGHTS AND FIGHTS

The Negro represents a minority in the midst of a more powerful and populous people; but

unlike minority races in the Balkan States, he
does not hope to win his cause by primary conflict. He must rely upon the essential righteousness of his claim and the aroused moral
sense of the nation. He is a coward who will
not exert his resistive power to its utmost for
the unlimited enjoyment of every right which
God or man has conferred upon him. There
are certain God-given rights which man may be
mean enough to deny but never can be mighty
enough to take away. The contest which the
Negro must wage incessantly and unceasingly
is not a conflict that would result in the destruction of the social fabric of which he forms a
part, but would rather lead to the fulfillment of
its declared aims and ideals. The Negro's
cause is right, and right must finally win. The
devils believe this, and tremble.

States' Rights

As a striking result of this new reconstruction, the old doctrine of States' rights, which
had its origin in the purpose to subordinate the
Negro and perpetuate his inferior status, will
be wiped away. This reactionary doctrine has
stood athwart every great moral reform which
our nation has undergone. It opposed unity of
the nation and the freedom of the slave. It
sought to defeat prohibition and women's claim

for the suffrage. Provincialism has been the bane of our national life. The Civil War created a new nation with dominant powers over the states. The World War will create a new world whose sanction will transcend that of any nation. Great reform movements, now sweeping through the world and the nation, will benefit all of the people, and no race or class can be shunted from the benefits thereof.

The Old Reconstruction and the New

The reconstruction growing out of the Civil War resulted in adding the Thirteenth, Fourteenth and Fifteenth Amendments to the Constitution of the United States. The Thirteenth Amendment, abolishing slavery and giving the Negro his freedom, is universally accepted and uncontested. The Fourteenth and Fifteenth Amendments, which made the Negro a citizen and clothed him with the elective franchise, have never been accepted in all parts of the nation. The refractory states have in a large measure nullified the intended effect of these Amendments. But the new reconstruction through which we are now passing must complete the work of the old, so that in truth and in deed, as well as in word and phrase, "There shall be no discrimination on account of race or color."

The failure of the old reconstruction, in so

far as it may be so considered, was due to the
fact that it never met with the unanimous acceptance of the American people, but was
forced by one section upon the unwilling acquiescence of the other. The new reconstruction, on the other hand, must meet with the
unanimous consent of the American people,
North and South, East and West. What
American dares rise up and say nay to the demands of democracy?

Government Based on Inequality

Alexander Stephens, the vice-president of the
Confederacy, stated in his inaugural address,
that the Confederate States would attempt to
found a government based frankly upon human
inequality. For four long years the bloody
struggle raged around this issue. Strange to
relate, the World War, waged upon the survival of the same issue, lasted for the same
duration of time. The Confederate cause was
lost. The German cause has been lost. Any
cause that openly advocates human inequality
is bound to be lost under the assault of democratic ideals. By the irony of history, the
political heirs and assigns of the advocates of
government based upon inequality were in
control of the affairs of this nation during the
World War, when it was committed most une-

quivocally to the doctrine of government based
frankly upon human equality. Woodrow Wilson was spokesman for democracy, not merely
for this nation but for all nations. It may be
said, in homely phrase, that the South was in
the saddle, but she was riding a democratic
horse which was headed to the goal of human
equality. She must ride straight or dismount.

REACTION

Reactionary voices here and there may be expected to rise, but they will be drowned in the
triumphant course of democracy. Over-buoyant expectation may meet with disappointment.
Negro soldiers, returning from across the seas
with laurels of victory, may here and there be
made to feel the sting of rebuff and insult by the
very people whose liberties they fought to
secure. Intense local animosities may be engendered in one place or another. Outbreaks
and murder may spasmodically occur. A comprehensive understanding of the far-reaching
effect of forward movements must discount all
this. Black laws followed the Thirteenth Amendment. The Ku Klux Klan came after reconstruction. There was a recrudescence of race
prejudice after the Spanish-American War, in
which the Negro had played a glorious part.
These are but backwaters in the current of

democracy. The tide is now at flood and cannot be stemmed. The most conspicuous opponents of democracy, for fear it might include the Negro, with dying gasp of defiance, were driven from places of public power under the excoriating lash of President Wilson, Southerner. The logic of events overrides the narrow purposes of men. The sign of democracy is written across the sky, in letters so bold and pronounced, that he who runs may read; and those who are too foolish to read will be compelled to run.

Rights and Duties

The Negro must not be allowed to make the same mistake in the new reconstruction that he was permitted to make in the old. All of his energies were focused upon the issue of political rights and privileges with little or no reserved power for economic and industrial advancement. Could Booker T. Washington have come upon the stage a generation earlier, preaching the doctrine of industry, thrift and economy alongside of Frederick Douglass, proclaiming in thunderous tones the gospel of human rights, the advancement of the race would have been built upon a foundation that could not be shaken. The desired product involves both factors. In this new day, the Negro must place equal emphasis upon rights and duties. He must deserve all that he demands, and demand all that he deserves.

Self-Reclamation

The government can give the individual only a fair chance. The race, he himself must run. No trick or contrivance of government can ennoble the Negro beyond the level of his work and worth. When democracy prevails, the upward struggle has just begun. Soil, sunshine, and moisture may abound, but the seed must send its own roots into the soil, and its blades into the air by the push of its own potency.

War energizes the powers, and liberalizes the faculties of man. In the wake of war, reconstruction always builds mightier structures than those that have been torn down. The United States is on the threshold of a mighty economic, educational, and moral awakening. The worker will feel a new zest, the thinker will have a new thought, and the poet will sing a new song. Opportunities will be open to every competent and willing worker for the best development and exercise of his highest powers and attainments. The Negro must contribute his bit and his best to the general welfare, and derive his just share from it. He must enter as a competent and willing participant in the new issues of life, and must not fail to help promote the glory of that new freedom whose beneficiary he devoutly hopes to be.

CHAPTER IV

UNREST AMONG WEAKER RACES

The inherent rights of man receive emphasis and new assertion at moments of social stress and strain. When society is in travail, liberty is born. During the long eras of leisure, the spirit of liberty languishes. Existing order is transformed, and all things made new amidst the fire and smoke of revolution. In times of quietude and peace, social evils accumulate and crystallize. The acquisition of wealth and the attainment of culture and refinement constitute the goal of endeavor. Discontent is decried and the soul seeks its ease. The voice of the reformer is denounced as tending to disturb social placidity and repose. The troublesome issues of the rights of man are banished from consciousness. Inequalities arise, aristocratic prerogative is asserted, and divine sanction assumed as the ordained scheme of social adjustment. When reform becomes impossible, revolution becomes imperative. It requires periodic upheavals to startle the soul from its complaisant slumber, discredit the dominance of material aims, and vindicate the rights of man as the highest attainable human value.

The permanent effect of any war is to be judged by its humanitarian outcome and moral aftermath. Sacrifice of blood and treasure is in vain unless there results a better social relationship. The American Revolutionary War released the Declaration of Independence, the embodiment of the democratic ideal. The French Revolution set the ears of the world atingling with the doctrine of "liberty, fraternity, equality." The war between the States produced the Emancipation Proclamation and extended the ennobling bonds of liberty to include the race farthest down.

The World War has exacted an unparalleled toll of human life and material values; but, alas, the world impatiently awaits a clear indication of corresponding moral contribution. The League of Nations, designed for the composure of the world, is frustrated by age-old jealousies, greed and ambition. Nations are vying for political and commercial ascendency as of yore. Race animosities have been aroused and stimulated. The weaker breeds of men have developed an assertive and defiant self-consciousness. Japan smarts under the stigma of race inferiority. The darker breeds of men resent the assumption on the part of the

whiter ones of everlasting lordship and dominion. In America, human beings are lynched,
tortured and burned alive at the exaction of
race prejudice; the land of liberty is in danger
of becoming the land of lynchers. The Ku
Klux Klan proclaims the revival of an invisible
empire based upon the principles of darkness
and evil. Is the World War to bring in the Anti-
Christ or the Christ that is to be? This query
must prick the Christian conscience to the core.
Race prejudice is the one dominant obstacle in
the world today which stands surely athwart
of the coming of the Kingdom of Heaven which
Jesus sought to set upon the earth. The
Christian church is vainly deluding itself in a
frantic endeavor to reconcile Christian duty
with racial caste. The chasm between races
cannot be bridged by a structure resting upon
such insecure foundation; the folly is as apparent as in building upon shifting sands
instead of enduring rock, or substituting coils
of smoke for bands of iron.

Yet we hope that, somehow, there is an imminent moral economy in human affairs. The
World War has brought together all peoples of
all lands and this incidental contact has, of
itself, aroused a consciousness of brotherhood
and of moral unity. It is the psychological
moment for the Christian religion to quicken

this consciousness into a keener sense of spiritual kinship and a more intense appreciation of
the oneness of human nature and of human
needs. Christianity must justify its claim of
being the world religion by meeting the needs
of the world at this critical time. The one
dominant purpose of the teachings of Jesus is
to promote peace on earth and good will among
men as was proclaimed by angelic heraldry on
the night of His birth. The dominant note in
Christianity is brotherhood, without restriction
or reservations. If a brother of the flesh should
impose upon his less fortunate kinsmen fixed
boundaries beyond which he dared not go, the
proffer would be rejected with scorn.

The man at the bottom is always the chief
beneficiary of social upheavals. As long as the
surface of the lake is calm and tranquil, the
sediments at the bottom are fixed in their place
by pressure of the superincumbent waters.
But when the storm arises, and lashes the
waters into fury, the bottom sediments arise
toward the top and settle themselves according
to their own specific gravity. The consciousness of the weaker races has been aroused by
the turbulency of war. Their erstwhile
lethargy and lassitude are giving way to the
stimulated urge of restlessness and divine discontent.

The war to destroy imperialism has left the world more imperialistic than before. The imperialism of race is more despicable in the eyes of the dominated races than the imperialism of empire. A noted American statesman based his objection to the League of Nations on the ground that it admitted the non-white races on a footing of equality with the whites. The terms "white" and "colored" today convey the same arrogant and intolerant significance as "Jew and Gentile," "Greek and Barbarian," "Christian and Heathen" in the days when the world was divided into such mutually exclusive classes with the implied hauteur and contempt of the former for the latter. Those who stand on the pinnacle of temporary advantage declare themselves to be the "chosen people," but they need not expect their claims to be allowed by the unchosen whom they hold in despite.

Can small nations, without the means of compelling power, maintain their self-sovereignty among larger nations with greater armies and navies? Can the weaker races assert their independence against the greed and rapacity of the stronger ones? are questions as ancient as the world-old issue between might and right. In the present posture of the world thought and conduct, the gospel of the heaviest battalion is the last word of authority, and the booming gun is the only sanction that has no doubt. But, somehow, the moral genius of mankind expects that the still small voice of conscience will triumph over the earthquake, the whirlwind and the devouring flame.

The restlessness of the weak lies at the basis of moral progress. No individual, nation or race is likely to abolish inethical procedure as long as it proves profitable. Idol makers will never destroy idolatry. Slavery has been banished from the civilized world by common consent of the exploiting nations, but only when it proved to be economically disadvantageous to the nations as a whole. Economic inequity quickly stimulates the sense of moral evil.

The man that feels the pain must utter the groan. The weak nation may not be morally superior to the strong one, but it possesses the moral advantage of weakness. It is a human instinct to heed the cry of the oppressed. But if the oppressed fail to give the outcry, there will be no indication for the oppressor to heed. The balance of powers is relied on to hold a turbulent world in equilibrium. The League of Nations is a polygon of forces in which the strongest components control the resultant. The two score of weaker nations are confessedly placed at the mercy and good graces of the five strongest powers. The weaker races of the world outnumber the stronger ones in the ratio of two to one. The mind is so prone to superficial indications that color has come to connote quality. "White" and "black" convey moral significance, like "up" and "down" in ethics.

The ultimate outcome of the war will hinge upon the relation of the stronger to the weaker races of mankind. All races, creeds and colors were brought into the conflict, and inspired with the hope that the bond of human brotherhood would become stronger than border, breed or birth. Their participation was invited on the basis of this assurance. The doctrine of self-determination became the moral watchword which gave zest and justification to the struggle. President Wilson made this phrase pregnant with vital meaning. He, doubtless, intended its application to be limited to the smaller and weaker states of Europe, which embraced his universe of moral discourse. But a word once uttered can never be recalled, nor can its application and meaning be limited to any prescribed races or preferred peoples. He that hath ears to hear, let him hear. "Liberty, fraternity, equality," originally intended for the Frenchman, became the moral watchword of mankind. The Declaration of Independence was intended to meet a political emergency in the relationship of England to her colonies. The de-

nunciatory phraseology and vehement assevera-
tions aimed at an obstinate monarch are dead,
and lie buried in the dust and cobwebs of oblivion, and possess only an antiquated interest.
The effervescence of the hour passes as the
winds that blow. The fundamental doctrine of
human liberty makes the universal appeal, and
renders the document immortal.

The Emancipation Proclamation of Abraham
Lincoln, though couched in terms of concrete
particulars, sounded the death knell of slavery
throughout the world. The doctrine of self-
determination is but a modified expression of
Lincoln's universal declaration, "No man is
good enough to govern another without his consent." Reëmphasis of this doctrine appeals
most keenly to the weaker races because their
ears are pricked to its kindly suggestion. To
the stronger races it conveys a certain con-
descension in loss of pride and lowering of
prestige; to the weaker ones it is the power
which makes for salvation. There exists
among modern statesmen and publicists the
complaisant delusion that they can indulge in
universal declarations of the rights of man,
while the ears of the weaker people are too dull
to hear and their minds too feeble to understand. But when Pandora's box is once opened,
it can never be closed. Ex-President Wilson's

attitude toward Mexico, Haiti and San Domingo spoke louder than the uttered word. The aggrieved groups quickly detected and repudiated the partiality of his meaning but insisted upon the universality of its import. The maxim is greater than the mouthpiece. The treasure is heavenly, though the vessel be earthen.

The minority cannot hope to dominate the majority for all time to come. The domination of the white race because of its whiteness would reverse all of received moral ideas of justice and righteousness. The stronger races today are the trustees of civilization, which they hold in trust not only for their descendants of the flesh, but for all the children of men. How can the advanced races best relate themselves to the backward ones, so as to lift them as expeditiously as possible to the attained level of civilization? is the ultimate question of statesmanship. That they can be, or should be, kept at a lower level so as to remain forever a field for exploitation finds no justification either in our ethical system or practical philosophy.

The present bias of mind of European nations is that the backward peoples are incapable of self-government according to the existing level of civilization, and, therefore, must be brought under alien dominion for the common good of all. But from another point of view it is also

apparent that any people, at whatever level of
culture, can govern themselves better than any
other agency can govern them. Self-government is more fundamental than good government; for self-government usually leads to good
government, but good government, however
benevolently imposed, will never lead to self-
government. President Wilson, in an un-
guarded moment, stated that the people of
Mexico should be allowed to spill all the blood
they pleased in the struggle for self-government, just as the people of Europe have done.
The deep, underlying thought of this suggestion
was obscured and left undeveloped by reason
of its political unwisdom. Much of the imperfection in the régime of the backward peoples
struggling up to the higher levels of civilization
is but incident to the upward struggle.

We scan the horizon in vain for an instance
wherein a stronger nation has conferred a lasting benefit upon a weaker one by the imposition
of its political authority. Japan is the most
illuminating instance in evidence. The Japanese wisely adopted and adapted whatever their
own genius could assimilate from the standards
of European culture and thereby rose swiftly to
the desired level of efficiency. She wove the
woof of alien attainment upon the warp of
native culture. Had any one of the European

states assumed control of Japan as a means of developing the natives, like progress would have been delayed by many centuries, if not made utterly impossible. American civilization came in touch with the Sandwich Islands with as high and holy a motive as ever an advanced culture approached a lower one. There was then quickened impulse of spiritual motive and missionary enthusiasm, but when the Stars and Stripes were lifted over the islands, it was but the symbol of death to the hope and ambition of the native population. Whatever the future position of these islands may be, it will not be for the welfare of the native Hawaiian. A shrewd missionary once described the blessings which Christianity brought to the natives by saying that it prepared thousands of them for the blissful hereafter to which it hastened them. The American Indians would possibly in time have developed the western continent to the highest level of civilization if left to their own autonomy. The marvelous expansion of the American continent has been in the interest of the white race and at the expense of the red. Lo, the poor Indian, looks stolidly on as he sees the paleface plant a glorious civilization in the wake of the death of his own race. The white man's glory is the red man's gloom.

The United States may do much in the Philippine Islands, but it is only by withdrawing its political authority and restoring the liberty of the people themselves that it can ever hope to lead to the development of the natives. Europe can never hope through political dominance to develop India or Africa. China must be left to her autonomous development if she would come into her own in the equation of civilization. It was President McKinley who devised the phrase, "benevolent assimilation." The strongest races can be of great advantage to the weaker races by proffering the right suggestion of friendly relationship, wholesome advice and kindly counsel. Moral mandates will bring help and encouragement; political mandates mean exploitation and death. Altruism is hardly a national virtue. A state exists to promote the welfare of the people within its borders and within the sphere of its operation. Avowed declaration on the part of statesmen of vicarious welfare of the weak must always be taken with a grain of salt. What nation would not gladly assume mandate of a rich and fertile area? On the other hand, who is willing to assume such responsibility for lands and peoples without resources of material or strategic value? An American humorist has shrewdly suggested that the United States would find quickly that the Philippines were hopelessly incapable of self-government if gold mines or oil fields should be developed in that distant archipelago.

Proximity is the fundamental process of socialization. Nearness begets dearness. This is a universal principle without deviation. Territorial unity lies at the basis of all national and racial spirit. Universal strivings of people everywhere show plainly that they seek a country. Abraham felt the impulse of his race for a homeland, and this impulse has been the inspiration of the Hebrew people from the days of Abraham to those of Einstein.

The Irishman, like the Jew, has a longing to reawaken the life and spirit of the harp that once shed the soul of music through Tara's Halls. When a people has become for a long time settled upon a given territory, and established reaction between the soil and the soul, they regard it as their eternal possession for themselves and for their seed after them, and the highest ideal is for self-government and self-direction in the land which the Lord, their God, has given them. Outside conquest can never overthrow this feeling unless it destroys the race itself, root and branch. Any racial element that cannot be exterminated will yearn to

regain dominion over its homeland. The
conquest of the white race over the regions of
the earth can only be temporary except where
it utterly destroys the native race, as in the case
of the Indian on the American continent, or the
native races in Australia. By universal agreement, the black and yellow races cannot be destroyed by contact with civilization, and are destined to dominate the lands that gave them
birth. There are two widely contrasted
theories of racial endowment; the one asserting that the European alone has inherent ability
to lift himself from a lower to a higher level of
culture; the other theory asserts that culture is
only the outgrowth of environment, and that
any race, under encouraging environment, will
develop the requisite powers to adjust itself to
a form of culture suitable to that environment.

The most striking evidence of the oneness of
the human race is that mankind everywhere
makes like response to the same stimulus. Not
only the weaker states of Europe have caught
the doctrine of self-determination, but aggrieved groups everywhere have been inspired
by it. Japan has opened the eyes of the world,
and has convinced the weaker races that culture is not an attribute of color, and that the
white race cannot claim a monopoly of those
faculties of mind and soul which make for ad-

vancement and civilization. The leaven of racial unrest is at work all over the world.

In India, it assumed form under the leadership of Ghandi who, embodying the genius of his race, based his propaganda upon non-resistance. The European for such a long time has ignored the doctrine which his borrowed religion inculcates that he has almost forgotten the meaning of its founder who declares that he who fighteth with the sword shall perish by the sword. The example of the Son of a subject race may yet teach the lordly European the wisdom of the essence of the Christian religion which he accepts and ignores. The World War has directly, or indirectly, killed off 40,000,000 or 50,000,000 members of the white race, approximately one-tenth of the Aryan population of the world. The white race is staggering under a burden of armament which all but breaks its back under the Atlantian load.

President Harding's conference on disarmament keenly realized the self-destruction of carnal warfare. So slow is the European mind to realize the wisdom of the Nazarene. This comparative race for armament is to determine which nation shall outdo the other in exploiting the resources of the weaker races scattered over the face of the earth.

All thoughtful minds are perfectly aware that in time the Indians will come into possession of their own sovereignty, if not through the passivity of Ghandi, yet through the inevitable racial aspiration for self-sovereignty.

Of all the weaker races, the Negro occupies the most interesting and most tragic situation. The continent of Africa is under their physical dominance, and in some blind, half conscious way it is looked upon as the homeland of this race. Scores of millions of African blood have been snatched from the motherland and distributed among the European peoples in all points of the earth. In the United States of America we have the most interesting fragment of this scattered race. And the outcome here will probably determine the future of Africa in the scheme of the world. No race question can be solved by dealing with scattered fragments, but the essential solution must be effective in the homeland of the race. The Irish question can never be settled by any adjustment of expatriated Irishmen to the nations and governments all over the world, but it must be determined by the genius of the race asserting itself in the native Erin. The Japanese question can never be solved by dealing with a handful of Japanese either in Australia or on the Pacific coast of America, but in the center of Japanese hope and aspiration, the island of Nippon itself. Even the question of the Jewish race will not be determined by dealing with the Jew in relation to the various nations and governments among which he is scattered over the face of the earth, but by the establishment of a Jewish state in Zion, where the race genius longs for Jerusalem, My Happy Home. And so, the African question cannot be settled in South America, or in the British Islands, or in the United States of America, until finally settled on the continent of Africa.

Valera, the Irishman, voiced the unrest of a branch of the Aryan race whose physical distinction has no significance, but whose racial passion demands self-guidance. Ghandi, the meek and lowly Hindu, spoke to the alien overlord of his race in the language of Moses to Pharaoh—"Let my people go." Marcus Garvey, a West Indian Negro, broke suddenly upon us like a voice crying in the wilderness for the redemption of Africa. Egypt joined the chorus. The scattered racial fragments throughout the world reëcho the refrain. Self-determination is and will be the goal of racial striving, unless or until, perchance, there arises a moral and spiritual sanction transcending the bonds of breed and birth, which shall ring out the feud of strife and blood.

CHAPTER V

RACE DIFFERENCES

So to Eternal Difference of Race

(Open Letter to President Harding and Reply)

Honorable Warren G. Harding,
  The White House,
    Washington, D. C.

Nov. 30, 1921.

MY DEAR MR. PRESIDENT:

Your Birmingham address marks an epoch in the history of race adjustment in the United States, if not throughout the entire world. You have doubtless received thousands of responses from all parts of the country expressive of every shade of thought, feeling and opinion. There is a sort of dilatory prudence in withholding the expression of one's opinion until others have spoken. But one thus runs the risk of being charged with hesitancy of opinion and deference of judgment. I trust, however, that this communication will not be regarded as being hopelessly belated or presented out of due season. The significance of your proposition is comprehensive and permanent. It pos-

sesses little or no news value or journalistic
timeliness. The principle which you lay down
and the policy which you approve are calculated to have enduring consequences upon the
tangled issue of race relationships. Indeed, the
hasty reaction will probably have no important
results. The race problem remains in all important respects the same immediately after
your delivery as immediately before it. Fundamental principles cannot be judged by instantaneous results. One generation sows the seed,
the next enjoys the fruition thereof.

The immediate effect of your declaration has
been to bring the eternal Negro question once
more to the forefront of current discussion.
There seems to be a conspiracy of silence on
part of the organs of public opinion to ignore
troublesome or distressing issues. Men are
prone by nature to seek easement of conscience
by affecting obliviousness of evils which menace
private repose and public tranquillity. In this
way is cherished the vain delusion that we may
gain surcease from menacing conditions which
we lack the moral courage to face. But the
ghost of evil conditions will not down at our
bidding. The bronchial tickling and the occasional cough remind the over-sanguine consumptive of the fatuity of his optimism. From the
foundation of the government until now there

has been no interval of long duration when the unwelcome issue of race has not forced itself on public thought and action. Just at a time when the South was flattering itself that its provincial régime of political and civic inequity had received the approval, or at least the connivance of the nation, and when the North, being so absorbed in economic exploitation, that its ear had grown dull to the complaints of the Negro, you came forward with the courage,— may I say without offense, with the temerity— to lend the weight of your high authority to renewed discussion of an issue which the people, if they could, would gladly relegate to the realm of oblivion.

The motive which prompted this bold and courageous utterance on your part has given rise to much speculation. Some have been disposed to consider its timeliness with reference to the Disarmament Conference as a preliminary pronouncement on the great issue of race which lies in the background of the international gathering now sitting in the city of Washington. This conference is a result of your statesmanship, and the world is looking with anxious expectancy to its effect upon the world-wide adjustment of nations and races. The race problem in America casts a shadow of suspicion upon the claims of democracy as the ideal form of government. A clear clarion pronouncement on this subject, coming from the highest authority in the nation, might well serve to allay this feeling of doubt as to the sincerity and genuineness of America's pretensions which the other nations have a right to entertain. Your declaration has been construed in some quarters as the answer which Great Britain and the United States, the two branches of the Anglo-Saxon race, have agreed to render in respect to Japan's demand for racial equality. It has been suggested that you may have been voicing the sentiment of the more intolerant Teutonic element of the white race in its endeavor to persuade the more liberal Latin element that the whiter races must adopt this policy in dealing with the darker ones.

On the other hand, there are those who are inclined to believe that your chief intention was to extend the influence of the Republican party in the Southern States which has, hitherto, been reduced to a nullity by reason of the race problem. In the last election the Republican party carried the States of Maryland, West Virginia, Missouri, Kentucky, Tennessee and Oklahoma. You would probably have received the electoral vote of every state in the Union if the race issue had not interfered. All genuine effort to remove this question from politics must meet with the approval of all right thinking American citizens. However, the recent overwhelming defeat of the Republican party in Virginia, which, it seems, anticipated much of your platform, is not reassuring.

The sudden abortive ending of the Ku Klux Klan investigation by the legislative and executive branches of the government lends color to the suspicion of some that your forthcoming deliverance would be relied on to squelch this nefarious organization, whose midnight wizardry seeks darkness rather than light because its deeds are evil.

It is not unreasonable to suppose that it was your purpose to lay down a comprehensive platform on which both races can stand and work out, with mutual confidence and coöperation, their common destiny. I am disposed to accept this interpretation of your motive.

There is all but universal commendation of your moral courage in injecting an unwelcome issue at so critical a juncture of the world's affairs. It is only the intolerable type of Southern opinion that questions either the wisdom or propriety of your doing so. As a Republican, elected mainly by Northern and Negro votes, you have gone into the heart of what Mr. Bryan would call the enemy's country, to reaffirm a doctrine which for two generations the white people of that section have united in oath-bound allegiance to combat. Every President of the United States, since Abraham Lincoln, with a single exception, has indulged in public declaration on the race question. Mr. Wilson, who relied on the soothing balm of pleasing phraseology to hold a restless world in poise, is the only President who did not deign a single word on this subject during his tenure of office. He probably felt that any utterance which he could afford to give would be violative of his declared principles of universal liberty and equality, and, therefore, preferred to remain silent rather than convict himself of illogicality and ethical inconsistency. The race issue was always shunted by his single-track mind. It will not be regarded as ungracious to say that he retires to private life with the unanimous approval of the Negro race. The esteem of the despised and neglected may seem to be of little import to one who treads the highway of world renown, but it is doubtful whether any American statesman, whatever his achievements, can receive the highest meed of permanent esteem if the least of his fellow-citizens justly have aught against him.

No President has spoken more clearly or with more genuine sincerity or with more evident indication of good will and generous spirit than that which characterizes your Birmingham address. But, Mr. President, any doctrine originated or adopted by one in high authority will not be judged in the future by the intention of its author, but by the meaning and significance inherent in the doctrine itself. A slaveholder penned the Declaration of Independence, but the motto: "All men are created free and equal" has gained an interpretation and significance that far surpass the restricted intention of its author and his aristocratic compeers who adopted it as a revolutionary watchword. Chief Justice Taney was considered a courteous, kindly and well-meaning jurist. His famous obiter dictum, that "the Negro had no rights which the white man was bound to respect," expressed, as he judged, with accuracy and appositeness the state of mind at the period which he undertook to describe; but the phrase itself rendered nugatory his meaning and purpose, and damns the author to "everlasting fame."

A phrase may be more potent than a fact. Opinion, crystallized in terse phraseology rules the world or throws it into confusion. The term "Social Equality" conveys deeper meaning and evokes quicker reaction than a volume of argumentation. The treatment which the Negro receives is always the outgrowth of the estimate in which he is held by his white fellow-citizens who for the time being occupy the superior position in our social scheme. When the Negro was regarded as a beast without a soul to be saved, he was dealt with in accordance with this low assumption. So long as he was held in the estimate described by Justice Taney's dictum, his legal and social status was adjusted in accordance. It was only by reason of the moral energy aroused by the anti-slavery discussion that the essential human recognition of the Negro found expression in the Thirteenth, Fourteenth, and Fifteenth Amendments to the Constitution. The thought is greater than the thing. Ideals are better than deals. A principle is greater than a program. Feeling is not only the greatest fact, but the greatest force in the world. Keep thy heart with all diligence, for out of it are the issues of life. Unless the public mind is held to the right attitude, we look in vain for righteous public action. If through the authority lent to the doctrine of race distinction by your great office it should prove convincing to the American people, the Negro would be branded with a stigma of inferiority, and laws, customs and practices would be based upon this foundation so long as its validity remains undisputed.

Mr. President, I know that it will grieve you

to learn that your colored fellow-citizens whom it was your chief purpose to benefit by your Birmingham platform, place upon it a construction which may be farthest from your intention and purpose. It is only out of a sense of duty to my race and to my nation that I write as I do. By voice and pen, I advocated your election as far as my limited opportunities would allow. I have hoped to have the chance to assist in your reëlection three years hence. I am not, therefore, writing in a captious spirit of criticism, but from deep conviction. Unfortunately, I have not yet learned the wisdom of the politician whose first principle of procedure is never to tell those in superior station the truth unless, perchance, he be first assured of its kindly reception. Candor compels me to say, Mr. President, speaking deliberately on behalf of the thoughtful element of the Negro race, that your platform based upon the assertion of "fundamental, inescapable and eternal differences" of race is calculated, in the long run, to do the Negro as great harm as the Taney dictum would have done, had not the aroused conscience of the nation negatived the interpretation which the author placed upon it. Since the foundation of the government no other president has ever lent the authority of his great office to the doctrine that the rights of American citizens should be conditioned upon recognition of indelible difference of race.

The fathers and founders of this republic, though dealing with the Negro race, then relatively more numerous than now, and on a decidedly lower level of progress and development, were scrupulously careful to exclude from the organic law all suggestion of race distinction. The federal administration should ever be kept true to the ideal of democracy. The fountain-head must be kept pure, although the streams which flow from it may gather impurities from its tributaries after leaving the original source. A corrupt fountain cannot send forth a pure stream.

The danger lurking in your platform, Mr. President, lies in its essential illogicality. You have attempted to derive a Northern conclusion from a Southern premise; and in doing so you have satisfied neither the North, the South, nor the Negro. The South accepts your premise, but rejects your conclusion; the Negro accepts your conclusion, but rejects your premise; while the North maintains a hesitant and lukewarm attitude towards both.

Senator Watson of Georgia, and Senator Heflin of Alabama, who typify the more radical Southern attitude, as well as Senator Pat Harrison, who occupies a medium position, were

quick to retort that your conclusion would at
once destroy your premise, and, therefore, must
be rejected. The governor of Alabama, who
presided at your meeting, gave a courteous and
cautious approval to your address as a whole,
but he will probably have to pay a heavy political price when the day of reckoning comes
with the junior senator from that state.

From the Negro's point of view you have attempted to build a superstructure of righteousness upon a fallacious foundation. Whatever
the intention of the builder, a house builded on
sand will not stand when the rains fall and the
floods descend and beat upon it. If you write
at top of the page the declared and accepted
doctrine of "fundamental, inescapable and eternal differences of race," it then makes no difference what you may write underneath, the Negro
would be degraded into an inferior caste which
would render any form of equality impossible.
The Negro's claim to political and civil equality does not rest upon any condition or concession, but grows out of his inalienable right
as a human being and his guaranteed rights as
an American citizen. When the Fourteenth
Amendment made the Negro a citizen, it was intended that he should enjoy all of the benefits
and fruitions of citizenship. There was not the
slightest suggestion or intimation that he would

be required or expected to assent to any assumption as a condition precedent to the enjoyment of his rights. These rights, instead of being stipulated upon the assumption of racial difference, were affirmed "without regard to race or color." The Negro, if he would, cannot barter away his rights, or hypothecate them upon the acceptance or rejection of any alleged theory of difference of race. If both races should accept or reject it, in whole or in part, the rights of the black man would be wholly unaffected by such agreement or disagreement.

So far as I have observed, the white press of the South has not in a single instance clearly and unequivocally adopted your platform of political, economic and educational equality for the Negro. But some of them, out of considerations of courtesy, and through ambiguity of language, and with evident mental reservation, have given cautious quasi approval of your position. On the other hand, the Negro press, in considerable proportion, either condemns your doctrine of eternal racial difference or ignores it in view of the hoped-for advantages to be derived from equality of opportunity. Your words are so much more pronounced and emphatic than any which this generation is accustomed to hear, that the over-optimistic Negro is carried away with the enthusiasm of the promise without stopping to consider the impossibility of its fulfillment. But in no single instance have I seen the Negro opinion which accepts in clear and unequivocal terms the doctrine of "fundamental, inescapable and eternal difference of race." Neither Major Moton nor Marcus Garvey would avow a categorical acceptance of this doctrine. Some are disposed to hope that the advantages which are calculated to flow from political, economic and educational equality would justify present silence, but not general acceptance of your premise. Others, I feel, have deluded themselves with the hope that if the conclusion be granted, the premise will speedily be overlooked or forgotten. The general drift of opinion, however, on part of the Negro press that has taken pains to give careful thought and analysis to the question, is that any form of equality will be impossible if your hypothesis becomes generally accepted. The Negro would thus sell his birthright for a mess of pottage, with no assurance that he will receive the pottage.

President Roosevelt, in his celebrated letter to a Southern publicist, declared that he would not shut the door of hope in the Negro's face. Your policy, Mr. President, contrary to your purpose, would latch, lock and bolt it to all eternity.

I am fully aware that you do not use the term "inferiority" in this discussion. Race difference does not in itself necessarily carry this connotation. There are marginal dissimilarities in racial attributes and endowments. The German is more phlegmatic than the Frenchman, the Celt is more hysterical than the Teuton, the peoples of Northern Europe show greater racial intolerance than those of Southern Europe. Italy has artistic temperament different from that of England. The Chinaman is more stolid than the Japanese. The Negro possesses patience, meekness, forgiveness of spirit which surpasses that yet manifested by any other race. In the sum total of racial endowment it is not a question of equality, but of equivalence. These differences or dissimilarities are doubtless the outgrowth of environment and long continued custom and practice. I think that no biologist or psychologist who has regard for his reputation would care to venture the opinion that such differences are inescapable and eternal.

Your words, Mr. President, were addressed to a Southern audience, and must have conveyed to them the meaning which they are accustomed to attach to such phraseology. In the vocabulary of the South, race difference means Negro inferiority. It would not be fair or courteous to you to suppose that you would employ words which would convey to your hearers strange and unusual meaning. Nor can we for a moment suppose that you intended that your words would convey one meaning to the white man of the South and another to the Negro. Your language, translated in terms of Southern interpretation and understanding, simply means that the Negro should be treated kindly so long as he is content to occupy the place which God and nature have assigned him. The man temporarily at the top is ever prone to set up fixed barriers between himself and the man at the bottom. This policy is as old as human oppression. But any insistence beyond these fixed limits leads swiftly to the reaffirmation of the Taney dictum that the Negro has no rights that the white man is bound to respect, but only restricted privileges which he is generous enough to bestow.

You recite with approval the views of Mr. F. D. Lugard set forth in the April number of the *Edinburgh Review*.

"Here then is the true conception of the inter-relation of color—complete uniformity in ideals, absolute equality in paths of knowledge and culture, equal opportunity for those who strive, equal admiration for those who achieve; in matters social and racial a separate path, each pursuing his own inherited tradition, preserving his own race purity and race pride; equality in things spiritual, agreed divergence in the physical and material.''

This conception is magnificent in theory, but unworked and unworkable in practice. It might conceivably be applied to races of widely separated residential boundaries like Japan and England, but is utterly impossible as a permanent solution where races are inextricably intermixed on the same territory. In the Hawaiian Islands there exists today a conglomerate racial situation composed of competing numbers of Europeans, Japanese, Chinese and natives, with a sprinkling of the Negro, together with various cross progenies. Such a permanent outcome of this tangled situation as Mr. Lugard proposes is but a beautiful dream.

One opinion in sociological matters suggests another. Surely the position of Professor Franz Boas, of Columbia University, would be as convincing to Americans as that of the author whom most American readers met with for the first time in your citation. Writing in the June number of the *Yale Review,* Professor Boas closes an illuminating article on ''The Problem of the American Negro'' with these words:

''Thus, it would seem, that man being what

he is, the Negro problem will not disappear in America until the Negro blood has been so diluted that it can no longer be recognized, just as anti-Semitism, until the last vestige of the Jew as a Jew has disappeared.''

When doctors of equal learning disagree, the layman is at liberty to accept the diagnosis of either, or reject both.

You have taken for granted a doctrine of universal importance without attempting to prove its accuracy or even to argue its validity. Without intending to do so, you have adopted the dogma of every pro-slavery advocate and of every present-day reactionary on the question of human rights. On this point you are in perfect accord with the late Senator Benjamin R. Tillman, and Mr. Thomas Dixon, Jr., author of *The Clansman*. This unintentional agreement, I am sure, will prove an uncomfortable one. The question of essential difference of race is one on which there are not sufficient scientific data to base any conclusion of value. The few psychologic tests already made are inconclusive.

On the other hand, the apostles of race prejudice assert with self-assumed infallibility that the difference of race is God-ordained, beyond a shadow of doubt or peradventure. These extemporaneous philosophers assume omniscience without taking the pains to acquire intelligence. They take their cue from the cuticle. On sight of color they seek no further proof. They assert without proof and argue without reason. Mr. Thomas Dixon, Jr., the chief effect of whose works is to stir up racial strife and ill-will, presents a fair specimen of the type of argument relied upon to prove the everlasting inferiority of the Negro. When the mind is already made up, confirmation is easy. Mr. Dixon's citations are hoary, his arguments trite and his rhetorical form of statement prescribed. Not a new fact or argument has been advanced on this subject since the days of Calhoun.

President Lincoln, in the heat of political discussion, in 1856, indulged in some general remark concerning the social distinction of the races, which is the only utterance from the Great Emancipator which Southern statesmen recite with approval. It is indeed disappointing to find a President of the United States at the end of the World War for democracy reverting to the undemocratic doctrine which has always been relied on to justify man's inhumanity to man.

Some time ago I wrote an open letter to Mr. Thomas Dixon, Jr., in which I undertook to controvert the whole fabric of his anti-Negro philosophy. I challenged him to point out a single intellectual, moral or spiritual discriminant which distinguishes the two races. So far the challenge remains unanswered. No reputable author has as yet isolated it.

In the present inflamed state of public feeling the question of social equality can be asserted only to be assented to. Opinion on a given question is of value only when the one who entertains it is equally free to espouse the opposite conclusion. Even the President of the United States could not discuss the question of social equality in Alabama, unless it was understood beforehand that his conclusion was in consonance with local sentiment. Rational discussion on this issue serves only to inflame the mind of its proponents.

"You may as well go reason with the wolf
  Why he has made the ewe bleat for the lamb."

The Negro does not wish to agitate this issue, but only asks that it be defined, so that he may understand the range and scope of its operation. If two races, from instinct or from calculated reasons, prefer to group themselves separately in all matters of personal and pleasurable intercourse, neither would have the right or reason to complain of the mutual exclusiveness. It is only because the plea of social equality limits citizens in their public and civil

rights that the Negro utters the voice of protest. The two races at present occupy separate
social spheres. Social prejudice, whether it be
based on color, race or religion, may be deep
seated and long abiding, albeit not eternal. All
peoples at times have recognized and acted
upon schemes of social distinction by acceptance, acquiescence and silence or by prudent
complaisance or compulsion. But one can hardly
expect the debased party to justify the grounds
of his debasement. The Negro finds himself in
a segregated social world. He is making the
best he can of this situation. He is not clamor-
ing for so-called social equality, and would be
wholly unable to assert his claim even if he were
clamorous. But surely it cannot be expected
that the race will meet in solemn conclave and
affirm its belief in and acceptance of "fundamental, inescapable and eternal differences."
This would justify the propaganda of the Ku
Klux Klan whose avowed purpose is to help the
Almighty carry out his plan of everlasting
white supremacy. Complaisant acquiescence on
his part could not mitigate the malignity of race
prejudice, but would serve to intensify it, if it
be natural, and to justify it if it be acquired.

You mention with approval Mr. Stoddard's
book on *The Rising Tide of Color*. This
book was under review by Mr. Lugard when

he proposed his platform of race adjustment based on race distinction. Mr. Stoddard is the apostle of the dominance of the white race by sheer right of its color. His doctrine sounds the death knell of democracy, Christianity and the brotherhood of man. Idolatry of race is more vicious than idolatry of graven images. Mr. Stoddard and all those of his persuasion would do well to ponder the fundamental purpose of the Second Commandment, "Thou shalt not make unto thee any graven image or likeness—Thou shalt not bow down thyself to them nor serve them." According to Mr. Stoddard it is more important that the world should be white than that it should be right. I wonder how this doctrine is received by the Japanese, Chinese and Hindu representatives who are now sitting in the world conclave at Washington. There is no attribute of the Almighty which is understandable by the darker races of mankind which dooms two-thirds of the human race to the everlasting domination of the other third by virtue of the pigmentation of the skin.

Mr. President, your platform conforms with considerable closeness to that of the late Henry W. Grady, the oracle of the new South, and to that of Booker T. Washington, the acknowledged race statesman of his day. Only you go farther in both directions than either of these

cared to go. Mr. Grady was ready to give the
Negro every consideration consistent with the
separateness and superiority of the white race.
He entertained certain misgivings as to the
eternal barrier of race and was frank enough
to declare that, if in his judgment natural antipathy were not enough to keep the races
asunder, he would stimulate race prejudice in
order that it might acquire and hold the
strength and stubbornness of instinct. Dr.
Booker T. Washington, in his epoch-making
Atlanta address, proposed the familiar hand
and finger policy as a working hypothesis. But
I find nowhere in his teaching nor in his practice
any recognition of a "fundamental, inescapable
and eternal difference of race."

Your doctrine of eternal difference is contrary to the scientific, ethical and social tendencies of the age. The human race is moving
toward unity, not diversity. The ancient barriers of caste, religion and race are being
thrown down by the onward sweep of cosmic
forces. The varieties of gifts, talents and attainments of different individuals, races and
nations of mankind are easily interchangeable
and modifiable by contact and culture. The
rapid means of communication and transmis-
sion of intelligence are bringing the ends of the
earth into momentary touch. No longer can

any race or nation expect to hold its peculiar
culture in airtight compartments. You and I,
Mr. President, are about the same age. It is
a reasonable hope and expectation that we shall
both live to see the time when aerial communication between Tokio and New York will be as
expeditious as land communication is at present between Washington and Chicago. Where
people meet and mingle, differences disappear
and unsuspected likenesses are revealed. The
culture of mankind flows from the higher to the
lower levels and tends, with increasing facility,
to cover the earth as the waters cover the sea.

Your audience must have received your re-
marks about the impossibility of amalgamation
with a measure of amusement mixed with
amazement. A glance over the colored section
of your audience would have convinced you
that amalgamation is not a theory, but a fact.
No discerning eye was keen enough to tell where
the white strain left off and the Negro began.
In face of these stubborn facts, your statement
is hard to understand. According to the 13th
census, there were over 2,000,000 mulattoes in
the United States. This albescent contingency
of the Negro race was not produced by the semi-
tropical climate of the Southland, as Southern
white men know full well. No wonder your
audience received this deliverance in silence.

It is idle for white men to prate about race purity while they practice race promiscuity. There is need of plain speaking on this point. It is needless to blink the facts, if I may be permitted to use your own expression, or, like the ostrich, to engage in complacent self-deception. The white man has never failed to mingle his blood with the darker races wherever he has met them in all the ends of the earth. According to President Roosevelt, Brazilian statesmen are convinced that their method of benevolent amalgamation is a more effective solvent of the race problem than the Anglo-Saxon policy of social segregation. In South Africa a million and a half Europeans have already produced one-half their number of mulattoes. The production of this composite progeny constitutes an important factor in the solution of the race problem not only in the United States of America, but throughout the world.

Several years ago I appeared before the House Committee to oppose a bill then pending forbidding intermarriage of whites and Negroes in the District of Columbia. I find that my words used then are pertinent now: "If you let people alone, of their own notion they do not usually amalgamate. The Jew will marry a Jew, the Italian an Italian, the Englishman will marry an Englishwoman. This is so in the natural course of things. Amalgamation of races is a slow and long process when you leave people alone. If you want to forbid intermarriage of races you must have in mind this fundamental principle. It makes no fundamental difference in the long run whether races are amalgamated legitimately or illegitimately. Students of history know that at one time in England there were two distinct peoples, the Normans and the Saxons, who finally became amalgamated very largely through the illegitimate process. But, after a few generations, when the social stigma had passed away, it made no difference. The social stigma of the father is visited on the children only to the third and fourth generations. For instance, the chairman of our delegation, though a colored man, is as white inside and outside as any member of Congress. If he chose to change his name and residence and to practice a little deception he could easily become a part of the white race. What he could do is only what 200,000 others could do in like situation.'' If God or nature had intended any indelible difference between the races, He could easily have accomplished the purpose by making them immiscible. It requires great human audacity to reënact laws of the Almighty, to say nothing of enacting laws for the Almighty.

You urge the Negro not to imitate the white man, but to set up his own racial ideals. The American Negro has acquired the European's consciousness and put on his spiritual clothes. He uses the same language, reads the same books, admires the same art, understands the same science, accepts the same standard of ethics and practices the same religion. When he builds a house or buys a suit of clothes or preaches a sermon or writes a poem, he must proceed along European lines. Whatever racial aims or ideals he might have developed if left in his native country have been destroyed by transplantation and by imitation of his captors. Fred Douglass used to say "there is none of the banana in me." It is no particular compliment to the white man that the Negro imitates him. The human race is ever prone to imitate admirable qualities wherever they appear. It is not color or racial indiosyncrasy that is imitated, but attainment, of which the color may be a negligible accompaniment. The Anglo-Saxon professes to imitate Jesus, the Savior of the World, although he may affect to despise the idiosyncrasies and race peculiarities of the Jew. It is not the race, but the ideal manifested by the individual. As in the water face answers to face, so the heart of man to the heart of man. The external incidents of race and color count absolutely for naught. Because the Negro's forefathers traveled in the dugout, there is no reason why his descendants may not use the steamship, the railway and the airplane. Whatever divergencies there may be in racial gifts and qualities serve as the spice of variety. It would be a curious philosophy that urged the Indian to put aside his ancestral and tribal ways and yet encouraged the Negro to revert to his African customs and traditions.

If I may be permitted to revert again to the deracialized millions of mixed breed, whose ethnic identity the white man has made doubtful, it would be interesting to know what traditions and racial ideals they should be encouraged to develop. Your advice to the Negroes on this point, Mr. President, though given with a generous purpose and kindly intent, is necessarily void of effect. No one can effectively advise another to be different from himself or to be content with anything less or anything different from that which he is willing to accept for himself. In vain does the millionaire advise the pauper to be content in his poverty. The well man need not urge the invalid to be satisfied with illness. The philosopher in vain preaches to the fool the contentment of folly. The teacher who would teach his pupil to be less than himself or different from himself loses the power of inspiration. No white man, however generous his spirit, is competent to advise the Negro in the domain of the segregated life which he must live apart.

> "The toad beneath the harrow knows
> Exactly where each toothprint goes.
> The butterfly along the road
> Preaches contentment to that toad."

Mr. President, your doctrine ties your hands and makes it impossible for you to accord the Negro political equality. You were supported in the last election by 100 per cent of the Negro voters. They naturally expect official recognition according to their weight and importance in the political equation. Their votes as much as any others helped to swell the magnitude of your majority. So far you have not seen your way clear to recognize this support by concrete tokens of political reward. The plaint of disappointment is all but universal. Your black political allies can scarcely refrain from the familiar lines

> "Behold a stranger at the door,
> He gently knocks, has knocked before,
> Has waited long, is waiting still;
> You treat no other friend so ill."

No one believes that this is in accord with your spontaneous feeling and attitude, but by reason of the recognition of race difference you hesitate to accord the Negro political equality. It is also stated that you have declared that you will not appoint a single colored man to office in the South where 8,000,000 loyal Republican Negroes reside. This is not because hundreds of Negroes are not well qualified to hold sundry offices as the white men whom you are likely to select, but because of alleged racial differences. Political equality must carry with it the right to vote and be voted for or to hold any office in any part of the United States. It is also stated that you have refused to appoint a colored man to the position of Register of the Treasury, a position accorded to the race for more than a generation, because 500 subordinate white employees in the Treasury Department petitioned you not to place a colored man over them. Racial segregation in the government departments, begun under Mr. Wilson's administration, is continued under yours. These instances are sufficient to prove conclusively that even a President of the United States cannot accord the Negro political equality as long as he defers to the doctrine of eternal difference of race.

It would be pleasing to suppose that the

Negro could get economic equality on the basis
that you have laid down but the hope is vain.
Every caste system in the world is based on
vocation. Social stratification rests upon employment. The Negro in Washington is not permitted to operate a street car as a motorman,
not because of his lack of ability to do so, but
by reason of his race alone. Any man who can
run an automobile in the open streets where
there are not tracks can surely guide a street
car which moves along fixed grooves. This
single citation is sufficient to show that you
cannot have democracy in industry as long as
you recognize inescapable difference of race.

In conclusion, Mr. President, you have called
the nations of the earth together to promote
peace and good will among men. Whatever
adjustments immediate exigencies may require,
whatever concessions weakness may be forced
to make at the behest of strength, the weaker
and darker races will not shut the door of hope
in their own faces by accepting the doctrine of
"fundamental, inescapable, and eternal difference" among the members of the human race.

The Negro has given his labor and his life to
build up American civilization. He is willing to
coöperate with his white fellow-citizens in all
constructive ways for the common weal. He
accepts without complaint the temporary humil-

iation of an inferior position. But he believes
that God Almighty has ordained America as the
trial ground of democracy where among all men
there shall prevail equality with the "i" dotted
and the "t" crossed.

Yours truly,
KELLY MILLER

29 November, 1921.

THE WHITE HOUSE,
Washington, D. C.,
December 6, 1921.

DEAR DR. MILLER:

Your long and very interesting letter of November thirtieth is before me.

I shall not at this time attempt anything like
a detailed consideration of it, but I do want to
thank you in the utmost sincerity for the effort
you have made to present so forcefully your
point of view.

I am sure you will not be disappointed if I
say that you have not convinced me, or, if I add
that I do not believe you will succeed in convincing a majority of the American people, of either
the white or black race. This problem has been
the subject of a good deal of thought and consideration on my part, as I know it has been on
yours.

I believe the suggestions advanced in the Birmingham address represent the possibility of a large and early amelioration of the condition of the colored people, and should greatly regret to have to conclude that they were unwilling to recognize this possibility and to avail themselves of it.

(Signed) WARREN G. HARDING.

Dr. Kelly Miller,
Dean, Howard University,
Washington, D. C.

CHAPTER VI

DISGRACE OF DEMOCRACY

(Open Letter to President Wilson)

Hon. Woodrow Wilson, President of the United
  States,
  The White House,
    Washington, D. C.

Aug. 4, 1917.

MR. PRESIDENT:

I am taking the liberty of intruding this letter
upon you because I feel that the issues involved
are as important as any questions now pressing
upon your busy attention. The whole civilized
world has been shocked at the recent occur-
rences in Memphis and East St. Louis. These
outbreaks call attention anew to the irritating
race problem of which they are but eruptive
symptoms which break forth ever and anon
with Vesuvian violence. For fully a generation
American statesmanship has striven to avoid,
ignore or forget the perplexing race problem.
But this persistent issue will not down at our
bidding, and cannot be shunted from public at-

tention by other questions, however momentous or vital they may seem to be.

I know that I am taking unwarranted liberties with the ceremonial proprieties in writing such a letter to the President of the United States at the present time. It may seem to partake of the spirit of heckling after the manner of the suffragists. Nothing is further from my purpose. No right-minded American would wish to add one featherweight to the burden that now so heavily taxes the mind and body of the President of the United States who labors under as heavy a load as human nature is capable of sustaining. Every citizen should strive to lighten rather than to aggravate that burden. It is, nevertheless, true that any suppressed and aggrieved class must run athwart the established code of procedure in order that their case may receive a just hearing. Ceremonial codes were enacted by those who are the beneficiaries of existing order which they wish to perpetuate and make unchangeable. They would estop all social and moral reform. The ardent suffragists find it necessary to violate ruthlessly the traditional and decorous modes of procedure in order to promote the reform which they have at heart. On one occasion you felt forced to terminate an interview with a committee of suffragists because they persisted in cross-examining the President of the United States.

There are 10,000,000 loyal citizens of African descent in the United States. They are rigorously excluded from a voice in the government by which they are controlled. They have no regularly constituted organ through which to present their case to the powers that be. They have no seat nor voice in the council of the nation. The late Doctor Booker T. Washington was the accepted spokesman and mediator of the race, but he has no successor. Under former administrations there was a small appointive official class of Negroes. Though derisively designated as the "Black Cabinet," they were on the inside of the circle of governmental control to which they had ready access in presenting the claims of the race. But under the exaction of partisan exigencies even these have been excluded from official position under your administration. Several weeks ago a delegation of colored men from the State of Maryland sought an interview with you concerning the horrible crime of East St. Louis. You were good enough to write Senator France that you were too busy with other pressing issues to grant the request of an interview. The failure of all other methods is my only excuse for resorting to an open letter as a means of reaching you and, through you, the nation at large, concerning the just grievances of 10,000,000 loyal American citizens.

The Negro feels that he is not regarded as a constituent part of American democracy. This is our fundamental grievance and lies at the basis of all the outrages inflicted upon this helpless race. It is the fundamental creed of democracy that no people are good enough to govern any other people without their consent and participation. The English are not good enough to govern the Irish. The Russians are not good enough to govern the Finns. The Germans are not good enough to govern the Belgians. The Belgians are not good enough to govern the people of the Congo. Men are not considered good enough to govern women. The white people of this country are not good enough to govern the Negro. As long as the black man is excluded from participation in the government of the nation, just so long will he be the victim of cruelty and outrage on the part of his white fellow-citizens who assume lordship over him.

These periodic outbreaks of lawlessness are but the outgrowth of the disfavor and despite in which the race is held by public opinion. The evil is so widespread that the remedy lies in the hands of the national government.

Resolutions pending before both houses of

Congress look toward investigation of the outrage at East St. Louis. I understand that you are sympathetically disposed toward this investigation by Federal authority. Such investigation is important only to the extent that it implies a tardy recognition of national responsibility for local lawlessness. There is no expectation that any additional comprehensive information will result. You may rest assured that there will be a half dozen similar outbreaks before this investigation is well under way. Indeed, since the East St. Louis atrocity there have already been lynchings in Georgia, Louisiana, Pennsylvania and Montana. Every intelligent American knows as much about the essential cause of this conflict as he will know after long and tedious investigation. The vital issues involved are apt to be obscured by technical wranglings over majority and minority reports. What the nation needs is not investigation of obvious fact, but determination and avowed declaration on the part of the President speaking for the people of the United States to put an end to lawlessness wherever it raises its hideous head.

I know that it has been steadily maintained that the Federal Government has no authority over lynchings and local race conflicts. This is not a political contention. This view was maintained under the administrations of Harrison, Cleveland, McKinley, Roosevelt and Taft. Indeed, President Cleveland, that great American democrat, came nearer recognizing Federal responsibility in such matters than any President before or since his time. During the administration of President McKinley, an atrocious riot occurred in Wilmington, N. C., the city in which you spent your boyhood as the son of a minister of the Gospel. Scores of innocent Negroes were killed and hundreds were driven from their homes. But it was maintained that the President had no authority to interfere. A horrible lynching took place at Alexandria, Virginia, a few miles from the White House, which the President might possibly have observed through his field glasses. And yet it was looked upon as a purely local affair for which the Federal Government had no responsibility nor concern. You recall the atrocities of the riot in Atlanta, a city in which you spent your young manhood as a practitioner of law. But here again even President Roosevelt could find no ground for interference.

These outbreaks are not limited to the Southern States, although they occur there more frequently than elsewhere because of the relatively larger number of Negroes in the total population. There have been lynchings and burnings in Illinois, Kansas, Delaware, Ohio, Indiana, Colorado and other Northern States. The evil is indeed national in its range and scope, and the nation must provide the remedy. Striking indeed is the analogy between the spread of lawlessness today and the extension of the institution of slavery two generations ago. Like slavery, lawlessness cannot be localized. As the nation could not exist half slave and half free under Abraham Lincoln, so it cannot continue half law-abiding and half lawless under Woodrow Wilson. The evil tendency overcomes the good, just as the darker overlaps the brighter phase in the waning moon. If the Negro is allowed to be lynched in the South with impunity, he will soon be lynched in the North, so easy is the communicability of evil suggestion. The lynching of Negroes has become fashionable in some parts of the country. When a black man is accused of wrongdoing, "Lynch the Negro!" is the cry that springs spontaneously to the lips of man, woman and child. The fashion is rapidly spreading throughout the whole nation. If slavery could have been isolated and segregated in the South that institution might have existed even down to the present time. And so, if lynching could be localized and limited to the Southern States, the nation as a whole would have less pretext for

interfering. But this cannot be done. Senator
Tombs of Georgia boasted that he would call
the roll of his slaves under the shadow of the
Bunker Hill monument, an ambition which,
doubtless, might have been gratified had not the
nation arisen in its moral might and blotted
out the iniquitous institution altogether. Unless
the aroused conscience of the American people,
efficiently asserting itself through Federal authority, shall stamp out the spirit of lawlessness, it is easy to prophesy that the Negro will
yet be lynched not only in the shadow of the
Bunker Hill monument, but on the campus of
your beloved Princeton. Already there have
been burnings of human beings in the bleeding
State of Old John Brown, and in the city where
lie the remains of Abraham Lincoln. During
the past thirty years nearly 3,000 Negroes have
been lynched in various parts of the country.
Scores of these have been burned at the stake.
Even the bodies of women have been fed to the
flames. Thousands of localities in the majority
of the States of the Union have experienced
these outrages. Our fair land of liberty is
blotted over with these foul spots which cannot
be washed out by all of the waters of the ocean.
It is not easy to calculate the number of persons
who have been involved in these lynchings,
either as participants or as acquiescent lookers-

on, all of whom were potential murderers. So general and widespread has become the practice that lynching may well be characterized as a national institution, to the eternal disgrace of American democracy.

Lynching cannot be confined to the Negro race. Hundreds of white men have been the victims of lawlessness and violence. While these words are flowing from my pen, news comes over the wire that a labor agitator has been lynched in the State of Montana. Although the Negro is at present the chief victim of lawlessness, like any other evil disease, it cannot be limited by racial lines.

It is but hollow mockery of the Negro, when he is beaten and bruised and burned in all parts of the nation and flees to the national government for asylum, to be denied relief on the ground of doubtful jurisdiction. The black man asks for justice and is given a theory of government. He asks for protection and is confronted with a scheme of governmental checks and balances.

Mr. President, you are commander-in-chief of the army and navy. You express the voice of the American people in the great world conflict which involves practically the entire human race. You are the accepted spokesman of the world democracy. You have sounded the trumpet of democratization of the nations, which shall never call retreat. But, Mr. President, a chain is no stronger than its weakest link. A doctrine that breaks down at home is not fit to be propagated abroad. One is reminded of the pious slaveholder who became so deeply impressed with the plea for foreign missions that he sold one of his slaves to contribute liberally to the cause. Why democratize the nations of the earth, if it leads them to delight in the burning of human beings after the manner of Springfield, Waco, Memphis, and East St. Louis while the nation looks helplessly on? You add nothing to the civilization of the world nor to the culture of the human spirit by the technical changes in forms of government. The old adage still remains true:

"For forms of government let fools contest—
What's best administered—is best."

If democracy cannot control lawlessness, then democracy must be pronounced a failure. The nations of the world have a right to demand of us the workings of the institutions at home before they are promulgated abroad. The German press will, doubtless, gloat with ghoulish glee over American atrocities against the Negro. The outrages complained of against the Belgians become merciful performances by gruesome comparison. Our frantic wail against the barbarity of Turk against Armenian, German upon Belgian, Russian upon Jew, are made with no effect. It cannot be said that these outbreaks are but the spontaneous ebullitions of popular feelings, without governmental sanction or approval. These outrages occur all over the nation. The nation must be responsible for what it permits. Sins of permission are as reprehensible as sins of commission. A few years ago a Turkish ambassador was handed his passports by you for calling attention to the inconsistency between our national practice and performance. The nation was compelled, with a spirit of humiliation, to accept the reproach which he hurled into our teeth: "Thou hypocrite, first cast out the beam of thine own eye; and then shalt thou see clearly to cast out the mote of thy brother's eye." Every highminded American must be touched with a tinge of shame when he contemplates that his rallying cry for the liberation of humanity is made a delusion and a snare by these racial barbarities.

It is needless to attempt to place the blame on the helpless Negro. In the early stages of these outbreaks there was an attempt to fix an evil and lecherous reputation on the Negro race as lying at the basis of lynching and lawlessness.

Statistics most clearly refute this contention. The great majority of the outbreaks cannot even allege rapeful assault in extenuation. It is undoubtedly true that there are imbruted and lawless members of the Negro race, as there are of the white race, capable of committing any outrageous and hideous offense. The Negro possesses the imperfections of his status. His virtues as well as his failures are simply human. It is a fatuous philosophy, however, that would resort to cruel and unusual punishment as a deterrent to crime. Lynching has never made one Negro virtuous nor planted the seed of right doing in the mind of a single American citizen. The Negro should be encouraged in all right directions to develop his best manly and human qualities. Where he deviates from the accepted standard he should be punished by due process of law. But as long as the Negro is held in general despite and suppressed below the level of human privilege, just so long will he produce a disproportionate number of imperfect individuals of evil propensity. To relegate the Negro to a status that encourages the basest instincts .of humanity, and then denounce him because he does not stand forth as a model of human perfection, is of the same order of ironical cruelty as shown by the barbarous Teutons in Shakespeare, who cut off the hands and hacked out the tongue of the lovely Lavinia, and then upbraided her for not calling for perfumed water to wash her delicate hands. The Negro is neither angelic nor diabolical, but merely human, and should be treated as such.

The vainglorious boast of Anglo-Saxon superiority will no longer avail to justify these outrages. The contact, adjustment and attrition of various races of mankind constitute a problem which is coterminous with the ends of the earth. The lighter and stronger races are coming into contact with the weaker and darker ones. The stronger breeds of men are relating themselves to the weaker members of the human family in all the ends of the earth. How does it happen that in the United States alone, of all civilized lands, these atrocious outrages are heaped upon the helpless Negro? The English nation has the largest colonial experience and success since the days of the Roman Empire, and has come into relationship with the various weaker breeds of men in all parts of the world. But everywhere under English jurisdiction law and order prevail. In the West Indies, where Negroes outnumber the whites 20 to 1, rape and lynching have scarcely yet found a place in the local vocabulary. In Brazil, under a Latin dispensation, where a more complex racial situation exists than in the United States, racial peace and good-will prevail. Belgium furnishes the only parallel of civilized nations, in the atrocious treatment of a helpless people placed in their charge. But even the Belgians were forced to modify the rigors of their outrageous régime in the Congo, under the bombardment of moral sentiment of the more enlightened nations of the world. America enjoys the evil distinction among all civilized nations of the earth of taking delight in murder and burning of human beings. Nowhere else do men, women and children dance with ghoulish glee and fight for ghastly souvenirs of human flesh and mock the dying groans of the helpless victim which sicken the air, while the flickering flames of the funeral pyre lighten the midnight sky with their lurid glare.

Mr. President, the American conscience has been touched and quickened by the East St. Louis outbreak as it has never been before. Press and pulpit have tried to forget these outrages. At each fresh outbreak they would lash themselves into a spasm of virtue and exhaust the entire vocabulary of denunciation, but, forthwith, would lapse into sudden silence and asquiescent guilt. By some fatuous delusion they seem to hope that the atrocities of Springfield, Wilmington, Waco, Atlanta, Memphis and a thousand other places of evil report would never be repeated, nor the memory rise up to condemn the nation. But silence and neglect merely result in compounding atrocities. The East St. Louis outbreak convinces the nation, as it has never been before, that the time for action has come. The press is not content with a single editorial ebullition, but by repeated utterances insists that the nation shall deal with its most malignant domestic evil. Reproach is cast upon your contention for the democratization of the world, in face of its lamentable failure at home. Ex-President Roosevelt, who is the greatest living voice now crying aloud for individual and national righteousness, has openly proclaimed, in dramatic declaration, that these outbreaks make our moral propaganda for the liberation of mankind but a delusion and a snare. Mr. President, can this nation hope to live and to grow in favor with God and man on the basis of a lie? A nation with a stultified conscience is a nation with stunted power.

Democracies have frequently shut their eyes to moral inconsistencies. The democracy of Greece conferred privilege upon a mere handful of freemen in the midst of ten times their own number of slaves. The Greek philosophers and statesmen were supremely unconscious of this moral obliquity. The Declaration of Independence which declared for the equality of all men was written by a slaveholder. The statesmen of the period, however, hoped that slavery would be of short-lived duration, and would effect its own solution in the process of time. But Thomas Jefferson was keenly sensitive of the moral inconsistency of this attitude that God is just, and that His justice would not slumber forever. Abraham Lincoln is perhaps the only great statesman of democracy who was absolutely consistent in his logical attitude and moral sincerity. He uttered no word of cryptic meaning. The people heard him gladly because the words that fell from his lips were not the coinage of his intellect, but the mintage of his heart. The embattled hosts under his high command marched to victory with the Battle Hymn of the Republic resounding in their souls:

"As He died to make men holy
Let us die to make men free—"

To them this phrase had no remote and deferred meaning, but was immediately applicable to their black brother in chains. It was not a barren ideality, but a living impulse. You have given the rallying cry for the present world crisis. But this shibboleth will be robbed of instant meaning and power unless it applies to the helpless within our own gates. If the sons and grandsons of the heroes who battered down the walls of slavery a half century ago could be made to feel with unreserved certainty a renewal of the moral energy which urged their fathers to that high resolve, they would, with heightened enthusiasm for humanity, demolish the Teutonic bulwarks of oppression across the seas.

Doctrine is more than deeds, if it be sound doctrine. Deeds are the outgrowth of doctrine. Doctrine lives forever with persistent potentiality. Doctrine rules the world or throws it into confusion. The power of words is far greater than the meaning of the author. It makes no difference what lay in the minds or practice of the statesmen of Greece. They planted the seeds of democracy, and all mankind will become the beneficiary of the sowing. The intendment of the signers of the Declaration of Independence boots but little. That document will stand for all time as the gospel of human liberty. When you speak of the democratization of the world and the liberation of mankind, you are setting up a standard to which the whole world must rise in the ages to come, despite its attitude at the present time. It may be far from the purpose of our present-day statesmen to admit the Negro into this democracy on terms of equality with the rest. But in spite of the purpose of this statesmanship, this must be the ultimate goal of human democracy. A democracy of race or class is no democracy at all. It is with projected imagination that the Negro will endure until these high-sounding phrases have borne their full fruition. Any other class of the American people, under the strain of distress to which the Negro has been subjected, would imitate Job's distracted wife, and curse the white God and die. The Negro will neither curse nor die, but grin and live—albeit beneath that grin is a groaning of spirit too deep for utterance. The Negro says to his country, "Though you slay me, yet will I serve you."

The Negro's patriotism is vicarious and altruistic. It seems to be an anomaly of fate that the Negro, the man of all men who is held in despite, should stand out in conspicuous relief at every crisis of our national history. His blood offering is not for himself or for his race, but for his country. This blood flows like a stream through our national history, from Boston Commons to Carrizal. Attucks was the first American to give his blood as an earnest of American independence. The Negro was with Washington in the dark days of Valley Forge, when the lamp of national liberty flickered almost to extinguishment. The black troops fought valiantly with Jackson behind the fleecy breastworks at New Orleans. Two hundred thousand black boys in blue responded to the call of the immortal Lincoln for the preservation of the Union. The Negro was the positive cause of the Civil War, and the negative cause of the united nation with which we face the world today.

The reckless daring of Negro troops on San Juan Hill marked the turning point in the struggle which drove the last vestige of Spanish power from the Western world. It was but yesterday that we buried with honor, at Arlington Cemetery, the Negro soldiers who fell face forward while carrying the flag to the farthest point in the heart of Mexico, in quest of the bandit who dared place impious foot on American soil. In complete harmony with this marvelous patriotic record, it so happened, that it was an American Negro who proved to be the first victim of ruthless submarine warfare, after you had distinctly announced to Germany that such outrages would be considered tantamount to war. In all of these ways has the Negro shown, purposely or unconsciously, his undeviating devotion to the glory and honor of the nation. Greater love hath no man than this, that he lay down his life for his country.

In the midst of the World War for the democratization of mankind, the Negro will do his full share. I have personally always striven to urge the Negro to be patriotic and loyal in every emergency. At the Reserve Officers' Training Camp in Fort Des Moines, there are over one hundred young colored men, who have come under my instruction. The deviltry of his fellowmen cannot devise iniquities horrible enough to drive him from his patriotic devotion. The Negro, Mr. President, in this emergency, will stand by you and the nation. Will you and the nation stand by the Negro?

I believe, Mr. President, that to the victor belong the spoils, especially if these spoils be human liberty. After this war for the liberation of mankind has been won through the Negro's patriotic participation, he will repeat the lines of the old familiar hymn somewhat louder than ever:

> "Behold a stranger at the door,
>   He gently knocks, has knocked before;
>   Has waited long, is waiting still;
>   You treat no other friend so ill."

As a student of public questions I have carefully watched your attitude on the race problem. You have preserved a lukewarm aloofness from the tangled issues of this problem. In searching your writings one finds little or no reference to this troubled phase of American life. It seems that you regard it as a regrettable social malady to be treated with cautious and calculated neglect. There is observable, however, a passive solicitude. You have kept the race problem in the back part of your mind. Your letter to Bishop Walters during your first campaign for the Presidency, expressing a generous concern for the welfare of the race, though of a general and passive character, caused many Negroes to give you their political support. Under the stress and strain of other pressing issues and the partisan demands of your political supporters, you have not yet translated this passive purpose into positive performance. There is, however, something of consolation in the fact that while during your entire career you have never done anything constructive for the Negro, you have never done anything destructive against him. Your constructive opportunity is now at hand. The time has come to make lawlessness a national issue, as a war measure if not from any higher consideration. As a patriotic and military necessity, I suggest that you ask the Congress of the United States to invest you with the power to prevent lynching, and to quell lawlessness and violence in all parts of the country during the continuance of the war. Or at least you might quicken the conscience of the nation by a stirring message to Congress calling attention to this growing evil which is gnawing at the vitals of the nation. It is entirely probable that before the war is over you will have to resort to some such measure to control internal disturbances on other accounts. It is inconceivable that this nation should spend billions of dollars and sacrifice the lives of millions of its citizens without domestic uprising and revulsion. In such a time it becomes necessary for the President to exercise all but dictatorial power. The country is willing to grant you anything you ask which, in your judgment, would promote the welfare of the nation in this crisis. You asked Congress to grant undiscriminated use of the Panama Canal as a means of securing international good-will and friendship, and it was granted. In face of the impending conflict you demanded that Congress should grant the eight-hour demand of the laboring men, and it was done. The suffragists who guard you going in and coming out of the White House were duly convicted under process of law, but were immediately pardoned by you to avoid embarrassment in this war emergency. You asked for billions of dollars and millions of lives to be placed at your disposal for the purpose of carrying on the great conflict, and it was willingly granted. The people have willingly placed in your hands more power than has ever been exercised by any member of the human race, and are willing to trust you in the use of that power. I am sure that they will grant this additional authority during the continuance of the present war in order to secure the unqualified patriotic devotion of all of the citizens and to safeguard the honor of democracy and the good name of the republic.

Mr. President, Negroes all over the nation are aroused as they have never been before. It is not the wild hysteria of the hour, but a determined purpose that this country shall be made a safe place for American citizens to live and work and enjoy the pursuits of happiness. Ten thousand speechless men and women marched in silent array down Fifth Avenue in New York City as a spectral demonstration against the wrongs and cruelties heaped upon the race. Negro women all over the nation have appointed a day of prayer in order that righteousness might be done to this people. The weaker sex of the weaker race are praying that God may use you as the instrument of His will to promote the cause of human freedom at home. I attended one of these 6 o'clock prayer meetings in the city of Washington. Two thousand humble women snatched the early hours of the morning before going on their daily tasks to resort to the house of prayer. They literally performed unto the Lord the burden of their prayer and song, "Steal Away to Jesus." There was not a note of bitterness nor denunciation throughout the season of prayer. They prayed as their mothers prayed in the darker days gone by, that God would deliver the race. Mr. President, you can help God answer their prayer. May it not be that these despised and rejected daughters of a despised and rejected race shall yet lead the world to its knees in acknowledgment of some controlling power outside of the machinations of man? As I sat there and listened in reverent silence to these two thousand voices as they sang,—

"On Christ, the Solid Rock, I stand,
All other ground is sinking sand——"

I could not think of the godless war which is now convulsing the world—a war in which Christian hands are dyed in Christian blood. It must cause the Prince of Peace to groan as in His dying agony when He gave up the ghost on the cross. The professed followers of the Meek and Lowly One, with heathen heart, are putting their trust in reeking tube and iron shard. God uses the humbler things of life to confound the mighty. It may be that these helpless victims of cruelty and outrage will bring an apostate world back to God.

Mr. President, ten million of your fellow-citizens are looking to you and to the God whom you serve to grant them relief in this hour of their deepest distress. All moral reforms grow out of the people who suffer and stand in need of them. The Negro's helpless position may yet bring America to a realizing sense that righteousness exalteth a nation, but sin is a reproach to any people.

Yours truly,

KELLY MILLER.

CHAPTER VII

THE NEGRO AND THE JAPANESE

I happened on the Pacific Coast when a committee of the United States Senate was inquiring into the Japanese situation. The stress of opposition was laid upon economic rather than racial differences. It was generally considered that the Japanese, by reason of their thrift and frugality, proved to be more than an equal competitor for the white man. They are able to increase the economic fraction by decreasing the denominator, whereas augmentation of the numerator is the only method that the American is willing to practice. Physiologically, the Japanese seem to be better adapted to truck gardening and other modes of agriculture on the Pacific coast; they are small in stature and can the more easily practice certain phases of agriculture which, like religious devotion, must be performed on the knee.

In addition to this, the Japanese have back of them a strong, aggressive and self-assertive nationality. With a territory too small to support its population, to seek a larger area for the expansion of its overcrowded life is the fixed policy of the Japanese government. It supports semi-officially large land and agricultural projects for its expatriated citizens. The American farmer, therefore, has to compete, not merely with individual Japanese, but also with the concealed hand of the Nippon government.

It is not contended that the Japanese have aspirations to become American citizens with singleness of spirit and detachment of aim, but after absorbing the substances of other lands, they long to return to their native land as the scattered Jew yearned for his native Jerusalem.

Mr. Harding, as the senator from Ohio, with statesmanlike comprehension of the issues involved, stated that America must be understood to possess the sovereign right to exclude any undesirable element from its borders, and must be the undisputed arbiter of the test of desirability. This he has done without wounding the racial pride or the just sensibilities of the nation involved in the issue.

I consulted many Californians, white and black, as to the attitude towards the Negro, and found that there existed on the Pacific coast no Negro problem in its frictional aspect. Where restrictive laws existed, they were inspired by the emergencies of the oriental situation and did not aim directly at the American Negro. The fact that the oriental situation had reached a stage of acute irritation tended to direct attention away from the Negro. It is not good policy to handle more than one troublesome issue at a time. Effort is frequently made to identify the attitude of the Pacific coast statesmen on the oriental question with that of the southerners on the Negro question. The two cases are in no sense identical.

The Negro is an American citizen whose American residence and citizenry reach further back than the great majority of the white race. He has from the beginning contributed a full share of the glory and grandeur of America and his claims to patrimony of American citizenship and privilege are his just and rightful due. The Japanese, on the other hand, is the eleventh hour comer, and is claiming the privilege of those who have borne the heat and burden of the day. If the case of the Negro were parallel to that of the Japanese, if the Negro were now for the first time claiming the right of unrestricted entry into the American industrial, political and social scheme, the situation would be entirely different; but he is as much a part of the constituent sovereignty as any other. He cannot, therefore, be deprived of any of the rights, privileges and prerogatives of American citizenship without violating every national and human obligation and stultifying the national conscience. Race adjustment, at best, constitutes an intricate and complicated problem, but considering the political aspect of the case, the political status of the Negro is so far removed from that of the Japanese that a comparison becomes odious.

Takao Ozawa is destined to become the Dred Scott of Japan. In the Dred Scott case the Supreme Court decided that the Negro race did not possess citizenship rights. In the Takao case the same tribunal has just declared that the Japanese race is not eligible to citizenship in the United States. Fortunately for the Negro race, this famous decision came at a time of intense moral agitation. The aroused conscience of the nation reversed the verdict of the court of next to the last resort. The American people arose in their moral might and utterly repudiated the repugnant verdict.

The people themselves constitute the court of last resort. The Fourteenth Amendment made a definition of citizenship which includes every person born in the United States and subject to the jurisdiction thereof. The learned jurist through whose voice the decision was announced became a byword of reproach to the American people. From that day until this, his name is never mentioned except in terms of denunciation or disgust. Had this iniquitous decision been handed down twenty years earlier or fifty years later, it doubtless might have met with a less unfriendly reception.

The Takao Ozawa decision came at a time when the American mind is not so sensitively concerned with the inherent rights of man to man. The rights of human beings, responsive to moral issues, must await the convenience of the interest of race. In all of the influential organs of public opinion, one looks in vain for a clear, straight from the soul, and straight from the shoulder condemnation of this Japanese decision. What is right and what is wrong is not determined by technical determination of the narrow letter of the law, but by the quickened or callous conscience of the people at that time.

According to the law passed in 1870, the white race and the Negro race are the only races eligible to naturalization. The Supreme Court has upheld the meaning and intent of the law. It is again fortunate for the Negro that this law was passed at a time when the American feeling on the Negro race question had reached its moral maximum. Well do I recall serving as spokesman of a delegation that called upon members of Congress to protest against a proposed law which excluded both Asiatics and Africans from coming to the United States. The Chairman of the House Committee on Immigration was a Democrat from Alabama. He stated that since the number of Negro immigrants was so insignificant, being but a handful of West Indians, and since these few settled in the North, and did not bother the white people of the South, he was perfectly willing to limit the restrictive provision to the Asiatics.

To some it may seem to be inexplicable that discrimination is here made in favor of the Negro rather than the Japanese. Ordinarily the higher meed of favor goes to the yellow Oriental. Here is a distinction with a deep difference. The claim of the Negro as a moral co-equal in this nation does not rest upon mere political expediency, or theory of race relationship, but is firmly founded upon basic principle of equity and justice. The white and black races came to this country at practically the same time. As many generations of blacks as of whites lie buried beneath her soil. They enjoy an inheritance of three centuries of ancestral toil. The white race has no claim to ownership of this nation that does not equally apply to the Negro. Both have contributed according to their talent and opportunity to her grandeur and glory. The contribution of the Negro as a spontaneous and cheerful co-worker has never been questioned. In industrial endeavor, in loyal devotion, in patriotic performance and in spiritual enrichment he has done his full share. The white race cannot, without violating every obligation of justice and honor, deny to the Negro any reward of privilege which as the fruit of their joint labor he claims for himself.

But with the Japanese it is not so. He has contributed nothing to the growth and grandeur of America. His claims rest solely upon the demands of international comity and the more abstract claims of human brotherhood.

Ozawa claimed that the Japanese should be classified as white by virtue of a common ancestry from which both races sprung. This claim was disallowed by the Supreme Court. The line of demarcation between the white and non-white races is clearly understood in a practical sense, which no amount of learned ethnological disquisition can seriously disturb. On the abstract side of the contention, the Negro cannot but sympathize with the Japanese point of view. The world cannot separate itself into air-tight compartments along lines of racial cleavage. The scientific, commercial and moral movements of the age make for moral unity. We can never have moral unity so long as any race smarts under the stigma of unfair discrimination.

The Supreme Court has never been the keeper of the conscience of the American people. Courts and jurists who deal in customs, traditions and precedents are apt to lag a generation or so behind the moral progress of the age. It was so in the Dred Scott decision. But in this instance it seems more likely that our highest tribunal has sensed the reactionary moral sense of the time. There is some faint glimpse of hope in the policy of the Department of Justice in requesting that the Supreme Court suspend consideration of this case pending deliberations concerning international disarmament. International harmony of action is dependent upon international goodwill. The Ozawa decision cannot possibly produce good feeling among the Japanese people. None of the non-white races of the earth will contemplate this decision with satisfaction. Will this decision be overthrown in time by the aroused moral sense of the nation as was its prototype in the days of Dred Scott or will it stand as a stumbling block in the way of international peace and good-will?

CHAPTER VIII

EDUCATION OF THE NEGRO IN THE NORTH

That "the Negro can earn a dollar in the South, but cannot spend it; and can spend a dollar in the North, but cannot earn it," is one of Booker T. Washington's most felicitous phrases. This was an apt accurate description at the time of its utterance. But social upheavals frustrate the wisdom of our profoundest philosophies. The war robbed this sententious assertion of its erstwhile truth and appositeness. The great educator had scarcely been dead a single year, when Negroes by the tens of thousand were rushing into the North to fill the vacuum in the labor market. The scale of wages seemed fabulous to the Negro workman, accustomed to the meager compensations in the South. The opportunities to earn and to spend were availed of with equal avidity. As a result of this labor demand, fully a half million Negroes were transferred from the South to the North.

Economic opportunity constitutes the prevailing motive in the movement of human population. Human greed is too hasty for immediate concrete results to calculate the far-reaching social consequences that follow in the train of the introduction of strange population for purposes of industrial and economic exploitation. The foreigner in America, the Negro in the South, and the Japanese in Hawaii and on the west coast were introduced to fulfill urgent labor demands, but their permanent social adjustments constitute the gravest problems of our national experience.

Fred Douglass used to say that wherever the Negro goes he takes himself with him. The sudden injection of a half million Negroes into the North will tend to make the question of race adjustment a national, rather than a sectional problem. The various features of the problem will gain new meaning and emphasis because of its widespread relationships. The educational significance of this northern movement of the Negro has hitherto received little or no attention, and yet it is calculated to be of the greatest significance in the educational life of the entire Negro race, and to influence the attitude of the whole nation. According to the reports of the Census Office, in 1920 there were 1,550,754 Negroes in the North, giving a decennial increase of 472,418 over the census of

1910. The great bulk of Negroes in the North
are found in the cities. The number of rural
Negroes in the Northern States has been gradually diminishing for the past three decades.
The Northern Negro creates an urban rather
than a rural problem. The following table reveals this city tendency in a most striking
manner:

NEGRO POPULATION—CITIES NORTH OF THE
POTOMAC RIVER

City	1910	1920	Increase
New York	91,706	153,088	61,382
Philadelphia	84,459	134,098	49,639
Washington	96,446	109,976	13,530
Chicago	44,103	109,594	65.491
Baltimore	84,749	108,...	......
St. Louis	43,960	69,603	25,643
Detroit	5,291	41,532	36,241
Pittsburgh	25,623	37,688	12,065
Indianapolis	21,816	34,690	12,874
Cleveland	8,448	34,474	26,026
Kansas City	23,566	30,706	7,140
Cincinnati	19,639	29,636	9,997
Columbus	12,739	22,091	9,352

These thirteen cities show an unusual increase, amounting in some cases to more than
fifty per cent. While this rapid growth was
due to special causes of limited continuance,

yet the numbers are not likely to diminish, but will show substantial increase with the coming decades.

There are six cities in the United States with more than 100,000 Negroes, all of which, with the single exception of New Orleans, are to be found north of the Potomac River. The border cities, Washington, Baltimore, St. Louis, and Kansas City, have separate colored schools, following the policy of the Southern States. In the other cities on the list there is no legal scholastic separation of the races. The city is the center of the educational life of the nation. The great systems of education, as well as the great seats of learning, are to be found mainly in the centers of population. A million and a half Negroes, constituting 15 per cent of the race, are thus brought into immediate contact with the best educational facilities to be found anywhere in the world. In the South the Negroes are found mainly in the rural district, where school facilities are meager and inadequate, and even in the large cities of this section the provisions for colored schools fall woefully short of the up-to-date standards of a well ordered system. In speaking of the education of the Negro, we should always keep in mind the widely contrasted educational advantages of these two groups.

Negroes in the North generally are admitted to all educational facilities provided for the general community, whether supported by public funds or based upon private foundation. The people of the North have devoted much of their resources and philanthropic energy to the education of the Negro in the South, while giving little or no consideration to the contingent of the race within their midst. The individual has been given an equal chance in the general educational provisions and has been expected to rise or fall according to the measure of his own merit. The rapidly increasing numbers focusing in the large centers of population will inevitably call attention to the special needs of this growing group separated in many ways from the life of the community of which they form a part.

The colored children have not seemed over-eager to avail themselves of the advantages provided for them. They have not felt the necessity of thorough educational equipment for the life tasks that lay within their reach. Being confined to the menial modes of service, they have not in large numbers been inspired to enter upon the higher reaches of education demanded in the more exacting lines of service. The eagerness of the Southern Negro for knowledge in the midst of meager facilities was in glaring contrast with the apathy of his Northern brother surrounded by such great advantages.

Until quite recently the fact of a colored student graduating from a high school in the North was so unusual as to demand general notice and flattering comment. For the most part the colored youth who pushed their way through Northern institutions of learning have been from the South with fresh incentive of the masses upon them. But as their numbers increase and concentrate in the larger centers, the circle of racial opportunity widens. The inspiration of racial life and uplift gives spurs to higher aspiration. The inherent needs and necessities of the masses create opportunities in the higher lines of leadership and service that demand the fullest educational equipment. Wherever the number of Negroes in a community is too small to create a center of racial life and activity, there is apt to be shown a corresponding lack of ambition and upward purpose on the part of colored youth. Wherever a handful of Negroes are gathered together in the North, there springs up a little church, which serves as an outlet for leadership and as a center of race aspiration. The largest Negro cities in the world are found in the North. New York, Philadelphia, Baltimore,

Washington, and Chicago contain each a sufficient number of Negroes to engage the highest human powers and faculties to answer the needs of so large a number of human beings. The ever widening field invites the highest ambition of Negro youth to rise to the level of the opportunity that awaits them.

In all of the Northern cities the Negro is concentrated in segregated areas and districts. This residential segregation creates a demand for leadership and self-direction. Large as his numbers seem, taken by themselves, the Negro constitutes only a small percentage of the total population except in several of the border cities. If they were evenly distributed throughout the white population, they would be practically unnoticed as a factor in the general equation. One hundred and fifty thousand Negroes in New York in the midst of six million whites, if evenly diffused, would count but one in forty, and would be a negligible entity in the general life of the metropolis. But a hundred thousand Negroes in Harlem constitute a city within a city. The racial needs of this large mass must be supplied by their own leadership, almost as if they constituted a separate community. Negro ministers, physicians, lawyers, editors, teachers, and business men must conform with reasonable approximation to the prevailing standards of the community. This opportunity gives incentive and ambition to the youth of the race to equip themselves with the fullest educational qualifications.

In most of the Northern States primary education is compulsory, so that every Negro child, in compliance with the law, must attend the public schools for a given period of years. In the near future we may expect that the Negro will approximate his full quota in high school, normal schools, technical schools, and colleges in the great centers of population where he is rapidly congregating.

There were more than four hundred Negro graduates from high schools in the class of 1920, and more than one hundred graduates from colleges and professional schools in the Northern States. This indicates the rapid growth in enrollment of the Negro in secondary as well as in higher institutions. There were probably 500 Negroes enrolled in colleges and professional schools of the North during the past year. This educational awakening in the North but indicates what may be expected in the near future.

The question naturally arises as to how far separate educational facilities will be deemed advisable for the Negroes in the Northern cities as their numbers tend to increase. This is al-

ready a mooted question in such cities as Philadelphia, Pittsburgh, Cincinnati, and Chicago.
In Washington, Baltimore, St. Louis, and
Kansas City, where separate colored schools
are maintained, there is a much larger enrollment of colored pupils in the higher levels of
instruction than in Philadelphia, New York,
and Boston, where the schools are mixed. The
separate systems seem to invoke a keener incentive and zest.

Will separate schools bring out the higher
aspirations of the Negro and lead to the un-
folding of his powers and possibilities? is the
question countered by the query: Will not
scholastic separation on racial lines vitiate the
spirit of democracy and lower the standards
of the less favored race? This controversy will
doubtless engender great heat of feeling and
animosity on the part of both races. The final
outcome should be determined in the light of
the best good to the Negro as well as that of the
community. The purpose of the schools is to
produce good and useful citizens. This objective should transcend all theoretical question of manner or method. And yet the great
democratic ideal must be kept constantly in
mind.

While the masses of the race remain in the
South, the educational center of gravity will be

shifting toward the North. Ambitious youth will flock to the centers of the best educational advantage, regardless of national or racial border lines. Northern institutions are filled with white Southern youth because they find there at present better educational facilities than the South provides. They saturate themselves with the aims and ideals and acquire technical facilities of these great centers of learning, and carry the acquisition back for the assimilation of their own section. Negro youth will be actuated by the same impulse and purpose.

Negro schools in the South have, so far, been planted and supported on the basis of the Northern philanthropy. This philanthropy has concerned itself largely with Negroes in the Southern States who have been suppressed below the level of educational opportunity and advantage. It has not contemplated that Negroes in considerable numbers would avail themselves of the best educational facilities afforded by colleges and universities of the North. It will be interesting to note the effect of this tendency upon the fate of the Negro's higher institutions of learning supported in the South on a philanthropic basis. Philanthropists are, naturally enough, disposed to place help where they deem it is the most needed. There is no particular need to help the Negro in the North, where he has only to stretch forth his hand and partake of the tree of knowledge which flourishes all about him. It is also natural that philanthropy will be inclined to foster institutions which encourage graduates to live and work among the masses in the South where the need is greatest. Negro students of Harvard, Yale or Chicago do not make the same philanthropic appeal as those in Atlanta, Fisk, and Tuskegee.

There is also a reserved feeling that it might be well to encourage separate Negro institutions, in order to keep too large a number of Negroes from entering white universities. This feeling will doubtless inure greatly to the benefit of Negro schools in the South. It must be determined whether the Northern universities are apt to impart to Negro students the social impulse and racial aspiration requisite to the best service of the race. These institutions are not adapted to the Negro's peculiar circumstances and conditions. They are founded and fostered to meet the needs, aspirations, and ambitions of the most favored white youth. The Negro must grasp the general aims and ideals and interpret and apply them to the situation and circumstances of his own race.

The schools of the South will be patterned after those in the North. The less-developed always pay homage to the better-perfected standards.   The Negro will gain acquaintance with the aims, ideals, and methods of the North, and will, perforce, exploit the attainment among his own people in the South.

In the educational world the law of supply and demand is inexorable.   The demand for Negroes in the higher levels of intellectual, moral, and social leadership in the North will be relatively small as compared with the larger field of the South.   The incidental hardships and inequalities of the Southern régime will be undergone in quest of a larger field for acquired attainment, quickened by sacrificial impulse of racial reclamation.   Thus the Northern movement of the Negro, actuated by purely industrial and economic motives, will yield significant educational fruitage.

CHAPTER IX

NATIONAL RESPONSIBILITY FOR NEGRO EDUCATION

The Fourteenth Amendment to the Constitution made the Negro a citizen of the United States. By fiat of law the status of the chattel was suddenly transformed into that of the citizen. The National Government is wholly responsible for the creation of Negro citizenship, a responsibility which involves the obligation to prepare him for his new function in the government. Carried away by the heat and hysteria of war, the statesmanship of that period did not consider all of the consequences growing out of this momentous act. It was deemed sufficient to invest the newly emancipated slave with a garb of citizenship, without preparing him to wear the unaccustomed garb becomingly. His education was left to the afflicted states, which had recently been disrupted and disorganized by the ruinous ravages of war. The ill-fated Freedmen's Bureau undertook in some slight measure to fulfill the national obligation. But for the most part the freedman was left to shift for himself in his upward struggle from ignorance to enlightenment. It was hoped that his enfranchisement might enable him to exert the requisite influence on the policy of the several states, leading to the establishment of adequate educational provision. Amidst all the imperfections and misdeeds of reconstruction, actual or alleged, there stands out in bold relief one clear redeeming feature. Actuated by the purpose of qualifying the Negro for the proper exercise of his citizenship function, the reconstruction governments established the public shcool system in the several Southern States. One searches in vain for any record of Southern statesmanship, before or since the Civil War, fraught with greater benefits to both races than the public provision for the education of all citizens, established by the much-maligned reconstruction governments.

But actual experience soon demonstrated what prudent provision should have foreseen, namely, that the recently impoverished and distracted Southern States were not, of themselves, able to maintain adequate school systems for the efficient education of both races. Their heroic efforts must be supplemented by national provision, or else the South for many generations must lag behind other sections of the nation, and the efficiency of the nation, as a whole, will be seriously impaired.

We are apt to be misled by statistics of illiteracy showing the remarkable rapidity with which the Negro is acquiring the use of letters. Beginning practically at the zero point of literacy, at the time of his emancipation, the rate of literacy had arisen to 70.6 per cent in 1900. The rapidity with which the Negro race has been literalized, has been considered the most marvelous attainment of the past century. In the period of fifty years a considerable majority of its members has learned the use of letters. This is a much larger per cent than is shown by many of the historic races of the Old World.

The mere technical acquisition of letters, however, is a matter of very simple attainment. A few months' schooling is sufficient to communicate to the individual the oral and phonetic symbols of knowledge, and the method of combining them into written and spoken speech. The letters of the alphabet constitute a key with twenty-six notches, which unlocks the accumulated storehouse of the wisdom and experience of mankind. But the mere possession of this mystic key is of little value unless the wielder has a previous appreciation of the wealth of wisdom which the storehouse contains. The Red Indian or any other savage peoples might acquire the ability to read and write within a single generation but if they still cling to their ancestorial and traditional ways, without the curiosity of incentive to understand the secret and method of civilization, their mere technical attainments would be of little more value than a curious intellectual gymnastic. Although 70 per cent of the Negro race can read and write, comparatively a small fraction of that number actually do make an efficient use of their attainments. In the states which require a literacy test for the exercise of franchise, the great bulk of Negroes are excluded because of their inability to meet this simple test; albeit the statistics of such states show a high average of Negro literacy. Of course it would be unbecoming to intimate that a sovereign state would be guilty of the deep dishonor of depriving its citizens of fundamental rights by cunning device or tricky contrivance. Statistics of illiteracy are misleading because the individual's pride which indisposes him to have his ignorance acknowledged and recorded, often leads him to render misleading answers to the query of the enumerator.

At Camp Dodge, where there were 3,600

Negro conscripts from Alabama, no one of whom, under the terms of conscription, was over 31 years of age, the Young Men's Christian Association found that over 75 per cent of them were unable to read or write effectively, notwithstanding the fact that the rate of Negro illiteracy in Alabama, according to the federal statistics, is only 40.1 per cent. There is one conspicuous outstanding fact, that the great majority of the Negro race are not able to make use of literary knowledge to improve their efficiency, or measure up to the standard of an enlightened citizenship.

When we consider the woeful inadequacy of provision made for Negro education, there is left no room to marvel because of this alarming result. According to reports just issued by the Bureau of Education, the State of Alabama expends $1.78 per capita for each Negro child, the state of Georgia $1.76, and Louisiana $1.31. These states expend from five to six times this amount per capita for the schooling of white children. It is conceded that even the provision for education of the white children of the South is scarcely more than one-third of that for the education of a child of the North and West. If it requires $25 per capita to prepare for the duties of citizenship in the North, a white child whose powers are reënforced by racial and social heredity, by what law of logic or common sense can it be expected that $1.31 will prepare a Negro child in Louisiana, who misses such reënforcement, for the exercise of like function?

I am not bringing this glaring discrepancy to light for the purpose of condemnation or denunciation, but merely to describe a situation furnishing a basal argument for the necessity of national aid to Negro education. Without such aid the Southern States must continue for generations under the heavy handicap of a comparatively ignorant and ill-equipped citizenship.

It is a fatal mistake to suppose that the efficient education of the Negro can be conducted on a cheaper scale than that for the whites. The fact that his home environment and his general grade of life is lower, makes adequate educational facilities all the more expensive. One dollar and thirty-one cents per capita applied to Negro education in Louisiana accomplishes even less, in effective results, than a like sum applied to the whites. Imagine the educational status of Massachusetts, if the state should suddenly reduce the provision of public instruction to the level of the cost of Negro education in Louisiana.

Philanthropy to a commendable degree has

served to supplement the deficiencies of the Southern States for Negro education. But neither the individual state nor the United States has the moral right to depend upon voluntary philanthropy to prepare its citizens for the responsible duties and obligations of citizenship. At best philanthropy is only a temporary and inadequate makeshift. As huge as philanthropic contributions seem to be in the aggregate, they amount to little more than one dose of medicine in the hospital, when compared to the magnitude of the task to which they are applied.

A generation ago Senator Henry W. Blair, of New Hampshire, devoted his public career to the promulgation of national aid to Negro education. The array of facts and arguments, which he marshaled in support of his propaganda, was undisputed and indisputable. The urgency of the need has been emphasized by a generation of neglect. It is said that the Athenians banished Aristides because they grew weary of hearing him called Aristides, the Just. By parity of ungracious procedure, Senator Blair was thrown out of public life because of his loquacious advocacy of national equity and justice. But his cause still remains. The nation has merely deferred payment on a debt which sooner or later must be liquidated with accumulated interest.

At the time of the Blair Educational Bill there were lurking suspicions in the minds of opposing statesmen of political and partisan advantage, and sinister sectional animosity concealed under the guise of Federal aid to education. The doctrine of local sovereignty was sharply accentuated; but opposition on these grounds has weakened with the intervening years. There still survives a statesmanlike duty of the nation to meet its moral obligation to the least of its citizens.

It was unfair to the Southern States to require them, unaided, to prepare the Negro for duties of citizenship at the time of his enfranchisement. The nation as a whole was responsible for the condition of the Negro. The fact that slavery became a localized institution was not due to the inherent deviltry of the South nor to the innate goodness of the North. Slavery was a national institution and became localized under the operation of climatic and economic law. It is equally unfair today, to require the South to bear the heavy burden alone. The Negro problem is the nation's problem; the remedy should be as comprehensive as the need.

In democracy, as in ethics, the individual is

the ultimate unit, and there must be essential equality among the units, or else the fabric of democracy, like the fabric of ethics, must fall. Under the traditional attitude of the white race toward the Negro, it was supposed that the guiding intelligence should be lodged in the white man's brain, and the muscular energy in the Negro's arm. But the circuit is too long. In a democracy each man must think as well as work. The country can no longer look upon the Negro merely for his utility as a tool, but must regard his totality as a man. An ideal American citizen is not that of a working man; but that of a man working. The presence of the ignorant Negro lowers the general average of efficiency of the community in which he lives and of the nation of which he forms a part. Georgia with half of its population practically illiterate can never hope to keep pace with Iowa, which strives to make every citizen intelligent and efficient. The United States can never reach the desired goal of efficiency, until it utilizes the undeveloped energies which lie dormant in the brain and brawn of every citizen.

So far I have dealt with the demands for Federal assistance to primary and elementary education, which imparts to each citizen a more or less well understood minimum of necessary knowledge and standard of efficiency. But there is a higher sense in which the nation is obligated to the cause of Negro Education. At the time of his emancipation the Negro was wholly without wise guidance and direction. The sudden severance of personal relation which had existed complacently under the régime of slavery left the Negro dependent upon his own internal resources for leadership of his higher and better life. The discipline of slavery had ill fitted him for this function. It had imparted to him the process without the principle; the knack without the knowledge; the rule without the reason; the formula without the philosophy. If the blind lead the blind they will both fall into the ditch. For want of vision people perish. The professional class constitutes the higher light of the race, and if that light within this race be darkness, how great is that darkness.

The Negro teacher meets with every form of ignorance and pedagogical obtuseness that befalls the white teachers; the Negro preacher has to do with every conceivable form of original and acquired sin; the doctor meets with all the variety of disease that the human flesh is heir to; the lawyer's sphere covers the whole gamut involving the rights of property and person. The problems growing out of the contact, attrition, and adjustment of the races involve issues which are as intricate as any that have ever taxed human wisdom for solution. If, then, the white man who stands in the high place of authority and leadership among the members of his race, fortified as he is by superior social environment, needs to qualify for his high calling by thorough and sound educational training, surely the Negro needs a no less thorough general education to qualify him to serve as philosopher, guide, and friend of ten million unfortunate human beings.

The Federal Government should make some provisions for those who are to stand in the high places of intellect and moral authority. In the Western States where philanthropical millionaires are scarce, and where the average citizen is not able to support the system of education on the higher level, the state undertakes the task of maintaining high institutions of learning for the leaders in the various walks of life. The Negro is unable at present to maintain such institutions for his own race; he is dependent upon a remote and vicarious philanthropy. The chief benefits of the higher workers among the Negro peoples inure to the community, to the state, and to the nation. Dr. James, the president of the University of Illinois, has for years advocated with great power of persuasion the establishment of a national university. All of his arguments may be multiplied by ten, when applied to obligation of the government to support at least one higher institution for the education of the Negro race.

Already through Land Grant and other federal funds, the government, in coöperation with the several states, is supporting agricultural and mechanical colleges for white youth. Some provision is also made for the Negro in the states where there is scholastic separation of the races. But these agricultural and mechanical colleges are essentially schools of secondary grade and cannot be maintained on high level of collegiate basis. It is easy for the Federal Government to extend the application by establishing and maintaining at least one institution of technical character and collegiate grade, which might serve as a finishing school for the work done in the several states. The Negro needs to be rooted and grounded in the principles of knowledge on the highest collegiate basis. The Federal Government has already acknowledged this responsibility in the moderate support which it gives Howard University as the national institution of the Negro race. This acknowledgment of a national responsibility, let us hope, augurs early ample provision for the education of a race in its upward struggle to the fullness of the stature of American citizenship.

It is needless to inject into this discussion the intricate and tangled issues of the race problem. Suffice it to say that ignorance is a menace to intelligence; sloth to efficiency; vice to virtue; and degradation to the dignity and decencies of life. Just as the Government through adequate Federal agency stamps out the yellow fever, cholera, and other infectious diseases, so it must, sooner or later, exterminate ignorance, which is more menaceful than any other plague that afflicts the nation.

CHAPTER X

THE PRACTICAL VALUE OF THE HIGHER EDUCATION OF THE NEGRO

The progress of the Negro race consists in improvement of the personal worth and social efficiency of its individual members. The value of any type of education must be appraised in terms of these standards. Any proposed scheme of social uplift which hopes to gain popular approval and support must be subjected to the concrete test of rendering the recipient more worthy in his individual qualities and of making him a more efficient instrument of service to his fellowman.

In this practical age there is little tolerance for abstract doctrine or fruitless theory that does not translate itself into the actualities of life. The whole educational world has been profoundly affected by the influence of this tendency. The stress of educational emphasis has been shifted from the passive to the active aspect of culture. To be somebody was the ideal of the old school education; to do something is the aim of the new. The one placed stress of emphasis on being; the other on doing.

This tendency towards the practical end of education is greatly emphasized when the application is limited to the colored race. The Negro's presence in this country, in the first place, was due to the belief that he was intended by the Creator to be an instrument of crude service. His traditional function was mainly mechanical, and scarcely more human than that of the ox which pulls the plow. His personality was at first denied, and afterwards ignored. Men spoke of the Negro as a "good hand" just as they spoke of a good ax or a good ox. The imputed virtue had exclusive reference to his utility as a tool. The traditional bias concerning the Negro's ordained place in the social scheme influences present opinion concerning the kind of education which should be imparted to him. As a consequence of this attitude, that type of education which fits him for his accustomed sphere and place has found ready appreciation and favor; he is to be educated for his work, rather than for himself.

As a matter of fact, the great bulk of this race must devote its chief energies to the cruder and coarser grades of service which fall to its lot as far in the future as our present vision can penetrate. The industrial education of the masses, therefore, becomes a matter of the highest concern to the practical statesman and philanthropist. Dr. Booker T. Washington, in his moments of greatest enthusiasm, has never over-stated the importance of industrial training as an essential agency of the general social uplift. But at the same time, it should never be forgotten that the Negro is a human being as well as a utensil of service. A wise educational economy will seek to make him a man working, rather than a working man.

The universities and colleges for the Negroes were founded on the wave of moral enthusiasm which marked the highest point that Christian philanthropy has ever attained. Upon the crest of this wave of enthusiasm for quickening the manhood of the Negro, educational facilities were provided for the race, which, up to that time, had been forbidden the use of letters, on the basis of the higher standards adapted to the requirements of the most favored European youth. If the practical phase was ignored, it was merely because industrial training was not at that time considered a vital part of the education of the white race. Indeed, it was reserved for General S. C. Armstrong to add a new chapter to American education. Industrial training has gained and will forever retain its important place in the educational program of the American people. Hampton and Tuskegee typify national, rather than racial educational ideals. General Armstrong and Booker T. Washington, his chief apostle, have become the schoolmasters, not merely to the Negro, but to the nation. Educational methods suggested by the needs of the Negro have been applied to the requirements of the white race. One is reminded of the lines of Kipling: "The things that you learn from the yellow and brown will help you a heap with the white."

As the heat of feeling engendered by the anti-slavery agitation cooled down, it was inevitable that there would be a reaction in public sentiment against the higher education of the race. Sentiment at the time when the general educational policy of the nation was being rewritten in terms of new demand, was such that it was to be expected that the so-called higher education of the Negro would be discredited and belittled. Under the partisan propaganda of the industrial advocates, the fountain of philanthropy was frozen to the appeal for a higher education.

Fortunately, however, the saner sense of the people is now reasserting itself. The two types of education are no longer contrasted as antagonistic and inconsistent, but compared as common factors of a joint product. Their relative claims should never have been made a matter of essential controversy, but merely a question of ratio and proportion. Negro colleges, following the lead of their white prototypes, are adjusting their curricula to the demands of the age. Economics, social science, and history are sharing with the traditional ingredients. The advocates of industrial training are now willing graciously to concede the value of the higher education if sensibly adapted and wisely applied.

There are ten million Negroes in the United States with the status of American citizenship, each of whom needs to improve his personal qualities and social efficiency. This improvement must be brought about through philanthropic assistance and by self-reclamation. The agency that will most effectively conduce to this end is the chief concern of wise philanthropy and statesmanship. Industrial and the higher education are both applied to the same task of uplifting and sustaining these millions of human beings and rendering them competent and willing co-workers for the common good of the nation. Industrial education is pushing up from the bottom, while the higher education is pulling from the top. Both elements are efficient; neither is sufficient.

The chief aim of the higher education is to produce an efficient leadership. According to the last available data from the Federal census, there are fifteen thousand Negro clergymen, about two thousand Negro physicians and dentists, twenty-one thousand Negro teachers, seven hundred Negro lawyers, and several thousand workers along the other lines of the higher callings and pursuits.

These constitute about one-half of one per cent of the race; but it is to this class that the ninety-nine and one-half per cent must look for leadership. The foreigners who flock to our shores are uplifted and sustained largely because they have intelligent and sympathetic leadership within their own race. The Catholic priesthood with its high standard of intelligence and practical statesmanship, saves the foreigner from becoming a national menace. The Negro must have a leadership within his own race to save him from a like fate. It is only through the higher training that such influence can be developed; this task is a practical one. It is of no more immediate practical advantage to the Negro, that the hungry should be fed, the naked clothed, and the houseless sheltered, than that the sick should be healed, the ignorant enlightened, and that the simple should be guided and the wayward reclaimed.

In the present temper of the American mind the Negro is confined to a separate social area which makes it necessary that his needs should be met by the professional class of his own race. Thus the Negro teacher, minister, physician, lawyer, and editor become a social necessity; hence the importance of the Negro college and university to train men and women of this blood for the higher offices to which their destiny calls them. Just in proportion as the spirit of racial segregation increases, the demand for internal leadership becomes intensified. No race, even through its most self-sacrificing members, can furnish intimate direction for a despised people, where general regulations compel them to ride in separate coaches, and to walk the streets apart, and to move in separate social spheres. It will be generally conceded that professional workers should have about the same degree of education regardless of the social advantages of the people among whom they will be called upon to labor. The Negro teacher certainly meets with the most difficult problems in pedagogy and psychology; the Negro physician must treat every form of disease that human flesh is heir to; the Negro minister has to deal with the gravest moral and spiritual problems growing out of original and acquired sin. There devolves upon the leadership of this race the handling of issues which are far-reaching in their relations and as intricate in their entanglement as any that ever taxed the human understanding. Surely, they need that kind and degree of preparation for their calling which have been found to be necessary by the experience of the ages. The function of the Negro college is to prepare the choice men of this race to stand in the high place of moral and spiritual authority as guides, philosophers and friends to their less fortunate brethren. For want of vision people perish, as well as for want of provision. The blind cannot lead the blind lest both fall into the ditch.

The graduates of Negro colleges and universities are sometimes derided in all the moods and tenses of irony and ridicule. We have all laughed ourselves to weariness over the account of the barefoot boy reading Plato between the plow handles, the kitchen scullion discanting upon Kant, and the hotel waiter reveling in the glories of the Renaissance. The Negro collegian is depicted as an impractical doctrinaire, who spends his time in impotent frenzy, screaming against the existing evils of society which he has neither the deep discernment to understand nor the practical wisdom to alleviate.

In the rapid rise of this class from the lower to the higher levels of life, instances of maladaptations and grotesque misfits might naturally be expected. But a wide acquaintance with the graduates of Negro colleges and universities, in all parts of the land, convinces me that such instances are exceptional, and do not, in the least, characterize them as a class. They are almost universally employed along lines of useful endeavor for the general betterment of the community and command the respect and good-will of the people of both races among whom they live and work.

As a concrete illustration of this principle, I cite the case of Howard University, which is the largest university of European type for Negro youth to be found anywhere in the world. This institution has a student body of fifteen hundred young men and women pursuing the various branches of collegiate and professional studies, and has sent into the world about three thousand graduates, and several times as many sometime pupils who have shared the partial benefit of its courses. These three thousand graduates and sometimes pupils are scattered throughout the length and breadth of the land, in almost every country and city with considerable Negro population, and are working along the lines of their callings as ministers, physicians, lawyers, teachers, and in the general activities for the welfare of the people. What is true of graduates of this university is equally true of those of other Negro colleges and of the men of the higher education as a class.

A few individual examples of Howard Alumni must suffice to justify this statement. Rev. Wm. H. Brooks, Pastor of St. Mark's Methodist Episcopal Church, New York City, has gone in and out among a congregation of nearly two thousand members for seventeen years, as their moral and spiritual example and guide. He is generally beloved and esteemed for his good works, and might well be described as the Good Shepherd of the colored people of New York City. Rev. George Frazier Miller, of the City of Brooklyn, a man of clean life and clear thought, high ideals and lofty endeavor, has endeared himself to the entire community as an exemplary moral and spiritual leader of men. Wm. E. Benson, founder of Kowaliga, Alabama, has established a self-supporting community involving ten thousand acres of land within the very heart of the black belt of the South. Hon. J. C. Napier, ex-Registrar of the U. S. Treasury, is a lawyer of substance and standing in the City of Nashville, and is universally respected and esteemed by the white and black alike for his manly life and wholesome influence. Prof. Hugh M. Brown, the reorganizer of the Colored Institute at Cheney, Pa., is perhaps the best expert of the country upon the application of industrial education to the teaching needs of the masses. Dr. W. A. Warfield is surgeon-in-chief of Freedmen's Hospital, Washington, D. C., an institution with two hundred and fifty beds, and perhaps the largest and best equipped hospital between Baltimore and New Orleans. Mr. J. E. Moorland, International Secretary of the Young Men's Christian Association, has been instrumental largely through the beneficence of Mr. Rosenwald, of Chicago, in promoting the erection of Y. M. C. A. buildings costing upward of $100,000 each, in large cities of the country; such buildings are already in full operation in Chicago, Washington, Indianapolis, and Philadelphia, and plans are under way for erection of like plants in a half dozen other cities. Under the leadership and direction of Mr. Moorland, the Young Men's Christian Association has become the most active field of social endeavor among the colored race within the last few years; the work already accomplished and under way involves more than a million of dollars. These are but samples of the effective work which graduates of this university are doing along all lines of endeavor for the general betterment of the people.

In the final analysis it will be found that there is no reasonable ground for conflict or misunderstanding between the two types of education. The late Dr. Booker T. Washington was a trustee of Hampton Institute and also of Howard University, and effectively served his race through the instrumentality of both institutions. Both types of school make the joint appeal to the philanthropy, statesmanship, and conscience of the American people: "This, ye ought to have done and not to have left the other undone."

CHAPTER XI

THE NEGRO BALANCE OF POWER

Significant political effects will result from the sudden influx of a half million Negroes to the North. This Negro migration was due primarily to the industrial necessities of the World War. The Negro is an inalienable Republican. He adheres to the fortunes of the party of Lincoln with a fealty that never falters. This adherence is not only due to gratitude for former favors, but also to the past, present and persistent hostile attitude of the Democratic party. To the mind of the Negro, the political appellations, Democratic and Republican, convey moral condonation. They convey contrasted ideas of good and bad, like up and down in ethics. A one party race occupies an unfortunate position in a two party state. Fluctuating political fortunes will ultimately put the one-sided adherent at the mercy of the political enemy. The ultimate political salvation of the race depends upon its enfranchisement from the bond which binds it to its salvators, and leaves it free, as other races, to form political allegiance. But, alas, there seems to be but little immediate hope. The Southern element is dominant in the Democratic party. The stubborn attitude of this Bourbon constituency makes affiliation with that party impossible. The recent experiment under the first term of Woodrow Wilson's administration proved disastrous.

The Negro newcomers to the North will adhere to the fortunes of the party which, in the past, gave their race freedom and the franchise, and at present offers more favorable consideration than its political adversary.

The solid Negro vote constitutes the balance of power in the closely contested states of the North and West which usually determine the issue between the two parties. Outside of New England there are few states in which prediction of success for either party can be relied upon with satisfied assurance in a presidential election. The tide of fortune turns according to the merits of the candidates and the issues espoused. The overwhelming result in the last election is no criterion. A political landslide slideth where it listeth. We feel the effect thereof, but cannot tell whence it cometh nor whither it goeth. It sweeps a given party in or out of power with equal celerity and suddenness.

Every new Negro voter counts for a certain addition to the Republican ranks and adds probability to success. European immigrants usually distribute themselves more or less evenly between the two dominant parties, and do not greatly disturb the political balance. But as this source of numerical augmentation has now been greatly diminished by stringent legislation, the Negro influx will receive greater consideration and emphasis. The enfranchisement of woman also lends advantage to the party to which the Negro belongs. Enfranchised white women divide their vote in about the same ratio as the white men. But the new Negro female vote adds a solid block to the Republican column. Negro men have been known, under appropriate inducement and persuasion, to vote the Democratic ticket, but the Negro woman is more cautious and conservative. No inducement or persuasion yet advanced can swerve her from allegiance to the party of racial deliverance.

The Negro in the North, especially the newcomer, is mainly adult, and yields a larger proportion of voters than is contributed by a normal population. It is reasonable to estimate that more than half of the half million Negro migrants are over twenty-one years of age. This would add at least 250,000 voters to the Republican strength in the Northern States.

The Northern influx of Negroes has been

confined mainly to a few industrial states which, curiously enough, are the states of greatest political uncertainty. The following table, giving the Northern states containing over 50,000 Negroes, and the decennial increment during the last decade, furnished interesting material for political speculation:

NEGROES IN THE NORTH

State	1919	1920	Increase
Entire North	1,078,336	1,550,754	472,418
Pennsylvania	193,919	234,494	40,575
New York	134,191	198,433	64,242
Ohio	111,452	186,183	74,731
Illinois	109,049	182,254	73,205
Missouri	157,452	178,241	20,789
New Jersey	89,760	117,132	27,372
Indiana	60,320	80,810	20,490
Michigan	17,115	60,082	42,967
Kansas	54,030	57,925	3,895
Total	927,288	1,295,554	368,266

Eighty-seven per cent of the Negroes in all of the North and West are found in these nine states, which also caught 88 per cent of the increase of Negro population. This shows that the race is growing slightly more rapidly in this area than in the other twenty-two more thinly settled states comprising the North and West.

Four hundred eighteen thousand Negroes, or 88 per cent of the Northern migration, went to the heavy Negro states above enumerated. In all of the remaining twenty-two states of the North and West there were only 151,048 Negroes whose numbers increased by 54,152 from 1910 to 1920.

Estimating that 25,000 voters will probably turn the tide in a closely contested election, it will be seen that the Negro easily holds the balance of power in the above enumerated states. There were at least 45,000 new voters added to the Republican party in New York, 32,000 in Pennsylvania, 37,000 in Ohio, 36,000 in Illinois, 10,000 in Missouri, 17,000 in New Jersey, 10,000 in Indiana, 22,000 in Michigan, and 3,000 in Kansas. The 205,200 Negroes scattered throughout the other twenty-two states have important political weight, amounting in some instances to a decisive factor.

On the whole, the Republican party represents the capital and organized business, on a large scale. The Democratic party is more largely composed of laborers and industrial workers. The conflict between labor and capital threatens the stability of our social order. The Negro's alignment with the party of conservative business integrity may serve to postpone the final issue of this conflict and, it may be, lead to permanent security of the existing order.

The Negro in the North is found mainly in the large centers of population. This city concentration will have great bearing, not only on municipal politics in general, but will enable the colored voter to utilize his ballot for the welfare of his group. For it will stimulate ambition to elect members of the race to official position.

The following table shows the cities with a Negro population of over 20,000, together with the decennial increase:

NEGRO POPULATION—CITIES NORTH OF THE
POTOMAC RIVER

City	1910	1920	Increase
New York	91,706	153,088	61,382
Philadelphia	84,459	134,098	49,639
Washington	96,446	109,976	13,530
Chicago	44,103	109,594	65,491
St. Louis	43,960	69,603	25,643
Detroit	5,241	41,532	36,241
Pittsburgh	25,623	37,688	12,065
Indianapolis	21,816	34,690	12,874
Cleveland	8,448	34,474	26,026
Kansas City	23,566	30,706	7,140
Cincinnati	19,639	29,636	9,997
Columbus	12,739	22,091	9,352
Total	477,746	807,176	323,901

The Negro in these cities increased by 72 per cent during the last decade, whereas the Northern contingent increased by only 46 per cent, the southern element by only 1.9 per cent, according to census reports. The race is not only flocking rapidly to the North, but much more rapidly to the large cities of that section. While this remarkable increase is due to causes of limited duration, yet the numbers are not likely to diminish, but will probably show substantial increase for the coming decades.

The segregation of the Negro in wards and districts in these cities has also important political significance. It will lead to political aspiration of the race for a measure of leadership and self-determination. If the Negroes were evenly divided throughout the entire population in such cities as New York, Philadelphia and Chicago, they would constitute a negligible per cent of the total population, and would have little or no direct political influence. But, because of residential segregation, they will, to a large degree, dominate the circumscribed areas in which they reside. Already Negro aldermen are elected to city governments in New York, Baltimore, Philadelphia, Chicago, Indianapolis and Cleveland. In the course of time, the race will be represented by its members in all city governments where they reside in large numbers and are restricted to circumscribed areas of domicile. Segregation also enables the race to elect members of the state legislatures as they dominate in the number of legislative districts. Already there are Negro members of the legislature in Pennsylvania, New York, New Jersey, Ohio and Illinois, based upon circumscribed numbers in segregated areas. Thus the Negro is not only gaining political power in local city affairs, but also in the state governments as well.

The Negro in the North is not an incurable Republican in municipal and state politics. The attitude of the Northern Democrat toward him is not less friendly than that of his Republican rival. In local affairs, they often affiliate with the party that offers the most advantageous consideration. In this way a basis of political influence is built up with both parties for the welfare of the race. The man with the votes is the man with the influence. The man without a vote is a nullity in the state.

It is a safe prophecy to predict that within the next half generation there will be Negro congressmen from New York, Philadelphia and Chicago. According to the present apportionment, it requires 211,877 to constitute a congressional district. Wherever the Negro constitutes the majority party, a Negro congressman may be nominated and elected by skillful manipulation. A Negro population of 60,000 or more might easily claim this distinction. The whites are more than apt to be divided among a number of parties with divergent political tenets. A solid party vote of more than one-fourth of the total might very easily dictate the final selection.

If the Negro population in New York, Philadelphia, St. Louis and Chicago were located in a single congressional district, they could easily elect members of their own race to Congress. But while they are segregated, these areas in which they reside are not contiguous so as to form a separate congressional district. By the political device known as gerrymandering, manipulators may regulate affairs so as to frustrate this ambitious purpose. But if the present tendency toward augmentation in numbers and segregation in sections continues, several of our great cities will contain districts with Negro political leadership.

In an important sense, the Negro constitutes a separate political entity from the whites. In prevalent parlance, the "Negro vote" is a racial entity without reference to hard and fast geographical lines. If all the Negroes in New York or Illinois could sense the necessity for a racial representative in Congress, they might so prevail upon the management of the Republican party, either to regulate congressional districts in their favor, or to throw the nomination to a Negro in districts even where they do constitute the majority of the dominant party. Trading votes is a practice well known to sagacious political management.

Self-determination is a phrase which President Wilson gave prominence to describe the spirit of the World War. Abraham Lincoln expressed the idea with greater aptness when he said that no man is good enough to govern another man without his consent. The same thought lay in the mind of Thomas Jefferson, who declared that all governments derive their just powers from the consent of the governed. The wise man is not wise enough to govern the fool. The good man is not good enough to govern the bad man. The rich man is not liberal enough to govern the poor man. The white man is not good enough to govern the black man without his consent and participation in the government. American women have full faith and confidence in American men; but they do not feel that they are qualified to govern them without their consent.

No class of people can have self-determination in the sense of a government separate and distinct from the whole people. All that can be expected is that every class shall have an equal say and an equal voice in the government by which it is controlled. An infant with no language but a cry exerts as large a share of self-determination upon the household as the wiser and older members of the family. Self-government is better than good government, for without self-government, good government has no enduring basis. Any class which is excluded from the governmental circle cannot expect to have its interests carefully considered and safeguarded. One Negro member of a city council or state legislature, or of the Congress of the United States, would be likely to accomplish more for the just consideration of his race than is possible for white representatives to do. The specific provisions securing public and civil equality of the races in Pennsylvania, New York, Ohio and Illinois have, for the most part, been proposed and pushed through by a single Negro member who happened to be elected to the legislature. Two or three Negro members of Congress with a comprehensive understanding, calm judgment and adaptable good sense would go far toward changing the national attitude on the public and political relations of the race. The Negro's political power is in inverse proportion to his relative numerosity. A handful of Negroes in Massachusetts have more political weight than a million of the race in Mississippi. It does not seem likely that the Negro will get his political power in the South within the near future, but whatever power the race asserts will come from the North.

The political oppression which tends to drive the black man to the North, and the proscriptive spirit which determines the metes and bounds of his habitation, will serve to give the race political vantage ground, and react to the undoing of the proscriptive tendencies of which he seems to be the helpless victim. Thus the Negro will become the negative beneficiary of circumstances which at first seemed calculated to work his political damage.

There is no likelihood that the North will resort to disfranchisement to deprive the Negro of his constitutional rights. His numbers are so small in proportion to the whole electorate that the scarecrow of Negro domination can have no terror.

The Negro voter in the North is actuated by altruistic racial motive in demanding full recognition for his race in the South. He will continue to keep the political agitation for constitutional rights which may serve to bring the nation to a realizing sense of its anomalous position when it would pose as the moral monitor of mankind and yet makes a scrap of paper of

its fundamental law. May it not be that this
Negro migration incident to industrial exigencies will, by the good fortune of circumstances,
lead to the fulfillment of the war amendments
of our Constitution, and make of that document
a charter of liberty indeed?

CHAPTER XII

THE HAITIAN MISSION

The unfortunate involvement of the United States in the affairs of the Haitian Republic constitutes as serious and as difficult a diplomatic tangle as any which the new administration is called upon to unravel. It is indeed the most troublesome issue which has been transmitted by the outgoing régime. The attempted rape of Haiti constitutes the most disgraceful chapter in the annals of diplomacy. This nation has always been too noble to play the rôle of oppressor, and too high-minded to take advantage of the weakness of the weak. America stands as the champion of the democratic ideal in the Western Hemisphere, and its vindicator in the eyes of all the world. A champion who ruthlessly overrides the weak will soon forfeit his reputation for chivalry and nobleness of nature. The rôle of the big brother and the big bully cannot be successfully played at the same time.

Theodore Roosevelt possessed a passionate instinct for righteousness. His was the first clarion call to the conscience of America against the shameful procedure in Haiti which convicts this nation of moral inconsistency, and belittles and belies our loud boastings about the widening bonds of democracy. The deed nullifies the doctrine. Exultation in the name of holy democracy becomes the empty mouthings of a hollow mockery. Those who sincerely believe in the democratic ideal as the ultimate form of human government must encourage its manifestation even in places where it thrives as the tender plant, and as a root out of dry ground.

What American statesman can have the heart, or rather the heartlessness, to snuff out the torch of liberty now flickering feebly in our black sister republic in the West Indies? A continuation of so great a shame and scandal by the present administration is unthinkable. To adjust this situation in harmony with the just aspirations of the Haitian people and in keeping with the democratic spirit of America demands a diplomatic representative of sane and sincere human sympathy and sound judgment, whose intellectual and moral authority will inspire confidence in the native, insure national satisfaction, and command international respect. This difficult task is worthy of the highest diplomatic genius. Such assignment

might be a temporary one until the intricate
tangle has been untied.

Since the days of reconstruction it has been
the policy to send a colored man as minister to
Haiti. This post is regarded as the highest
political prize awarded the colored race for
party devotion and political service. The idea
of a Negro representative for a Negro government is doubtless intended as a compliment.
The most eminent colored men, including Frederick Douglass, John M. Langston, and George
W. Williams, have been assigned this post.
But, on closer analysis, this official segregation
involves a compromise rather than a compliment. It is undemocratic, to say the least, to
circumscribe the official privilege of any group
of American citizens to a limited and peculiar
area. A representative with deep race affiliation and sympathy is hardly the ideal American diplomat who must, first of all, represent
the government which sends him and not the
government to which he is sent.

We have, in our cosmopolitan citizenship,
naturalized or native born citizens whose blood
ties bind them to every race and nation; and
yet we would hardly send an Italian as ambassador to Italy, or a Frenchman to France,
or a Russian to Russia. We should certainly
not send an Irishman to Ireland did these mili-

tant people secure complete diplomatic independence. The race spirit has become so intensified in Haitian diplomacy that a colored representative would necessarily be placed under great temptation of divided allegiance. We cannot expect to discredit the Negro at home and hope that he will be esteemed abroad. San Domingo has expressed resentment at our sending as representative a citizen of an ostracized group. If the American Negro is not deemed good enough to represent his government in the general diplomatic service, he will not long be acceptable in this capacity by governments of his own race and color.

At one time the American Negro was appointed to the consular service in several European centers and served acceptably to all concerned. President Garfield offered the ministership to Brazil to Senator Bruce, who, doubtless, would have been appointed and confirmed had he not declined the proffer. President Cleveland appointed a colored man as minister to Bolivia, who failed of confirmation on account of stubborn opposition of Southern senators. Mr. Cleveland's policy was to send a white man to Haiti and a colored man to a white government, so that the colored race would not lose official recognition, but would rather gain, broadening the hitherto prescribed area. The statesmanlike wisdom of this policy was unfortunately frustrated by the narrow provincial spirit which gained the upper hand of his own political party.

Much of the misfortune of the present predicament in Haiti is due to the unwise policy of appointing a Southern white man as minister and filling the important fiscal stations with men of Southern birth and attitude on the race question. The dogma that the Southern white man knows best how to handle the Negro has long been exploded. A slave driver knows best how to drive slaves, if slaves must be driven; but it would be most difficult for him to readjust his attitude so as to deal with an erstwhile chattel on terms of equality. The Southern white man is apt to have a provincial mind, and a limited spirit and local outlook so far as race relationship is concerned. He genuinely mistakes his narrow traditional spirit for the universal mind on this question, and where he does not find it so, he quickly inaugurates a missionary propaganda to make it so. The intensity of his zeal for racial traditions necessarily militates against his success as diplomatic agent among the people held in social disesteem.

It might prove to be practical wisdom to send a member of the Hebrew race on this delicate mission to Haiti in this delicate crisis. This race is characterized by unquestioning national loyalty, broad human sympathy and international understanding. All elements concerned will have confidence in the righteousness of his judgment. It is our traditional policy to send a Jew as ambassador to Turkey because of the intricate racial and religious situation. England sent a member of this race as viceroy to India to compose the racial turmoil. President Wilson recently appointed a member of this race as personal representative and mediator in Armenia.

At any rate it is to be hoped that some way out of this awkward situation may be found by the present administration.

CHAPTER XIII

ENUMERATION ERRORS IN NEGRO POPULATION

The Bureau of the Census was established for the purpose of enumerating the population of the United States, and for the collection and coalition of other statistical data bearing on the social welfare of the nation. The government bases its calculations upon the information furnished by this bureau. The ratio of congressional representation, military conscription and other federal regulations is based upon the census enumeration within the limits of the several states. Publicists and social philosophers base their conclusions upon the same data. It is, therefore, a matter of the greatest importance that the enumeration should be reliable and trustworthy. The Bureau of the Census ranks as a scientific department of the government. Constantly repeated errors of this bureau tend to impeach its scientific reputation and to vitiate the conclusions based upon its output. Numerous complaints have been made by competent critics not only repudiating the results, but also impugning the motive. Manipulation in behalf of sectional and partisan advantage has been freely charged. Senator Roger Q. Mills, in an article in *The Forum,* bitterly complained that the South was deprived of its due quota of representation by the imperfection of the enumeration of 1890. Indeed, the alleged inaccuracies of the eleventh census provoked a flood of condemnatory literature.

Various enumerations of the Negro population by the Census Office since 1860 have not been very flattering to the scientific reputation of that bureau. These enumerations have been not only inherently erroneous, but so conflicting and inconsistent as to demand calculated corrections. It may be taken for granted that the enumerations up to 1860 were reasonably accurate and reliable. The Negroes, up to that time, were in a state of slavery, and the master had merely to hand the list of his slaves to the enumerator, just as he would the list of his cattle or other forms of chattel. There was every facility and every reason for accurate returns. The Negro population up to 1860 was inflated by importation of slaves from Africa, and, consequently, it was impossible to check the accuracy of the count by the ordinary statistical tests. Beginning, however, with the census of 1870, this population has been cut off from outside reënforcement and has had to depend upon its inherent productivity for growth and expansion. It, therefore, becomes an easy matter to apply the ordinary statistical checks to test the accuracy of enumeration.

It is conceded that the enumerations of 1860, 1880, 1900 and 1910 were accurate within the allowable limit of error. According to these enumerations, the growth was more or less normal and regular, and conformed to the requirements of statistical expectation. But the enumerations of 1870, 1890 and 1920 are so flagrantly discrepant as to demand special explanation and correction. A miscount at one enumeration upsets the balance for two decades. If it be an undercount it makes the increase too small for the preceding decade, and too large for the succeeding one. Accordingly, the only consecutive decades upon which we can rely for accuracy concerning the growth of the Negro population would be the 1850-1860 and 1900-1910. In order to escape obvious absurdities, the figures for the other decades must be supplied by reasoned interpolations. The mere exhibit of the several enumerations by the Census Office will convince the student of their inherent improbability.

NEGRO POPULATION AT EACH CENSUS, AND
DECENNIAL INCREASE, 1860–1920

Year	Number	Decennial Increase	Per Cent of Increase
1860	4,441,830	803,022	22.1
1870	4,880,009	438,179	9.9
1880	6,580,793	1,700,784	34.9
1890	7,488,676	907,883	13.8
1900	8,833,994	1,345,318	18.0
1910	9,827,763	993,769	11.2
1920	10,463,013	635,250	6.5

The irregularities of these figures are as whimsical as if produced by the sport of the gods. The normal growth of population uninfluenced by immigration or emigration shows a gradual increase in decennial increment and a gradual decline in the rate of increase. Wherever there is found to be a wide divergence from this law, it must be accounted for by special contributory influences. The column giving the decennial increments, instead of showing a gradual behavior, jumps back and forth with unaccountable capriciousness. A sudden drop from 803,022 to 438,179 is offset by an alarming rise to 1,700,784 for the next decade, when, lo and behold, there is a swift decline to 907,883 for the following ten years.

We look aghast at the upward bound to 1,345,-318, thence a downward drop to 993,769, followed by a still further startling decline to 635,250. It makes the head swim to try to keep track of such whimsical variations. The decadal increase per cent shows similar irregularities. The rhythmical rise and fall of these figures impresses one as the alternate up and down motion of boys playing at seesaw. Why should the ordinates of a curve, which should move smoothly downward, drop suddenly from 22.3 to 9.9, then rise to 34.9 and drop again to 13.9, then rise to 18.0 and decline again to 11.2 with a final slump of 6.5? Such variability has, perhaps, never been experienced by any human population. The internal evidence of error is overwhelming. The Census Bureau has sought to make corrections for the evidently erroneous enumerations of 1870 and 1890. But the equally discrepant figures of 1920 remain so far undisputed.

The census of 1870 has been universally discredited. The greatest error of enumeration falls, naturally enough, on the Negro race. This race had just been set free, and had not reëstablished itself in definite domiciles. Political conditions in the South were in the flux and flow of readjustment. The machinery of the Census Bureau was not sufficiently efficient to cope with so complicated a situation. Statisticians, recognizing the evident error, have tried to correct the mistake by statistical computation. The Census Bureau estimates the error in the Negro population for the decade to be 512,163. An acknowledged error of a half million, it would seem, would put this bureau on the lookout for similar errors in the future. But the census of 1890 was notoriously faulty. Here again the undercount, it is obvious, fell mainly in the South, and largely among the Negro population.

The Census Bureau, in commenting upon the apparent irregularities of returns for 1890, states: "According to the returns, the rate from 1880 to 1890 was very much lower than even the last rate, that of 1870-1880, and the rate for 1890-1900 was much higher than during the preceding or succeeding decade. Such abrupt changes in a class of the population which is not affected by immigration seem very improbable and almost force the conclusion that the enumeration of the Negroes in 1890 was deficient." In a special volume on *Negro Population of the United States 1790-1915*, the director further declares:

"The presumption of an undercount at the census of 1890, therefore, rests upon the improbability of the

decennial rates of increase themselves as developed
from the census returns; the inconsistency of the
indicated changes in the rates from decade to decade
with the changes in the proportion of children in the
Negro population, and upon the improbability of
the decennial mortality indicated for the decades
1880-1890 and 1890-1900. . . . The number of omissions at the census of 1890 cannot be accurately determined, but it would seem to be a fair assumption that
the decline in the rate of increase from decade to
decade was constant, and that the rate fell off in each
of the two decades, 1880-1890, 1890-1900, by approximately the same amount.   On this assumption, the
probable rates of increase for the four decades, 1870-
1910, are 22.0, 17.9, 13.8, 11.2. . . . A rate of 17.9 for
the decade 1880-1890 would give a Negro population
in 1890 of nearly 7,760,000, which, in round numbers,
exceeds the population enumerated at the census of
1890 by 270,000.   This is probably the number of
omissions of Negroes at the census of 1890, on the assumption that the retardation in the rate of growth
in the 20 years, 1880-1900, was constant.''

By making the estimated corrections for acknowledged error in the counts of 1870 and
1890, decadal growth from 1880 to 1890 would
be reduced and from 1890 to 1900 increased, so
as to produce reasonable conformity with the
laws of normal growth.   A gradual decline in
the rate of growth from 22.3 per cent to 11.2
per cent in 60 years will prove that the Negro

element conforms to the regular law of human population. This decline would appear even more gradual if we consider that the rate of 22.1 from 1850 to 1860 was contributed, in considerable measure, by African importation. The Census Bureau offers the following table with corrected numbers for 1870 and 1890:

NEGRO POPULATION—DECENNIAL INCREASES, WITH ESTIMATED ALLOWANCES FOR 1870 AND 1890

Year	Number	Decennial Increase	Per Cent of Increase
1910	9,827,763	993,769	11.2
1900	8,833,994	1,073,994	13.8
1890	7,760,000	1,179,207	17.6
1880	6,580,793	1,188,621	22.0
1870	5,392,172	950,342	21.4
1860	4,441,830	803,022	22.1

According to the recent bulletin issued by the Bureau of the Census, the Negro population showed a surprising and unexpected decline during the last decade. In 1910 there were 9,827,763 Negroes, and in 1920 10,463,013, giving a decadal increase of 635,250 or 6.5 per cent. If these figures were added to the table corrected to 1910, the disparity would be as glaring as any which has yet come from the Census Bureau. The sudden drop in decadal increase from 993,769 to 635,250, or from 11.2 per cent to 6.5 per cent, is so strikingly out of harmony with the more or less regular movement of the table as to call loudly for correction or explanation. The table shows a gradual increase in the decennial increment from 1880 to 1910, a decline of 194,852 in three decades. But now we are called upon to accept a sudden decline of 358,519 in a single decade.

The decennial rate of increase dropped from 11.2 per cent between 1900 and 1910 to 6.5 per cent between 1910 and 1920, whereas we should have expected a gradual decline of not more than one or two points. On the face of the figures it seems probable that the Census Bureau has again committed an error in the enumeration of the Negro population. As this bureau has admittedly committed grave errors in enumeration of Negro population in two preceding censuses, it is but reasonable that the obvious discrepancy can be most reasonably accounted for by an error in the present count.

Aside from the internal evidence itself, there is sufficient reason to suppose that this count might have been erroneous. The mobile Negro population has been greatly upset by the World

War. There was a mad rush of Negroes from the South to fill the vacuum in the labor market caused by unsettled conditions. Thousands of Negro homes were broken up and their members scattered without definite residential identity. In the cities especially, it seems probable that the count was greatly underestimated. The Negro migrants lived for the most part in improvised lodgings and boarding houses whose proprietors had little knowledge of and less interest in the identity of the boarders. The census official, visiting such boarding houses with a large number of Negro boarders would, in all probability, receive an innaccurate underestimate by the ignorant and uncaring proprietors. As an illustration of such inaccuracy, I cite a quotation from an editorial of the *Dispatch* of Oklahoma City:

"If the Census enumerators over the United States were as careless in the count as they were shown to be by this publication during the poll of the population last year, the general charge is right that the black man has made a much larger numerical advance than the official, yet faulty, records show. It will be remembered that the *Dispatch* made the charge during the enumeration that there was a laxness and really seeming desire to overlook the black man in this city. Our charge was printed in the daily papers. To cap it off, the irate enumerator in the section of the city where the *Dispatch* is located, appeared on the evening that the charge was published, and demanded of the editor the basis of the charge. We took him out into the 300 block on East Second Street and found 33 black men whom he had not counted, folk who told him so, and whose names he did not have on his lists.''

If the presumption of undercount was justified by the statistical indication for 1870 and 1890, surely a like presumption would obtain for the census of 1920. There are but three methods of accounting for this sudden slump in the growth of the Negro population. First, an undercount of the Census Bureau; second, a sudden increase in the death rate; and third, a decrease in the birth rate of Negro population.

It is known that the death rate of the Negro is decreasing rather than increasing under improved sanitary conditions and general social environment. The Director of the Census states that ''the death rate has not changed greatly.'' Instead of adhering to the ''fair assumption'' of a steadily declining rate of increase, as was done for the faulty enumerations of 1870 and 1890, the Director of the Fourteenth Census accepts the violent leap from 11.2 to 6.5 and endeavors to vindicate the count of 1920, by assuming a sudden decrease in Negro birth rate.

On this point the Census Bureau explains:

"The rate of increase in the Negro population, which is not perceptibly increased by immigration or emigration, is by far the lowest on record. This element of the population has been growing at a rapidly diminishing rate during the last 30 years, its percentage of increase having declined from 18 per cent between 1890 and 1900 to 11.2 per cent during the following decade and to 6.5 per cent during the 10 years ended January 1, 1920. Such data as are available as to birth and death rates among the Negroes indicate that the birth rate has decreased considerably since 1900, while the death rate has not changed greatly."

The statement, "this element of the population has been growing at a rapidly diminishing rate during the past 30 years," that is, since 1890, presupposes the accuracy of the census of 1870, which presumption the Census Office itself discredits in a previous statement. It entirely overlooks the fact that the rate rose suddenly from 13.8 for 1880-1890 to 18.0 for 1890-1900. With the indicated corrections the rate of increase has declined within the expected limits of fluctuation from 22 per cent for

the decade 1850-1860 to 11.2 per cent for the
decade 1900-1910, making a drop of 10.8 points
in six decades. The sudden downward drop by
4.6 points in a single decade certainly calls for
a more satisfactory explanation than a sudden
and unaccounted for decrease in birth rate.
The only statement which the Census Bureau
vouchsafes to account for this rather startling
conclusion is a very hesitant and uncertain one:

"Such data as are available with regard to birth
and death rate among Negroes indicate that the birth
rate has decreased considerably since 1910, but the
death rate has not changed greatly."

On examining the data on which this conclusion is based, we find that they are wholly insufficient to justify the sweeping conclusion imposed upon it. The mortality statistics are
based upon returns from the registration area.
Only five Southern states are now included in
the area; namely, Maryland, Virginia, North
Carolina, South Carolina and Kentucky, from
which birth and death rates are collected annually, and even these states were not admitted
to the birth registration area in 1900. Thus
the computation of birth and death rates for
the colored population of these states is neither
adequate nor convincing.

BIRTH RATE OF NEGRO POPULATION IN SPECIFIED
REGISTRATION STATES, 1900 AND 1919
(COMPARATIVE)

States and Color	Birth Rate	
	1900	1919
Maryland:		
White	25.7	19.0
Colored	27.9	26.7
Virginia:		
White	31.5	25.9
Colored	33.1	27.8
North Carolina:		
White	34.3	29.3
Colored	36.5	28.5
South Carolina:		
White	32.3	27.1
Colored	38.2	26.2
Kentucky:		
White	31.2	24.7
Colored	25.2	17.7

Those are the only heavy Negro states within
the registration area.

These states were not all included within the
registration area for 1900. Mortality statistics
in the non-registration area are notoriously inaccurate and unreliable. Birth registration is
especially unsatisfactory even in the registration area.

Return of Negro births would naturally be most inaccurate. Negro births, especially in rural and small urban communities, are not always attended by regular physicians or certified health officials. The midwife still plies her trade. There is a relatively large number of illegitimate births among Negroes. Official returns in such cases would not be apt to be rendered fully for prudential reasons. It is therefore evident that the rapidly declining birth rate revealed by the census is based upon no comparable and adequate data.

Even the apparent rapid increase in the white death rate awaits fuller explanation before the figures can be relied upon with assurance. It is curious to note that the birth rate among the whites in South Carolina fell from 32.3 in 1900 to 27.1 in 1919, the death rate rising but slightly from 10.4 to 10.6 during the same interval. And yet the white population of that state increased from 557,807 in 1900 to 808,538 in 1920. There was a vigesimal increment of 250,731 with little or no reënforcement from immigration. This unexplained increment in the white population seems also to discredit the reliability of the recorded mortality statistics within the states so recently added to the registration area.

It is well understood that these states, except

South Carolina, have shown a comparatively slow rate of increase in Negro population for thirty years preceding the census in question. The facts are indicated in the following table:

DECENNIAL RATE OF INCREASE OF THE NEGRO POPULATION IN CERTAIN REGISTRATION STATES: 1880–1910

| Name | Rate of Increase | | |
	1890	1900	1910
United States	13.5	18.0	11.2
Maryland	2.6	9.0	−1.2
Virginia	.6	4.0	1.6
North Carolina	5.6	11.3	11.7
South Carolina	14.0	13.6	6.8
Kentucky	−1.2	6.2	−8.1

From the table it will be seen that the increase in Negro population in the Southern states within the registration area has been considerably lower than that for the country at large. In Maryland, there is an actual decline in the Negro population of 1.2 per cent, from 1900 to 1910, and the small gain of 2.6 from 1880 to 1890. In Virginia the highest rate of increase during the past thirty years was 4 per cent. In Kentucky there was an actual decline for two of the three decades. The low rate of increase in the border states is due to the large emigration of the Negro from these states to the nearby Northern states and cities. It is well known that the Negroes who migrate to the North and the large cities are largely younger people of both sexes, who, if they had remained at home, would naturally tend to increase the birth rate.

The low birth rate revealed by the census in these states is due to the migration of the Negro population of reproductive age from those states within the registration area. This, of course, does not affect, necessarily, the birth rate of the Negro population as a whole. A better view of the birth rate of the Negro population may be secured by considering the growth of the population in the more typical Southern states not so much affected by migration during the same period.

DECENNIAL RATE OF INCREASE OF THE NEGRO
POPULATION IN CERTAIN NON-REGISTRATION
STATES: 1880–1910

Name	1890	1900	1910
United States	13.5	18.0	11.2
Georgia	18.4	20.5	13.7
Alabama	13.1	21.9	9.8
Mississippi	14.2	22.2	11.2
Louisiana	15.6	16.4	9.7

Thus it will be seen that four heavy Negro states, with an aggregate Negro population of nearly four million, show a rate of increase far greater than those in the registration area. The increase in these states was due wholly to excess of births over deaths. But this does not tell the whole story. While the stream of migration was not so pronounced from these states as from the northern tier of Southern states, still there has been a considerable northern movement for the past three or four decades.

From a comprehensive view of the whole situation, it seems perfectly clear that the sudden decline of the Negro population as revealed by the census of 1920 is due to miscount rather than to the declining birth rate. If we should estimate an error in count of 300,000, scarcely greater than that conceded by the Census Bureau itself for the count of 1890, the Negro population during the last sixty years would have followed more or less consistently the ordinary laws of growth. Let us accept the substantial accuracy of the census of 1860, 1880, 1900 and 1910 and estimate the error for 1870 at 512,163, for 1890 at 270,000, as conceded by the Census Bureau, and let us still further allow an error in the count, 300,000 for 1920, as here suggested.

The growth of the Negro population since 1850 would be as follows:

NEGRO POPULATION

Year	Number	Decennial Increase	Per Cent of Increase
1920	10,763,013	935,250	9.6
1910	9,827,763	993,769	11.2
1900	8,833,994	1,073,994	13.8
1890	7,760,000	1,179,207	17.6
1880	6,580,793	1,188,621	22.0
1870	5,392,172	950,342	21.4
1860	4,441,830	803,022	22.1

The table makes the Negro population behave more or less normally, and is certainly more reasonable than the startling deviation revealed by the face of returns, and the explanation is more acceptable to reason than that urged by the Census Bureau, of a sudden and unexplainable decline in the Negro birth rate.

It is a source of surprise to note that the American mind seems to expect that any fact which affects the Negro will deviate from the normal course of human values. It is prone to accept with satisfaction wild assertions and unsupported theories, without subjecting them to the test of logic and reason. If it is seen in

the Census, it is so. Any statement issued upon
the authority of the government which seems
to be belittling to the Negro will be seized upon
by the would-be social philosophers and exploited throughout the nation to the disadvantage of the race.

De Bow, relying upon the low rate of increase
in the Negro population, revealed by the census of 1870, proved to the entire satisfaction
of those who were satisfied with this type of
proof that the Negro could not withstand the
competition of freedom and would, forthwith,
fall out of the equation as an affected factor.
The census of 1880, showing the unheard of increase of 34 per cent, set all of De Bow's philosophy at naught. But thence arose another
school of philosophers which declared that this
unheard of increase in the Negro population
threatened the numerical ascendency of the
white race, and, therefore, the black man
should be returned to Africa whence his ancestors came. The census of 1890 refuted this conclusion by showing only an increase of 13.8 per
cent; but, no whit abashed, another type of
anti-Negro propagandism arose, declaring that
the rapid decline in the race indicated inherent,
degenerative physical tendencies threatening
to the health and stamina of the American
people. The census of 1900, showing a rise of

decadal growth of 8.0 per cent, produced a calm
in the domain of social speculation. It seems
to be the nature of the prophet to ignore the
failure of the fulfillment of his prophecies.
But the preceding prophecies of evil are still
of record.

It is particularly unfortunate that such loose
and unscientific propaganda can be bolstered
up by data from government documents which
the uninquiring mind is disposed to accept with
the authority of holy writ. The calamity philosophers have already dipped their pens in ink
to damn the Negro race to degeneration and
death by reason of the latest census figures.
The thought, and perhaps the conduct, of the
nation may be misled on the basis of erroneous
data, backed up by governmental authority.

The broader question arises in the scientific
mind: If the data on Negro population furnished by the census cannot be relied on, as is
clearly shown by past enumerations, what assurance is there that collateral information,
such as death rate, birth rate, occupation,
illiteracy, etc., is to be given full credit and
confidence? The Negro problem is the most
complicated issue with which we have to deal.
Straight thinking and sound opinion based upon
accurate data are absolutely necessary to enable
us to reach any conclusion of value. The Cen-

sus Office has now become a permanent bureau which, it is hoped, will take rank with other scientific departments of the government.

Statesmen and publicists should have serious concern about the accuracy of Negro statistics in view of the importance of the political and sociological conclusions based upon and derived from them.

The problem of eugenics is receiving much attention from students of sociology at the present time. The future welfare of society depends very largely upon perpetuating and carrying forward the best characteristics derivable from physical heredity and social environment. The application of eugenics to the colored race of the United States suggests several new and interesting lines of inquiry.

A study of the number of children, contributed by the fifty-five colored teachers in Howard University, Washington, D. C., throws an interesting side light on the question of eugenics as it affects the Negro race. Howard University is an institution for the higher education of the Negro, comprising a student body of over fifteen hundred. The Negro members of the faculty maintain, on the whole, perhaps, a status as high as any other group of colored people to be found in the United States. The present study is limited to the teachers of the academic faculties, as they constitute a coherent social entity, whose life focuses about the institution.

As outgrowth of sudden change of condition due to the Civil War, the Negro has developed a small upper class with a wide fissure between it and the great mass life of the race. There are about fifty thousand Negroes belonging to the professional class, who earn a livelihood by some form of intellectual endeavor; while the great bulk of the race lives mainly by manual exertion. All social stratification rests ultimately upon occupation. The Negro has no considerable middle class, such as is found in well regulated societies, which shades imperceptibly in both directions. According to the occupational test, the demarcation between the professional and laboring classes of the Negro is as sharp as a knife-cut line.

It becomes a matter of sociological interest to know how far this upper class is self-sustaining through its own reproductivity. I have, therefore, undertaken to make a study of race eugenics in so far as this particular group is concerned. In the fifty-five families from which these teachers were derived, there were 363 children, or an average of 6.5 for each family. On the other hand, these fifty-five teachers who have passed from the lower to the upper section of Negro life, have, so far, contributed only 37 children, or an average of .7 for each potential family involved. Of this number there are 41 males, 14 females; 22 are married, and 33 are single; the number for each family so far formed is 1.6; the largest number of children in any family is 6; four of the families are barren and four have one child each. The average age of the single members is over 32 years. This strongly indicates that the upward struggle defers the age of marriage to a time when only limited progeny might be expected. Considering all the probabilities in the case, it seems to me entirely likely that these fifty-five potential families, when the whole record is in, will not produce more than an average of two children to each family, while the fifty-five parent families, under the old régime gave rise to 363 children. The new issue will scarcely produce sufficient progeny to perpetuate its own numbers.

There is always a certain sort of social restraint, in the case of an individual advancing from a lower to a higher level of life. The first descendants of foreigners in this country have a lower birth rate than any other element of our population. The intolerant social environment created by the white race may also produce a strong deterrent influence. Animals, in captivity or under restrained environment, do not breed as freely as when placed under free and normal surroundings. The educated Negro, especially when submerged in a white environment, is under a sort of social captivity. The effect of this psychophysical factor upon reproductivity awaits further and fuller study, both in its biological and psychological aspects.

From a wide acquaintance with the upper life of the Negro race, under wide variety of conditions and circumstances, I am fully persuaded that this Howard University group is typical of like element throughout the race so far as fecundity is concerned. The upper class is headed towards extinction, unless reënforced from the fruitful mass below. It is doubtless true that the same restraining influence is exerted upon the corresponding element of the white race. But as there is not the same sharpness of separation between the social levels, nor such severe transitional struggle, the contributing causes do not perhaps operate with the same degree of intensity.

The prolonged period of education delays the age of marriage. The Negro during the first generation of freedom acquired his education at a later period than the white children and, by reason of the hard struggle he has had to undergo, his scholastic training was completed at a somewhat advanced age. The high standard of living, which the professional Negro feels he must maintain, still further delays the age of marriage. A single illustration will serve to clarify this point. I half-jocularly asked one of our bachelor instructors, who has passed beyond his fortieth birthday, why he did not take unto himself a companion and helpmate. His reply was that his salary was not sufficient to allow him to support a family in the style and manner which he deemed appropriate. My reply was: "If your parents had been constrained by like consideration, you would probably not be in existence." His father was a laboring man with a family of eight children. It was the opinion of Grant Allen, the eminent English literary and scientific authority, that the human race would become extinct if all females deferred marriage beyond the age of twenty-six.

The conscious purpose of race suicide doubtless contributes somewhat to the low birth rate. There are some of sensitive and timid spirit who shirk the responsibility of parenthood, because they do not wish to bring into the world children to be subjected to the proscription and obloquy of the Negro's social status.

Will this tendency, which threatens the extinction of the higher element of the Negro race, continue to operate in the future with the same degree of intensity as at the present time? Probably not. The first generation after slavery was subjected to the severe strain and stress of rapid readjustment. The sudden leap from the lower to the upper levels of life was a feat of social acrobatics that can hardly be repeated under more orderly scheme of development. The life of subsequent generations will be better ordered and, therefore, we may expect that the resulting effect will be seen in the family life. The birth rate of the mass of the race is not affected by like considerations. They feel little or nothing of the stress and strain of the upper class, and multiply and make merry, in blissful oblivion of these things. The rate of increase of the upper class is scarcely a third of that of the bulk of the race, as is clearly indicated by the relative prolificness of the Howard University faculty as compared with that of their parents. The higher or professional class in the Negro race will not be recruited from within its own ranks, but must be reënforced from the great mass below. This will produce healthy current throughout the race which will serve somewhat to bridge the chasm produced by the absence of a mediatory class.

The whole question suggests the importance of a more careful and extended study in this field of inquiry which is as fruitful as any other in its far-reaching effect upon the general social welfare.

CHAPTER XIV

BOOKER T. WASHINGTON FIVE YEARS AFTER

"The evil that men do lives after them; the good is often interred with their bones." These words were placed in the mouth of Marc Antony, with Shakespearian adroitness, to appease the passion of the hostile multitude. This propitiatory utterance contradicts the universal propensity and experience of mankind. Contemporaneous faults and foibles of genius are never permitted to obscure their permanent contribution to the sum total of human good. Lifetime reputation is an unsafe measure of the influence of a great man. His acts must be judged in the calm retrospect, and disengaged from the predilections and prejudices of the period, in order to determine his proper place and appraisement.

Booker T. Washington has been dead five years. Even now too short an interval has elapsed to disentangle his real work and worth from partisan zeal and animosities, and to weigh calmly his genuine contribution to the welfare of his race and nation.

For almost a generation the name of Booker T. Washington occupied a large share of the attention of his fellowmen. The nation delighted to mark the wisdom of his sayings and to write his speeches in its books. He occupied as large a place for as long a time in public esteem and favor as any man of his generation. He bore the stamp of natural greatness. His wisdom was intuitive. According to African lore he was born with a caul over his face. He knew without learning, and understood with the certainty of instinct. Like Abraham Lincoln, he possessed an infallible inner sense whose guidance he followed with satisfied assurance. He possessed the genius of common sense, and the philosophy of simple things. His was a universal mind. While he dealt with the most complex and distressing social particulars, his spirit always rose above the temporary intricacies of besetting conditions and lived in an atmosphere that was calm and serene. Booker T. Washington was, perhaps, the only man of eminence of his day who was free from race prejudice. He neither despised nor esteemed any man because of his race. Race prejudice is often extolled as a virtue, but the moral genius of mankind reprobates it as a vice. Though corporally aligned with the Negro race, morally and spiritually he was heir of all the ages. Flesh and blood did not reveal to him the truth by which he guided his path. Progress from enmity to amity is the highest mark of human culture. "Love your enemies; do good to them that hate you," is the goal of human strivings which the carnally minded still deem impossible of realization.

His spiritual inheritance was reënforced by the folk sense and the folk feeling of the Negro race. The Negro embodies the assemblage of Christian virtues and graces to a degree unequaled by any other member of the human family. Meekness, humility and forgiveness of spirit are undetachable coefficients of his blood. He is incapable of deep-seated hatred and revenge. He endures with passivity and quick forgetfulness outrage and contumely which would make other races curse God and die. When he is reviled, he reviles not again. The Negro nature strangely fulfills the apostolic definition, "Charity suffereth long, and is kind; charity envieth not; charity vaunteth not itself, is not puffed up, doth not behave itself unseemly, seeketh not her own, is not easily provoked, thinketh no evil; rejoiceth not in iniquity, but rejoiceth in truth; beareth all things, believeth all things, hopeth all things, endureth all things." To the revengeful and vindictive spirit, this racial virtue is an amazing grace;

but to the Negro it is assuredly a saving one. By no other endowment could he possibly survive in the midst of an arrogant and rapacious civilization with which he has neither the power to cope nor the spirit to contest. The Indian showed resentment; and is dead. The Negro submits and survives. There are thirty million Negroes in the Western world who are clearly destined to inherit the full measure of European civilization and culture. History affords no more striking fulfillment of the beatitude with a promise, "Blessed are the meek, for they shall inherit the earth." The vehement and inflammatory utterances of part of a certain type of temperament are but the temporary effervescences of an excitable mood, and do not express deep-seated or serious purpose of the people whose cause is thus espoused. The Negro spiritual breathes in blind, half-conscious poetry the spontaneous feelings of his soul without bitterness or hate. Booker T. Washington fathomed the feelings of his race as well as his own personal disposition when he said, "No man can be mean enough to make me hate him." This apothegm ranks with the great moral maxims of mankind, and takes its place alongside of the wisest sayings of saints and sages of all time. Let other races conquer through the exploitation of power; the Negro will triumph through the manifestation of love. Mr. Washington also embodied the mother wit and never-failing good humor of his race. Next to his submissive spirit, the Negro's humor is his greatest salvator. He laughs where others weep; he smiles where others frown; he grins where others groan. He thus relieves the pressure upon his overburdened spirit which would otherwise pine away under the weight of impressing ills. His humor disarms his enemies. The race that laughs is the race that lasts.

Booker Washington possessed the qualities of naturalness, moderation, and simplicity which are not usually considered to be attributes of the Negro race. He had poise without pose. Extravagance in word or deed was foreign to his nature. Amidst turmoil and confusion he maintained a calm and unruffled exterior, albeit there may have been inner groanings of soul too deep for utterance. A quick appreciation and proper appraisement of values are characteristic of men of long experience in handling practical affairs. What others acquire by experience, he gained through instinct. Walt Whitman speaks of himself as "meeter of gentleman and savage on equal terms." Booker T. Washington could mingle with kings and potentates with the dignity and nonchalance of one to the manor born, and could sup with a peasant in a log cabin in Alabama and make himself an agreeable guest in this humble environment. He received a gift of a million dollars from admiring philanthropists and endured the bitter abuse of his own race with equal equanimity and composure. Excitability of temperament is considered characteristic of the Negro race, and yet he was steadied by a natural ballast that held him in stable equilibrium. A simple, unadorned story of his life in *Up from Slavery*, recorded without the least ornamentation or studied style, takes rank with the great biographies of celebrated men. It was easy to believe the genuineness and sincerity of his purpose because of the naturalness and simplicity of his spirit.

With this secret and method, Booker T. Washington entered upon the scene of action more than a quarter century ago. A superlative nature needs no nurture. A soul surcharged with moral and spiritual potencies requires only the suggestion and the occasion to wake it into life and power. Samuel Chapman Armstrong gave the suggestion and the Negro situation in the South furnished the field. Ingersoll says of Shakespeare: "Give him an acorn, and he will create the forest; give him a grain of sand and a drop of water, and he will

create the seashore and the mighty ocean."
The man met the opportunity.

Assigned to a little Alabama town with an
Indian name, in no sense different from a hundred similar communities with like designations, in a few years he gave Tuskegee a name
as renowned as our great metropolitan centers.
This institution grew out of the personality of
Booker T. Washington as surely as the oak
grows out of the acorn. It is but the outward
embodiment of his inner spirit.

His whole propaganda was based upon the
philosophy of peace and good-will between the
races. The apostle Paul advises that we should,
if possible, live at peace with all men. Booker
Washington always found it possible. His task
was a most difficult and delicate one. He preserved the equilibrium of a triangle of forces.
Up to his time the white man of the South, the
white man of the North, and the Negro were of
divergent minds as to a proper plan of racial
adjustment. There was something of coöperation between the North and the Negro, but the
Southern white man was left out of account.
He essayed, and in large measure succeeded, in
bringing these three factors into harmonious
coöperation. An ardent disciple of General
Armstrong in promoting the gospel of industrial education, he gave that doctrine an em-

phasis and application which it was impossible for the founder of Hampton to do. The unpreparedness of the Negro to compete in the skilled pursuits of life with requisite expertness gave him the strategical advantage in promoting this practical gospel. This was not a one-sided obsession on his part. He saw the present, pressing need, and urged its fulfillment with all of the ardor and earnestness of his nature. He was a partisan advocate only in the sense that he stressed with unreserved emphasis the things he felt to be of the greatest need for the time and place with which he was dealing. If advocates of other types of effort were worsted in the controversy, it was because they were unable to match his earnest urgency and persuasive plea. His advocacy of industrial education was not limited to the Negro race, but was as wide as the circle of human needs. It meant most to the Negro only because he needed it most. He aimed to reach the man farthest down.

No man of his day did more, if as much, to put practical education in the program of our educational systems throughout the country. He became the exponent and spokesman of this practical ideal, not only for the Negro, but for the nation. The utilitarian tendency in education owes as much to Booker T. Washington as to any other contributant agent or agency. They called him the wizard of Tuskegee, not because of his working in the darkness after the manner of the traditional wizard, but because of the wonderful works which grew, as it were, out of the wizardry of his august personality.

The apostle of the new method came upon the scene at a critical time in the history of race adjustment. The reconstruction program which attempted to enforce political equality had been overthrown. The carpetbagger, native white, and Negro politician had been driven from power, but were still hanging to the lingering hope to regain the blissful seat. The sectional hatred engendered by the war was gradually yielding to the mollifying influence of time. The attitude of the North was hesitant and equivocal; that of the South was growing assertive and hopeful. Political discussion hinged upon the wisdom or unwisdom of enforcing the war amendments to the Constitution. Force bills were introduced in Congress to compel the South to yield to the declared and decreed will of the nation, but were defeated by skillfully manipulated combinations. Economic discussions began to vie with political rights in the arenas of public debate. The question of the industrial and economic rehabilitation of the South was supplanting agitation for political reconstruction. The wounds of war were slowly healing. The North and South were gradually gravitating towards a basis of common understanding. The Nation was growing tired of the continual agitation of the race question, which for fully a generation had all but absorbed public attention. Up to this time every Negro leader had ardently espoused the old political platform. The industrial and economic development of the race had been given little earnest consideration. The gospel of race development, according to Armstrong, was deemed decidedly unorthodox. The Northern philanthropists and friends of the Negro had espoused the same view. Institutions for the so-called higher education of the Negro, fostered by philanthropy, flourished like the bay tree.

The public mind, by the well-known laws of social psychology, will not hold one sentiment intently for a long time. It is always in quest of some new thing. The time was ripe. The public sentiment was ready for a change. A brilliant colored man with attractive public powers was all that was needed to launch the new propaganda. The time was ripe to exploit any Negro leader who would abandon the old method and advocate a new policy more in consonance with changing public sentiment. Booker T. Washington stepped into the breach. He understood the point of view of the Southern white man, as well as that of the Northern white man and the Negro himself, and endeavored to hold a just balance among conflicting states of feeling and belief. As ambassador for the Negro he was accepted at the court of the white race, and spoke before the bar of public opinion for his people boldly, as an ambassador ought to speak. He did not demand more than he had the power to enforce or the ability to persuade. He who demands only what he can command is wise; he who demands less is cowardly; he who demands more is a braggart.

Booker T. Washington was a pragmatist of the first water. He believed in attempting the thing possible and postponing the unattainable to the time of increased ability and power. He knew with an instinctive certainty just how far the prejudice of the white race would permit the Negro to go, and just how far the Negro with his traditional weakness and ineptitude, could go without such permission. The bar was placed at the exact height which the athlete could leap with his present training and strength, and raised to higher levels according to developing prowess and skill. There was sharp criticism on part of his race because he did not place the bar at an ideal height whether the acrobat could jump it or not.

Dr. Washington was often denounced by critics of his own race because, as spokesman, he did not demand all that they were entitled to in theory. But no one has ever demonstrated that he ever asked for less than it was probable, or even possible, to secure. He was the philosopher of the possible, and believed in reaching the ideal by gradual approximation. His was the patience of knowledge. The one who comprehends the whole equation refuses to become unduly excited over any unfavorable factor. He knew the Negro and he knew the white man as none before or since has known, for his knowledge rested upon the infallible foundation of intuition.

Booker T. Washington had a deep and abiding faith in the ultimate possibilities of the Negro, although he fully appreciated his present defects and imperfections. In his belief the white race had already contributed about all it was calculated to do through direct and intimate ministration. Race reclamation must come through self-directed activities. Up to this time white men had worked for the Negro. Dr. Washington taught that the Negro must henceforth work for himself. Tuskegee was built on the basis of this idea. Negroes conduct all of the activities of this institution in its various features and ramifications. It was declared that the Negro could not safely be put in charge of large interests, such as the construction of large buildings, and the management and manipulation of large plants. He did not argue the point, but produced the concrete results. This institution, which sprang up as if by magic, under Negro enterprise and skill, still remains the largest and most complicated project under race direction and intimate management. Not only so, but Tuskegee became the center of race energy and enterprise ramifying in all directions throughout the country. White philanthropists were easily persuaded òf the wisdom of this policy and were willing to furnish the means to give the experiment a full and fair trial. There is perhaps no other philanthropic enterprise that promises so much for the ultimate development and reclamation of the race. The only help that is worth while is the help that helps the helpless to help themselves.

Dr. Washington minimized politics and stressed economics as the immediate step in race development. And yet he believed that the Negro should have all the political rights he could get, just as he believed that he should have all of the higher education he could use. The storm center raged around his political policy. The whites, North and South, were easily persuaded of the importance of economic development as contrasted with political power. He became not only the spokesman, but the oracle of race adjustment and relationship. So complete was the confidence imposed in him by the white race that he was chosen as the referee of such political patronage as it was deemed wise to assign to the Negro leaders. In this capacity his position was anomalous. The avowed advocate of political relinquishment becomes the controlling dispenser of political power. But where the carrion is, there will the vultures be also. It did seem amazing with what ease the erstwhile Negro politicians were won over to the Washington practical and pacific program after Roosevelt selected him as the political referee for the race. So great is the persuasive power of patronage. In this seemingly anomalous capacity, Dr. Washington, after all, was not inconsistent. He believed to the fullest extent in the rights of the Negro, in so far as he was able to secure and maintain those rights. And he did not deem it inharmonious with his asserted policy of political quiescence to help him as far as feasible on the road to political power and prestige. The putative apostle of the Negro's political elimination wielded more political power than has befallen the good fortune of any other Negro before or since his time. The assumption of this rôle, strangely enough, did not offend the white men of the South, whose avowed purpose was to exclude the Negro from politics, and who relied upon the program of Dr. Washington to facilitate this exclusion. There was the reserved feeling that whatever he did was right.

There always existed a small group of assertive Negroes which Dr. Washington never was able to bring to his point of view. This group was composed mainly of college bred men of liberal culture who were unwilling to compromise their intellectual integrity by surrendering the abstract claim of political rights. They could not tolerate the suggestion of inferiority which his program implied. Even his control of political patronage was not able to convert the most stubborn of these. The man with the theory always has the advantage of the man with the thing, in abstract disquisition. Since Mr. Washington's death, this group has gained the ascendency in dominating the thought and opinion of the race, but has not been able to realize to the least degree the rights and recognition so vehemently demanded.

A statesman is one who possesses the sagacity to formulate a program of procedure and who has the force to impress it upon his day and time as an effective policy. Booker T. Washington is the only Negro who has been able to force upon the acceptance of the American people a policy and program for his race. From this point of view he may be denominated the one commanding race statesman yet to appear. It is true that his policy has not solved the race problem, but it has laid down certain lines which must be followed in any plan of future solution. His program is not complete, but it is funda-mental as far as it goes.

Booker Washington died before America entered into the World War. He left no successor. Those who come after him absorb and apply such measure of his method as may be appropriate to their nature and understanding. Others will take advantage of his demise to disparage such of his doctrine as does not meet with their approval. None have caught a full portion of his secret and method. The white race regard his loss as irreparable and hardly expect to look upon his like again.

The last five years have wrought great change in the spirit of aggrieved groups in all parts of the world. A new sense of self-assertion has been aroused in the Negro. The white race has become more determined and intolerant. The Ku Klux Klan is a concrete expression of this intolerance. The two races are facing each other with suspicion and distrust. There is no Booker Washington to lay propitiating hands upon them both. Had Booker Washington survived to this time his wisdom to deal with the shifting exigencies of the problem is conjectural. Who can tell what effect the perplexing issues of reconstruction might have had upon the reputation and fame of Abraham Lincoln had he survived to that time? We only know, in case of the one as of the other, that his pacificatory spirit and his enlightened common sense would have been a sobering and steadying influence in any emergency.

The titanic struggle has greatly modified many of the conditions with which he had to deal. He urged the Negro to remain in the country; the war thrust him into the city. The war created unforeseen industrial demands. Five hundred thousand Negroes rushed to the North to fill the vacuum in the labor market. The advocate of political inaction is apt to be hooted by the multitude whose passion has been heated by strife. There is little patience with the counsellor of patience when the beat of the war drum dins in the ear. The radical rides on the rising tide of war. That "the Negro could earn a dollar in the South, but could not spend it; and spend a dollar in the North, but could not earn it," ranks among Mr. Washington's most apt and pithy sayings. But the truth and appositeness of his sententious assertion were suddenly reversed with changing industrial conditions. The new situation of the Negro frustrates much of the philosophy that used to pass as the last words of wisdom. Programs are always subject to the exigencies of shifting conditions; principles will abide.

Booker T. Washington's pacificatory doctrine of racial peace and good will, his sound, sober appraisement of the importance of practical education, his urgent insistence upon economic development instead of too confident reliance on political action, his common-sense gospel of industry, thrift, and economy, his philosophy of accomplishing the possible rather than attempting the unattainable, must be at the basis of any future scheme of race reclamation and relationship.

His place in history is secure. His contribution is permanent. His influence will abide. Booker Washington will be remembered by posterity, not only as a great Negro, but as a great American, and as a great man.

CHAPTER XV

RACE COOPERATION

The permanent effect of any war is to be judged by its humanitarian outcome and moral aftermath. Sacrifice of blood and treasure is in vain unless there results a better social relationship. The Revolutionary War released the Declaration of Independence, the embodiment of the democratic ideal. The French Revolution set the ears of the world tingling with the doctrine of "liberty, fraternity, equality." Our Civil War produced the Emancipation Proclamation and extended the ennobling bonds of liberty to include the race farthest down.

The World War has exacted an unparalleled toll of human life and material values; but, alas, the world impatiently awaits a clear indication of corresponding moral contribution. President Wilson's loudly declared doctrine of bigger and better definition of democracy is now repeated only with a sneer or with a smile. The League of Nations designed for the composure of the world is frustrated by age-old jealousies, greed and ambition. Nations are vying for political and commercial ascendency as of yore. Race animosities have been aroused and stimulated. The weaker breeds of men have developed an assertive and defiant self-consciousness. Japan smarts keenly under the stigma of race inferiority. The darker breeds of men in all lands resent the assumption of the whiter ones of everlasting overlordship and dominion. In our own land human beings are lynched, tortured and burned alive at the exactions of race prejudice. The land of liberty is in danger of becoming the land of lynchers. The Ku Klux Klan proclaims the revival of an invisible empire based upon the principles of darkness and of evil. Did the World War bring in the Anti-Christ or the Christ that is to be? This query must prick the Christian conscience to the core. Race prejudice is the one dominant obstacle in the world today which stands squarely athwart the coming of the Kingdom of Heaven which Jesus sought to set up on earth. The Jewish race held so tenaciously to the tenets of racial and religious prejudices that they rejected altogether the new doctrines of social, moral and spiritual democracy. The Southern slaveholders sought to reconcile Christianity and slavery and hoped to gain easement of conscience by such complacent reconciliation. The Christian church today is vainly deluding itself with a frantic endeavor to reconcile Christian duty with racial caste. But the chasm between the races cannot be bridged by a structure resting upon such an insecure foundation. The folly is as apparent as it would be to build upon the shifting sands instead of enduring rock, or substitute coils of smoke for bands of iron.

And yet we hope that somehow there is an imminent moral economy in human affairs. The World War has brought together all peoples of all lands and this incidental contact has of itself aroused a consciousness of brotherhood and moral unity. It is now, in this period of reconstruction, that there comes the psychological moment for the Christian religion to quicken this conscience into a keener sense of spiritual kinship and an intenser appreciation of the oneness of human nature and human needs. Will the church give the teachings of Jesus a chance to function, or will it adhere to the conception of that sundown disciple of Jesus who held the unity of the flesh to be greater than the unity of the spirit? Christianity must justify its claim of being the world religion by meeting the needs of the world at this critical time. But the one dominant purpose of the teachings of Jesus is to promote peace on earth and good will among men as was proclaimed by angelic heraldry on the night of His birth.

The dominant note in Christianity is brotherhood, without restrictions or reservations. If a brother of the flesh should impose upon his less fortunate kinsmen fixed boundaries beyond which he dared not go, the proffer would be rejected with scorn. The fate of Ananias who openly allowed full acceptance of Christian platform, but cherished secret reservations, should stand as a solemn warning to all who would imitate his example.

Programs grow out of principles. The one depends upon the shifting emergencies of the circumstances and conditions, and the other abides forever. The constructive program of interracial and racial relations must be based upon principles above enunciated. No other foundation can be laid than the one that is laid. If the fundamentals of our platform are so based, we need have little concern about planks and provisions which must, of necessity, be adapted to the existence of time, place and condition.

In the construction of our platform, let us bear in mind: First, it is a universal principle that all peoples who must perforce dwell together find a modus vivendi and accommodate themselves to it. Indeed, this is true of the animals of the forest. The moving picture camera set up in the heart of Africa faithfully

portrays the modus vivendi among the denizens
of the jungle. In a region where there is but
one water hole in a radius of many miles, the
elephant, the lion, the tiger, the goat, the fox,
the jackal, the fierce animals and the mild ones,
all use this common fountain. They come and
go with as much orderliness and decorum as
prevails at a well-ordered breakfast table. We
may, therefore, rely upon the inherent propensity towards human adjustment and face the
race situation without fear and trembling.

In the second place, there can be but one
ethical standard to be applied to human beings,
irrespective of race or color. The laws of
science are absolutely uniform in their operation. The force of gravitation takes no heed of
distinctions among men, and so the ethical laws
admit of no variation to accommodate racial
arrogance or pretension. It would be as disastrous to treat the two races by different moral
formulas as it would be to adopt a double
standard of weights and measures. The physician who would treat the Negro patient afflicted
with the same ailment by a different method
than that applied to a white patient would violate the integrity of his profession. The merchant who would mete out his goods to Negro
customers by one yard stick and to his white
customers by another would very soon acquire

the deserved reputation of dishonesty. The merchant, the physician, the druggist, the lawyer, the business man, the man of practical affairs find that they must apply one invariable formula to white and black alike or stultify their own conscience and dishonor their profession. The Christian can do no less.

In the third place, the Negro is a human being and is endowed with all the potential faculties and powers of humanity, albeit he may be belated and retarded in their development and exercise. The white people at present represent the advanced section of the human family and are trustees of human culture and civilization, a trust vouchsafed to them not for themselves alone or for their sons and daughters after the flesh, but for all the children of men. Those who entered the vineyard at the eleventh hour were received on terms of compensatory equality with those who had borne the heat and burden of the day. Other men have labored and we have entered into their labors.

With these fundamental propositions in mind we may approach the question of race coöperation with assurance that our efforts will be not in vain. It is not necessary that men should agree on all issues in order that they may work effectively together for certain definitely understood objects which promote the common good.

Men differing widely in religion may work together in politics, and those with diverse political views may be of the same household of faith.

There are certain general advantages which apply to both races alike and numerous ills which afflict them both. Character, intelligence, industry, thrift, economy are virtues of universal value. There need be no apprehension that as the Negro advances in the scale of excellence he will become more menaceful to the white race. But vice is a menace to virtue, disease to health, ignorance to intelligence, and degradation is a menace to the decorum and decencies of life. The germs of disease gnaw with equal avidity at the vitals of white and black alike, and have an unobstructed passage from one to the other. Ignorance, sloth, inefficiency, moral turpitude, by whatever element manifested, impair the standard and tone of the community in which they prevail. The two races should coöperate to the fullest extent to wipe out the evils and promote the good measures which are universal in their scope and application.

"One touch of nature makes the whole world kin." Pity and need make universal appeal in the human heart. The Negro makes the greatest demand upon social endeavor, because for the present his need is greatest and a Good Samaritan will rise up to bind his wound and soothe his bleeding heart. The very presence of the Negro, with his wide circle of needs, is indeed a benediction to the people among whom his lot has been cast. It will serve to free them from that pharasaical hauteur which vaunts itself—"I thank the Lord that I am not as other men."

Indeed, the Negro's presence, with his needs, imperfections and delinquencies growing out of his state, should lead those who are more fortunate, not to harden their hearts against his lot, but to increase their feeling for human awakening and improvement. Let both races, through their best representatives, join hand and heart in this field of human service, the Negro placing strength upon the Ten Commandments and the white man upon the Golden Rule. And if we do not succeed in solving the race problem, we will accomplish that which is to us of infinitely more importance—we will have done our duty.

CHAPTER XVI

THE NEGRO'S PLACE IN THE LABOR STRUGGLE

The battle for bread and the adjustment of races constitute the two great world problems of our day. Each complicates the other. Settle the battle for bread, and the race problem would still survive. Adjust the race problem, and the battle for bread would continue to rage. In the United States today we have the two problems operating simultaneously. The resultant and significance of the outcome are as interesting as any other social phenomena with which we have to deal.

The strike is on; common sense is off. Labor and capital are at it again. The issue is as old as human greed. It is with us always. Half the energy of the human race has been wasted in friction instead of being conserved by co-operation for useful ends.

It seems as if it must needs be so. The offense must needs come, notwithstanding the woe and misery which follow in its train. How long will mankind waste their while in strife and exhaust their might for that which satisfieth not? The universality of senseless strife among men is the amplest proof of the theory of evolution. Nature is red in tooth and claw. Man is an animal in all of his lower propensities, responding but slowly to the light of reason. No one can accept with full satisfaction the one definition that man is a rational animal, after the awful experience of the last eight years of irrational strife which engulfed the human race. Not a single intellectual, moral or spiritual principle has been advanced by this universal deluge of blood and tears. The wanton waste of tens of millions of lives and hundreds of billions of material substance, convicts the human race of utter irrationality. Had half of this wasted energy and destroyed values been utilized in constructive advantage, ignorance, misery and want could have been banished from the face of the earth.

But man learns his lesson slowly. The winding stair of progress slopes gradually upward. The lesson of yesterday we ignore today, and forget tomorrow.

Labor and capital will fight it out until by extermination or mutual exhaustion, they learn the folly of strife. By senseless antagonism, they fill the land with misery and want; by harmony of action they might bring peace, plenty and prosperity. Labor and capital now stand

opposed to each other in hostile camps, each
vowing its own advantage at the expense of
the other. The selfish end obscures the common weal. The terms labor and capital suggest contrasted significance, like friend and foe,
each ready to fly at the face of the other on
slightest provocation. They should stand as
complementary designations, like bow and
arrow, man and wife, where each is essential to
the proper functioning of the other. If capital
or labor should win, where were the victory?
Capital is labor in the passive voice. Labor
is capital in the present tense; without labor,
capital is useless. Without capital, labor is
impotent. Without the two hundred thousand
laborers of the Pennsylvania Railroad, the
billion dollar capital would be nugatory and
dead. Without the capital, the laborers would
be in idleness and want. They are complementary factors of the same product. Production is the end in view; capital and labor are
the means employed. They are equally indispensable instruments. The divisive issue
grows out of the distribution of profit. It is too
much to hope that this issue will be satisfac-
torily settled until selfishness can be still further reduced as a controlling element of human
motive. The present strike will shortly be settled on the basis of compromise and temporary

conciliation. But the roots of discord remain
for the future. The buds will resprout as long
as there is life in the roots. The issue would
have become acute long before now had not the
World War shunted attention in another direction of foreign profiteering. Both labor and
capital fattened so grossly on the common
booty that they, for the moment, forgot their
mutual antàgonisms.

But, now that the industrial and economic
flush of the war is over, and the profits of production are gravitating to the normal level, the
age-old issue recurs. One of these days, in the
sweet by and by, when reason and common
sense shall have gained sway as the monitors of
human motive, then capital and labor will
coöperate in friendly unison like the right·and
left hands of the human body. Until then, we
may expect constant recurrence of destructive
collisions, and more and more perfect adjustment as the outcome of recurrent shocks.

The industrial world may be divided into
three classes: (1) Those who work with the ten
fingers of two hands, (2) those who work with
three fingers of one hand, and (3) those who
work with the brain. The function of the industrial secretariat, which merely records the
work of the hand toilers and registers the will
of the brain workers, is secondary and inter-
mediate. Those engaged in the primary tasks

of mental and muscular effort are divided into
wide-apart camps. The mental workers have
fortified themselves behind the breastworks of
capital. The muscular laborer must rely upon
his bodily strength. The one uses the mailed
fist, the other the bare hand.

Where does the Negro stand in this nation-
wide, yea world-wide issue between capital and
labor? Logic aligns him with labor, but good
sense arrays him on the side of capital. The
race issue frustrates all of the conclusions of
logic. The Negro is essentially a manual
worker and, therefore, is vitally concerned in
whatever advantages may accrue to the toiling
world. He shares in every concession wrested
from capital by the militant demands of labor.
But the issue between the white and colored
workman is sharper than that between capital
and labor. Capital, white labor and the Negro
constitute the eternal triangle of the industrial
world.

The Negro was brought to this country because it was thought that his animal and mechanical powers could be easily exploited for
the benefit of his white captor. It was deemed
the prerogative of any white man to exploit the
Negro for his economic benefit. It is hard for
the white race today to rid itself of this traditional conceit. The Negro is regarded as the
ordained workman, the surplus fruitage of

whose labor should inure to the advantage of the overlord. In a similar way capital looks upon all labor as an agency to swell the magnitude of its own profit. If there were no surplus productivity of labor, the capitalists would have no need of him. The workman who consumes as much as he produces is an unprofitable servant. The Negro is regarded as a field of double exploitation. He shares the estimate of capital towards all labor heightened by the world-wide and age-old conceit that it is the white man's prerogative to profit at the expense of the darker races of men.

The fact that the Negro constitutes only a small fraction of the labor fund of the nation greatly complicates the question of industrial and racial adjustment. All caste and class systems in the world rest fundamentally upon the stratification of labor. If there were Negroes enough to man the lower levels of industry and to do all of the rougher forms of work, their industrial subordination would be simple and easy. But it is plainly impossible to maintain any permanent separation of peoples who must perform the same tasks at the same time with the same compensation. There are not enough Negroes to fill the quota of any of the great lines of industry, and, consequently the number must be supplemented by white men. If all Negroes were domestic servants and all domestic ser-

vants were Negroes, the line of racial and industrial cleavage would be clear. But in New
York City there are only 150,000 Negroes out
of a total population of 5,000,000. If every
Negro man, woman and child were engaged in
domestic service in that city, the number would
be insufficient to fill the quota of the menial
calling. The Negroes are unevenly distributed
throughout the whole nation and scattered
through the whole field of employment in the
catalogue of listed occupations. Even in the
South the Negro constitutes but one-third of
the population, and forms only a fractional
part of the manual labor of that section. The
attempt to force occupational separation of the
races under such circumstances becomes impossible. The democratic idea will not sanction
the suggestion that the line of demarcation be
maintained by awarding the Negro lower wage
for the same work as his white competitor. In
South Africa, it is said that a native receives
twenty-five cents for painting the upper half
of the pole, and a white man a dollar for painting the lower half.

The capitalist has but one dominating motive, the production and sale of goods. The
race or color of the producer counts but little.
The work is listed with material assets as an instrument of production. A good engine and a
good engineer are equally essential factors in

the process of transportation. Manhood and mechanism are merged. There is little margin of favor between the white and black workman except as reflected in productive efficiency. There is no personal closeness or intimacy of contact between employer and employee. Race prejudice finds no room for manifestation. The capitalist is prone to a kind and generous attitude toward the black workman. The Negro is acceptable to him according to his merit and efficiency merely as a tool of production. There is also involved in this attitude the thought that, on the whole, the Negro may be a little cheaper than the white man, and is more easily manipulated.

The source of friction arises between the black and white workmen assigned to the same task at the same time. This implies racial equality which wounds the white man's sense of pride. If the capitalist shows race prejudice in his operations, it is merely the reflected attitude of the white workman. The colored man who applies at the office for skilled employment meets with one unvarying response from the employer: "I have no objection, but all of my white workmen will quit if I assign you a place among them."

In all the leading lines of industry the white workmen organize and either shut out the Negro or shunt him aside in separate lines with a lower level of dignity and compensation. The brick-layer must be white, the hod carrier may be black. The Negro may, indeed, bring the brick to the scaffold, but should he dare adjust it in its place on the wall, the white man would throw down his trowel with indignant protest.

In so far as the labor unions recognize the Negro, they are forced to do so by the attitude of capital. It seems easier to them to handle the black competitor through the union than to have him as a standing menace on the outside. The regulations of labor unions, however fair they may seem on their face, always work to the disadvantage of the Negro in practical applications. What boots the Negro carpenter to have a union card in his hand if the white workmen refuse to work with him. There is no practical advantage to the Negro in maintaining the same level of wages at the same craft, if at the same time the black man is not permitted to enter upon that craft?

The capitalist stands for an open shop which gives to every man the unhindered right to work according to his ability and skill. In this proposition the capitalist and the Negro are as one.

The political revolution in the South grew out of the conflict between white and black labor. The Southern aristocrat who had no doubt or misgivings as to the superiority of his status, stood ready to form political alliance

with the Negro on the basis of the amended constitution.   So declared Wade Hampton of
South Carolina. "Not so!" shouted Ben Tillman. "This would put the Negro and the poor
white laboring man on the same level, with the
old aristocrats as the overlords of both."
Under Tillman's leadership, the reins of power
were snatched from aristocrat and Negro, and
the laboring white man so manipulated the machinery of government as to keep the Negro
workman in the subordinate place. It is essentially the labor problem which keeps the Negro
from the franchise in the South.

The Negro is the weaker industrial vessel.
He has not as yet the developed capacity to
organize and conduct enterprises under his own
initiative. Growing indications in this direction are interesting and encouraging, but not of
sufficient magnitude to affect the general status
of things. He must look to the white man for
employment. The poor white man has nothing
he wants. His dependency is wholly upon the
capitalistic class.

The employing classes have been wonderfully
helpful to the Negro by way of generous philanthropic contributions. They have built his
schools and colleges and made the betterment of
the race possible. Whenever a sharp issue is
drawn between those who have, and those who
have not, the Negro's instinct aligns him with

wealth and power.   It is also true that the capitalistic element at present possesses the culture and moral restraint in dealing with the Negro which the white workman misses.   There is nothing in the white working class to which the Negro can appeal.   They are the ones who lynch, and burn and torture him.   He looks to the upper element for respect of law and order and the appeal to conscience.

But the laborers outnumber the capitalists more than ten to one, and under spur of the democratic ideal must in the long run gain the essential ends for which they strive.   White labor in the South has already asserted its political power.   Will it not also shortly assert its dominancy in the North and West, and indeed, in the nation?   If the colored race aligns itself with capital, and refuses to help win the common battle of labor, how will it fare with him in the hour of triumph?

Sufficient unto today is the industrial wisdom thereof.   The Negro would rather risk the ills he has than fly to those he knows not of.   Here again the laws of logic fail to apply.   The Negro has an instinct for expediency.   His quick-witted African instinct will enable him to catch the manners living as they rise.   But his present-day wisdom, heedless of logical consistency, says to the industrial overlord: ''Surely the captain may depend on me.''

CHAPTER XVII
CHRISTIANITY AND BACKWARD RACES

We read in a recent issue of the New York *Times*: "Mr. Mark O. Prentiss, special representative of the American Near East Relief, said that Noureddin Pasha, second in command of the Nationalist Army, told him that Turkey was through with all missionaries, including Americans, and it was going to be 'Turkey for the Turks.' If the Americans wanted to help Turkey, Noureddin advised, they could send technical men, but no more missionaries." This is as sad a comment on the failure of modern day interpretation and application of the Christian religion to assuage political and racial animosities as one has heard in recent days. But this is by no means an isolated instance. India is saying to the Western world: "Give us Christ, but not the kind of Christianity that you practice."

The World War and its selfish aftermath have robbed the missionary of the magic of His mission. How can the disciples of the Prince of Peace deluge the world with blood and tears for the purposes of greed and gain? For three

years the Christian nations of the earth have
been wrangling over the division of the spoils
of war. The pious people who on a Sunday
recite the commandment which says: "Thou
shalt not kill," go straight down from the house
of God breathing out hatred and slaughter
against their fellowmen. The inconsistency of
the Christian is discrediting the teachings of
Christ. The professed disciples frustrate and
bring to naught the gospel of the Master.

In our own country, the white Christian is
causing his black brother to stumble. The
Negro no longer respects the white man's pretensions to Christianity. A religion that cannot cross the color line will not meet the needs
of the world. The despised man will not take
a religion that must be handed to him with the
left hand across the great divide. Christ said
to His disciples: "Where I go, there ye may
be also." The white Christian says to his black
co-religionist: "So far and no farther." It is
a psychological impossibility for a self-thinking
mind to accept the religious teaching of the
overlord who denies him the right to vote, makes
him ride in Jim Crow cars, shuts him out from
hotels, deprives him of a part in the government which he is taxed to support, and refuses
him the right to work on a level with his powers
and preparation. A religion which stultifies

the soul cannot save it. For what is the value
of a stultified soul even though it be saved?

I believe profoundly in the saving power of
religion. But the saddest experience which
worries my soul is to see the educated young
Negro of this day and generation repudiate religion because the un-Christianlike attitude of
his white professing Christian causeth him to
offend. I can only urge upon the intelligencia
of the race to adopt a deeper philosophy.
Christianity does not belong to the white race.
Because this race violates its spirit and essence
is no valid reason for the Negro to repudiate it.
You would not discredit the multiplication table
because some unscrupulous business firm manipulated it to your disadvantage in a shady
business transaction. Then why discredit or
decry Christianity because the white man fails
to live up to the level of its requirements? I
make no universal indictment of the white race.
There doubtless be some who have not bowed
the knee to the Baal of racial idolatry. A
righteous man might have been found in Sodom,
had Lot possessed the sportsmanship to push
the process of elimination far enough.

The apostasy of the white man gives the
Negro the moral advantage of exemplifying the
value of the Christian virtues and graces, at a
time when such exemplification is a consumma-

tion devoutly to be wished.   The race problem, of which the black man bears the brunt, cannot be solved by science, or politics, or trade or economics.   If there is any solvent it must be looked for in religion.   Though all men should repudiate Christianity, yet should not the Negro.   To him indeed it is the power of God unto salvation.   The old hymn runs: "What sinners value I resign."   But with the Negro it should rather be: "What the white man resigns, I value."

The Turk is perfectly willing to accept the science and technical skill of the European, but not his religion with its assumptions of racial arrogance and inescapable differences.   This again is the attitude of the backward world.   It seeks to gain the efficiency and technical skill of the European, but eschews its racial arrogance which seems to run too deep to be effaced even by religion.

But it was not ever thus.   It is not necessarily so.   The good missionaries of God who came to the Southland immediately after the war were received in fullest confidence by the people whom they came to benefit.   They were regarded as elder brothers who were willing to undergo any sacrifice to lift the younger brothers to the level to which a more propitious fortune had lifted them.   The same faith and confidence still obtains in scattered instances.

Is Christianity incompatible with race prejudice? This constitutes the most fraughted and the most fateful query that can be put to mankind today. The poise of the world, the moral and social unity of mankind, hang on the answer. This query was once put to the Jew. He answered in the negative, and the scepter passed to the Gentiles. It is now put to the white race. Its fate as a permanent world influence hinges on the answer to the ancient query.

Bernard Shaw, the eccentric Irish philosopher demands that Christianity be given a chance. The deviltry of human nature has never given the doctrine of the Nazarene a fair chance to function in the affairs of the world.

We believe that Christ will yet triumph over caste, and will yet bring peace on earth and good will among men. As the Jew failed to exemplify this world function of Christianity, the opportunity was passed on to the Gentiles. If they fail, it may be transferred to the Negro. Will he then be any more obedient to the heavenly opportunity than those whom he now denounces for their lamentable failure?

CHAPTER XVIII

TAGORE

The *Literary Digest,* during the summer of 1922, contained a very interesting account of the advice which Sir Rabindranath Tagore, the famous Hindu poet, gave to an English missionary in India. This native philosopher urged the British evangelist to lay aside all presumption of superiority and to identify himself with the natives in habits and in love. He then proceeded to give this sound advice: "If you have in you pride of race, pride of sect and pride of personal superiority strong, there is no use trying to do good to others. They will reject your gift, or even if they accept it, they will not be morally benefited by it. You have repeatedly stated that your standard of living is not likely to be different from that of the natives, but one thing I ask of you: 'Will you be able to make yourself one of those whom you call natives?'

"But when a man tries to usurp God's place and assumes the rôle of giver of gifts, and does not come as merely a purveyor of God's love, then it is all vanity."

The situation in India is in every particular

on a parallel with that of the Negro in the United States. The good missionaries who came South immediately after the Civil War exhibited little or nothing of the hauteur of racial superiority. They came in the simple spirit of love and human service. If the Negro, by reason of age-long suppression, stood in need of reclamation, they came to him in the level spirit of helpfulness as a more favored to a less fortunate brother. The response on part of the black beneficiary was spontaneous and immediate. The service proffered in simple sincerity was accepted with child-like reverence and devotion. The grateful heart of the unsophisticated Negro endowed the good missionaries from the North, not with race superiority, but with angelic excellence. The heart of man always responds to the heart of man when the appeal is genuine and direct. But when artifice enters, the heart never responds. The early missionaries inspired the race with the impulse to better ways and the nobler modes of life. The Negro can never repay the debt of gratitude he owes these devoted servants of God who did the Master's work in the Master's spirit.

But with the lapse of time, the race consciousness began to assert itself. Race distinction began to be insisted on. The superiority of the white man must be assumed as a condition precedent to all things else. All of the artificial barriers of the Southern white man must be respected and observed by the Northerner who came to work among colored folk. Service to the Negro was hypothecated on social distinction.

The weakening of the results at once became apparent. Where there is a lack of complete mental and moral freedom between pupil and teacher the lesson can never be adequately taught. The spirit of the teacher must meet the spirit of the taught. A Negro mathematician could not teach the multiplication table to white pupils in Atlanta, Ga., because there could be no meeting of the minds.

The southern white man has acted upon the assumption from the beginning. He holds the Negro in contempt, and therefore does not deem himself qualified to become his teacher, because he would not put himself on his plane.

It may be said that no particular class of individuals is responsible for this change for the worse in public sentiment. The South has set up a social régime and compels all white men and women to conform to it. The Negro is kept in his assigned place by the stern hand of compulsion. The white worker could not, if he would, relate himself to his field as he was wont to do in former days. The white bishop over a Negro conference in Georgia does not dare or does not deign to sit in at the same table with the people whom he serves. His usefulness can only be partial and limited. A bishop who cannot mingle with his people is a poor representative of the Head of the church who came eating and drinking with publicans and sinners.

The Negro school and college is laboring under the heavy handicap of racial assumption. A gift that is handed down is never so acceptable as one that is handed out. The most helpful hand is the one stretched out on the horizontal, and not on the incline.

The white man has, indeed, brought good gifts. He has built schools and colleges and organized and operated helpful agencies for the general welfare of the race. Many of them in days gone by have given themselves in devoted service.

And yet, the words of Tagore are suggestive and significant. The moral advantage of a gift does not depend upon its munificence, but upon the spirit of him that gives and of him that receives.

All of this serves to remind us that the Negro problem in the United States is not an isolated thing apart from the whole human equation. The relations of the whiter races to the darker ones constitute one vast problem with local and national complexities and variations. But there underlies it all one common thread of human kinship which arrogance cannot destroy, and prudence should not ignore.

CHAPTER XIX

LLOYD GEORGE ON METHODISM

Lloyd George, the wily Welshman and crafty statesman, has been suing for the good graces of America. As premier of Great Britain, he acknowledges the debt which his country incurred on account of the World War. Since the overthrow of his cabinet, he has given himself to philosophical speculation in quest of a moral offset for material values. In a recent notable address, he declares that America derived more in permanent advantage from England through Whitefield and Wesley than England gained from us through the gigantic loans advanced to enable her to fight the central powers. This leads to the idea of a common divisor of values belonging to different categories. The highest services to mankind cannot be compensated in terms of monetary units. We cannot reckon the service of Abraham Lincoln to the nation nor of Frederick Douglass to the Negro by the standard coin of the realm. Spiritual and moral contributions transcend economic achievements. All other manifesta-

tion of power shall vanish away; faith, hope and
charity alone survive. Solomon was reputed
to be the richest man in the world of his
day, and yet his wealth does not interest a
single human being. He was also considered
the wisest man of his time. That wisdom is
the eternal possession of mankind. Moses,
Buddha, Jesus and Mahomet command the faith
and obedience of all mankind through their
moral and spiritual accomplishments.

Lloyd George affirms that it was Whitefield
and Wesley that led America to participate in
the World War, and that they will yet lead this
nation to enter into the League of Nations.
This is an unexpected tribute to the permanent
influence of moral and spiritual impressions.
It was John Wesley and George Whitefield who
planted and promoted the Methodist church on
the American continent. The nation is still
urged forward by the moral impulse of that
movement. When Methodism was first brought
to America, it had to confront an interesting
psychological situation. Existing modes of
worship tended to repress the emotions rather
than give them free scope and play. People of
a lower level of culture always seek the easiest
outlet for pent-up feelings. The ministry of
Methodism came to the great mass of country
folk who sought for dramatic portrayal of

spiritual manifestations. The song, the shout, the groan, the prayer meeting, the class meeting, the revival and the camp meeting met the requirements and answered the needs of existing conditions. The impression made was deep and abiding. The people then appear to have risen several degrees higher in the scale of culture since that day. Modes of worship have been modified in greater conformity to this social progress. The groaning and shouting at camp meeting and revival are heard no more. But the influence of those earlier days survives as an unconscious influence that counts for national righteousness. The Methodist Church, in all of its differentiated bodies, constitutes the largest branch of the Protestant church of America. On all great questions of national concern it is found on the side of sound national policy. No amount of money consideration can pay for such a heritage as this.

In the same connection Lloyd George also alluded to the priceless value of the services contributed to America by Roger Williams, who planted the Baptist church in the wilderness of the New World. The appeal of Roger Williams met response by the same social grade. The methods were very similar to those of the Methodists with vital doctrinal differences. These two branches of the Christian church constitute

not only the numerical bulk, but the moral backbone of the Christian church of America.   They
constitute the church of the common people, the
proletariat, where we must always look for the
moral stamina of a nation.   Imagine if you can
the moral vacuum that would have existed
had these great arms of the Christian church
not been in operation during our national
history.

What has been said so far applies to these
churches as a whole.   But when we limit the
application to the Negro contingent the stress
of emphasis should be doubled.   Roger Williams, Wesley and Whitefield are indeed the
great benefactors of the Negro race.   The question is often raised why the Negro takes to
the Baptist and Methodist churches so much
more readily than to any other modes of worship.   The answer is easily rendered.   These
churches, especially in the earlier day, made
the easiest appeal to the people of a given level
of culture.   The appeal must be dramatic, the
response spectacular.   Emotion is the dominant
element in any religion.   A religion without
passion is a religion without power.   An illiterate and unenlightened people cannot express
their pent-up emotions in the refined and
recondite fashion of the elect and the elite.   The
joy of service, devotion to duty, the inner

revelry of the soul are too abstract for their simple concrete experiences. The song, the shout, the groan, the bodily contortions are more immediate and manifest.

As the people advance in culture and inner understanding, it will not become necessary to change their religious adherence. The dignity and decorousness of the mode keeps pace with the intellectual and social advancement of the people. The Salvation Army today is supplying the place once occupied by the Methodist and Baptist churches. The method shifts to suit varying conditions. The moral and spiritual good abides forever.

The suggestion of Lloyd George contains a most valuable lesson for the American people on the midst of their rush after the God of Mammon. Doubly valuable is the lesson to the Negro, that the highest values in life consist in moral and spiritual excellence and are beyond money and beyond price.

CHAPTER XX

THE ORDER OF MELCHISEDECH

Richard Henry Boyd and Elias Camp Morris, respective leaders of rival factions of Negro Baptists, have recently passed from work to reward, within a few days of each other. These two great leaders typify and embody the spirit and the work of the priesthood which has developed the Negro church during the past half century. They were born in the midst of slavery, with no advantage of early education, and came to manhood about the time of the Emancipation Proclamation.

They both possessed native energy of mind and vigor of spirit. They came upon the scene of action at a time when the demand of the moral and spiritual vineyard could not wait upon the slow process of the schools. They picked up fragments of knowledge and bits of information and consecrated them to the great task of human betterment. The situation was urgent. The demands were immediate. Millions of human beings were pining for the saving knowledge of truth. The ignorant cannot be made intelligent, the vicious cannot be made virtuous, corruption cannot take on incorruptibility, crudeness cannot be clothed with decorum in a moment in the twinkling of an eye. The work of social, moral and spiritual regeneration must be applied to existing human conditions, just as they are without one plea. Just after emancipation, when the entire fabric of social life had been upset, a serious situation impended. The dead must be buried, lovers must be united in holy wedlock according to the Christian ritual, infants must be baptized, forms of public worship must be established and maintained, churches must be built and manned, the religious estate must be organized and ordered. God, Himself, was impatient. He could not wait upon the slow process of the school and the seminary for an educated and enlightened priesthood. The field was ripe unto the harvest.

Then up rose Boyd and Morris, with thousands of their compeers, from cornfield and plowhandle responding with deepest sincerity of soul, "Here am I, send me." There sprung up a spontaneous priesthood after the manner of Melchisedech. They grew up as a tender plant, and as a root out of dry ground. They heard the voice and heeded the Macedonian cry. They were not disobedient to the heavenly vision. God placed the heavenly treasure in earthen vessels.

Some would say that they were unlettered men, but theirs was the kind of ignorance that God winks at and utilizes. The dynamic feature of knowledge is not found in books, but in the spirit and will to do. The more intelligent Negro ministry today may well indulge the contemplation, whether God was not able to use the ignorance of the elders to greater advantage in promoting the cause of His kingdom than He is now making of the high literary intelligence of their successors. The spirit is more than the letter. The will will find a way. "Who so doeth My will shall know the doctrine." But those who know the doctrine do not always do the will. Boyd and Morris possessed the spirit of service and devotion, and a requisite degree of the letter was vouchsafed them. The Apostles were crude, unlettered men. But they received power and understanding by coming in touch with the source of all power. Education cannot give capacity, but merely facilitates its development and expression.

Boyd and Morris possessed moral enthusiasm, and hitched their energies to a great cause. Consecration to a noble purpose quickly develops the best powers and possibilities. There is today a lamentable lag in the effective powers of the Negro intelligencia. Our educational opportunities are expanding, facilities are multiplying, thousands of our young men are being educated in the highest terms of the technical letter. But the impotency of the letter is painfully apparent. This is because their moral energies are not released, and geared up with the machinery of great social tasks. The spirit of Boyd and Morris will rise up and condemn this generation. The spirit without the letter is more effective than the letter without the spirit.

Speaking typically of our illustrious dead, it might be said that they found millions of the race who, like sheep, were scattered abroad without a shepherd, and brought them into the fold. They built up a communion of over three million souls. Their work in the promotion of the Kingdom of God has not been paralleled anywhere in the world during the past two generations. The noblest ambitions of the thousands of Baptist priests that follow them might well be to carry on and carry out and carry up the great religious estate which they have inherited from their spiritual fathers.

By means of the microscopic criticism it might be easy to discover great faults and serious imperfections in the lives of these two great leaders. The cynic delights in exploiting the faults and foibles of the great. Let him find flaws who will; I prefer to magnify the virtues of imperfect humanity.

The splitting asunder of a great Christian estate over a paltry property dispute is deeply to be deplored. These men were rivals. Neither spared the other in the heat of the controversy. The whole Baptist denomination was aligned in hostile camps contending with as much heat and bitterness as was consistent with Christian charity and grace. May this controversy end at the graves of its leaders. Great men often accomplish more in their death than by their lives. So may it be with Boyd and Morris.

Three million Negro Baptists welded into one compact militant body under intelligent and consecrated leadership would constitute our greatest agency for social, moral and spiritual betterment.

Boyd and Morris, though divided in heated contention, were essentially alike in origin, opportunity, power and purpose. They have wrought well. They have exploited to the full the talents with which they were endowed. They have earned the gratitude of three million Baptists and of ten million Negroes.

"Their bones are dust, their good swords rust,
    Their souls are with the saints, we trust."

CHAPTER XXI

THE COLLEGE BRED NEGRO AND THE CHURCH

The collegian of this day and generation is not spiritually minded. He gives little or no attention to things that look God-wards. We live in a material age. The basic principle of our civilization is metallic. Charles Darwin gave a shock to the religious world from which it has not yet recovered. The church has not yet assimilated and absorbed the scientific diet. All religious systems must institutionalize the state of knowledge current at the time of their establishment. As science advances, ancient scientific truth becomes present error. The conflict between science and religion becomes inevitable. As always happens, the church first combats, then tolerates, and finally accepts a newly discovered scientific truth. The old bottle often cracks in its endeavor to hold new wine. Such has been the case with the theory of evolution. The new impulse contributed by Darwin has dominated the thought and opinion of the thinking people of the world for half a century.

It has met not only with universal acceptance, but with enthusiastic acclaim throughout the world. The church, being more cautious and hesitant, has lagged in the rear, which has caused the college man to assume an attitude of intellectual disdain and moral indifference. The whole religious world today is in the throes of theological transition. The old truth must be restated in terms of the present-day thought and knowledge. This task should challenge the highest energies and enthusiasm of the college man.

It was unfortunate that the Negro was brought into the intellectual arena at the time of this raging controversy, when science seems to be gaining the upper hand. The intellectual and spiritual life of the race is based upon the everlasting foundation—"In the beginning, God." The Negro mind is characterized by a deep spiritual nature and lively mode of manifestation. But the seductive influence of modern teaching and its material exploitation have served to swerve him from the line of spiritual interest which clearly marks the destiny of the race.

The Christian ministry offers the best field for the outlet of Negro capacity and genius. The pulpit constitutes the most attractive leadership of the Negro masses, not only in matters moral and spiritual, but within the wider scope of social activities. At least one-third of our college output should recruit the ranks of the ministry in the various denominations. The Baptist and Methodist churches, which count their adherents by the millions, furnish a field for the high-talented, high-minded and high-souled young men to administer and perfect these great moral and spiritual estates. The cry goes out to the Negro collegian with more than Macedonian urgency.

It is needless to plead that white college men are turning away from the ministry into the more alluring secular and material pursuits. Where conditions are different, comparisons are odious. The pulpit today offers no such relative opportunity to white youth as it does to youth of Negro blood. Secular pursuits have less relative attraction and rewards. Graduates of Yale, Harvard and Princeton a hundred years ago rushed into the ministry not merely because of the fact that the ministry of that day furnished the most alluring remunerative and attractive field for the outlet of their talent and training. The educated Negro of today stands where the white collegians stood a century ago with reference to the appealing and imperative field of service.

But, alas, alas, the apathy is appalling! I

have peculiar opportunity to study and understand the attitude of college youth toward the
Christian ministry. In the junior college of
Howard University there are about five hundred young men, about three hundred of whom
have indicated medicine for their chosen profession. Not a half dozen have indicated the
ministry. I daresay that a somewhat similar
proportion runs throughout our colleges and
universities. In the high schools the disposition
toward the ministry is equally appalling and
disappointing. Of the large graduating classes
from the Washington, Baltimore and St. Louis
high schools, as well as the young men in the
high school of Philadelphia, New York and
Chicago and other well-equipped secondary institutions of learning, few indeed are they who
show any inclination or give any indication toward the sacerdotal office.

What is to be the future of the Negro church
and of our great religious denominations unless
leadership is assumed by the best mind and
heart and conscience of the race? The pulpit
must keep in advance of the people, else the
people will repudiate the pulpit. We can rely
to a certain extent upon the spontaneity of
spiritual power. Those who are moved by the
spirit always have and always will manifest a
certain degree of intelligence and practical en-

ergy. The Negro church, so far, has been built up mainly by men who had not had the fullest opportunity of preparation and culture. If they were ignorant of the technical letter, it was the kind of ignorance that God winks at, and utilizes. But He will not wink at ignorance in this day and generation, nor yet will He utilize it to promote his spiritual estate. God always uses the best instrumentalities at His command, and unless the Negro church in the coming generation shall be manned and commanded by educated men fully abreast of the knowledge and culture of the day, great will be our condemnation and the curse will fall on our heads.

The theological opinion of the world is becoming more and more liberalized. The college man need no longer hesitate concerning the ministry because of old theological exactions which compromised his intellectual integrity. The one great task before the Negro college world is to infuse into the rising generation of educated youth the wisdom and necessity of dedicating their lives to the great task of moral and spiritual leadership, in the name of God, humanity and the race.

CHAPTER XXII

THE SPORT OF THE GHOULS

The maxim of Alexander Pope,

> "Virtuous and vicious every man must be,
> None in the extreme, but each in the degree,"

expresses a doctrine which is as true of nations as of individuals. Every nation has its characteristic vices as well as its virtues. The German kultur would reach the attainment of efficiency through ruthlessness of method. England attains her political aims with a bland and complaisant pharaseeism. The seductive hedonism of France renders her the most attractive state in Europe. The democratic ideal of America is tainted with a disregard for law, the only foundation upon which a democracy can endure. She is impelled by a wild and reckless intrepidity of spirit.

> "That bids her make the laws she flouts—
> That bids her flout the laws she makes."

The United States has the largest percentage of murders and homicides and the lowest average of legal executions of any civilized institution on the face of the earth. Ex-President, now Chief-Justice Taft, in a notable address some years ago, stated that there had been 131,951 murders and homicides in the United States between 1885 and 1908, and only 2,286 legal executions. In 1912, there were 9,152 homicides and only 145 executions.

Lawlessness is universally deplored as America's overshadowing national sin. In partial explanation of this deplorable state of things, it might be said that in a new country where the self-assertive Saxon was confronted by two primitive races, his personal authority was subject to little or no legal restraint. His word was law, and his judgment the final source of appeal. It was the imperialism of race that destroyed the Indian and enslaved the Negro. The spirit of self-sufficiency of judgment in dealing with primitive races survives long after evoking conditions have passed away.

Lynching is a peculiar American institution. This country has contributed a new word to the English language. The term, itself, is said to be derived from a Virginia slaveholder named Lynch who was in the habit of taking the law into his own hands in dealing with runaway slaves and white outlaws who sought shelter in the Dismal Swamp. Mr. Lynch is said to have contributed the name to Lynchburg, Va. The word has come to mean the infliction of summary punishment without due process of law. But the process is so generally applied to the Negro offender that it has grown to connote a mode of racial punishment.

Since the beginning of time, when the feelings have been wrought to fever heat, and the sensibilities outraged by some flagrant offense, men have resorted to condign punishment under spur of the inflamed passion of the moment. When the primitive instincts are aroused, the mob is impatient of judge and jury. Appeal to passion renders swifter vindication than the court of reason. Lord Bacon speaks of vengeance as a kind of wild justice. This is a primitive method of procedure where the baser impulse gains the upper hand over the better judgment. The ape and tiger die slowly. Wild justice yields reluctantly to the orderly process of civilized procedure.

The practice of lynching is apt to be manifested on the frontiers of civilization where a lower culture is brought into contact with a higher. The sons of God are prone to wreak summary vengeance upon the children of men who dare dispute their higher prerogative. The flaming sword of wrath still guards the forbidden fruit from the excluded aspirant of lower degree. Race hatred is the cause of most human outrages. The massacre of Armenian by Turk, pogroms of the Poles against the Jews, and lynching of Negroes in America grow out of the same basal instinct.

In most cases the outbreak between races takes on the form of mass assault and is inspired by political, religious or economic motive. Race riots, a somewhat new phase of race conflict in America, partakes largely of this nature. In case of lynching, the mob forms around an individual who is alleged to have committed some flagrant offense, and proceeds to execute the offender without waiting for the formal sanction of the court of law.

Violence is usually limited to the individual offender and does not involve wholesale slaughter. While the Negro is the usual victim of lynching, he is by no means the only one. During the thirty years, 1889-1918, there were 702 white men lynched in the United States. A larger number of white men were lynched in America than in all the rest of the civilized world. When the evil passion has once been aroused, it is impossible to limit its viciousness to any one race or class. The iniquities visited upon the Negro today will be meted out to the white man tomorrow. The evil inherent in race contact consists in a double standard of dealing.

The methods devised for special application to the inferior race will inevitably tend to the demoralization of all. Water seeks its lowest level. So evil practice always tends to gravitate to the lowest ethical standard.

It is interesting to inquire why lynching is almost wholly limited to the United States of America. The self-reliant spirit of democracy, especially in pioneer communities, makes the individual feel that, in the final analysis, he is a law unto himself. The individual and not the social conscience becomes the immediate guide. The self-responsible individual or group that feels that its sensibilities have been ruthlessly outraged, justifies itself in wreaking summary vengeance upon the offender, especially when he falls outside the pale of its own race and class. In the anti-slavery controversy, those who went on the side of liberty often appealed to what they called the higher law, which took precedence over the law of the land. This is a dangerous doctrine, to be indulged only in case of extreme moral emergencies. If it is allowed to become the practice of individuals or groups not accustomed to exercise rigid-self-restraint, it is sure to lead to gross abuse. In a democracy such ultra procedure is apt to be indulged either for good or ill.

Each Southern plantation constituted a juris-

diction within itself where the owner was juror,
judge and executioner. He possessed the power
of life and death over his slaves. His influence
over public sentiment was so powerful that his
will and judgment became the law of the community. The slaveholders were to the manor
born, and felt that they rightfully exercised the
power of life and death over their slaves for the
good of society. When the master murdered
his slave, he was considered the chief loser.
The community felt little concern. The con-
straint of conscience and the restraint of self-
interest tended to reduce the practice to a minimum under the old régime of master and slave.
But the slaveholders constituted a relatively
small proportion of the white population of the
South. Not one in ten of the white population
of the Southern states belonged in this class.
The poor whites who were unable to own slaves
were held in a degree of contempt and disesteem
scarcely above the level of the blacks. They
were subject to the direction and control of the
aristocratic class, and were as amenable to their
personal and public authority as slaves themselves. Their color, which preëmpted them
from forced servitude, was the principal advantage which they enjoyed. They naturally
developed a hatred for the Negroes who were
their indirect industrial rivals, and felt that,

as white men, they were required to live on a higher level than the blacks, and as freemen they could not enter into competition with the slave labor.

After the emancipation of the Negro and the overthrow of the reconstruction régime in the South, the non-slaveholding whites, for the first time, gained consciousness of their political power. Animosity against the old aristocratic white element was scarcely less vehement than their venom against the Negro. The voice of the new man became dominant in the state. They drove the slaveholding oligarchy from power and took the reins of government into their own hands. Public feeling was lashed into fury against the Negro. Lynching was urged as a suitable mode of punishment whenever the black man threatened or jeopardized the prerogative of the white race. The late Senator Benjamin R. Tillman was the mouthpiece and oracle of this ruthless program. It is noticeable that under slavery lynchings were rare and almost unheard of. Under the reconstruction government they were infrequent. The practice rose simultaneously with the rise of the non-slaveholding whites to power in the states.

A people who begin their existence with violent protest against authority to which they were once subject are apt to carry the protestant spirit beyond the limit of its original intendment. The Protestant religion will reach its logical goal when all ecclesiastical authority is abolished over the individual conscience and judgment. The Boston Tea Party embodied the spirit of disregard for law as much as a mob of lynchers. If it is rejoined that the Puritan lawbreakers were impelled by patriotic motives which rose above the law, so the mob might retort that its hasty passion is also promoting immediate or ultimate social aims. The lawless habit acquired for some worthy purpose seeks exercise on unworthy objects when that purpose has been subserved. It is to be hoped that the democracies which are achieved by more orderly and regular procedure will escape this evil concomitant.

The term "social equality" has come to signify the deadline of relationship between the races. Any semblance of attempt on part of the Negro to cross this deadline in the South is vested with summary punishment. Every white man feels that he bears a racial commission to act in the emergency. His acts, however outrageous, will be sure to meet with public favor, if he can show that they were committed in the name and at the behest of social equality. The phrase has taken on frenzied meaning. It has

become the tocsin and rallying cry of the white
supremacy propaganda. Men worship and bow
down at its shrine as a heathen before his
graven god. No crime is too heinous to be committed at its dictation. That the races must be
kept apart is the gospel of the South, more
sacred than Holy Writ. There is no provision
of the sacred Scripture that may not be violated
to attain this great objective. Any act on the
part of an individual or group of individuals
which tends to this end is justified in public
opinion.

Lynching is sought to be justified on the
ground of assault on white women by colored
men. But it is not the crime so much as the
color of the criminal that provokes the punishment. The assault of a Negro on a white woman
arouses all of the passion and animosity of the
white race. It is easier to inflame public opinion over the color of the criminal than over the
nature of the crime. Social intimacy and physical mixture of the races must be prevented at
all hazards, is the philosophy of those who
justify lynching.

Race hatred and lynching do not heed the
obvious facts and formulas of logic. The mixture of the races has already taken place on a
gigantic scale. The presence of three million

mulattoes indicates clearly that the danger of intermixture does not come through assault of the black male upon the white female. The result will be just as effective through the lust of the white male after the black female. The fact of mixed progeny is stubborn and persistent. The laws of biology care nothing for the social creeds of the day. It makes little or no difference how mixed progeny is produced. The essential thing is the product, not the process.

Lynching of Negroes does not involve risk of danger, nor does it evoke the manly qualities of courage or daring. It is a safe pastime which appeals to the coward and the bully. There is a total lack of the zest of sportsmanship. A mob of five hundred men armed to the teeth wreaking vengeance on a defenseless Negro already in custody of the law does not present an heroic spectacle. The complacent sheriff is easily "overpowered" and renders the keys for the asking. The culprit is spirited away to be strung up to the limb of a tree. His body is riddled with bullets and ticketed with a placard to remind all Negroes of the superiority of the white race. In the South a white man is rarely ever punished for killing a Negro. Of the thousands of homicides and murders of black men during the past fifty years, instances of legal execution may be counted on the fingers of one's hand. The white man in the South, either as an individual, or as part of the mob, may kill a Negro with all but absolute impunity. Lynching is apt to continue until the participant is made to pay the penalty for his part in the murderous pact. Men will override the law at their convenience when they can do so with impunity. Salutary fear of the law is persuasive to obedience of law.

Although lynchings occur most frequently in the South, they are by no means confined to that section. They have occurred in all but six states of the United States. They are not limited by geographical boundaries or lines of latitude.

The following table indicates the number of white and colored persons lynched in the United States from 1889 to 1920:

Year	Total	White	Colored
1889	175	80	95
1890	91	3	88
1891	194	67	127
1892	226	71	155
1893	153	39	114
1894	182	54	128

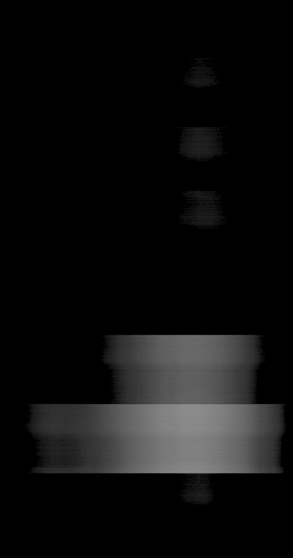

Of 3,224 of these cases of lynchings the causes or alleged causes are as follows:

NUMBER OF PERSONS LYNCHED, BY OFFENSES CHARGED
AND BY COLOR, 1889-1918

	Murder	Rape	Attacks upon Women	Other Crimes against the Person	Crimes against Property	Miscellaneous Crimes	Absence of Crimes
White ...	319	46	13	62	121	135	6
Negro ...	900	477	237	253	210	303	142
Total	1219	523	250	315	331	438	148

Only 19 per cent of the lynchings of Negroes were on account of allegement of rape, and 9.4 per cent for attack upon women. It must always be borne in mind that the offenses were only alleged. In few cases have they been proved by a court of competent jurisdiction. In numerous instances mistaken identity has been established after the victim has been dispatched to his doom. Hundreds have met their fate with the protestation of innocence on their dying lips.

Effort has been made to besmirch the Negro race by branding it with evil reputation. Lynching has sought justification because of the alleged lecherous propensity of the Negro race.

of being the only civilized nation of the earth whose people take delight in the burning and torturing of human beings. Nowhere else in the civilized world do men, women and children dance with glee and fight for ghastly souvenirs of quivering human flesh, and mock with laughter the dying groans of the helpless victim which sicken the air while the flickering flames of the funeral pyre light up the midnight sky with their dismal glare.

But the United States is seriously conscious of the evil reputation which lynching imposes upon the nation. And yet it cannot plead exculpation on the ground that only the evil-minded few perpetrate and participate in this evil. Any nation is held justly accountable for the characteristic conduct of its citizens. The practice is too widespread in time and space to plead national irresponsibility. The nation commits what it permits. The American people, when clothed in their right mind and speaking with their true voice denounce the evil practice in every mood and tense of condemnation. They hope and pray that the reproach might be rolled away. When the nation would assume the asserted place as moral monitor among the nations of the earth, and condemn other people for their sins, it must face the age-old retort: "Thou hypocrite, first cast out the beam out of thine own eye."

our own. I say plainly that every American who takes part in the action of a mob or gives it any sort of countenance is no true son of this great democracy, but its betrayer, and does more to discredit her by that single disloyalty to her standards of law and right than the words of her statesmen or the sacrifices of her heroic boys in the trenches can do to make suffering people believe her to be their saviour. How shall we commend democracy to the acceptance of other peoples if we disgrace our own by proving that it is after all, no protection to the weak. Every mob contributes to German lies about the United States what her most gifted liars cannot improve upon by way of calumny. They can at least say that such things cannot happen in Germany except in time of revolution, when law is swept away.

WOODROW WILSON.

July 25, 1918.

But in spite of the President's proclamation there were 83 lynchings in 1919, 65 in 1920, and over 60 in 1921. The conscience of the nation is pricked to the core. All of America's resourcefulness must be asserted to exterminate this national disgrace lest the home of freedom in the Western World lose its boasted reputation as the land of liberty, and become known among nations as the land of lynchers.

deem him stricken of God and afflicted. He was cut out of the land of the living that the land might live. He made intercessions for us and gave his life as a ransom for many; and with his stripes we are healed.

Abraham Lincoln is the one commanding moral genius that has risen out of the Western World. Material attainment, intellectual shrewdness and political talent have engrossed the chief energies of this hemisphere and even the Christian Church on this continent deteriorates toward the lower level of things concrete and material. The anti-slavery agitation produced a spasm of national virtue; but like a hasty spark it scarcely survived the attrition which produced it. John Brown, William Lloyd Garrison, and Charles Sumner were filled with moral indignation against a specific wrong. But Lincoln's moral sense was instinctive and all-embracing. His reaction against wrong was not born of the heated issues of the passing hour. His moral understanding was instinctive, his ethical knowledge intuitive. "If slavery is not wrong, then nothing is wrong." This moral proposition is as clear, concise and convincing as any axiom of Euclid.

When but a bearded youth, he saw a man's body at auction in the slave market in New Orleans, his moral nature instinctively revolted.

much of his secret as was appropriate to their understanding.

Immediately after the battle of Antietam, it is said that, with hands behind his back, he walked up and down the cabinet room, oblivious of the presence of his advisers, and indulged in inner groanings of the spirit too deep for vocal utterance. But finally he ejaculated: "I promised God, I promised God, I promised God that if He would give me victory at Antietam, I would do this thing." The Emancipation Proclamation was a covenant made in Heaven. It was submitted to the cabinet for its information only as a vow registered on high. After receiving the sanction of Heaven on this Proclamation, he no more thought of submitting it to the council of his advisers than Moses dreamed of submitting the Ten Commandments to the approval of the host which he led.

Behold a man without animosity or bitterness of soul! He had no special loves and no particular hatreds. He freed the Negro without loving him and subdued the South without hating it. "With charity for all and malice toward none," was the moral axiom upon which his mind moved. His devotion surpassed the ordinary human understanding. Others knew in part and understood in part and loved in part; he comprehended the whole. His contem-

would have been an abortive attempt to free the Negro if the Union had been destroyed? "If I can save the Union by retaining slavery, I will do it." "If I can save the Union by destroying slavery, I will do it." "If I can save the Union part slave and part free, I will do it."

These were the utterances of a sagacious and far-seeing statesmanship. But immediately his moral genius asserted itself and forced him to register the impulse of his soul: "And yet I wish that all men might be free." The moment he discovered that the national body had developed the moral resistance to withstand the shock, he issued the Emancipation Proclamation. He knew as none other when the psychological moment had arrived. The Proclamation was issued with a timeliness of intuitive wisdom, not too soon, nor yet too late.

The Negro race is accustomed to celebrate the first of January as the date of their deliverance, but the great word was issued on the 22d of September, and marked the beginning of all that we are and all that we hope to be on the American continent. Let every Negro, with unalloyed devotion and reverence of spirit, bow in honor of the name of Abraham Lincoln, the Great Emancipator who freed the Negro and saved the nation.

and preserved in the title: "The Fisk Jubilee Singers." The founders of Fisk University at Nashville, Tenn., unconsciously built a phrasal monument to their endeavor which will outlast the institution of learning which they established for the uplift and enlightenment of the down-trodden and oppressed.

The early missionaries to the Southland during and immediately after the Civil War were motivated by deep religious consecration and zeal for humanity. They had been told that the Negro did not possess the higher attributes of human nature, and there was nothing in him that would respond to the higher human appeal. But their faith triumphed over skepticism. Belief in God compels acceptance of the corollary, belief in man. Faith is its own foundation where evidence is wanting, but tangible proof and concrete demonstration double its validity and divests it of all semblance of doubt. The Northern missionaries were keenly on the lookout for the manifestation of those human qualities that would justify their faith and vindicate their devotion in the eyes of a doubting world. Then their ear first caught the melodic suggestion, their joy knew no bound. It was but the smothered soul of a race striving for expression through weird wailings and plaintive lamentation like that of the captured Jews who

through which the voice of the Negro carried its own meaning and mission to the nation, and indeed to the world. The new song gushed from the heart as the trill from the throat of the bird. The nation listened with moistened eyes. Kings and queens heard it and wept. The response was spontaneous and immediate. The civilized world was easily persuaded to a sympathetic and generous attitude towards a people who cried out of the depth of their distress. "The Fisk Jubilee Hall" stands today as a reminder of the substantial response evoked by this appeal. Other institutions were also in the field. The foundation of many a Negro school and college was laid on the basis of the jubilee music. These bespeak better things for the Negro race.

But the early missionaries and school marms exploited only one feature of the Negro's emotional endowment. The spirituality of the Negro's song not only convinced the nation of the worthiness of the object of their sacrifice and devotion, but also proved profitable to their enterprise. We naturally extol the things which we prefer and by which we profit, and are prone to deny or ignore the things which frustrate our aims. The early missionaries were of the Puritan temperament and mold of mind. They, naturally enough, sought to create the

higher power of expression. We listen for it in Harry Burleigh and Roland Hayes the same as in the untutored choir of a Baptist church.

The jazz was later in receiving recognition than the jubilee because of the different method of exploitation. The missionaries had the Negro tell his own story in his own voice. The fork-faced minstrels of the earlier days essayed to portray the jazz phase of the Negro life by means of alien impersonalization. A Negro performance without the Negro performer is at best a tepid substitute. No one race can portray the soul of another. Roman tears will not moisten British eyes. The white man is a colorless misfit whether he attempts jubilee or jazz. We always prefer the original to the substitute. The one is a play; the other a performance.

The Negro is at present becoming his own interpreter both as to jubilee and jazz. Negro authors are putting a new emphasis and meaning in both. After two generations of constant singing, the jubilee songs have still the moving and melting power of the earlier years. The musical authorities of Europe tell us over and over again that we have not yet begun to explore the possibilities of the musical endowment of the transplanted race. The Negro is becoming educated in musical art and technique.

CHAPTER XXV

PESSIMISM OF THE NEGRO

The Negro poet, Fenton Johnson, ejaculates:

"It is better to die than to grow up and find out that you are colored."

Here is the epitome of pessimistic philosophy in a nutshell. Race prejudice is a fact which the Negro did not create and which he cannot control. He may indeed modify its malignity or mitigate its intensity by wise and sensible procedure. But lachrymose lamentations will avail him nothing. Shall he yield up the ghost as the coward does in the face of unfavorable fate? Or shall he meet the outward pressure of circumstances with the inner resistance of soul. The inane critic of creation makes a sorry spectacle in face of cosmic law. The physical coward flees before testing the adequacy of his strength against opposing obstacle. He sees lions in the way and trembles without determining whether or not they are chained. The moral coward is more despicable. He makes an unconditional surrender of the soul. When one surrenders his will he paralyzes his ener-

living? What human or divine end can be served thereby? Suicide is the one sin that shall never be forgiven. If our poet desires to die in order to terminate his own line and escape the hardships of his color it is his personal prerogative so to do. The one commendable act in the record of the life of Judas Iscariot is that "he went out and hanged himself." But would to God that the poet had taken the decisive step before penning these fatal words. The race might well have rejoiced at the riddance. But the viciousness of evil doctrine consists in its suggestiveness, especially to those of weak will and feeble spirit.

Unfortunately, Fenton Johnson does not stand alone. His brand of moral imbecility is widespread and contagious. The race abounds in weak-souled pessimists without faith, hope or courage, ashamed of their kind and of their own progeny. They live without hope and die without issue. They are even devoid of that salutary cowardice of conscience which makes them think rather of the ills they have than face the far-flung consequences of personal or social suicide.

Race suicide discredits the Creator and defeats the ends of creation. Man alone possesses this power. He is the only biological pervert who thwarts his own existence. "Multiply, re-

"The mind is its own palace,
    And of itself can make a heaven of hell, a
        hell of heaven."

All is not lost if the mind is not lost. The unconquerable will always finds hope in despondency and resolution in despair. If there can only be injected into the mind of the Negro this much of the spirit of Milton's devil, we shall never again listen to a pessimistic wail counseling supine yielding to an unfavorable fate. That would be an infamy beneath the deepest downfall under the compulsion of supernal power. Satan's counsel to his overthrown hosts applies with special pertinency to the Negro of today.

ation moves. Herein lies the Negro's protective device and defensive philosophy.

Endurance is the dominant virtue that crowns the apex of the pyramid of human strivings. He that endureth to the end shall be saved. All things in this life and in the life to be are reserved to him that overcometh.

In the meantime let us pray that Fenton Johnson, for the excited moment, was inebriated with the delirium of poetic fantasy; but that in his soberer mood he will recant his evil utterance, and apologize for the insult to God who made him and to the race which must bear the brunt of his inanity.

THE END